Physiology and Fitness

Dean Hodgkin, B.Sc.

THE
GREAT
COURSES

PUBLISHED BY:

THE GREAT COURSES
Corporate Headquarters
4840 Westfields Boulevard, Suite 500
Chantilly, Virginia 20151-2299
Phone: 1-800-832-2412
Fax: 703-378-3819
www.thegreatcourses.com

Dean Hodgkin, B.Sc.

Mathematics and Management Studies,
University of Portsmouth
Certificate in Exercise and Health Studies,
Physical Education Association
of Great Britain and Northern Ireland

International fitness expert Dean Hodgkin has presented master classes and seminars to fitness instructors in more than 36 countries, including the IDEA convention for the world's largest association of fitness and wellness professionals. Voted Best International Fitness Presenter at the One Body One World awards in New York, he has appeared on numerous television and radio shows worldwide, including appearances in Taiwan, Mumbai, Warsaw, Amsterdam, and New York. He has taught classes all over the world, including in South Africa, Russia, Japan, India, China, Germany, Spain, Italy, France, and Sweden.

His feature articles on fitness and physiology have appeared in the leading newspapers in Great Britain, including *The Times*, *The Sunday Times*, and the *Daily Express*. In addition, Hodgkin writes regularly for the top men's and women's health magazines throughout the world, including *GQ*, *Esquire*, *Men's Health*, *Women's Fitness*, *Health & Fitness*, and *Weight Watchers*.

Hodgkin also publishes in the medical press, including *Nursing Times*, the British dental magazine *Vital*, and the diabetes magazine *Sweet*. A coauthor of *The Men's Maintenance Manual*, which was published internationally, he is now working on an advanced fitness book for women.

Hodgkin was 3 times the World Karate Champion and 2 times the European Karate Champion as well as a member of the British Karate Squad for 10 years. He was also voted the Most Outstanding Competitor at the world championships in Calgary, Canada.

At the 2012 International Fitness Showcase—Europe's largest group exercise event, attracting over 7000 participants—Hodgkin received a Lifetime Achievement Award for his services to the fitness industry. Among many other accomplishments, he served as the Fitness Coach for Nike Basketball Camps, training prospects for the NBA and 2012 Olympics, and he was named an Ambassador for the Special Olympics in 2010.

His teaching includes training sports and fitness professionals, adults, and children for a wide range of activities, and he has taught tens of thousands of students around the world. Hodgkin has also worked as a consultant to a number of corporate clients, such as The Royal Automobile Club, Remington, and Reebok International, Ltd. Additionally, he consults for the leading U.K. spa, Ragdale Hall, as well as for LeSPORT, voted the world's best destination spa by *Condé Nast Traveller*.

After receiving a Bachelor of Science honors degree in Mathematics and Management Studies from the University of Portsmouth, Hodgkin continued his education at Leicester College, where he was awarded the Certificate in Exercise and Health Studies by the Physical Education Association of Great Britain and Northern Ireland, the leading qualification in the field at the time.

Fascinated by the human body, Hodgkin continues to educate himself, obtaining numerous certifications in health safety and health club management as well as industry-specific qualifications such as fitness yoga, spinning, FLEXI-BAR, and Zumba, among others. He is renowned for his practical skills in presenting a wide range of themed master classes and workshops—from mind-body wellness to dance and from core strengthening to aquatics—and he even offers juggling seminars that are aimed at improving mental agility and tackling stress. By keeping up with the latest physiological research on cardio and resistance training, Hodgkin tailors workout sessions to maximize the beneficial effects of exercise for your heart, lungs, bones, and mind.

Hodgkin's mission is to educate people of all ages and all cultures so that they understand the many benefits and experience the many joys of getting and staying fit. ■

Table of Contents

Table of Contents

Physiology and Fitness

Scope:

There's a wealth of scientific evidence that shows that appropriate exercise has a positive impact on the health of human beings in many ways. There's a whole industry of gyms, DVDs, articles, TV shows, and books that introduce us to the world of personal trainers, sports scientists, and health promotion workers. We all know that exercise is something that we should be doing if we're able, but within the bombardment of fitness-related information, there's very little insight into how and why changes occur in our bodies during regular physical activity. This course is designed to equip you with a basic understanding of how your body works and to enable you to set and meet your own health and fitness goals—including permanent weight loss, completing a charity run, or simply having more energy to live your day-to-day life with gusto.

Studies have shown that about 60% of adults don't get enough exercise and that 25% of adults don't get any exercise at all. The recommended guidelines are 150 minutes per week, and if you double that, you could reduce your risk of coronary heart disease by 20%. You could extend your life and reduce your risk of heart disease, diabetes, and cancer just by doing 15 minutes or more of exercise each day. Many people don't engage in 15 minutes or more of exercise each day—even though it's clearly beneficial—because of lack of time, energy, motivation, and information. This course is designed to help you tackle and overcome these most common obstacles.

Throughout this course, you'll discover ways to fit exercise into your daily life, and you'll begin to understand what exercise does for your body so that you'll feel more motivated to make a habit of exercising. In addition, you'll learn various tips on how to squeeze exercise into your day—whether you're at work or even in the car.

The journey through many aspects of health and fitness that this course will take you on will teach you how your body is structured and how it functions. You'll learn various principles of exercise with practical examples based on thoroughly researched facts rather than on fad or fashion. In addition, you'll encounter common health issues that occur through various stages of life so that even though some might not currently relate to you directly, you could become a vital conduit for your family and friends, who may be facing their own specific challenges and opportunities.

In general, there's a split between how people view exercise: There's a group of people who exercise regularly, even fanatically, but don't necessarily understand the science of physiology, and there's another group that reads about the science of physiology, but they don't necessarily apply that knowledge to consistent workouts. These 2 aspects of physiology are rarely interwoven so that scientific knowledge can improve the exercise or so that exercise can improve the understanding of physiology. In other words, you need both knowledge and practice to create a successful and consistent program of exercise for the rest of your life.

You can intensify any of the workouts explained in this course by adding more weight, more repetitions, more sets, or perhaps by combining workouts as you become fitter. You need to work your whole body in a variety of different ways to manage life's demands—from having to reach for a jar on a high shelf, which requires balance and mobility, to preventing injuries, which requires strength and flexibility.

To participate in this course, you can use some very simple tools, such as weights, resistance bands, training balls, medicine balls, benches, and steps. There are also some simple substitutions you can make for these items, which are available from most sports retailers, so that you can do the exercises at home. It is important to know that you don't need fancy equipment to participate—all you need is the will to exercise. ■

Walk Your Way to Fitness
Lecture 19

P erhaps due to its proven simplicity and comparably easy access, walking is the most undervalued of all the exercise formats. In general, many people view it as only being suitable as a route to fitness for the elderly or for the very out of shape. However, both the American Heart Association and the American College of Sports Medicine recommend walking as an exercise intervention that can improve a number of health measures. In this lecture, you will learn the value of walking as a workout mode and how to do it correctly to ensure optimum health benefits.

The Benefits of Walking

- Race walkers can cover a mile in just over 5 minutes and a full marathon in around 3 hours. Although over 40% of journeys in the United States are less than 2 miles, only 10% of these short trips are not made by car. These short trips offer a lot of opportunity for walking.

- Walking a mile burns just as many calories as running—it just takes longer. Walking has been proven to be an effective treatment for mild depression, reducing symptoms by 47%.

- Walking for fitness first gained popularity in the United States in the 1980s after cardiologist James Rippe, a graduate of Harvard Medical School, published details about how beneficial walking was for his patients recovering from a heart attack. His results showed that walking can not only reduce important health parameters such as high blood pressure and cholesterol, but can also significantly aid weight loss.

- Studies have shown that exercise doesn't have to be vigorous to reduce cardiovascular risk factors; even strolling can reduce the risk of cardiovascular disease.

3

- As with any activity, walking uses energy, so adding walking to your daily activity will burn extra calories. As long you don't compensate by eating extra food, regular fitness walking will result in weight loss. In addition, if you walk up a steep incline or increase your pace, you burn more calories.

- Race walking speeds of over 5 miles per hour will burn as many as 600 calories per hour. A 12-minute-per-mile pace, about 5 miles per hour, can burn as many as 50% more calories than a 20-minute-per-mile pace, which is 3 miles per hour. If you're walking faster, you'll not only burn more calories, but you'll also spend less time each day exercising.

- As a weight-bearing exercise, walking can also positively impact bone density. Osteoporosis reduces the density of bones and can be life threatening. Several studies have reported that regular walking at moderate to brisk speeds increases bone density—even for just 30 minutes a day.

- Regular aerobic conditioning, which is precisely what walking is, can help reduce stress. A walking program has been shown to produce significant gains in self-image, confidence, and feelings of well-being in addition to reducing depression.

- Exercise-related injuries are shown to be much lower for walking than for most other exercise formats. For example, during running, the body has to absorb impacts equal to around 5 times your body weight, but walking causes impact stresses of only around 2 to 3 times your weight. Therefore, walking is less likely to produce injuries and is consequently being recommended as a rehab activity for injured runners.

- Studies have shown that increasing the intensity of a walking program, unlike other modes of exercise, doesn't carry any increased risk of injury.

- When it comes to exercise for seniors, it can be argued that walking is the foremost option—although, of course, every type of exercise has some risk associated with it. However, because walking is a low-impact activity, the risk is lower compared to other forms of exercise, such as running.

The Walking Motion

- Starting at the top of the body, the shoulder muscles are used when you pump your arms vigorously while walking, and they provide balance as they swing in opposition to your legs.

- Walking with an upright posture is the most efficient way of locomotion, so pulling in the deeper abdominal muscles is important. The hip flexor muscles at the front and top of the thigh are responsible for lifting leg and swinging through the striding phase of the walk.

- The quadricep muscles on the front of the thigh are used to extend the knee as each leg is straightened. Your hips sway from side to side as you walk, and the glutei are responsible for this motion. Drawing the leg back and pushing off the ground requires hip extension, which uses the back of the thigh and the glutei.

- The **tibialis anterior** is on the front of the shin and raises the toes as the leg swings forward to ensure that your heel touches down first. The calf muscles provide the upward and forward momentum from the push off the ground as the heel lifts and you project forward.

- The **heel strike** describes the moment the foot first touches the ground and lasts for a split second. This is followed by the **early flatfoot stage**, which is defined as the point at which the whole foot is in contact with the ground, and the body's center of gravity, located in the pelvis in front of the bottom of the spine, is moving forward through the foot. This is an important stage because this is where shock absorption takes place, which is a key to preventing injury.

- The **late flatfoot stage** is the point at which the center of gravity passes forward of the neutral position, and subconsciously, the whole body structure changes from being flexible, in order to absorb shock, to being more rigid, enabling the body to propel forward.

- The final phase is called the **toe-off stage**, the point at which the swing of the leg begins again. This is where the difference between walking and running is most obvious; in walking, the next heel strike occurs immediately on the other foot, but a runner will go through the **floating stage**, describing the moment where both feet are momentarily off the ground.

Common Questions
- Is walking as good as a form of exercise as running? In fact, walking is a much healthier choice because you get all of the benefits of running—such as toning the muscles, improving the cardiorespiratory system, strengthening the immune system, and

Walking is a great alternative to running, especially because it has a lower impact on your joints.

controlling blood fats and stress hormones—but without the same risk of injury to your joints.

- Can walking really help you lose fat? It can, but the caveat is that just like any other form of exercise, the more effort you put in, the better the results you will achieve.

- To turn a simple walk into a workout, vary the intensity by alternating between a moderate but brisk pace and sprinting, pumping your arms as you vigorously move yourself across the ground. Just 30 minutes of this, including 30-second sprints and 1-minute slow paces for recovery, will lead to serious calorie burn.

- Walking is not just a simpler, easier version of running; you actually burn more calories walking fast than you do running. The 2 activities are obviously similar and offer common benefits, but walking also has the bonus of reducing the likelihood of impact injury. It also affords an opportunity to keep your fitness level up by exercising with certain injuries that running might not allow.

- Walking also provides the ideal gentle workout mode on the day following a race or a particularly heavy training session. Furthermore, it allows partners of disparate abilities to exercise together because the fitter person speed walking will be working hardest if trying to keep up with the less fit person who is running.

Walking Tips
- When outdoor temperatures are high, profuse sweating leads to considerable water loss. This reduces the amount of blood returning to the heart, which could result in cardiovascular stress as indicated by very high heart rates. On a hot day, you must take a water bottle with you.

- When humidity is high and air temperature is up, the body's ability to dissipate internal heat produced during exercise is impaired. Therefore, you may need to reduce your speed or continue walking during extreme conditions because it could result in heat exhaustion or perhaps heat stroke. To improve the body's ability to stay cool, you need to choose light, loose clothing that will allow air to circulate around the body.

- If the sun is strong, a hat or visor may be advisable, and a smear of petroleum jelly across your forehead just above your eyebrows will prevent sweat from running into your eyes. In addition, petroleum jelly is useful to lubricate the tops of the legs and under the arms to avoid chafing.

- On a cool or cold day, layering clothing will keep walkers warm at the start of the exercise. As the body becomes warm, outer layers can be removed before the under layers become wet from perspiration. If your clothing becomes wet, it should be changed as soon as possible. Gloves and a hat are advisable if the weather is very cold because a lot of heat is lost through the hands and head.

- In wet weather, you'll chill very quickly unless you protect yourself from the rain, but try to avoid plastic garments because they don't allow perspiration to escape, so you could end up becoming chilled. In addition, windy conditions can significantly alter the intensity of exercise, so adjust your workouts accordingly if you need to.

- Walkers who are accustomed to exercising at lower altitudes will need to decrease their exercise intensity and increase their warm-up and cooldown periods at higher altitudes until they have acclimatized to the new conditions.

- The mechanics of walking are quite distinct from other sports, and thus, there are different requirements for walking shoes. A good walking shoe must be flexible in the forefoot and stiff in the heel with a slightly firmer yet still comfortable middle sole.

- In addition, wear well-fitting, seam-free socks—that are made of cotton or of a wool mix—to prevent chaffing and to absorb perspiration.

Walking Workouts

- The following walking technique includes 3 distinct intensity levels. For level 1, called health walking, focus on your posture by lifting up through the center of your body, trying to maintain a large space between your rib cage and your pelvis. Relax your shoulders, and swing your arms in rhythm with your stride

- Keep your arms swinging naturally and comfortably, and relax your elbows as you swing your arms in opposition to your legs. The length of each stride should be comfortable, with stride length varying from one individual to another.

- For level 2, called fitness walking, keep the same posture as in level 1, but bend your elbows so that your arms will swing faster. Swinging your arms faster will cause you to increase your stride frequency.

- Level 3 is known as speed walking and should only be used in short spurts due to the effort involved. As your arms swing from your shoulders, focus on driving your elbows back and keeping them close to the sides of your body. Concentrate on increasing stride frequency—not stride length.

- Like any other exercise class, begin your walking workout with a warm-up, then do the aerobic training section, and follow with a cooldown or stretch.

- Level 1 walking is ideal as a warm-up. Then, start to increase your walking speed from level 1 to level 2, concentrating on good posture.

- Next is the aerobic section, where the aim is to elevate your heart rate for a specific period of time. This section should form the major part of your walk and should feature alternate bursts of level 3 with level 2 for recovery.

- Your cooldown will return your body to its pre-exercise state by reducing your heart rate and breathing rate gradually to more normal levels, followed by stretching the muscles used to maintain or develop flexibility.

Important Terms

early flatfoot stage: The stage of walking at which the whole foot is in contact with the ground. This is an important stage because this is where shock absorption takes place, which is a key to preventing injury.

floating stage: The moment for runners at which both feet are momentarily off the ground.

heel strike: The split second at which the foot first touches the ground when walking.

late flatfoot stage: The stage of walking at which the center of gravity passes forward of the neutral position, and subconsciously, the whole body structure changes from being flexible, in order to absorb shock, to being more rigid, enabling the body to propel forward.

tibialis anterior: A muscle that is located on the front of the shin and is responsible for raising the toes as the leg swings forward to ensure that the heel touches down first when walking.

toe-off stage: The stage of walking at which the swing of the leg begins.

Walk Your Way to Fitness
Lecture 19—Transcript

Perhaps due to its proven simplicity and comparably easy access, walking is the most undervalued exercise format that exists. As a sweeping generalization, a lot of people view it as only being suitable as a route to fitness for the elderly or the very out of shape. How wrong this statement is.

Both the American Heart Association and the American College of Sports Medicine recommend walking as an exercise intervention that can improve a number of health measures. So there must be some weight behind these claims. Over the next 30 minutes I will convince you of its value as a workout mode, prove to you it's not a soft option, and teach you just how to do it correctly to ensure optimum health benefits.

Firstly let's look at a few facts about walking, and I find some of these, well nothing short of amazing. Race walkers can cover a mile in just over 5 minutes and a full marathon in around 3 hours. Although over 40% of journeys in the U.S. are less than 2 miles, only 10% of these short trips are not made by car. These short trips offer a lot of opportunity for walking. Walking a mile burns just as many calories as running, it just takes longer. Walking has been proven to be an effective treatment for mild depression, reducing symptoms by 47%. Walking can reduce your risk of type 2 diabetes by 58%, and a 2011 study by Erin Richman showed that brisk walking, at least 3 miles per hour for 3 hours or more a week, lowered the risk of prostate cancer progression.

Walking for fitness first gained popularity in the United States in the '80s after Cardiologist James Rippe, a graduate of the Harvard Medical School, published details of how beneficial walking was for his patients recovering from a heart attack. Dr. Rippe wanted to know if these benefits could be extrapolated to the general population. With a team of researchers, he set up the Rockport Walking Program in Massachusetts.

In 1989 when the results were published, they caused quite sensation in the mainstream media and led to a sudden boom in fitness walking across the nation. The program showed how walking can not only reduce important health parameters such as high blood pressure and cholesterol, but could also significantly aid weight loss. So let's take a look at what the research tells us.

Firstly let's consider whether walking can truly be effective as a training stimulus. Rippe's study tested 500 people and found that 67% of the men and 90% of the women could reach their target heart rates by walking 4 to 4 and 1/2 miles per hour. Dr. Astrand found that during competitive walking, intensity reached approximately 85% of maximum heart rate. It was even higher uphill.

In another study, Michael Pollock at the University of Florida's Center for Exercise Science found that middle-aged men who walked to the pace of 3 and 1/2 to 4 and 1/2 miles per hour for 40 minutes, 4 times per week had the same cardiovascular improvements as men the same age who jogged for 30 minutes 3 times a week. These walkers didn't reach the same level of intensity as the runners, yet the increased duration and frequency of walking gave the walkers similar aerobic benefits.

Now I'll specifically consider the area of cardiovascular disease. A British study by Adrianne Hardman looked at the effects on the health of previously sedentary women who walked regularly for 1 year. The women walked on average 2 and 1/2 hours per week at about 4 miles per hour. This added up to approximately 10 miles per week at around 70% of maximum heart rate.

The results of the study showed enhanced exercise tolerance, improved metabolic response to exercise and changes in the lipid profile of the blood, significant enough to predict a decreased risk of coronary artery disease in the walking group when compared to controls. The conclusion: Exercise doesn't have to be vigorous to reduce cardiovascular risk factors. In other words, even strolling can reduce the risk of cardiovascular disease.

One of the most comprehensive and renowned of these studies looked at the physical activity of 17,000 Harvard alumni across 20 years. Ralph Paffenbarger and his colleagues concluded that walking can reduce the risk of cardiovascular disease and reduce the risk of a heart attack by 28% or more. You can do this in 5 30-minute walking sessions per week.

Now clearly for a lot of us weight management, weight loss is the primary motivation. So how effective is walking in this domain? As with any activity, walking uses energy and therefore adding walking to your daily activity will use extra calories. So long as you don't compensate by eating extra food, regular fitness walking will result in weight loss.

Back to Dr. James Rippe, he estimated that brisk walking for 45 minutes per day, 4 times per week is sufficient to lose an amazing 18 pounds over a year even without dietary change.

Not surprisingly, if you walk up a steep incline and/or increase your pace you burn more calories. For example, if you weigh 150 pounds, that's 68 kilos, and you walk 3 and 1/2 miles per hour, that's about 5.6 kilometers per hour on flat ground, you're going to burn about 300 calories an hour. However, if you walked up just a 4% incline, you'd burn 400 calories an hour. If you walked up a 10% incline, you'd burn a whopping 500 calories per hour. Now if you pick up the pace as well, say to just 4 miles per hour or 6.4 kilometers per hour on level ground, you'll burn 350 calories in an hour. And that's pretty good for just walking.

Race walking speeds of over 5 miles per hour will burn as many as 600 calories per hour. A 12 minute mile pace (around 5 miles per hour) can burn as many as 50% more calories than a 20 minute mile pace (which is 3 miles per hour). If you're walking faster you'll not only burn more calories, but you'll also spend less time each day exercising. For example, walking 3 miles at a 12 minute mile pace 5 days per week will save you 2 hours per week over a person walking 3 miles at a 20 minute mile pace. As a weight bearing exercise, walking can also positively impact upon bone density.

Osteoporosis is a major health problem affecting around 25% of women and 8% of men in the UK and some 15 million people in the U.S. Osteoporosis reduces the density of bones and can be life-threatening since many older people die as a result of complications suffered from broken bones. Several studies have reported that regular walking at moderate to brisk speeds increases bone density, even just walking for just 30 minutes a day.

As we discussed in our lecture on stress, exercise can help reduce stress, particularly regular aerobic conditioning, which is precisely what walking is. A walking program has been shown to produce significant gains in self-image, confidence, feelings of well-being, and just reducing depression. In one particular study, A. F. Kramer and his colleagues examined the effects of brisk walking on mildly obese sedentary women and found that walking markedly improved their psychological well-being. So it's easy to understand why Hippocrates is quoted as saying, "Walking is man's best medicine."

But where walking really displays its value is in the area of injury, as exercise related injuries are shown to be much lower than for most other exercise formats. During running for instance, the body has to absorb impacts equal to around 5 times your body weight, but walking causes impact stresses of only around 2–3 times your own weight. This means that walking is less likely to produce injuries and is consequently being recommended as a rehab activity for injured runners. Studies have shown that increasing the intensity of a walking program, unlike other modes or exercise doesn't carry any increased risk of injury. During one 24 week study, not 1 of the 59 participants who walked 5 days a week at speeds of between 3 and 5 miles per hour sustained a walking-related injury that necessitated consulting with a physician. Another 28-week study compared the injury rate of subjects running versus those doing fitness walking 4 days a week at 80% of their maximum heart rate for 40 minutes. Preliminary results indicated that runners lost 11.1 days of training due to injury, but fitness walkers only lost an average of 1 and 1/2 days of training.

When it comes to exercise for seniors it can be argued that walking is the foremost option. Although of course every type of exercise has some risk associated with it. However, because walking is a low impact activity, the risk is lower compared to other forms of exercise such as running.

Now for those of you who might consider walking too easy or maybe even too boring to adopt as a fitness technique, I'm going to give you a challenge. Pop on the treadmill next time you're at the gym and just 2 miles an hour, set the pace at 2 miles an hour, but every 30 seconds I want you to increase the speed by 2 miles an hour. Somewhere around 5 miles per hour you'll naturally want to break into a jog because biomechanically it's more efficient for your body to do this but at this point don't. Don't run, just walk faster and see how it feels after about 5 minutes. I'm pretty sure you'll then be convinced of the fitness credentials of walking.

Walking obviously uses similar muscles to running but let's look at how your body achieves the walking motion. Let's work from the upper body downwards and see what's really going on here. The shoulder muscles are used when you pump your arms vigorously while walking and of course they provide balance as they swing in opposition to your legs.

Walking with an upright posture is most efficient way of locomotion so, pulling in the deeper abdominal muscles is important. Moving a little lower the hip flexor muscles at the front and top of the thigh are responsible for lifting the leg and swinging through the striding phase of the walk.

The quadricep muscles on the front of the thigh are used as to extend the knee as each leg is straightened on that reach. Your hips actually will rock from side to side as you walk and the gluteals are responsible for this motion. Now drawing the leg back and pushing off requires hip extension which is working into the back of the thigh also into the gluteals.

The tibialis anterior is on the front of the shin and that'll raise the toes as the leg swings forwards to ensure your heel touched down first. The calf muscles will provide that upward and forward momentum from the push off as the heel lifts and you project forward. As you might imagine though, the real science is going on down in the feet. So let's investigate a little more closely what's really going on here.

The heel strike describes the moment the foot first touches the ground and lasts for literally, just a split second. This is followed by the early flat foot stage, defined as the point where the whole of the foot is now in contact with the ground and the body's center of gravity located in the pelvis just in front of the bottom of the spine is now moving forwards through the foot. This is an important stage as this is where shock absorption takes place which is a key to preventing injury.

The next phase is called the late flat foot, and at this point this is where the center of gravity actually passes forward of the neutral position and subconsciously the whole body structure changes from being flexible to absorb shock to being more rigid, enabling us to propel forwards.

Around 2–3 times the body weight pass through the foot as the heel raises, something that happens between anywhere from 3–10 thousand times each day. So it's not surprising that the foot can suffer chronic injury due to repetitive stress.

Then the final phase obviously, the toe-off, the point at which the swing begins again. This is where the difference between walking and running is most obvious, since in walking the next heel strike occurs immediately on the other foot. But a runner will go through what's called floating stage, describing the moment where both feet are momentarily off the ground.

As an experienced trainer, I've been around a while and I'm always being asked questions, all sorts of questions. But these 2 are really common and they relate to walking. I've been asked these questions so many times I've lost count over the years. "Surely walking can't be as good for me as running." Actually it's a much healthier choice as you'll get all of the benefits of running such as toning the muscles, improving the cardiorespiratory system, strengthening the immune system, controlling blood fats, stress hormones, but without the same risk of injury to your joints. Runners put a strain on their joints as I mentioned earlier equal to around 5 times their body weight with each impact, in stark contrast to what we just learned about walkers.

Another question: "Can walking really help me to lose fat?" Without doubt although the caveat here is that, just like any other form of exercise, the more effort you put in, the better results you'll achieve. To turn a simple walk into a workout, vary the intensity by alternating between a moderate but brisk pace and then some full out sprints in inverted commas, pumping your arms as you vigorously move yourself across the ground.

Just 30 minutes like this, including 30 second sprints and 1 minute slow pace for recovery will lead to a serious calorie burn and so will considerably help you in your weight loss efforts.

Another question, I'm already running, if I'm running what's the point in walking? Well this completely misses the point because unfortunately, walking is not simply just a simpler, easier version of running. For, as we've already discovered, you actually burn more calories walking fast than you do jogging.

The 2 activities are obviously similar and offer common benefits but walking also has the bonus of reducing the likelihood of impact injury as we've seen. It affords an opportunity to still keep your fitness level up by exercising with certain injuries that running might not allow.

It also provides the ideal gentle workout mode on the day following a race or a particularly heavy training session. Finally, it allows partners of disparate abilities to exercise together as the fitter person speed walking will be working hardest if trying to keep up with the less fit person who's jogging.

So now hopefully you're convinced; here's a few tips to get you started. Exercising outdoors, perhaps even in extreme conditions, can dampen your enthusiasm to walk, so a few necessary precautions are needed in such conditions.

When temperatures are high, profuse sweating leads to considerable water loss. This reduces the amount of blood returning to the heart which could result in cardiovascular stress as indicated by very high heart rates. So on a hot day then, you must take your water bottle with you.

When humidity is high, say over about 60%, air temperature is up, the body's ability to dissipate internal heat produced during exercise is impaired. So you may need to reduce your speed or continued walking during these extreme conditions because it could result in heat exhaustion or perhaps heat stroke.

Now the symptoms of heat exhaustion include weakness, dizziness, headaches, nausea, pale skin, profuse sweating, and a weak but rapid pulse. And the best treatment for this condition is replenishment of fluids and prolonged rest in a cool location. So on warm days you need to choose light, loose clothing that will allow air to circulate around the body and thus improve the body's ability to stay cool. If the sun is strong, a hat or a visor may be advisable and smear of petroleum jelly across the forehead just above the eyebrows will prevent sweat from running into your eyes. By the way petroleum jelly is also useful to lubricate the tops of the legs and under the arms to avoid chafing. Layering clothing will keep walkers warm at the start of the exercise on a cool or cold day. As the body becomes warm, outer layers can be removed before the under layers become wet from perspiration. If your clothing becomes wet it should be changed as soon as possible.

Dressing advice for cold days is to start with a thin layer of thermal fabric that traps the air but releases moisture next to the skin, followed by a warm synthetic such as a sweatshirt or a fleece. All these layers should allow perspiration to escape so they need to be nonabsorbent and dry quickly. There are many lightweight thermal garments on the market designed for walking, and whilst not essential they will help to ensure your comfort. Obviously gloves and a hat are advisable if the weather is very cold as a lot of heat is lost through the hands and head.

In wet weather you'll chill very quickly unless you protect yourself from the rain but try to avoid plastic garments as these don't allow perspiration to escape so you could end up getting chilled.

Windy conditions can significantly alter the intensity of exercise. For example, on a calm day, a 3 mile walk on level ground could be completed in an hour at a level intensity that feels somewhat hard. The same person however may find the same 3 mile walk very hard in windy conditions. So adjust your workouts accordingly if need be.

You might, by the way, talking about walking outdoors, want to try Nordic Walking. Now this has been around for a while now but involves using poles so you're using your upper body. And that can help to burn a few more calories if it's done correctly. If possible avoid vigorous exercise in areas with high levels of air pollution. While environmental hazards in highly polluted areas can be reduced by walking in the early morning, late evening, or weekends, it might be better to exercise indoors.

Bear in mind that at even in just moderate altitude your circulatory system might find it more difficult than usual to deliver as much oxygen to the exercising muscles as is required. Walkers who are accustomed to exercising at lower altitudes will need to decrease their exercise intensity and increase warm-up and cool-down periods at higher altitudes until they have acclimatized to these new conditions. It usually takes weeks to adapt to major changes in altitude.

A lot of people ask me about walking shoes. A walking shoe is a performance product designed specifically for this activity, just as basketball shoes and running shoes are designed for those activities. The mechanics of walking are quite distinct from other sports and thus there are different requirements for the footwear. Firstly, a walking shoe doesn't have to absorb as much force as a running shoe and so it should have a slightly lower heel. However it should still have adequate cushioning at the heel strike point. The lower heel, which usually has a slight bevel in the rear, also accommodates the heel strike and forward roll of the foot seen in walking. A higher heel will tend to cause the toe to slap down rapidly, possibly even causing soreness on the shins. The shoe must be flexible in the forefoot. It should also have good toe-spring to further aid in the forward roll of the foot from heel to toe. A runner's shoe will only need to allow for probably around 30 degrees of bend. But a walkers shoe really needs to allow for around 45 degrees. A stiff heel lends lateral support when the heel first contacts the ground. And we'll choose a slightly firmer yet still comfortable mid-sole, and this also improves lateral stability and increases the durability of the shoe since the firmer material is less likely to compress over time. There's no need for the sometimes bulky, lateral support structures found in the forefoot of basketball, tennis, aerobics and similar shoes. These only add weight and are unnecessary in an activity which has little side-to-side movement and is essentially linear such as walking. Just another tip, wear well-fitting, seam-free socks to prevent chaffing and to absorb perspiration. They need to fit well and cotton, wool mix is usually most comfortable and more absorbent.

I'll now take you through a walking technique, introducing 3 distinct intensity levels. We'll start at level 1, and this is referred to as health walking. First, focus on your posture by lifting up through the center of your body, trying to maintain a large space between your rib cage and your pelvis. Relax your shoulders down and back and swing your arms in rhythm with your stride. Keep your arms swinging naturally and comfortably, relax your elbows as you swing your arms in opposition to your legs. The forward swing should never cross the center of the body and the arms should swing from the shoulder and not from the elbow.

The length of each stride should be comfortable, with stride length varying from one individual to another. Stride length is determined by leg length, hamstring tightness, and pelvic rotation. A person with short legs, tight hamstrings, and limited pelvis rotation will therefore have a shorter stride length than someone with longer legs, flexible hip joints, and greater amount of rotation.

When you plant your heel, your forefoot and toes are raised towards the shins, this is called dorsiflexion. Then you lower your foot to the ground with control, not slapping or pounding. Finally your foot rolls from heel to toe. Of course the faster you bring your rear leg forward, the faster your walking rate.

Level 2 is called fitness walking as although posture remains as in level 1, there are various technique modifications that will enable you to increase the pace now. For fitness walking, bend your elbows so that your arms will swing faster. Swinging the arms faster will cause you to increase your stride frequency.

Don't cross the body with the arms, it should be a forward and backward movement coming from the shoulders rather than the elbows. Fix your elbows at about a 90 degree angle. Swing and hold the forearms close to the side, keep your hands in loose fists, in line with your forearms.

By the time your foot is planted on the ground, your leg should be almost fully extended. Be careful not to lock your knee—that is to push your leg so straight that it is rigid and can't move back any more. If you find yourself bobbing or bouncing somewhat as you walk, you may be bending your knee prematurely.

Your hips should be rotating slightly as you walk, so one hip will be forward while the other hip is back. Let this hip rotation occur naturally; don't wiggle your hips to make it happen. If you're walking properly you'll notice the rotation. As you speed up you're naturally going to lean more forward, now make sure this is from your ankles up. Don't bend just from the waist forwards, as this can cause pain and discomfort in your lumbar spine.

Level 3 is known as speed walking and is an effort of around 9 on a scale of 1–10. So it can't be maintained for long durations but should be used in short spurts. The technique is as follows. As the arm swings from the shoulder focus on driving your elbows back and keep them close to the sides of the body. As we said earlier, pumping your arms as fast as you can will naturally increase your stride frequency.

Concentrate on increasing stride frequency, not stride length. The hips move or rotate forwards and backwards with a minimum of side to side motion. Remember our aim is to get from A to B in a straight line forwards. So we want our movement to be forwards not side to side. As the hip of the advancing leg reaches maximum forward rotation, the hip will drop or tilt down slightly. So there's a fair bit of movement going on around the pelvis.

Ensure you keep the ball of the rear foot on the ground until the heel of the forward leg has contacted the ground. At the heel plant, the ankle should be dorsiflexed to about 90 degrees, i.e., the toe lift should be more pronounced. The point of contact between the foot and ground moves smoothly from the heel to the ball of the foot in a continuous rolling motion, with a strong push off the ball of the foot. At these higher walking speeds, the placement of the foot should form a continuous straight line with the inner edge of one foot landing in front of the inner edge of the other foot. Almost like walking on a tightrope rather than walking on tram lines.

For most people the toes are turned outward from the heels approximately 10 degrees and this angle tends to decrease as you increase your speed. However, this angle of gait varies from one individual to another.

Lean forwards from your ankles as this will give you a feeling of being able to push against the ground harder. It will also help you to avoid over striding that can slow you down. Leaning too far forward however, can cause you to land flat-footed or to lift the rear off the ground prematurely.

Now that you know the 3 levels of walking, let's talk about structuring your walking workout for maximum benefits. Like any other exercise class, begin with a warm up, then do the aerobic training section and follow with a cool down or stretch.

As we've discussed previously, the purpose of the warm up is to prepare your body for exercise by increasing the internal body temperature about 1 or 2 degrees, increasing the blood flow to the muscles, and lubricating the joints by pumping synovial fluid into them. Level 1 walking is ideal for this purpose. This should be followed by a pulse raiser to bring your heart rate up, increase blood flow to the working muscles, and provide neuromuscular activity that mimics that of the training section of the class. Simply start to increase your walking speed then from level 1 to level 2, concentrating on good posture, relaxed technique with the foot rolling motion. You're aiming to reach an intensity of around 5–6 on a scale of 1–10.

Next is the aerobic section where the aim is to elevate your heart rate for a specific period of time, leading to calorie burning, improved fitness, reduction in the risk of lifestyle related diseases. These are all the benefits we're after. This section should form the major part of your walk and should feature alternate bursts of level 3 with level 2 for recovery. You could work for set time periods or perhaps 30 seconds on, 30 seconds off, or use physical markers. For example walk level 3 between 2 trees and then level 2 between the next 2 trees alternating the speed.

Your cool down follows, as this will return your body to its pre-exercise state by reducing the heart rate and breathing rate gradually to more normal levels, followed by stretching the muscles used to maintain or develop flexibility. For a selection of stretches don't forget to take a look at the stretch workout at the end of this series.

So what are you waiting for? Even if you don't fancy striding out solo, there are plenty of options to help you get started. It's easy enough to locate a mall walking, race walking, American Volkssport Association or Nordic Walking Club near to you so you can have company while you're getting fit.

Now you may have heard the saying that good things come to those who wait, but I hope you'll agree with me now, we've uncovered there's so many health and fitness benefits that go with walking that actually, good things come to those who walk. And remember, walking might be cheap but life is priceless.

The Amazing Benefits of Stretching
Lecture 20

Flexibility is considered to be one of the health-related components of fitness, and poor flexibility can lead to alignment issues that could increase your risk of postural problems, which can potentially negatively affect your quality of life. In this lecture, you'll learn how to stretch effectively to help keep you mobile well into your later years, and you'll discover a range of techniques that will help improve your flexibility—along with an understanding of why the various techniques work.

Joints and Flexibility

- Flexibility refers to the range of motion around a joint or group of joints. It varies from person to person, but for each individual, it also differs from joint to joint. It's primarily dependent upon the specific joint structure and is significantly influenced by the connective tissues around each of the joints.

- There are 3 different types of joints: joints that are fused and exhibit no movement (the skull), joints with limited movement (the spine), and synovial joints (the elbow and knee) that allow for a higher degree of movement.

- Synovial joints rely upon both a capsule that envelops the whole joint and the supporting ligaments to hold the bones together. The capsule fills with synovial fluid to lubricate the joints, making movement easier, but it's also tough enough to restrict potential damaging movements.

- The ligaments are made of fibrous tissue similar to the capsule and serve to attach bone to bone. Importantly, they also give the joint stability by preventing movement that could cause dislocation, for example.

- Joint health is related to activity levels, age, and gender, and a clear link exists between the amount of exercise taken and the mobility of the joints—with even just regular walking positively affecting the range of motion in the hips and lower spine. Because tightness in these areas can be a contributory factor in the incidence of falls in the elderly, joint health has great value in maintaining good quality of life.

- The American College of Sports Medicine recommends stretching to promote enhanced flexibility as an essential preventive measure. Regular stretching also has been found to significantly reduce lower back pain.

- As we age, there's a gradual slowing of the cell function in muscles, tendons, and ligaments that leads to a buildup of **collagen**, the main component of connective tissue, which becomes denser and less resistant to lengthening. Because connective tissue surrounds the joint, reduced mobility is the result. However, regular stretching can help to maintain the elasticity of connective tissue and reduce the effects of this aging process.

- In general, females tend to have better flexibility than males at most joints, and this can be attributed to small differences in the joint structures and the associated connective tissues. The effect of age on flexibility, however, is considerably greater than gender.

- Body temperature affects range of motion because it improves with increasing heat, which explains the reason that exercise always begins with a warm-up period. Contrary to common belief, rather than shortening your muscles and making them stiffer, weight training exercises that work through your full range of motion will improve your flexibility.

- During pregnancy, the joints and ligaments in the **lumbopelvic area**—which includes the lumbar, stomach, pelvis, and hips—are relaxed to allow for growth and movement of the fetus and to make delivery a little easier. This change is due to increased levels of the relaxin hormone, which drops to normal levels after the birth, so the connective tissues tighten up again.

- Improving flexibility requires a stretching program that aims to increase the range of motion and that takes into account the factors regarding the joints. Careful consideration should be given to designing a plan to ensure that it's safe, appropriate, and effective.

© Jupiterimages/Thinkstock.

Flexibility can be completely maintained throughout your life by doing stretching exercises.

- Research shows that regular stretching has been shown to produce enhanced range of motion, reduced risk of injury—and the degree of injury if injury occurs—increased sports performance in terms of endurance and skill, improved posture, and a positive impact on mental health by providing a vehicle for physical relaxation.

Stretching Techniques
- Stretching can be active, brought about by contracting the opposing muscle group to move the limb to a position where the target muscle is lengthened, or it can be passive, whereby the limb is moved by a partner, yourself, or a prop. Stretching techniques are divided into 3 main categories: ballistic, static, and proprioceptive neuromuscular facilitation (PNF).

- **Ballistic stretching** involves swinging or bouncing a limb into a position beyond the normal joint range, thereby lengthening the associated muscles. It's a common technique for elite sportspeople, but it's not recommended for the public because it is difficult to execute safely.

- **Static stretching** is the most common method of practice, requiring a gentle movement toward the end position that slowly lengthens the muscle. Then, you hold the point at which there's mild tension for between 15 and 30 seconds. A good tip is to use imagery; try to actually picture the muscle lengthening as you stretch.

- **Proprioceptive neuromuscular facilitation (PNF)** stretching techniques were originally devised as a therapy for patients suffering from muscle-related diseases and work by using the body's nervous system to encourage extended lengthening of the muscles. It uses 3 key responses: the myotatic reflex, the Golgi tendon organ reflex, and the principle of reciprocal inhibition.

- The **myotatic reflex**, also known as the stretch reflex, is an automatic contraction within the muscle. It's a response to a change in the length that is detected by muscle spindles, which lie within the muscle fibers. This is a self-preserving response to the possibility that the muscle might be stretched too far and could cause a tearing of the fibers. This reflex is the reason ballistic stretching carries some risk.

- The **Golgi tendon organ reflex**, also known as the inverse stretch reflex, is the opposite of the myotatic reflex. This receptor is located at the point where the muscle joins the tendon, and it detects tension. If it detects very high tension, it interprets it as a possible threat to the muscle—potentially causing it to tear—so it forces the muscle to relax, thereby removing the threat.

- **Reciprocal inhibition** describes the process whereby one muscle relaxes to some degree if its cooperating pair contracts. These sensory responses are used in combination with a technique called contract-relax-antagonist-contract. First, the target muscle group is stretched slowly, in a passive manner, which avoids initiating the myotatic reflex. Then, it's held in a position while a voluntary contraction of the muscle is exerted for about 6 seconds without it moving, which will stimulate the Golgi tendon organ reflex that relaxes the muscle. Then, the opposite muscle group is contracted strongly, and by reciprocal inhibition, the target muscle relaxes even more and can then be stretched to a much greater degree. This has been shown to be the best stretching method to improve flexibility.

- A technique that works on the principle of reciprocal innovation is called **active isolated stretching** and is suitable for just about anyone—including elite athletes and those not accustomed to exercise. The body positions are comfortable and easily manageable, and the stretches are gentle and relaxing. Unlike the other techniques, this is an active technique that is performed with a partner.

- Start by contracting the muscles to move through a full range of functional motion. This will result in the opposite muscles switching off and relaxing, allowing a partner to assist the stretch by gently extending the range of motion. This assist should only last for about 2 seconds, and each stretch should be performed 10 times.

Flexibility Guidelines
- As with any form of exercise, you should follow a plan when dealing with flexibility. However, unlike cardio fitness and strength training, there are no universally agreed upon programs for flexibility. Therefore, applying common sense and committing yourself to regular stretching will lead to increased range of motion.

- Try to stretch daily if possible. Withhold static stretches at the point of mild tension for 15 seconds to maintain flexibility but closer to 30 seconds to improve it. Ensure you're warm before stretching—either after some cardio exercise or a warm bath.

- Be aware of your posture; ensure that you are in a comfortable position to stretch that allows you to focus on the target muscle. Perform stretches that target the joints that feel particularly stiff or that replicate movements you need for your chosen sport.

- Use deep breathing, gentle music, and some visualization to help your efforts by helping to relax the muscles. If at any time you feel a sharp or stabbing pain, release the stretch immediately.

Myths and Misconceptions of Stretching

- There are many myths and misconceptions about stretching that, unfortunately, are even held by some lesser qualified fitness professionals.

- Flexibility is not related to your shape because height, weight, arm span, and leg length do not significantly affect range of motion.

- It's easy to assume that weight training leads to stiffness. However, there's no link between muscle size and immobility. In fact, because resistance training results in improvements in the elasticity of the muscles and the tensile strength in the tendons and ligaments, it can increase your range of motion over time—even without stretching.

- Furthermore, flexibility training can actually improve your strength. By increasing your flexibility, the muscles are able to operate over a greater range of motion, thereby recruiting more muscle fibers and generating more force.

- In preparation for exercise and sporting pursuits by engaging in a warm-up, the increased body temperature through movement will stimulate the flow of synovial fluid into the joints that lubricate them. Respiratory speed will increase to introduce more oxygen to generate fuel, and the heart rate will increase to transport nutrients to the working muscles.

- Most importantly, as temperature increases, so does the speed of nerve impulses, and this is the key to reducing the risk of injury. For example, if you stumble on uneven pavement, as your ankle begins to roll, the Golgi tendon organs detect extra tension in the area, and a message gets sent through the spinal cord that orders the muscle to contract, helping you stand back up.

- The faster that message transfers, the less risk there is of injury. The nerve fibers are incased in the myelin sheath, which serve to insulate the nerve fibers because the warmer you are, the faster those messages will transfer.

- In order to reduce the risk of injury, those muscle messages need to transfer extremely quickly. In this case, the key to reducing the risk of injury is to warm up, and the warm-up should focus on mobility and increasing temperature.

- In fact, studies confirm that pre-exercise stretching actually increases the risk of injury by rendering the joints less stable. Stretching to develop flexibility is best left until the end of the session—when you're warm.

- Our final controversy concerns the much-heralded value of stretching in preventing muscle soreness experienced the day following exercise. In fact, muscle soreness is the sum of several factors, including microtrauma to the muscle fibers—inflammation within the cells and irritation of the nerve endings due to additional enzyme activity.

- Because stretching cannot impact these processes that lead to microtrauma, it can't affect muscle soreness. Therefore, if you exercise intensely today, expect muscle soreness tomorrow and embrace it because it's a sign that you worked hard enough to set in motion the adaptive responses that will lead to positive change. A cooldown will help remove waste products, such as lactic acid, and reduce the inflammation to some degree, and stretching can be part of that cooldown.

Important Terms

active isolated stretching: A stretching technique that uses the synchronization of paired muscles to allow for coordinated movements and is performed with a partner.

ballistic stretching: A type of stretching that involves swinging or bouncing a limb into a position beyond the normal joint range, thereby lengthening the associated muscles.

collagen: The main component of connective tissue.

Golgi tendon organ reflex: An automatic relaxing within the muscle that is a response to a change in muscle tension.

lumbopelvic area: The area of the body that includes the lumbar, stomach, pelvis, and hips.

myotatic reflex: An automatic contraction within the muscle that is a response to a change in the length that is detected by muscle spindles.

proprioceptive neuromuscular facilitation (PNF): A stretching technique that works by using the body's nervous system to encourage extended lengthening of the muscles.

reciprocal inhibition: The process in which one muscle relaxes to some degree if its cooperating pair contracts.

static stretching: The most common method of stretching that requires a gentle movement toward the end position that slowly lengthens the muscle. Then, you hold the point at which there's mild tension for between 15 and 30 seconds.

The Amazing Benefits of Stretching
Lecture 20—Transcript

The main function of muscles is to provide the driving force that brings about movement of the skeleton's complex system of levers. If they can operate through a wide range of motion then they'll quite obviously be more effective in creating movement of the limbs, and this range of motion is what's known as flexibility.

You may remember from our very first lecture that flexibility is considered one of the health related components of fitness. A poor score in this area is likely to lead to alignment issues that could increase your risk of postural problems with the potential to negatively affect your quality of life.

So it would be useful to know how to stretch effectively to help to keep you mobile well into your later years, and that's a key part of this presentation, as I intend to equip you with a range of techniques to promote your flexibility and the understanding behind why they work. You'll also learn a few interesting facts about stretching along the way. For instance, does stretching before activity really help to reduce the chance of you injuring yourself? Is it truly the route to reducing feelings of muscle soreness? Can stretching actually make you stronger? You might be quite surprised to learn the answers to these questions.

Let's start by defining flexibility in a little more detail. We know flexibility refers to the range of motion around a joint or a group of joints, and it not only varies from person to person but for each individual it also differs from joint to joint. It's primarily dependent upon the specific joint structure and is significantly influenced by the connective tissues around each of the joints.

As discussed in my lecture on the joints, there are 3 different types. First are those joints that are fused and exhibit no movement, such as those found in the skull. Secondly, there are joints with limited movement such as the spine. And then thirdly there are synovial joints, such as the elbow and knee that allow for a higher degree of movement, and clearly it is the latter group that are our focus is in a stretching program.

These joints rely upon both a capsule that envelops the whole joint and the supporting ligaments to hold the bones together. The capsule can actually be friend or foe, as it fills with synovial fluid to lubricate the joints and that makes movement easier. But fortunately, it's also tough enough to restrict potential damaging movements.

The ligaments are made of fibrous tissue similar to the capsule and serve to attach bone to bone. Importantly they also give the joint stability by preventing movement that could cause dislocation, for example.

Since joint health is related to activity levels, age, and gender, then it's no surprise these are key considerations in determining our flexibility. A clear link exists between the amount of exercise taken and mobility of the joints; it's well established, with even just regular walking positively affecting the range of motion in the hips and the lower spine. Since tightness in these areas can be a contributory factor in the incidence of falls in the elderly, you begin to appreciate its value in maintaining good quality of life.

The American College of Sports Medicine recommends stretching to promote enhanced flexibility as an essential preventive measure. Regular stretching also has been found to significantly reduce low back pain. As we age there's a gradual slowing of the cell function in muscles, tendons and ligaments, and that leads to a buildup of collagen, the main component of connective tissue, becoming denser and so somewhat less resistant to lengthening. As these surround the joint, then, reduced mobility is the result, to the extent that some of us lose as much as 50% of our range of movement in some areas. The good news is however, regular stretching can help to maintain the elasticity of this connective tissue and so reduce the effects of this particular aging process.

I asked Dr. Novella if you can recover flexibility even if you've gone years without stretching. Listen to what he had to say.

> **Steven Novella, MD**: Other things that can also happen, that commonly happen with age is a loss of flexibility and balance, but these things are not inevitable. They are not as much of an inevitable

consequence of just the aging process as is the issues with muscles and bone physiology.

Flexibility can be completely maintained by doing stretching exercises. There are specific diseases that may limit that, for example arthritis. If you have inflammatory arthritis, you're not going to be able to undo the effects of that with simple stretching. But stretching exercises will deal with the otherwise inevitable loss of flexibility that just happens as a natural consequence of aging.

Dean Hodgkin: So unless you have a serious injury, say a stroke or broken limb that requires therapy, it's really a matter of persistent stretching to build up your flexibility.

In general, females tend to have better flexibility than males at most joints and this can be attributed to small differences in the joint structures and the associated connective tissues. The effect of age on flexibility, however, is considerably greater than gender.

In addition to the 3 fundamental determinants of flexibility, age and sex, there are 3 other less influential items that are nonetheless, worthy of consideration.

Body temperature affects range of motion, as it's known to improve along with increasing heat, hence the reason for exercise always beginning with a warm up period. Contrary to common belief, rather than shortening your muscles and making them stiffer, weight training exercises that work through your full range of motion will improve your flexibility, but more about that later.

During pregnancy, the joints and ligaments in the lumbopelvic area, that's your lumbar, stomach, pelvis, hips combined, are relaxed to allow for growth and movement of the fetus, plus to make delivery a little easier. This change is due to increased levels of the relaxin hormone that drops to normal again after the birth, and so the connective tissues tighten up again.

Improving flexibility then requires a stretching program that aims to increase the range of motion, and that takes into account the previous factors regarding the joints. Careful consideration should be given to designing a plan to ensure it's safe, appropriate, and effective. If it is, then research shows that regular stretching has been shown to produce the following positive adaptations: enhanced range of motion, that's a given; reduced risk of injury and the degree of injury if that occurs; increased sports performance in terms of endurance and skill; improved posture leading to reduced risk of low back malady; positive impact on mental health through providing a vehicle for physical relaxation.

As we noted in a previous lecture, stretching can be active, brought about by contracting the opposing muscle group to move the limb to a position where the target muscle is lengthened or it can be passive, whereby the limb is moved by a partner or yourself or a prop using say, a towel.

However, stretching techniques are divided into 3 main categories, namely ballistic, static, and PNF, and these are defined as follows. Ballistic stretching involves swinging or bouncing a limb into a position beyond the normal joint range and so lengthening the associated muscles. It's a common technique for elite sportspeople, especially gymnasts and martial artists, but it's not recommended for the public at large, as it is difficult to execute safely. Static stretching on the other hand is the most common method of practice, requiring a gentle movement toward the end position that slowly lengthens the muscle and then we hold at that point, as a little bit of mild tension for somewhere between 15 and 30 seconds. Let's have a look at that.

So let's look at the static stretch in action. So our aim here is to try to lengthen the muscle slowly and we're going to do this with the hamstring. I'm going to use for the next few examples, the hamstring muscle group. So what Cameron is going to do for us, is show us this static stretch. So we're going to go with just one leg first of all because I want you to be aware that you could definitely have difference from one side to the other. This could be due to past injury issues, all sorts of reasons why you might have a difference. So I'd like you to separate, do one leg, each side. Now the other foot you can have it tucked to the side, you can rest the leg out, you can rest the foot flat and have the knee up. You could go to the hurdle position, it really doesn't matter, whichever position is comfortable for you, and more importantly is this front leg.

We're going to sit up nice and tall, we're then going to begin to hinge from the hip rather than round the spine, and we'll start to feel that stretch, that lengthening through the hamstring at the back of the thigh. You're going to find your comfortable position and hold it there, try to keep the breathing relaxed. Now this is what will happen: The amazing thing is after around 6–8 seconds, somewhere there, you'll start to get something called collagen creep. What will happen there is that the connective tissues will start to align themselves and it'll start to give you a little bit more stretch. So if you take a deep breath you'll find that in that position you'll be able to go a little bit further. And again, we're going to the point of mild tension, you're trying to get to that point where we feel the stretch. It's not painful but we can feel that mild tension as the muscle stretches.

And a good tip here, if you ease yourself out of that position for me please, and we'll swap over legs, a good tip here is to use imagery. So try to actually picture the muscle lengthening as you do it. So set yourself up, and remember we said switching from side to side. Try to analyze if there's any difference from one side to the other.

That deep breath first, we lower ourselves down to the point of mild tension and hold it there. Now we're looking out for that collagen creep, then taking a deep breath and easing a little further into it because I know that it will stretch that little bit further when you hold that position.

Now to get out developmental stretches we're looking really for at least 15 seconds, probably around about 30 seconds is a much better way to do that. So that's how your static stretch works.

Let me show a few other positions you can use this technique in. As you can see these are fairly easy to execute and we'll be doing these at the end of each of our workouts later.

PNF or proprioceptive neuromuscular facilitation stretching techniques were originally devised as a therapy for patients suffering muscle related diseases and work by using the body's nervous system to encourage extended lengthening of the muscles. It uses 3 key responses, the myotatic reflex also known as the stretch reflex, the Golgi tendon organ reflex, and the principle of reciprocal inhibition.

So the myotatic reflex, this is an automatic contraction within the muscle. And it's a response to a change in the length being detected by what are known as muscle spindles that lie within the muscle fibers. This is a self-preserving response to the possibility that the muscle might be stretched too far and could cause tearing of the fibers. This reflex is the reason ballistic stretching carries a little bit of risk.

The Golgi tendon organ reflex is the opposite of the above and that's why it's also sometimes referred to as the inverse stretch reflex. This receptor is located at the point where the muscle joins the tendon and it detects tension. If it detects very high tension, it interprets this as a possible threat to the muscle, again potentially causing it to tear, so it forces the muscle to relax, so removing the threat.

The third neuromuscular response, reciprocal inhibition describes the process whereby because muscles work as co-operating pairs, one muscle has to relax to some degree if the other contracts. So for example if I'm using my bicep to left my arm, my tricep has to relax.

These sensory responses are used in combination in a technique called contract-relax-agonist contract, it's a strange title. Firstly, the target muscle group is stretched slowly, in a passive manner. This avoids initiating the myotatic reflex. Then it's held in a position while a voluntary contraction of the muscle is exerted for around 6 seconds without it moving and this will stimulate the Golgi tendon organ reflex that relaxes the muscle.

Now the opposite muscle group is contracted strongly, and by reciprocal inhibition, the target muscle relaxes even more and so can then be stretched to a much greater degree. This has been shown to be the best stretching method to improve flexibility. Let's have a look at how it works.

Let's now have a look at that proprioceptive neuromuscular facilitation (PNF) in action. So we're going to work again as I said earlier, with the hamstring muscle group. And the important thing here is you need to work with your partner, you need to communicate on this one because we've got to very carefully get to that point where we feel the tension. And you've got to know where that is; we don't want to go too far with this.

So I'm going to start with Cameron's right leg. So we're going to take the leg up, first thing we're going to do is straighten the leg out but we're not locking out at the knee, okay. I'm going to get into a position where I can apply the pressure. What I'm going to do, start to take it forwards, let's keep the hips down to a point where we feel a mild stretch in the hamstring in the back of the thigh. Let me know when we get to that point, a little nod will do, fabulous. So we've got to that point now, we're getting that stretch, that mild tension through the back of the thigh. I need to now hold that, listen carefully, hold that position, it can't move.

Now what Cameron is going to do is use the hamstring muscle to press against me. So really press hard against me now with that leg. He's trying to force it back but I'm not letting it move. I've got to work against this. What's happening here is we'll start to stimulate because of that tension. And relax; it's only about 6 seconds, the Golgi tendon organ reflex, that'll make the muscle relax.

If we use the front of the thigh we can draw that foot a little further back, did you see how that's gone a little bit further? Then I can get a hold of it and we can start the whole process again. So you can see how we're increasing the flexibility here. So let's relax, we'll take that stretch until we feel that point where we get that mild tension, try not to stimulate the myotatic reflex, brilliant. We're going to hold it, fix it, same thing again. Let's push back against me; I'm going to hold it. We've got that strong tension through the hamstring muscle. I'm holding onto it, 6 seconds, and we'll relax it off. Use the front of the thigh to draw the leg closer towards you, and then we'll ease off and I think you'll have seen there, how we manage to increase the flexibility through the legs. So you need to work together on this one and of course you need to balance, make sure you're working both legs. That's your

PNF stretching technique; let me show you a few other positions in which we can use the same technique.

A final technique is called active isolated stretching, suitable for just about anyone, whether elite athletes or couch potatoes. The body positions are comfortable and easily manageable, plus the stretches are gentle and relaxing. Unlike the other techniques we have looked at, this is an active technique you perform with a partner. So it can be a little bit more fun than the others. This technique uses the last of the sensory responses we looked at earlier regarding synchronization of paired muscles to allow for coordinated movements. So we begin by contracting the muscles to move through a full range of functional motion. This will result in the opposite muscles switching off and relaxing, allowing a partner to assist the stretch by gently extending the range of motion. This assist should only last for around 2 seconds and each stretch should be performed 10 times. Let's have a look at this one in action.

Our final stretching technique is the active isolated stretch and remember this works on the principle of reciprocal innovation. So by using one muscle group, the other muscle group relaxes. So the way we're going to work, this is again, look at it, how it applies to our hamstring muscle group at the back of the thigh. We're lying down in comfortable position—again be aware of your neutral spine. What's going to happen here is Cameron is going to swing that right leg for please, it's under control.

It is a slightly ballistic movement but it's controlled. Now what's happening here is we're really switching on the front of the thigh, the hip flexors to pull this leg up. While that's happening, then the hamstring muscle is having to relax and stretch, that's our reciprocal innovation. Now what happens is, if we get too far and it gets to a point where, hang on a minute, this is going to be too much of a stretch, the hamstring muscle group will kick in and try to put a break on the movement, yes. But what I'm going to do is, just before it gets to the end of the movement, before the hamstrings have decided to put a break on, I'm going to add just a little bit of a push. It allows us to go, as I think you'll see just a few degrees further. So we're increasing that dynamic flexibility, increasing that range of motion by using this principle of reciprocal innovation. The strength on the front before the hamstring at the back has time to switch off, I'm going to add just that little extra push.

Now the important thing is it doesn't stop; it's a continuation of the movement. So you need to watch it a couple times first, be aware of how it works and then just add that little extra push at the end. Now we're looking for 10 repetitions of that exercise, that's the target figure, it's a key figure, 10 repetitions of each exercise. Now here's a few other ways you can use that technique. As with any form of exercise, you should follow a plan. But this is where flexibility becomes the black sheep of the exercise physiology community, as unlike cardio fitness, strength, et cetera, there are no universally agreed upon programs.

Rest assured, however, applying a smidgeon of common sense and committing yourself to regular stretching will bear fruit in the shape of increased range of motion. As a guideline, then, I'll offer you the following advice. Try to stretch regularly—daily if possible. Withhold those static stretches at the point of mild tension for 15 seconds to maintain flexibility but nearer to 30 seconds to improve it. Ensure you're warm before stretching, either after some cardio exercise or a good time is when you're fresh out of the warm bath.

Be aware of your posture; ensure you are in a comfortable position to stretch that allows you to focus on the target muscle. Perform stretches that target the joints in which you feel particularly stiff or that replicate movements you need for your chosen sport. It's a good idea to use deep breathing, gentle music, and sometimes a little visualization to help your efforts by helping the muscles to relax the muscles. But if at any time you feel a sharp or stabbing pain, release the stretch immediately.

Now I'd like to off on a slight tangent here and tackle few myths and misconceptions related to stretching that, unfortunately, are not just held by members of the public but some lesser qualified fitness professionals unfortunately harbor a few of these uncertainties. So be warned, some of these may come as a slight shock and could be almost contrary to what you may have previously heard or read.

Firstly to answer the most basic question I'm often asked on this subject, flexibility is not related to your shape, as height, weight, arm span, and leg length do not significantly affect range of motion.

Resistance or weight training, a topic we looked at earlier when we discussed flexibility, often causes confusion. It's easy to assume that weight training leads to the stiffness; we've all seen huge bodybuilders who can only scratch their backs by adopting the technique made famous by Baloo the bear in the Jungle Book, if you remember him leaning against the rock. However, there's absolutely no link between muscle size and immobility. In fact, because resistance training results in improvements in the elasticity of the muscles and the tensile strength in the tendons and ligaments, it can increase your range of motion over time, even without doing stretching.

Having said that resistance training can improve flexibility, you might not be totally surprised to learn this is a reciprocal relationship. So yes, believe it or not flexibility training can actually improve your strength. By increasing your flexibility, the muscles are able to operate over a greater range of motion. So we recruit more muscle fibers and so we generate more force.

Now another item that causes much misunderstanding is the place of stretching in warm up. Preparing for exercise and sporting pursuits. Should we stretch beforehand or not? The clue here to the purpose of the warm up is in the title, as increased body temperature through movement will stimulate the flow of synovial fluid into the joints that lubricate them. Respiratory speed will increase to introduce more oxygen to generate fuel, and the heart rate will increase to transport nutrients to the working muscles.

Most importantly, however, as temperature increases, so does the speed of nerve impulses and it is this that is the key to reducing the risk of injury. So let me give you an example. Imagine you're walking down a road, it's an uneven surface. You may have experienced this where you get a little twist of the ankle on something uneven and automatically without you thinking, it corrects itself, yes.

Now what's actually happened there, is as we've begun to roll over here, those Golgi tendon organs have detected, hang on a minute, there's a lot tension going on here. There's a message that gets sent on what's called a neural arc that comes up here, through to the spinal cord, come back down and this message goes, hang on a minute, I'm going too far here, there's going to be some injury unless something happens. The message that comes back down is we need to contract this muscle quickly and get ourselves back in that position before something goes wrong.

So this is what happens, and all of that happens in that split second, without us having to continuously correct ourselves. Now, the beauty of this is, the faster that message transfers, then the less risk there is of injury, yes. The beauty of the nerve fibers, is there incased in something called the myelin sheath. The myelin sheath is purely there, it serves one purpose, to insulate the nerve fibers to keep them warm, because guess what. The warmer you are the faster those messages will transfer.

Clearly then, in order to reduce this risk of injury, I need those muscle messages to transfer really, really quickly, yes. So the key to reducing the risk of injury has nothing at all to do with whether I've spent time, and I've never yet seen anybody do this before they exercise, stretching what's called the perineal muscle on the outside of the ankle and lower leg. You wouldn't it. So warm up is absolutely vital, stretching I'm afraid, won't make any difference in that example.

There are actually now a number of studies that confirm that not only does pre-exercise stretching does not reduce the risk of injury as even school of thought that suggesting that it increases the risk of injury by rendering the joints less stable. So the warm up, then, should focus on mobility and increasing temperature. Stretching to develop flexibility is best left until the end of the session when you're warm.

Our final controversy concerns the much heralded value of stretching in preventing muscle soreness experienced the day following exercise. You may well have heard the advice: You must stretch after your workout or you'll feel stiff tomorrow. Well, muscle soreness is actually the sum of several factors including microtrauma to the muscle fibers, basically it's inflammation within the cells and irritation of the nerve endings due to additional enzyme activity.

Now since stretching cannot impact upon these processes that lead to that then it can't affect muscle soreness. So if you exercise intensely today, you've got to expect muscle soreness tomorrow and then embrace it because it's a sign that you've worked hard enough to set in motion the adaptive responses that will lead to positive change.

Please note however, a cool down will help to remove waste products, that lactic acid we talked about in an energy systems lecture, and in turn reduce the inflammation to some degree.

It also, of course helps for your heart rate and respiration to slow down gradually instead of abruptly, remember we talked about this as well. So your workout should finish with a cool down, and stretching can be part of that cool down. But it's not the fact that you're stretching that makes the difference, just the fact that you are doing something active to gradually bring you back to homeostasis, rather than stopping dead in your tracks.

So now you know that flexibility is a key player in maintaining a good quality of life into your later years and you're armed with an array of stretching techniques you can employ to not just retain but actually improve your mobility.

When it comes to flexibility, you can do it alone or with a friend, you can do it indoors or out, you can do it in the morning or at night, you can do it every day or just every other day. But the important thing is, to borrow a well-known phrase from one of the sportswear giants, just do it.

Stay Active—Defy the Aging Process
Lecture 21

Exercise is a key factor in maintaining a good quality of life. Research confirms that fitness levels achieved in your younger years can impact not just your physical, but also your psychological health in later life. If you continue to be active throughout your life, then you can expect to retain a desirable quality of life well into your advanced years. In this lecture, you'll learn about the aging body and investigate how it changes as the years go by. You'll also discover the value that exercise has in helping you resist the aging process.

Fitness and Aging

- The aging process is influenced by a number of factors—but primarily by genetics, disease, and lifestyle. In particular, lifestyle has been shown to be susceptible to manipulation and capable of impacting life span.

- An active lifestyle is recommended for good health regardless of your age, but some researchers even suggest that the older you are, the more important it is. While exercise is of benefit at any age, it's been proposed that age 50 is a critical point at which engaging in regular exercise can protect against the physical and psychological deteriorations associated with getting old—such as frailty and disability.

- The benefits of regular exercise apply at any age, so it's never too late to start a new exercise regime. Exercise can not only add years to your life, but it will also put life in your years—even if you're currently not active.

The Bones and Aging

- A drop in calcium levels is the most noticeable result of aging, and it occurs more in women than in men due to the postmenopause reduction in estrogen levels. As a result, the bones become brittle and more likely to fracture. Decreased calcium levels introduce the risk of an exacerbated curvature of the spine, leading to poor posture, increased risk of falls, and extra pressure on key joints.

- Inactivity is a major contributor to osteoporosis, and weight-bearing exercise can retain bone mineral density, so regular exercise is encouraged from an early age as a preventive measure.

- Older adults who commit to 1 hour of exercise each day can reduce their risk of hip fracture by as much as 50%. Tennis and jogging are favored in comparison to walking and gardening, which have showed no effect on the rate of fracture incidence.

- Osteoporosis sufferers may already exhibit reduced mobility, so exercise will need to begin gentle. Aquatic exercise is a recommended option to help improve movement, but the buoyancy of the water reduces the weight bearing, which is needed, so switching to dry land is recommended as soon as possible.

- A common feature in older adults is a slight forward bend at the hip and in the lumbar spine, so it's recommended to stretch the muscles at the front of the body, particularly in the hip flexors.

The Joints and Aging

- The most obvious consideration in the joints is the decreased range of motion caused by the stiffening of the connective tissue around them—in combination with the muscles losing their elasticity.

- In addition, the production of synovial fluid decreases and becomes more viscous, so the cartilage that covers the ends of the bones can actually tear and lose fluid, reducing the cushioning effect when the joints move.

- These changes not only restrict movement but can also cause pain. Previous injury is one of the causes for these changes, but leading a sedentary lifestyle can also be a significant cause.

- In the spine, the disks between the vertebrae that are made of cartilage begin to lose their fluid, and increased calcium deposits are noted, so their ability to soften movement in these vital joints is somewhat impaired. These combined changes lead to reduced movement, most noticeably in the ankles, knees, and hips, but this can be overcome through regular activity.

- When considering exercise as an intervention for arthritis, the most common ailment associated with old age, the first thing to appreciate is that exercise will not make the condition worse, which is a common misconception. Not only will it help to improve cardiovascular profile, increase muscular strength, and improve your flexibility, but it can also have a positive impact on mental health.

The Muscles and Aging

- The changes in muscles over time are similar to the changes in bone: There's a progressive loss of tissue with advancing years, but the general decline is more often associated with inactivity rather than age.

- Older people who remain active display better strength and ability to perform their tasks than sedentary counterparts. Research suggests that as we age, there is a decline in fast-twitch muscle fibers due to the speed of their contraction. As a result, power reduces.

- Potential maximum tension is unaffected because the motor unit, which is the nerve and muscle combination, will still perform as designed. Therefore, any decease in strength is due to other influences.

- Reductions in the number of blood vessels, enzyme concentration, and the ability to store energy in the muscle cells contribute to a decline in muscular endurance.

- Exercise prescription incorporates strength training because gains can be made at any age, and the associated increase in the ability to perform everyday tasks and the reduced risk of falls also promote a psychological boost.

The Cardiovascular System and Aging

- Age-related changes within the cardiovascular system are less pronounced than in the bones and muscles. The heart retains the capability to supply blood to the body, allowing it to perform everyday tasks.

- Most of the changes that occur—including decreases in the heart muscle performance, the efficiency of the blood vessels

Engaging in regular exercise throughout your life will positively affect the quality of your life in later years.

to transport oxygen, and the ability of the skeletal muscle to use oxygen—are due to inactivity rather than age.

- Fortunately, these drawbacks can be significantly mitigated by regular exercise, which can lead to increases in stroke volume, total blood volume, and good cholesterol. Therefore, adherence to a suitable exercise program can afford a high protection against cardiovascular disease, hypertension, and diabetes.

- Furthermore, although our breathing apparatus is fully grown by our mid-20s, the efficiency of gaseous exchange continues to improve into our early 40s. This is why endurance athletes, such as marathon runners, reach their peak a little later than athletes in other disciplines.

Physiological Changes and Aging

- Lung volume decreases as the lung tissues in the chest wall lose elasticity. There's a reduction in the number of cilia—the tiny hairs that remove particles from the airways—which can increase the risk of infection.

- Collagen builds up around the alveoli, leading to a reduced surface area and diminishing the exchange of gases, which leads to less available oxygen. Calcification affects the trachea and the rib cartilages, leading to a stiffness that reduces the ability to expand and take in more air.

- These factors combine to initiate a gradual increase in the rate of breathing that tends to be shallow-chest breathing. This doesn't preclude exercise, but deep breathing is consciously encouraged, and alternating intervals of higher and lower intensity are preferable.

The Nervous System and Aging

- In regards to the nervous system, evidence shows that coordination declines with age. Interestingly, research has shown that active older people have faster reactions than inactive younger people, suggesting that a sedentary lifestyle is the key factor rather than age.

- In addition, neurons decline naturally, but physical challenges, such as learning new motor skills, can lead to development of an unlimited number of neural pathways. If a muscle is not regularly used, the motor units that control it can shrink, so the neuron becomes less efficient, proving that inactivity accelerates the aging process.

- Due to the cardiovascular changes that take place, blood supply to the brain may decline, restricting the oxygen provided. Without this fuel, brain processes can be prolonged, which is what can cause loss of coordination and an increased risk of balance issues.

- Diminished neural activity can also lead to a slowed reaction to requirements for redistributing blood supply that results in **blood**

pooling, the term given to blood remaining in the extremities, which can cause dizziness. This can manifest itself in a drop of blood pressure that occurs when standing up quickly from a sitting or lying position—called **postural hypotension**.

Seeing and Hearing with Age

- Aging is linked to degeneration in both sight and hearing ability. The lens loses elasticity, making it harder to focus, and the iris muscles weaken, so the amount of light entering the retina is reduced.

- In terms of hearing, the ability to detect higher-pitch tones becomes difficult, but other sounds can be a problem if there is a high level of background noise.

- While many elderly people are unwilling to accept the reduction in these senses, it clearly happens, and it's a contributory factor in balance issues.

- Regular exercise can lead to improvements in the cardiovascular system, breathing function, and muscle performance, and all of these will enhance the efforts of the central nervous system.

Functional Fitness

- Physiologists refer to **functional fitness** as the fitness that is relevant to day-to-day living; it's the difference between independence and potentially becoming a burden on those close to you as you age.

- In order to develop and retain a desirable degree of functional fitness, cardiovascular fitness, muscular strength and endurance, flexibility, balance, and motor skills are the targets for improvement.

- Cardiovascular training will induce improvements in your maximal oxygen uptake, leading to an enhanced ability to walk, cycle, or swim without discomfort. Increasing cardiac outputs, lowering heart rate, and reducing hypertension are key bonuses. The blood supply and enzyme concentration, leading to better muscle endurance, will increase.

- To bring about these changes, aim to exercise every day if possible—even if you have to build up to this. Try to avoid high-intensity exercise; instead, aim for medium-intensity exercises that last for about 30 minutes. The exercise mode should incorporate movements of the large muscle groups, so walking, cycling, and swimming are the favored options.

- Training for muscular strength and endurance, you can expect increased strength—the ability to lift and carry things at home—and better endurance, enabling you to walk up and down stairs much more easily.

- Increased lean muscle tissue helps to boost metabolism, control body composition, and enhance bone density.

- To bring about these improvements in muscular strength and endurance, include exercises for all the major muscle groups 3 times per week with, ideally, a day's rest in between to allow the muscles to rest.

- Overload is the key, so workouts must lead to muscular fatigue. Expect to spend about 30 minutes performing 2 to 3 sets of an exercise with 10 to 12 repetitions of each exercise.

Guidelines for Flexibility Training
- Flexibility training can bring several positive benefits, including increased range of motion, lengthening of key postural muscles, improved balance, less stiffness, and less pain when moving.

- Begin with just 2 stretching sessions each week and build up to 5. Remember to always warm up first with at least 5 minutes of gentle cardio-type activity.

- Mix dynamic stretching techniques—but not bouncing—with static stretches that are held at the end point of mild tension for 15 to 30 seconds.

- Try to include stretches for the whole body, targeting problems that may exist. When doing your stretching exercises, try to keep your breathing relaxed.

- To train to improve balance, adopting wide-, narrow-, and single-leg stances for basic exercises such as squats will help to develop static balance. Use movements in all directions to promote gains in dynamic balance, and include exercises that employ functional training equipment, such as core boards and wobble boards.

- Motor skills can also benefit from balance exercises, and playing catch with an uneven ball or with a partner will lead to further gains in coordination and will help you develop quick reactions.

Important Terms

blood pooling: The term given to blood remaining in the extremities, which can cause dizziness.

functional fitness: The fitness that is relevant to day-to-day living.

postural hypotension: The drop of blood pressure that occurs when standing up quickly from a sitting or lying position.

Stay Active—Defy the Aging Process
Lecture 21—Transcript

According to the U.S. Census Bureau, during the 20th century the population under 65 tripled, whilst at the same time their relatives over 65 increased by a factor of 11. As a proportion, shifting from a ratio of 1 in 25 to a considerable 1 in 8. Now projections suggest this will be around 1in 5 by halfway through this century. So clearly then, it's important for the population to develop and maintain good health moving into later years, in order to reduce the risk of illness, injury and disease that will predicate loss of independence and significantly increase healthcare costs. More importantly however is the concept of maintaining a good quality of life, and the good news is that to a great degree, this lies in our own hands, with exercise being a key factor as supported by the National Institute on Aging making it a platform for its Go4Life campaign.

There's now an abundance of research to confirm that fitness levels achieved in our younger years can impact upon not just the physical but also our psychological health in later life. In addition, all the signs point to the fact that if we continue to be active then we can expect to retain a desirable quality of life well into our advanced years. So in this lecture we'll take a journey through the aging body and investigate just how it changes as the years go by. We'll also look at what value exercise has in helping us to resist the aging process and draw up a plan of just what form that should take.

Whilst I don't deny we all have a biological clock, if you stay with me for the next 30 minutes, I'll equip you with the tools to seriously slow it down. Be warned though, I'm about to challenge some of your firmly held beliefs about growing old.

The aging process is influenced by a number of factors but primarily genetics, disease and lifestyle. It is this later variable, in particular, that has been shown to be susceptible to manipulation and capable of impacting life span. Not only is an active lifestyle recommended for good health whatever your age, there's a school of thought that now suggests the older you are the more important it is.

But what about that old saying, you can't teach an old dog new tricks? Is that really true? Let's go to Professor Sapolsky for just a minute and find out what happens in the brain when you pick up something like exercise as an adult.

> **Robert Sapolsky**: An amazing finding, one of the biggest revolutions in neurobiology in the last 20 years, is the fact that the brain, the adult brain, makes new neurons—new neurons in a part of the brain having to do with memory.
>
> If you took an introductory neurobiology class anytime since the pharaohs, the first thing they teach you is, your brain doesn't make new neurons by the time you're 3 years old.
>
> Massive revolution, that there is actually (jargon) "adult neurogenesis." So what triggers this? What stimulates this? It's environmental stimulation; it's learning new things; it's exercise, as well. And what is one of the coolest things about it is making new neurons in response to stimulation, enrichment, exercise, all of that.
>
> That is not just the purview of 20 year old jocks. What the studies already show is, get a 90 year old more stimulated through any of those routes and afterward when you examine the brain there are new perky adolescent neurons there going about their rejuvenating business. Aging is no more a time of life where stress is an inevitability than at any earlier stage.

Dean Hodgkin: Now that's encouraging, isn't it? So you don't have an excuse if you've never been active up until now. Of relevant note is that whilst exercise is of benefit at any age, it's been proposed that age 50 years is a critical point at which taking regular exercise can protect against the physical and psychological deteriorations associated with getting old, in other words, frailty and even disability.

When we consider the benefits of regular exercise it's important to stress that these apply at any age, so it's never too late to embark upon a new exercise regime and enjoy the lower risk of heart disease, stroke, diabetes, falls, stress, and even depression.

Now add to that improved strength, flexibility, balance, self-esteem, better sleep, and social contact, and you start to wonder why anyone would not voluntarily not partake.

It's true to say that exercise can not only add years to your life but will certainly put life in your years, even if you're currently not active. Before we can prescribe appropriate exercise advice, we need to understand the changes that occur in the body as we age.

So let's begin with the bones. We know from our earlier lecture on this topic that a drop in calcium levels is the most noticeable result of aging, more so in women than men due to the issue of reduced estrogen levels post-menopause. Now this manifests itself in bones becoming brittle and more likely to fracture as we age. It also introduces the risk of changes in the spine, notably exacerbated curvature leading to poor posture, also increased risk of falls, and extra pressure on key joints. Fortunately though, there is a wealth of evidence to show that inactivity is the major contributor to osteoporosis, and that weight bearing exercise can retain bone mineral density. This is why there is so much emphasis on encouraging regular exercise from an early age as a preventive measure.

However, older adults who commit to 1 hour each day could reduce risk of hip fracture by as much as 50%, although the type of activity is important. Tennis and jogging for example are favored in comparison to walking and gardening which have showed no effect on the rate of fracture incidence. This is the first point at which we notice the idea that exercise can actually slow the aging process, although listen carefully as this will become a recurring theme. Since osteoporosis sufferers may already exhibit reduced mobility, clearly exercise will need to begin gently with aqua options, for example, being a recommended option to help improve movement, although the buoyancy of the water reduces the weight bearing which is needed, so switching to dry land will be necessary as soon as possible.

A combination of cardio and strength training is the ideal recipe to begin with, and these exercises should focus on improving the ability to perform daily activities. It's also important to remember from our lecture on bones that adaptations to exercise are site specific, so a program must incorporate a total body approach. A common feature in older adults is a slight forward bend at the hip and in the lumbar spine, this sort of position like so. So it's recommended to stretch the muscles at the front of the body, particularly if we take the hip flexors.

So I'd take a stretch where I'd take one foot behind and then a little tilt of the pelvis forwards will start to stretch through here. But also to strengthen the posterior chain of muscles, so exercises that will work through the muscles that protect the lower back. And if you look at our lecture on the spine, you'll find several examples there of how we can do that.

Let's move on to the joints. The most obvious consideration in the joints is the decreased range of motion caused by stiffening of the connective tissue around them, in combination also with the muscles losing their elasticity. Also the production of synovial fluid (that's the fluid that lubricates the joints) decreases and actually becomes more viscous. The cartilage that covers the ends of the bones can actually tear and lose fluid, so reducing the cushioning effect when the joints move. These changes not only restrict movement but can cause pain, although previous injury is one of the causes for these changes but also a sedentary lifestyle can be a significant cause.

In the spine, the disks between the vertebrae that are also made of cartilage begin to lose their fluid and increased calcium deposits are noted. So their ability to soften movement in these vital joints is somewhat impaired. As mentioned, then, these combined changes lead to reduced movement, most noticeably in the ankles, in the knees, in the hips, but this can be overcome through regular activity.

Arthritis is the most common ailment associated with old age and actually includes a large number of different conditions that lead to degeneration and inflammation of the joints, examples being osteoarthritis, rheumatoid arthritis, ankylosing spondylitis, and gout.

When considering exercise as an intervention, the first thing to appreciate is that it will not make the condition worse, which can be a common misconception. Not only will it help to improve cardiovascular profile, increase muscular strength, and improve your flexibility, it can also have a positive impact on mental health through additional social contact as we mentioned earlier, enhanced self-esteem, and reduced feelings of depression.

But even better than this, some studies have shown that exercise can help to relieve pain symptoms in nearly half of arthritis sufferers. So here are some exercise guidelines for this population. Firstly we need to consider the low impact activities and try to avoid prolonged one-leg work. We need some balance work but make sure we're switching side to side. Focus on strength and flexibility at first and avoid positions that involve you kneeling for prolonged periods. Repeated short bouts are a better option than a long workout.

Let's have a look now at the muscles. If we now look at muscles, the changes are similar to bone, in that there's a progressive loss of tissue with advancing years but, again, the general decline we see is more often associated with inactivity rather than age. Older persons who remain active display better strength and ability to perform their tasks than sedentary counterparts. Research suggests that as we age, there will be a decline in type 2 muscles fibers, known as the fast twitch variety due to their speed of their contraction. So as a result of this, our power will reduce and so it's fair to assume sprinting speeds for an example, will decrease with age.

Potential maximum tension however, is unaffected as the motor unit which is the nerve and muscle combination, will still perform as designed. So any decease in strength is due to other influences. This is why some bodybuilders have been able to compete well into their later years.

Reductions in the number of blood vessels, enzyme concentration and the ability to store energy in the muscle cells, and all these factors, will contribute to a decline in muscular endurance. Exercise prescription then, is clearly going to incorporate strength training, as gains can be made at any age. The beauty of strength and endurance training is that the benefits will not solely be restricted to the physical, as the associated increases in the ability to perform everyday tasks and the reduced risk of falls promote a psychological boost also.

In support of the argument that exercise can bring positive changes at any age, a 2007 study showed that after 26 weeks of progressive resistance training, a group of elderly persons with an average age of 68 years were found to improve their relative strength from 59% lower to only 38% lower than the a control group with an average age of 24 years. You could even argue that in this case, exercise doesn't just slow the aging process, it actually reverses it.

Let's move onto the cardiovascular system and we find that age-related changes here are less pronounced than in the bones and muscles as we've just discussed. The heart retains the capability to supply blood to the body and allowing it to perform everyday tasks. So again the theory here is that most of the changes we see are due to inactivity rather than age. There'll undoubtedly be decreases in the heart muscle performance, the efficiency of the blood vessels to transport the oxygen and the ability of the skeletal muscle to use it. But fortunately, these drawbacks can be significantly mitigated by regular exercise which can lead to increases in stroke volume which is the total amount of blood pumped with each beat, the total blood volume and high density lipoproteins or the good cholesterol. So adherence to a suitable exercise program then, can afford a high protection against cardiovascular disease. The sort of things we associate with aging, for example hypertension and diabetes.

Next let's consider breathing and how aging affects the mechanics of respiration. Although our breathing apparatus is fully grown by our mid-twenties, the efficiency of gaseous exchange continues to improve into early forties. You'll recall that the gaseous exchange is simply the process of carbon dioxide and oxygen circulating between the blood and the lungs.

This is why endurance athletes, such as marathon runners, will reach their peak a little later than athletes in other disciplines. Ingeniously, the respiratory system is designed with extra capacity so that when a decline begins from age 40 onwards, it isn't noticed in the course of carrying out common daily activities. Changes are more likely to restrict the ability to accommodate strenuous exercise.

So let's consider some of these physiological changes. Firstly the lung volume will decrease as the lung tissues in the chest wall lose elasticity. There'll be a reduction in the number of cilia (the tiny hairs that remove particles from the airways) and that can increase the risk of infection. Collagen builds up around the alveoli, those little air bubbles leading to a reduced surface area and so diminishing the exchange of gases, leading to a little less oxygen being available. Calcification affects the trachea and the rib cartilages, leading to a stiffness that reduces the ability to expand and take in more air. These factors combine to initiate a gradual increase in the rate of breathing that tends to be shallow chest breathing. This doesn't preclude exercise, but leads to the suggestion that deep breathing should be consciously encouraged and alternating intervals of higher and lower intensity will be preferable.

Positive adaptations have been noted in asthmatics who engage in regular exercise, although in this case recommendations are to begin gently and gradually increase to a medium intensity. A training program should also include exercise to encourage good posture, especially in the thoracic region, as this will clearly impact upon breathing mechanics.

Finally in our tour of how aging affects the body and its functions, we'll consider the nervous system. Here evidence shows that coordination declines with age. But interestingly, research has shown that active older people have faster reactions than inactive younger people, again suggesting that a sedentary lifestyle is the key factor rather than the passing sands of time.

In our look at the brain we established that neurons do decline naturally but physical challenges, such as learning new motor skills, can lead to development of an unlimited number of neural pathways. A notable point here is that if a muscle is not regularly used, the motor units that control it can shrink and the neuron becomes less efficient, so proving that inactivity accelerates the aging process. In addition, due to the cardiovascular changes that take place that we discussed earlier, blood supply to the brain may decline, restricting the oxygen provided and without this fuel, brain processes can be prolonged, which is what can cause loss of coordination and an increased risk of balance issues, with of course the potential for falls.

Diminished neural activity can also lead to a slowed reaction to requirements for redistributing blood supply that results in blood pooling, the term given to blood remaining in the extremities which can cause dizziness. This can manifest itself in a drop of blood pressure if standing up quickly from a sitting or lying position, something that's known as postural hypotension.

So as you'll be aware already, aging is linked to degeneration in both sight and hearing ability. The lens loses elasticity and so making it harder to focus, in addition to which the iris muscles weaken and so the amount of light entering the retina is reduced and hence the problems. The light adapted eye of a 20-year-old receives 6 times more light than that of an 80-year-old. In dark adapted conditions, the 20-year-old eye receives about 16 times more light. In comparison to younger people, it is as though older persons were wearing medium-density sunglasses in bright light and extremely dark glasses in dim light. With hearing, it's mainly being able to detect higher pitch tones that becomes difficult, although other sounds can be a problem if there is a high level of background noise. Whilst many elderly persons are unwilling to accept the reduction in these senses, it clearly happens and it's a contributory factor in balance issues, especially when combined with the slower speed of information transfer from the skin, vibratory sensors and the muscle and joint receptors. You may remember we talked about the muscle spindles and Golgi tendon organs in our stretching lecture.

As we've already discovered in previous sections, regular exercise can bring about improvements in the cardiovascular system, also breathing function, muscle performance and all of these will enhance the efforts of the central nervous system. Thus far we've only really scratched the surface in the domain of exercise prescription, so let's dig a little deeper.

A critical phenomenon to take on board at this stage is an appreciation of diversity amongst the older population. So to support this, bear in mind the oldest person to complete a marathon was, get ready for this, 98 years old. Yet a U.K. study revealed that over a third of people over 50, who have no restrictive medical conditions, just simply don't exercise regularly.

In the U.S., national data shows that only 31% of those aged 65–74 participate in 20 minutes of moderate physical activity on 3 or more days of the week. Only 16% report 30 minutes of moderate activity 5 or more times a week. And the figures decline even more for the truly vigorous physical activity that can really to help maintain your cardiovascular health. So when we try to define the concept of aging, it's clear it has relative, social, functional, and chronological dimensions. The gym is the home of an incredibly wide variety of exercise and program variations but a proportion of these are for purely aesthetic gains.

For the older exerciser, however, the desired goals are more likely to be the ability to carry the groceries, being able to stand up from a chair without emitting a groan, that I noticed I've started to do, and having the energy take the family dog for a walk in the park. This is what the physiologists refer to as the functional fitness. It's totally relevant to day-to-day living and it's the difference between independence and potentially becoming a burden on those close to you. So your quality of life both today and tomorrow is at stake here. So this then, provides the framework for us to build an exercise regime. In order to develop and or retain a desirable degree of functional fitness, the following components are the targets for improvement.

Firstly: cardiovascular fitness, our muscular strength and endurance, flexibility, balance, and motor skills. So let's look at these in order, look at them in a little bit more detail. Cardiovascular training will induce improvements in your maximal oxygen uptake, leading to an enhanced ability to walk, cycle or swim without discomfort, in addition to giving a general feeling of having a good energy level.

Cardiac outputs, lowering heart rate, and also reducing hypertension are key bonuses. The blood supply and enzyme concentration, leading to better muscle endurance will increase. And so we've got various improvements here but the requirements to bring about these about are that we need to aim for something every day if possible, even if you have to build up to this.

Try to avoid high intensity exercise; we're looking at medium intensity, around 5–7 out of 10 on an intensity level, depending on your current fitness level. Thirty minutes is the target, but remember benefits can be accrued in a piecemeal fashion. So 2 lots of 15 minutes or 3 bouts of 10 minutes will produce the same gains so suddenly, it doesn't seem so onerous. I'm sure you can manage 10 minutes. The exercise mode should incorporate movements of the large muscle groups, so walking, cycling, swimming are the favored options.

If we move now to training for muscular strength and endurance, these are the kind of things that we can expect, we can expect increased strength and so the ability to left and carry things at home. We can look forward to better endurance, enabling us to walk up and down the stairs much more easily.

Increased lean muscle tissue, helping to boost metabolism and so control body composition is a welcomed change. And of course enhanced bone density, decreasing the risk of fractures.

So how do we bring about these improvements in muscular strength and endurance? This is how we do it. Firstly we need to include exercises for all the major muscle groups and that's in common with our cardiovascular training, 3 times per week with ideally with a day's rest in between to allow the muscles to rest.

Overload is the key, so workouts must lead to muscular fatigue, so you may need to build up to this at first. Again expect to take around 30 minutes, performing maybe 2–3 sets of an exercise, and we're looking for 10–12 repetitions of each exercise. For those who are comfortable, gym workouts are an option, but beginners may prefer the comfort of home workouts, using just your body weight as resistance, and we've got a specific workout later for you later in this series to do just that.

Let's have a look at flexibility training and this can bring several positive benefits such as increased range of movement making it easier to perform our daily tasks. Lengthening the key postural muscles, leading to better static and dynamic posture plus improved balance, less stiffness, less pain on moving, wouldn't that be welcomed.

So let's look at the guidelines for flexibility training. How do we get these improvements? Begin with just 2 stretching sessions each week and build up to 5. Remember to always warm up first with at least 5 minutes of gentle cardio type activity. Mix dynamic stretching techniques, but not bouncing, with static stretches that are held at the end point of mild tension for 15 to30 seconds, again have a look at our flexibility lecture for some tips there. Try to include stretches for the whole body, targeting problems that may exist, for example stiffness due to old sports injuries or maybe rounded shoulders and short hamstrings due to years of working in a seated position. Remember when doing your stretching exercises: Try to keep your breathing relaxed.

Next on our shopping list is balance. As we have seen, balance is a composite of several functions working in harmony and will be directly affected by the previous fitness components, muscular strength, flexibility, especially in the lower limbs. Now balance, as we've already established can be static or dynamic and is governed by 3 senses. There's the visual, the vestibular, where sensors in the inner ear detect position of the head and then somatosensory which includes touch.

So how do we train to improve balance? Firstly adopting wide, narrow, and single leg stances for basic exercises such as a bicep curl or squats will help to develop static balance. Use movements in all directions to promote gains in dynamic balance. So try not to always be working forwards, backwards and side to side. Let's move at diagonals as well. Include exercises that employ functional training equipment, the core board, the wobble board, the TRX (the straps that you can hang from the ceiling), and things like flexi-bar or bodyblade (the things that we have to shake and use the vibrational energy).

Finally let's have a look at motor skills that will, unfortunately, deteriorate but can fortunately benefit automatically from the previously mentioned balance exercises. However, including the following also will lead to further gains in co-ordination. Playing catch with a knobby ball, an uneven ball or a partner to give an element of surprise will develop quick reactions. Performing your exercises at different speeds, simple things like walking your usual route to the shop but in a different direction, learning a new swimming stroke. All of these things will help.

Whilst much of this presentation has focused on the multifarious benefits of exercise for the elderly, we've also established that regular exercise throughout our lives will build a degree of protection against many conditions and make a big difference to quality of life in later years. So let's try and put together a blueprint, then, to help you to adapt your exercise regime to the challenges of aging, ensuring you derive the maximum benefit. Let's break it down by decade. We'll start in your 20s. At this point bone density is increasing, so it's vital to exercise appropriately, in order to lay down as much bone tissue as possible before the decline begins. Cardio activity should be weight bearing therefore, so opt for high impact aerobics and aim for 2 weight training sessions per week.

If the free weights area of the gym is not your cup of tea, try a group exercise class, maybe something like Body Pump, group resistance. Your target working heart rate is at its maximum now, so your cardio sessions should be intense, you should be pushing yourself, maybe up to 90% of your recommended range, which you calculate by subtracting your age from 220.

You're also at your most flexible around now, but don't let this lead you into a false sense of security. This will decline as you age so don't skip your stretching, particularly after your workout. Allow at least 10 minutes and aim to lengthen the muscles in the whole body. It's a great time to start including yoga or tai chi in your workouts for example.

Moving on to your 30s is when the first signs of the aging process will really to begin to manifest, with the loss of muscle tissue most noticeable in the back of the upper arms sometimes unsympathetically labeled as bingo wings. Unfortunately, losing lean body tissue also leads to a slowing of your metabolic rate, so this is when the pounds might begin to pile on.

Increase weight training to 3 times per week now, target your problem zones, the triceps, the abdominals, the buttocks. As this could be the decade of child-bearing, so this can be an issue, busy moms be aware that you need those cardio workouts. But we've said 3 times 10 minutes is just as effective in terms of calorie burning as a 30 minutes bout. Bone density here is at its peak, so choose weight-bearing exercises such as jogging.

The metabolic rate begins to slow in your 40s, together with changes in hormone levels, so you may notice the storage of extra pounds. In addition, your target heart rate declines, so it's important to lower the intensity but therefore increase the duration of your cardio workouts if you want to burn fat. Start to think about protecting your joints from wear and tear by opting for low impact exercise.

So switch jogging for power-walking, high impact aerobics for spinning, indoor cycling, weight training should remain a staple of your exercise diet. Not only to counter the inevitable muscle loss we've already spoken about but also to give the requisite strength to tackle your daily tasks, such as carrying the shopping to the car or digging the garden.

Moving onto your 50s, it's vital to maintain activity levels as the risk of heart disease increases and bone density decreases due to the lowering of the estrogen levels, post-menopause. Circuit training here is ideal; it'll combine cardio and strength work, so it ticks both the boxes for us.

The best option here is the PHA format we spoke about that in a different lecture, alternating upper and lower body exercises at each station, as this give a greater calorie burn. Now this is the time when stiffness is noticeable, particularly in the lower spine, so flexibility work is seriously recommended. Consider yoga and core conditioning, to improve posture and protect your back.

The good news is that after 60 it's actually better to be slightly overweight, caution the words slightly. And this is because the risk of osteoporosis and fractures is higher if you're too thin. Now don't let this deter you from the prescription to maintain cardio exercise to burn calories.

Think about activities here that are easier on the joints, as the thinning of cartilage and stiffening of the tendons and ligaments can leave them a little more susceptible to injury. So this is where aqua workouts are perfect since this allows for the muscles to work against the water resistance for toning benefits, but the buoyancy supports the joints.

Walking should be the prime cardio option here, whether in the form of a country hike, early morning mall walking before the shops open, whatever it is, a stride session on the treadmill or a weight loss power-walk. If you carry some weight while you walk, you'll also help maintain your bone density. So a couple little dumbbells in the hands perhaps.

Whilst not an obvious choice for most pensioners, gym sessions are also vital, particularly if practicing functional strength work on the cable machines to mimic everyday movements, so doing chopping type movements will mimic the idea of picking things up and putting them on a shelf.

I remember a few years ago, one of the leading sportswear brands gave birth to the slogan, "Fitness is a race with no finish line," and I certainly hope I've now convinced you of that. The quality of your life in later years is only loosely linked to your actual age; rather the most important factor is your activity level.

Although often muttered as an off the cuff phrase, the concept of use it or lose it carries much greater meaning than it first appears to. If like many of us in this day and age, you're looking for the secret of eternal youth, I think that in exercise you may just have found it.

Sitting Disease
Lecture 22

L eading a sedentary lifestyle can have a significantly negative impact on your health, with recent research stacking up to highlight just how dangerous inactivity can be to your future well-being. It's now a proven fact that spending too much time seated will shorten your life. In this lecture, you'll discover the dangers associated with long periods of sitting, and you'll learn a wide range of tactics that you can employ on a daily basis. Whether at work, at home, or on the journey between the 2, you can start to make changes today that will improve your health tomorrow.

Leading a Sedentary Lifestyle
- According to the American Institute for Cancer Research, approximately 100,000 new cases of breast and colon cancer each year are linked to sedentary lifestyles.

- A study at the University of South Carolina showed that people who were inactive for more than 23 hours per week had a 64% greater risk of death from heart disease when compared to a control group, who were sedentary for less than 11 hours per week.

- It's estimated that up to 100,000 people die each year from blood clots, and sitting in one position for too long is the key factor.

- The dangers of sitting were discovered in the late 1950s, when we realized that men who were employed in manual labor roles were less likely to suffer coronary artery disease than those whose jobs were not physically active.

- Research has concluded that there's a significant link between time spent seated and mortality. More importantly, being active doesn't balance out the negative effects of being seated much of the time.

The Physiological Implications of Being Sedentary

- A 2008 study published in *Current Cardiovascular Risk Reports* showed that if we don't stand, electrical activity within the muscles effectively ceases, leading to a drop of up to 90% in the levels of **lipoprotein lipase**, which is an enzyme that draws fat out of the bloodstream for use as fuel, because it wouldn't be required. This leads to a higher concentration of blood fats that are known to increase the risk of cardiovascular malaise.

- In addition, sitting appears to lead to about a 20% reduction in high-density lipoprotein, or good cholesterol, increasing the risk of suffering from a cardiovascular disease.

- Sitting only requires contractions of the small muscles in the hands and forearms—for example, when typing or changing the television channels with a remote control—and these use up small amounts of energy when compared to the large muscles in the legs, buttocks, and lower back. As a result, your metabolism plummets, so calories are not being consumed but absorbed, a fact that will more than likely manifest itself in the waist area.

- Remaining sedentary for more than 24 hours impairs the ability of our insulin to uptake glucose, which then raises the risk of diabetes. In addition, blood circulation is, to a certain degree, dependent upon movement. When the legs are not moving, the leg muscles are not contracting, and the risk of blood pooling in the lower limbs is increased, potentially leading to a number of health-related issues—including **deep vein thrombosis (DVT)**, which is a clot in the leg or groin, and feeling dizzy when standing. Furthermore, the lymphatic system is solely reliant upon the massage effects of muscles due to movement.

- Even if you hit the gym straight after work, an 8-hour day spent sitting at your desk is going to take its toll in time. Unfortunately, whether you're out of shape or in good shape, too much sitting can be deleterious to your health.

- The human body adapts specifically to the demands that are placed on it; sitting, in effect, trains your body to do nothing and leads to physiological adaptations that reduce your functionality.

- Because the hazards of too much sitting can affect us even when we're active, we need a blueprint to reduce sedentary behavior that involves taking stock of our daily routine and attempting to find opportunities to reduce the time spent seated—particularly for long, uninterrupted bouts.

- This doesn't necessarily mean heading for the gym and a full hour-long workout, but it does involve engaging in non-exercise activity thermogenesis (NEAT), a label coined by Dr. James Levine of the Mayo Clinic in Rochester, Minnesota. NEAT involves finding ways to introduce exercise into your daily routine, thereby reducing the amount of time you spend sitting.

Preventing Sitting Disease

- At work, where the likelihood of being stationed at a desk is an issue, take breaks by walking to the water fountain. In addition to the exercise in getting you there, water has known benefits to health. Furthermore, stand whenever you're taking a phone call, or earn your coffee break by walking up and down the stairs a few times beforehand.

- You can schedule a 5-minute activity period for both the morning and afternoon to take a walk. Even if you can't leave your chair, you can still tone your abdominals by sitting upright with your shoulders drawn back, taking hold of the front edge of the chair with both hands for support, and slowly lifting your knees toward your chest.

- If you're downloading large files, use the time to get out of your seat and do a few squats. If you're photocopying, try some rear leg lifts. If you can hold mobile meetings, try discussing work matters while you stroll around the building or, better still, outside so that you get the boost of fresh air and vitamin D from the natural light.

- Even if you can't leave your desk, a few seated stretches will still bring benefits, so try to repeat the following moves a few times during the day, holding each static position for about 15 seconds.

- First, work through the neck. Take your head, drop your ear down to your shoulder, and then take your opposite hand out to the side and press it away from you. You'll feel a stretch come down through the neck and into the shoulder. Hold the stretch for about 15 seconds.

- Lift your head back up and twist your head to the side, releasing through the neck on the opposite side. You'll need to work on both sides, holding each stretch at the end position to ease the tension and returning back to the center.

If you work at a desk, perform seated stretches throughout the day to ease the tension in your shoulders, neck, and upper back.

- Then, lift your hands up in front of your chest, interlock your fingers, and keep your elbows bent but reach your arms forward, rounding the shoulders and dropping the chin down. Try to stretch your shoulder blades apart, stretching through the muscles in your upper back.

- Ease out of that stretch and balance it by taking your hands around behind your back in the lower back region. Then, squeeze your shoulder blades together, bringing your elbows toward each other, and you'll feel that stretch through the chest and through the front of the shoulders. Then, take one arm across your chest, take your hand above the elbow, and squeeze it in, feeling a stretch into your shoulder.

- To stretch your triceps, lift your hand up, drop your hand behind your head in between your shoulder blades—with your other hand on your elbow—and gently press down so that your fingertips are sliding down between your shoulder blades. Remember to do both sides and to hold all stretches for 15 seconds.

- At home, the major concern is sitting down in the evening to watch television, so try to stand up or march in place during the commercial breaks. Purchase a piece of home cardio equipment so that you can cycle, walk, or step while watching your favorite shows or movies.

- Do a few tricep dips off the end of the couch or chair while you're waiting for your favorite program to begin. Stand on one leg and keep your balance while the theme song plays at the beginning and end of the show, or if you're waiting for a particular show, switch to the music channel and dance along with whatever is playing for a few minutes.

- You could also try using a fitness ball in your office and home. Instead of sitting in a chair to watch television, you can sit on a fitness ball and gently bounce.

- If you're reading, put your book down, stand up, and walk in place for 2 minutes after reading every 6 pages.

- Keep a resistance band in the kitchen drawer so that you can pump rubber while dinner is cooking.

- The World Health Organization warned that sitting on a plane for more than 4 hours can double your chances of developing a blood clot. In fact, it's estimated that 5% of all air travelers suffer clots, but some people may not know it because the clots may become reabsorbed within the circulatory system. For those who already suffer from circulation problems and for the elderly, the risk of clotting and, therefore, the possibility of deep vein thrombosis (DVT) is increased.

- If a clot breaks away from the wall of the vein and travels within the bloodstream, it may cause a blockage or possibly even lead to a heart attack. If you fly regularly, it's important not to simply ignore leg pain or assume it's just a cramp. If caught early enough and treated with a blood-thinning agent, clots can be relieved before becoming a problem.

- To help reduce your risk of DVT on your next flight, take a few minutes every hour to circle your ankles, to flex and point your feet, to lift and lower your heels, and to lift and lower your thighs. Stretch the calves by placing the toes on the footrest and pressing the heels down to the floor, lengthening the back of the lower leg.

- In addition, get up and walk the length of the aisles at regular intervals, drink plenty of water, and try to avoid diuretics such as alcohol and coffee because dehydration is thought to be a contributory factor.

- You can also make good use of your spare time on a plane or as a passenger in a car by relieving tension and stress with a total body self-massage.

Posture and Breathing
- There is no doubt that long periods of sitting are linked with poor posture, which is a crucial factor in back pain issues. A big problem with being seated is that it's too easy to switch off your core muscles, and your alignment suffers as a result. A disengaged core manifests itself in rounded shoulders and a forward chin position.

- A surprising cause of poor posture is poor breathing technique. When breathing is not effective, the nervous system will attempt to bring about changes that allow for more oxygen to be taken on board and then delivered to all the cells within the body because they need this life-giving fuel. Unfortunately, this can initiate changes in posture.

- While the diaphragm plays a vital role in contracting to give more space in the thoracic cavity, producing a pressure drop that leads to inhalation, its action is supported by the pectoralis minor and sternocleidomastoid muscles, which lift the rib cage. If breathing is not adequate, the nervous system will influence posture to put these muscles in a position that will allow them to better assist respiration—where it's easier for them to lift the rib cage.

- Moving the shoulders and chin forward results in these 2 muscles having a better line of pull; rather than pulling slightly backward, they are able to pull directly upward, which helps to expand the rib cage and create more space for air to enter.

- The greatest concern is that as these muscles work harder, they also become stronger and stiffer, so it's harder for them to return to a more natural posture. Fortunately, breathing exercises can help you overcome this.

Important Terms

deep vein thrombosis (DVT): A clot in the leg or groin.

lipoprotein lipase: An enzyme that draws fat out of the bloodstream for use as fuel.

Sitting Disease
Lecture 22—Transcript

Throughout this series we've looked at the body's amazing structure and the incredible processes that take place within it, in all cases discovering that regular exercise can bring positive changes leading to improvements in health status.

We've seen there's evidence to suggest that we can reduce our risk of suffering from heart disease, diabetes, osteoporosis, and certain cancers and also control weight management simply by committing to being active. The flip side of this coin however, is that a sedentary lifestyle can have a quite significant negative impact on one's health, with recent research stacking up to highlight just how dangerous inactivity can be to our future wellbeing.

If you take into account that due to the technological age in which we now live, most of us will be sedentary for around 70% of the day, be that driving the kids to school, working at a computer, eating at the dinner table, or simply flaking out on the couch in front of the television, we should perhaps all take a moment to consider whether we spend too much time on our backsides and if there's a possibility that we're at risk of succumbing to sitting disease.

Now don't be fooled, this term isn't simply marketing speak, consider the following statistics. According to the American Institute for Cancer Research, around 100,000 new cases of breast and colon cancer each year are linked to sedentary lifestyles. A study at the University of South Carolina showed that people who were inactive for more than 23 hours per week had a 64% greater risk of death from heart disease when compared to a control group who were sedentary for less than 11 hours per week. It's estimated that up to 100,000 people die each year from blood clots, and sitting in one position for too long is the key factor. We've known the dangers of sitting for a long time now, these were discovered back in the late 50s, when we realized that men who were employed in manual labor roles were less likely to suffer coronary artery disease than those whose jobs were not physically active. This was supported by the relatively large Canadian Fitness Survey in 2009, published in *Medicine & Science in Sports & Exercise* that looked at more than 7,000 men and nearly 10,000 women over a considerable 12 year period. The study participants ranged in age from 18–90 years, so it was an unusually broad study. The researcher concluded that there's a significant link between time spent seated and mortality. More importantly, the study revealed that being active doesn't balance out the negative effects of being seated too much of the time. So even if you achieve the recommended minimum target of 30 minutes, 5 times per week, spending too many of your waking hours parked on your backside is not good for you. This doesn't negate the fact of course that you still need to be active, but you do need to break up bouts of sitting.

At this point you may be wondering, just how does sitting down have such a bad effect on health? Well, let's take a look at the physiological implications of being sedentary. A 2008 study published in *Current Cardiovascular Risk Reports* showed that if we don't stand, electrical activity within the muscles effectively ceases, leading to a drop of up to 90% in the levels of lipoprotein lipase, which is an enzyme that draws fat out of the bloodstream for use as fuel, as it clearly wouldn't be required. This then leads to a higher concentration of blood fats that are known to increase the risk of cardiovascular malaise.

In addition, sitting appears to lead to around a 20% reduction in high-density lipoprotein, known as the good cholesterol, for its positive effect on the circulatory system, so again, increasing the risk of suffering from a cardiovascular disease. Unsurprisingly, sitting probably only requires contractions of the small muscles in the hands and forearms; I'm thinking of a computer here or a phone handset or maybe even a television remote control. And these will use up little amounts of energy when compared to the big muscles in the legs, in buttocks, in the lower back. As a result, your metabolism plummets, so calories are not being consumed but absorbed, a fact that will more than likely manifest itself in the waist area.

The story gets worse, as remaining sedentary for more than 24 hours, for example when on bed rest due to a serious debilitating injury or illness, impairs the ability of our insulin to uptake glucose. Now this in turn raises the risk of diabetes, as found in a study at the Pennington Biomedical Research Center. It's also worth noting that blood circulation is, to a certain degree, dependent upon movement. Yes, the heart is a pump, it's key in getting the oxygen-rich blood around to all the extremities within the body. But venous return is assisted by the squeezing effect of the muscles on the veins when they contract. So when the legs are not moving, the leg muscles are not contracting and the risk of blood pooling in the lower limbs is increased, potentially leading to a number of health related issues such as deep vein thrombosis which is a clot in the leg or groin and feeling light headed when standing. Of more concern however, is the impact on the lymphatic system, as it is solely reliant upon the massage effect of muscles due to movement.

What this tells us then, is that sitting like any more accepted illnesses, has an associated pathology and this is the reason why even if you hit the gym straight after work, an 8 hour day spent sat at your desk is going to take its toll in time. Unfortunately, whether you're carrying a little excess baggage and totally out of shape or even a finely honed Olympic athlete, too much sitting can be deleterious to your health.

Dr. Toni Yancey, co-director of the Kaiser Permanente Center for Health Equity at the University of California, Los Angeles, has conducted considerable research into this topic and sums up the situation excellently in the following quote,

> We just aren't really structured to be sitting for such long periods of time, and when we do that, our body just kind of goes into shutdown. If there's a fountain of youth, it is probably physical activity. So the problem isn't whether it's a good idea, the problem is how to get people to do more of it.

This really should come as no surprise for, in this course, we have learned that the human body adapts specifically to the demands that are placed upon it. For example, in our look at the skeleton we discovered that loading the bones through resistance training stimulates growth at a cellular level and so bone density increases leading to a reduction in the risk of osteoporosis. So it follows, then, the converse will also be true, thus sitting is in effect training your body to do nothing and leads to physiological adaptations that reduce your functionality.

Since the hazards of too much sitting can affect us even when we're active, what we need is a blueprint to reduce sedentary behavior. Obviously, this involves taking stock of our daily routine and attempting to find opportunities to reduce the time spent seated, particularly long, uninterrupted bouts.

Now this doesn't necessarily mean heading for the gym and a full hour-long workout but engaging in what is referred to as non-exercise activity Thermogenesis, or NEAT for short. This label was originated by Dr. James Levine of the Mayo Clinic in Rochester, Minnesota, who in 2005 published results of his detailed analysis of metabolism.

Dr. Levine was trying to uncover why it is that 2 people can eat an identical diet but one might gain weight while the other doesn't. He tracked not only food consumption but also activity, and I mean every activity. He used motion-tracking underwear to detect even the smallest movements, enabling him to notice that those people who don't gain weight move more.

Amazingly, those who didn't put on weight during the study were also the same people who, without even thinking about it, felt an urge to be active, to take the stairs, for instance, rather than the elevator. He found that the weight gainers sat for 2 hours longer each day, on average, than those who didn't put on pounds. The great news is, in the NEAT world, little things add up to big changes.

Unfortunately, we can't just all give up our jobs and then take up a physical vocation so what's required is some creative thinking to introduce more movement to your daily routine and so reduce the amount of time you spend sitting. As an example, did you know that there already exists a first grade classroom with no chairs where children are encouraged to crawl and climb whilst performing basic literacy and numeracy drills? In addition, treadmill desks are not the stuff of science fiction movies, but can actually be found in some more health conscious offices.

Since sitting disease affects us at the desk at work, in front of the television or computer at home, on flights and behind the wheel of our cars, here's a 4-pronged defense strategy that can serve as a critical dose of preventive medicine.

Firstly at work where the likelihood of being stationed at a desk is the issue, take your breaks by walking to the water fountain as well as the exercise in getting you there, H_2O has known benefits to health also. When you need to powder your nose, walk to the furthest away toilet in the building, stand whenever you're taking a phone call. Earn your coffee break by walking up and down the stairs a few times immediately beforehand.

Can you schedule 5-minute activity periods for both the morning and afternoon, as if it were a meeting in your diary? You could just simply take a walk. You can still tone your abdominals, even if you can't leave your chair, by sitting upright with your shoulders drawn back, take hold of the front edge of the chair with both hands for support and now slowly lift your knees towards your chest.

If you're downloading big files, use the time to get out of your seat and do a few squats. Have a stretch whenever you're talking to colleagues. If you're photocopying, try rear leg lifts. And can you hold mobile meetings, discussing work matters while you stroll around the building or better still, outside so you get the boost of fresh air and Vitamin D from the natural light?

Even if you can't leave your desk, a few seated stretches will still bring benefits so try to repeat the following moves a few times during the day, holding each static position for around 15 seconds. In fact, you can do some of these with me right now.

Firstly let's work through the neck. So take the head, drop the ear down to the shoulder, and then take the opposite hand out to the side and press it away. You'll feel that stretch come down through the neck and into the shoulder. Remember you need to hold these stretches for about 15 seconds, but we're going to move through them to give you a good range.

Lift the head back up, this time we're going to twist the head, twist to the side releasing through the neck on the opposite side. You'll need to work on both sides and again remember holding each stretch at the end position to ease the tension, and back to the center. This time we're going to lift the hands up in front of the chest, interlock the fingers and you're going to keep the elbows bent but reach the arms forwards, sort of really rounding the shoulders, dropping the chin down.

And we're trying to stretch the shoulder blades apart here, really getting into the upper back, into the rhomboids, into the trapezius, really stretching through the muscles in the upper back. We'll ease out of that and we'll balance it by taking the hands around behind, you'll need to sit forward in the chair slightly, here. Hands are in the lower back and now we squeeze the shoulder blades together, bring the elbows towards each other, and you'll feel that stretch through the chest and through the front of the shoulders.

Again, move into the position, hold your end position, you'll feel the tension release, the muscles begin to stretch and we'll ease back. We're going to take one arm across the chest, take the hand above the elbow, and squeeze it in, and here we're getting a stretch into that shoulder.

Now remember there's a lot of tension held in the shoulders, the neck, the upper back if we're working at a desk, so this is an ideal stretch, and ease that off. And 1 more final for the triceps, you're going to lift the hand up, drop the hand behind the head in between the shoulder blades, the other hand on the elbow and gently press down so the finger tips are sliding down between the shoulder blades, and that's a little stretch for the triceps at the back of the arm, and ease that off. Remember you've got to do both sides and hold those stretches for 15 seconds.

At home the major concern is sitting down in the evening to watch television. So could we try these tactics? Stand up or march on spot during the commercial breaks when you're watching. Purchase a piece of home cardio equipment so you can cycle, walk, or step while watching your favorite DVD.

Do a few triceps dips off the end of the couch or chair while you're waiting for your favorite program to begin. Stand on one leg and keep your balance while the theme tune plays at the start and end of the show or if you're waiting for a particular show, switch to the music channel and dance along with whatever is playing for a few minutes.

You could try a fitness ball, maybe one in the office and one at home, so instead of sitting on a chair to watch television you can sit on a fitness ball and gently bounce. If you're reading, not watching television, put your book down, stand up and walk on the spot for 2 minutes after reading every 6 pages. Keep a resistance band in the kitchen drawer so you can pump rubber while the dinner is cooking.

But what about travelling? The dangers of flying were highlighted by the World Health Organization, in suggesting that sitting on a plane for more than 4 hours can double the chance of you developing a blood clot.

In fact, it's estimated that 5% of all air travelers suffer clots, although some of us may not even know it, as they may become reabsorbed within the circulatory system. For those people who are already suffering circulation problems and the elderly, the risk of clotting and so the possibility of deep vein thrombosis, also called DVT, is increased.

If a clot breaks away from the wall of the vein and travels within the bloodstream, it may cause a blockage or pulmonary embolism and possibly even lead to a heart attack. If you fly regularly then, it's important not to simply ignore leg pain or assume it's just cramp. The good news is that if caught early enough and treated with a blood thinning agent such as Warfarin, clots can be relieved before becoming a problem. But here are a few tips you can deploy on or next flight to help you to reduce your risk of DVT.

Every hour take a few minutes to circle your ankles, to flex and point your feet, to lift and lower your heels and lift and lower your thighs. Stretch the calves by placing the toes on the footrest and then pressing the heels down to the floor to lengthening the back of the lower leg. Get up and walk the length of the aisles at regular intervals, and dehydration is thought to be a contributory factor, so drink plenty of water and try to avoid diuretics such as alcohol and coffee.

The following exercises won't help reduce the risk of DVT directly, as they don't affect the lower limbs but remembering the NEAT principle we talked of earlier, they'll certainly still be of benefit to our health.

We can start with a simple bicep curl, just bending the elbows, lifting the arms up to shoulder and back down, just lightly clinch the fists. And just about 5 repetitions of each exercise will keep the upper body mobile, in your seat, and hold that there.

Bring them up to chest level, take the elbows out to the side, and push the hands forwards in front of the chest, careful not lock out your arms, getting that range of movement through the shoulder, good challenge for the core strength here as well, keep your abdominals pulled in tight.

And we're going to change that slightly, take them out to the side, lift the hands up, squeeze the elbows together in the center. Bring the elbows together, a little bit of work for the pectorals, but again working that mobility through the shoulders and a chance to work on your core strength, keeping your abdominals in tight. So you're sitting up away from the back of the seat, and hold them when there in the center.

Now we're going to press up to the top and back down with that little twist, fabulous. Keeping those shoulders moving, keeping the arms moving, we're getting that extension through the elbow, we're getting a little bit of elevation through the shoulder girdle.

And bring them back down; rest them on the top of your thighs. And then the head we're just going to go from side to side, a little tilt and across the other side with a tilt, and across. I'm going to do a little half circle now that goes from the side to the front, around to the other side but then come straight back, don't go back, don't tilt the head backwards.

Tilting the head backwards can squeeze the blood vessels at the back of the neck, also the nerve so we don't tilt backwards necessarily but we just roll from side to side. Now whenever you think about it, if you can run through these exercises, it'll keep your upper body mobile.

Probably the most restrictive of situations, when we're seated and have to remain so is when we're driving. Now clearly, there are no stretches or exercises that can be safely performed when your vehicle is moving, but just because your car comes to a stop, doesn't mean your journey to a healthier you also has to stall. Next time you're stuck in a jam, try the following exercises.

To exercise the chest, put the hands on the wheel, at the numbers 3 and 9, imagine you're working with a clock. Now we're doing isometric exercises here, and you may remember form our lecture on muscles, that involves contracting the muscles but no movement. So what we do here is, keeping the elbows slightly soft, squeeze the hands in towards each other. What we're doing here is working the pectoral muscles in the chest, squeezing the hands closer together, holding that contraction for about 5 seconds, and then we ease off. Now that's something you'll repeat, we're going to do it just once here but you'll need to repeat that 3 times for each exercise.

To work the upper back, we're going to left the hands up now to the 1 and 11, and the arms are nearly straight again. And this time we're going to press down, so the feeling is pressing down and we're working into the latissimus dorsi, the back of the armpit, large muscle in the upper back as we start to press down. Again holding that contraction for around 5 seconds and then easing off.

We're taking the hands back to 3 and 9 for a little work on the shoulders. What we're doing here is trying to open out, so grab a hold of the wheel and now as if you're pulling it apart, the elbows are slightly lifted as if you're pulling it open. Trust me you're not going to strong enough to pull the steering wheel apart, again around 5 seconds. Feeling that work in the shoulders, holding that contraction before we release.

We're going to work into the biceps and triceps now, and for these exercises you need to move yourself forward slightly on your seat so that you're towards the front of the seat now.

We're going to put the hands underneath the wheel, at 5 and 7. And now the aim is to lift upwards, as if you're lifting palms upwards, starting to work into the biceps on the front of the arm. Hold that contraction, the stronger the contraction, the better. Try not to hold your breath on these isometric exercises, and release that off. Remember you're going to repeat each exercise around 3 times.

Take the hands up to top, to the 1 and 11 again, this time the elbows drop in, and now we're pressing down with the palms. So now this is slightly different than the upper back where the arm was long, we're now working through a bent elbow, trying to straighten the arm out, working into the triceps, that problem area at the back of the arm, and we'll ease that off.

We can relax the hands now. What we're going to do is a little bit of work for the gluteals, for the hamstrings at the back of the thighs, and the way we do that is simply pressing into your heels and trying to lift your back side as if you're lifting it just slightly off the seat.

You won't be able to leave the seat but that squat position, really pressing the heels down into the floor will enable you to get some work for the glutes and into the hamstrings.

Then finally we lift up the heels onto the balls of the feet as high as we can, and then press the balls of the feet down into the floor. Really push down with the balls of the feet, working into the calves, and ease the heels down and a good idea to finish, rest the hands on top of the thighs and just take a few deep breaths.

Of course, as a passenger you're not bound to only move when the car doesn't, so try some of the stretching and mobilizing exercises proposed earlier for when you are at your workstation and or sitting on a plane. In addition, you can make good use of the time by relieving tension and stress with a self-massage. Here's a seated manipulation routine for you to try right now while you're watching this and to then take away and use in the office, on the plane and in the passenger seat.

Let's start on the right side. Use your right hand and find the trapezius muscle which is just below the base of your skull. Tilt your head towards the left shoulder, and while you press deep into the muscle with the right hand, slowly drag the fingers down and out towards the right shoulder. Repeat this movement about 5 times, and switch over to the other side. From the base of the skull, press into the muscle and drag down, keep the pressure on with the fingertips.

To massage the shoulders, place your left hand on your right shoulder and with your right hand cup the bottom of the left elbow. This will support it and keep it stable as you massage. Keep the fingers of your left hand together and press them deep into the shoulder muscle, and now gently walk the fingers into the muscle forwards and backwards for a few seconds. So rather than squeeze and release, keep the squeeze on but rock forwards and backwards and then just change the position slightly so we get a different portion of the muscles. Squeeze it and rock forwards and backwards. Keep changing the position so that we cover the entire muscle, really getting into the deltoid and we can change sides. So reach to the shoulder, cup the elbow, squeeze, and rock forwards and backwards. Remember again to move the hand to different positions to cover the entire shoulder muscle.

Moving on to the upper back, particularly the latissimus dorsi, we're going to lift the left hand up, put it behind the head. Elbow will be pointing up towards the ceiling. Reach your right hand across your chest, reaching into the back of the armpit into the latissimus dorsi. Now squeeze the fingers together in the right hand and massage downwards. Keep squeezing and move down, squeeze and move down, squeeze and move down, all the way down to the hip, and once you get there, take it back up, and start again. From the top, squeeze, squeeze, squeeze, and keep moving down, and again we'll repeat this 5 times. When you've done that we'll change sides, really squeeze the fingers in, and move down. Around 5 repetitions is your target.

Now, it's true to say that just about all of us, whatever our vocations or hobbies, can benefit from loosening the lower back, so to achieve this we've got a little tool. We're going to use a tennis ball for this exercise, any kind of ball that gives you a little bit of resistance that's not too squishy. So we're going to lie on your back, you're going to bend the knees and you're going to out the ball under your lower back. Now lie yourself down onto the floor, and all we're going to do here is, gently using the hands and the feet, allow yourself to rock side to side, forwards and backwards. It's really quite random, the movement is up to you, just get that little roll about; take your time. Nice and slowly, rolling forwards and backwards, side to side, just getting that little massage effect all the way through the lower back. You can use as much or little of your body weight as you wish by putting a little more weight on the hands or the feet bearing that position.

Let's move on to the hamstrings now, particularly important for any of you who are runners, tight hamstrings are a common problem. So what we're going to do here is lying on your back, you're going to bring your right leg over the top of the left, fabulous. We're going to place the hands on thigh, and you're going to press the fingers into the middle of the hamstring, thumbs by the knee, and as you press the fingers in, you now start to drag the fingers back towards the hip. Really pressing into that hamstring muscle all the time as we're doing it, then take it back up and start again. Press the fingers into the back of leg, and we drag the hands up the thigh applying the pressure as we go. Still on the hamstring, move onto the other side, beautiful. Pressing those fingers in and dragging down and switching back to the other side. Hamstrings again because this is a tight area, so same position but this time what you're going to do is dig the fingers in and you're going to rub side to side and then move down slightly, rub side to side, and keep moving side to side with the hands working up and down the thigh, changing over to the other side after a couple of minutes.

To balance out we'll move onto the quadriceps now onto the front the of thigh, so if you sit yourself up for this one, and the leg can be out in front. So let's take the right leg first off all, what you're going to do is put one hand on top, near the hip and then put the other hand on top and press down into the palm. So that gives us that extra pressure.

Now we begin to slide down towards the knee, slowly sliding down towards the knee keeping the pressure on. You really need 2 hands to do this, and then come back up to the top and start again. So make sure you've got plenty of pressure into the muscle and gently move down from the top of the thigh towards the knee cap and we change the angle slightly so we move a little bit to the outside, a little bit closer to the middle. That way we're really getting to our 4 of those quadriceps muscles, obviously 4 being where the term quadriceps comes from.

Let's take the right leg first and bring it up, you're going to wrap the hands around below the knee, digging the thumbs into the calf. What we're going to do then is begin to slide down, keeping the pressure with the thumbs into the calf muscle and down into the Achilles, slide it down and then work your way back up. Literally pressing the thumb in, sliding down towards the

Achilles, and then sliding back up. We'll go back to the other side, but this time digging the thumbs in. What you're going to do is press them into the middle and draw them apart, work down, press in, draw them apart. Press in, draw them apart, like you're really kneading that calf muscle—a couple of minutes on each leg. We're now going to take one foot over the top of the other and simply get some rotation through the ankle, and let's keep alternating directions. So one way, circle back the other; just really release that pressure through the ankle.

And hold that there, keep the foot there. What we're going to do now is dig the thumbs into the sole and then start to slide the length of the foot up to the end. We'll do that a couple more times, start from the heel, really press in, and work right the way through the longitude in the arch all the way up to the top. This time when you get there, just start to spread the toes apart. Pull them apart, work your way through each pairing, releasing that tension through the feet. Then when you've done that we'll swap over to the other side.

Finally into the forearms, last exercise so sitting comfortably. What we're going to do is turn one hand up, let's take the thumb pressing in, starting just above the elbow. We'll start to circular massage to work our way down towards the wrist, really dig the thumb in, and then we'll come back up and do it again. Really press in, little circles, work your way down to the bottom and again. Then to get into the front, we're going to turn it over, you're going to dig the thumb in and then just simply contract and relax the muscle by clenching and opening the fist.

Move it down, press in, and then you'll feel the muscle move under the thumb. Then move it down a little lower and do it again. All you need to do is really press with the thumb and let that contraction of the muscle do the massage; and swapping over to the other side, first of all the palms up, little pressing in with the thumbs, circular movements working your way down. Then when you turn it over, dig the thumb in and open and clench the fist. Move it down a little, press it in, and relax your hands down. And there's your total body self-massage.

You don't need to be a genius to link long periods of sitting with poor posture, and in our look at the spine we established that poor posture is a crucial factor in back pain issues. A big problem with being seated is that it's too easy to switch off your core muscles and your alignment suffers.

Take a look around an office, it won't take you too long to spot someone with a disengaged core manifesting itself by way of rounded shoulders and a forward chin position. One surprising cause of this actually might be poor breathing technique.

In previous lectures we touched on the concept of homeostasis which is the body's natural desire to return itself to optimum functioning, usually via subconscious actions. When breathing is not effective, the nervous system will attempt to bring about changes that allow for more oxygen to be taken on board and then delivered to all the cells within the body as they need this life-giving fuel. Unfortunately, this can initiate changes in posture.

Let's just remind ourselves of the basics of breathing mechanics. We investigated in our specific lecture on this topic. Whilst the diaphragm plays the vital role in contracting to give more space in the thoracic cavity, so producing a pressure drop that leads to inhalation, its action is supported by the pectoralis minor and sternocleidomastoid muscles.

These effectively lift the rib cage. If breathing is not adequate, the nervous system will influence posture to put these muscles in a position that will allow them to better assist respiration, in other words putting them in a position where it's easier for them to left the rib cage.

So moving the shoulders and the chin forwards actually results in these 2 muscles having a better line of pull, rather than pulling slightly backwards there now pulling directly upwards. And that helps to expand the rib cage and so create more space for air to enter.

The greatest concern is that as these muscles work harder, they also become stronger and stiffer, so it's harder for them to return to a more natural posture. Now I recommend that you look at Lecture 6 for some breathing exercises to overcome this.

So, now you know of the dangers associated with long seated periods and you're armed with a wide range of tactics you can deploy on a daily basis, whether at work, home, or on the journey between the two, you can start to make changes today that will improve your health for tomorrow.

It's now a proven fact that too much time on your backside will literally shorten your life. But, just like the growing numbers of employees at both Google and Facebook who have traded their traditional workstations for standing desks, you don't have to take it sitting down.

Exercise for Weight Loss
Lecture 23

R esearch shows that excess body fat carries an increased health risk. Therefore, more importantly for health instead of for aesthetic reasons, weight management and, particularly, weight loss should be a focus of every individual. The goal of this lecture is to analyze the role of exercise as a tool to achieve weight loss, helping you to understand how and why exercise works. By the end of the lecture, you should feel confident that you have the requisite knowledge of exercise for weight loss to make the right choices for your body—today, tomorrow, and for the rest of your life.

BMI and Obesity
- **Body mass index (BMI)** is calculated as your weight in kilograms divided by the square of your height in meters. For example, a person who is 5 feet 9 inches tall and weighs 125 pounds has a BMI of 18.5.

- The Centers for Disease Control and Prevention suggest that a BMI of 18.5 to 24.9 is a healthy range, with 25.0 to 29.9 being overweight and more than 30 being classified as obese. This is merely a guideline that correlates to the amount of body fat in the general population, and athletes or extremely muscular individuals will score falsely high on this scale.

- The percentage of overweight individuals is growing because of a very simple mathematical equation: the sum of calories in minus calories out. If more calories are consumed in the form of food than are used up through activity and metabolism, the result is weight gain.

- Fortunately, dietary restriction and increased exercise will lead to a calorie deficit and, therefore, to weight loss. Unfortunately, however, this technological age in which we now live has led to a predominantly sedentary lifestyle for most of us, and essential movement for everyday tasks has become minimized. When this is combined with the incredibly easy access to calorie-dense foods, it's easy to understand how the equation works against us, leading to weight problems.

- We've evolved as a species that was occasionally threatened with famine and that required considerable physical effort to acquire food, and as a result, we developed the ability to take in and store food in the form of fat tissue. The existence of readily available food and the removal of the necessity to hunt for it have led to an expanding global waistband.

- When you eat and how much you sleep are factors in being overweight, but those are largely choices we can influence.

- There are other contributors to being overweight, including genetics. There's no doubt that heredity plays a role in our physical makeup—or, rather, it can explain disorders that contribute to increased weight—but genetics cannot account for a significant portion of obese people.

- In general, women carry more body fat than men but, usually, around the hips and thighs—known as a **gynoid**, or pear-shaped, body—while men's fat deposits tend to be around the stomach, which is referred to as the **android**, or apple, shape. For men, the increased abdominal fat is likely to lead to a greater risk of cardiovascular disease.

Storing Fat
- We store fat in the body in the form of **triglycerides**, which are composed of 3 fatty acid molecules found within specific fat cells known as **adipocytes**. There is also a small amount of fat residing within the muscle cells, ready to be used as fuel for exercise, although most will come through the bloodstream.

- The release of fat from storage to be used as fuel is regulated by 2 enzymes: hormone-sensitive lipase and lipoprotein lipase.

Hormone-sensitive lipase is located in the fat cell and acts to break apart the triglyceride, releasing the 3 fatty acids into the bloodstream. This is influenced by the hormone **epinephrine**, which increases in concentration during cardio exercise. The responsiveness of hormone-sensitive lipase increases during cardio exercise as well.

- A training effect of regular exercise is that this phenomenon improves; as we get fitter, the enzyme responds to lower levels of epinephrine and, therefore, more readily breaks apart the triglycerides to be used as energy.

- Conversely, the lipoprotein lipase is found on the walls of the blood vessels and acts as a transporter, mopping up triglycerides in the blood and taking them to storage sites to be used as fuel later.

- Exercise, especially when combined with reduced calorie intake through sensible eating, is the optimum approach to sustained weight loss—not only decreasing body fat but also enhancing cardiovascular profile, improving insulin sensitivity, and lowering blood pressure.

Misconceptions about Losing Weight
- Losing weight through exercise can be somewhat confusing. For example, cardio machines in the gym recommend built-in fat-burning programs at around 60% to 70% of maximum working heart rate—which we calculate by subtracting your age from 220—although this is a fairly low intensity.

- This is based on the premise that at lower intensities, the majority of the calories burned are from fat stores—rather than carbohydrate, which is stored in the muscles and liver. It is true that as the intensity increases, a lower proportion of the fuel will be provided by fat, but the important factor is the total number of calories expended.

- Therefore, a vigorous workout may burn a lesser percentage of calories from fat stores, but the total amount could be greater than working out for the same length of time at a lower intensity. As your fitness level starts to improve through regular activity, your ability to achieve and maintain higher intensities will also improve, and therefore, your capacity to burn fat during exercise will increase.

- It's important to begin exercise gently, particularly if you have not done it in a while, but accelerated results will come from increasing the intensity of exercise, so you should try to do that as soon as possible. In addition, consult your physician before embarking on a new exercise regime.

- Another common misconception is that fat burning during exercise only begins after a set period, usually quoted as being around 20 or 30 minutes. Fat metabolism is, indeed, a slow starter because transport to and utilization in the muscles requires time to work effectively. After a while, the switch takes place from carbohydrate to fat for fuel, and this switch occurs sooner for fitter people because the fitter you are, the more fat you will be able to burn during exercise.

- Studies have shown that there are a number of physiological adaptations as a result of cardio exercise that help to shift body fat, and regular exercise helps us become better at using our fat stores.

Exercising for Weight Loss

- An exercise-for-fat-loss program will depend on frequency and duration. Because the aim is to burn as many calories as possible, exercising more often and for longer will help tip the energy balance equation toward a negative calorie deficit.

- When considering exercise for weight loss, thought should be given to the influence of **excess postexercise oxygen consumption (EPOC)**, which is the number of calories that are burned immediately after exercise has ceased. This is due to the increased metabolic effect of your body removing waste products from the cells and then refueling. EPOC is dependent upon the intensity of the workout.

- Fat can be burned at any exercise intensity, and low-intensity exercise is recommended for those with a low fitness level because it is more likely to encourage them to stick with it.

- While the percentage of fat compared to carbohydrate being used as fuel varies with intensity, the most important figure is the total number of calories consumed. Frequency and duration need to be high enough to have a significant impact on reducing body fat, and EPOC contributes significantly to calorie expenditure and is greater for higher-intensity exercise sessions.

- Although exercise can make a big difference in the amount of calories used up, weight loss will only be achieved if you don't eat too much. Regular resistance training results in a short-term boost in fat burning after exercise but a long-term increase in muscle tissue, which is associated with an increase in resting metabolic rate.

- The best exercise prescription is to combine intense cardio and resistance training modes. Because low-calorie diets lead to a slowing of the metabolism, resistance training is a vital tool to counter this and is highly valuable to help you maintain weight-loss progress— as long as you're combining exercise and food restriction.

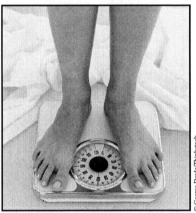

© George Doyle/Thinkstock.

- You get out of exercise what you put in, so resistance training needs to be intense and progressive. Weights should be selected to produce momentary

Research shows that people who lose a significant amount of weight and keep it off frequently step on scales to keep track of their progress.

muscular fatigue at around 12 to 15 repetitions and then increased once it becomes too easy.

Getting Results

- High-intensity interval training requires 10 sets of 4 minutes at 95% of your maximum working heart rate with 2 minutes of rest in between.

- A resistance training circuit involves about 20 repetitions at each of 12 weight-training stations with little or no rest, and the stations ideally should alternate between upper and lower body for a good calorie burn.

- Sprint interval training involves maximum effort for 30 seconds followed by 4 minutes of light exercise—repeated 6 times.

- Fartlek training involves interspersing a steady pace with quicker bursts of varying duration in an unstructured format.

- Metabolic conditioning is the idea of working continuous cardio at a moderate intensity of around 70% of your maximum working heart rate for around 40 to 60 minutes.

- Step-up interval training begins at an easy cardio pace, and speed increases perhaps every 4 minutes by about 15% until you reach the set target of between 20 and 60 minutes.

- As you start to become fitter, another technique is near-maximal training, which involves 5 sets of 5 minutes at 95% of your maximum working heart rate followed by 5 minutes at 50%.

Losing Weight and Keeping It Off

- Both research and anecdotal evidence suggest that most of us are capable of successfully losing weight, but the bigger challenge is maintaining our new weight. The triggers to weight regain can be divided into 3 distinct categories: lifestyle, stress, and hormones.

o   Being involved in sports, especially team sports, can be a great motivator to remaining regularly active. Marriage is commonly accompanied by a reduction in exercise levels and an increase in food intake—particularly for men. Those who give up smoking may find that weight increases because nicotine speeds up metabolic rate, and withdrawing it causes a decrease. Holiday seasons present the risk of gaining back lost weight, but standing away from the buffet table, for example, will help.

o   In addition, restrained eaters can sometimes worry less about their weight when under stress and then throw caution to the wind regarding food intake, so efforts should be made to try to adhere to regular patterns. Bereavement can lead to comfort eating and a lack of motivation to exercise. Divorce can be associated with feelings of depression and a break in routine that affects both eating and activity patterns.

o   Furthermore, changes linked to menopause are known to generally lead to a shift in body composition, so resistance training is particularly useful at this time. Pregnancy will lead to an increase in body weight, but it's important to try to restrict this to about 10 kilograms. Fat cells multiply during growth spurts and are then retained for life, so restraining junk-food consumption is key during periods of growth such as puberty.

- A recurring problem is, after a concentrated weight-loss effort, gaining more weight than was lost. Those who successfully keep the weight off have been shown to exercise for 250 minutes per week, frequently step on a scale, never skip breakfast, and maintain a written record of their weight-loss progress and a food diary.

- Exercise can help tackle cellulite—the result of fat protruding from the subcutaneous layer into the skin due to laxity in the connective tissue within the skin—by helping to reduce the presence of body fat and by toning the muscles.

Important Terms

adipocyte: A fat cell.

android: The apple shape associated with men's bodies.

body mass index (BMI): Calculated as your weight in kilograms divided by the square of your height in meters.

epinephrine: A hormone that increases in concentration during cardio exercise.

excess postexercise oxygen consumption (EPOC): The number of calories that are burned immediately after exercise has ceased—due to the increased metabolic effect of your body removing waste products from the cells and then refueling.

gynoid: The pear shape associated with women's bodies.

hormone-sensitive lipase: An enzyme that is located in the fat cell and acts to break apart the triglyceride, releasing the 3 fatty acids into the bloodstream.

triglyceride: A group of 3 fatty acid molecules found within specific fat cells known as adipocytes.

Exercise for Weight Loss
Lecture 23—Transcript

A few years ago the Madrid Fashion Show hit the headlines for taking a stand on the issue of stick-thin models, by not permitting any girls with a body mass index of less than 18, i.e., below the healthy range, to take to the catwalk. This was seen as a major step forward, not just for the sake of the models' health but also for the legions of girls across the world who see them as role models.

Whilst the pressure to be thin, and the trend for size zero, and the stigma occasionally attached to being overweight are unwelcome attitudes held within certain population subsets, the truth is that a wealth of research has proved that excess body fat does carries an increased health risk. More importantly for health rather than aesthetic reasons, weight management is an important issue and particularly, weight loss in light of the National Health and Nutrition Examination Survey that calculated that 34% of American adults are overweight, 33% are obese and a further 6% are extremely obese. The leading health policy journal, *Health Affairs*, estimated that medical costs associated with obesity, total an incredible $147 billion in 2008.

The aim of this presentation is to analyze the role of exercise as a tool to achieve weight loss, helping you to understand how and why it works. Over the next 30 minutes, I will equip you with the vital knowledge to ensure you win at losing!

Firstly, since the word "obese" appears so regularly in mainstream press and on television and in everyday conversation, it seems pertinent to start with a definition. Body Mass Index, or BMI, is calculated as your weight in kilograms divided by the square of your height in meters. For example, a person who is 5 feet 9 inches tall, weighing 125 pounds will have a BMI of 18.5.

The Centers for Disease Control and Prevention suggests that a BMI of 18.5–24.9 is a healthy range, with 25.0–29.9 being overweight and more than 30 being classed as obese. Be aware, however, this is merely a guideline that correlates to the amount of body fat in the general population and athletes or heavily muscled individuals will score falsely high on this scale.

So why is it that the percentage of overweight is growing, literally in all senses? It all comes down to very simple mathematical equation: the sum of calories in minus calories out. If more calories are taken on board in the form of food than are used up through activity and metabolism, the result will be weight gain.

Let's consider a specific example taken from an article by Doug McGuff. "An hour of jogging will burn only about 150 calories above your basal metabolic rate, but it only takes about 20 seconds to eat 150 calories of cookies."

Fortunately, however, dietary restriction and increased exercise will lead to a calorie deficit and so to weight loss. Unfortunately, however, this technological age in which we now live has led to a predominantly sedentary lifestyle for most of us and essential movement in everyday tasks has become somewhat minimized. When this is combined with the incredibly easy access to calorie dense foodstuffs, such as fast food, then it's easy to understand how the equation we just mentioned works against us, leading to weight problems.

We've evolved as a species that was occasionally threatened with famine and that required considerable physical effort to acquire food, as a result of which, we developed an ability to take in and store food, in the form of fat tissue. Now we can see how readily available food and the removal of the necessity to hunt for it have led to an expanding global waistband.

One surprising effect on your body mass turns out to be the amount you sleep. I asked Professor Heller about this, since sleep is his primary area of research. So let's go to him and see what he had to say.

> **Craig Heller**: So there is a relationship between sleep and weight gain, and the relationship is short sleep tends to correlate with excess weight gain. A large epidemiological study was done in which all sorts of characteristics of lifestyle were compared to

body composition, percent body fat. It was found that everything else being equal, individuals who fell into the short sleep category, people not getting more than 6 hours of sleep a night, they tended to have excess body mass. Whereas those individuals who were getting 8 or more hours of sleep per night, they were the individuals who had the lowest percent body fat.

Now, you might ask why that might be so. Well, one of the factors that perhaps comes into play is when you eat. People who are short sleepers, who are up late at night, they tend to snack late at night, they tend to eat late at night, and in a different study, it has been shown that calories, everything else being equal, calories consumed after 8 pm have a greater impact on body mass than calories consumed earlier in the day.

Dean Hodgkin: When you eat and how much you sleep are factors, then, in being overweight. But those are largely choices we can influence, unless you work the late shift, which is a high-risk category because you're off your natural circadian rhythm.

Clearly there are other contributors to being overweight, genetics often being cited. Now there's no doubt that heredity plays a role in our physical make-up, or rather it can explain disorders such as Bardet-Biedl, Prader-Willi and Cushing's syndromes, all of these can contribute to increased weight. But it's widely accepted this cannot account for a significant portion of the obese, hence the previously mentioned factors having more impact than genetics.

Let's consider gender next. In general women are known to carry more body fat than men but usually around the hips and thighs, known as the gynoid or pear-shaped body, while men's fat deposits tend to be around the tummy, referred to as the android or apple shape. Please note these are just sweeping generalizations, with much variance about these norms on both sides. It is well documented, unfortunately for the men out there, that the increased abdominal fat is likely to lead to a greater risk of cardiovascular disease.

How do we store fat? We store fat in the body in the form of triglycerides, as the name suggests this is made up of 3 fatty acid molecules found within specific fat cells, known as adipocytes. There is also a small amount residing within the muscle cells ready to be used as fuel for exercise, although most will come via the bloodstream.

The release of fat from storage to be used as fuel is regulated by 2 enzymes: hormone sensitive lipase and lipoprotein lipase. The first of these is located in the fat cell and acts to break apart the triglyceride, so releasing the 3 fatty acids into the bloodstream. This is influenced by the hormone epinephrine, which increases in concentration during cardio exercise, and also the responsiveness of the hormone sensitive lipase increases at this time.

Interestingly, a training effect of regular exercise is that this phenomenon improves, so as we get fitter, the enzyme responds to lower levels of epinephrine and so more readily breaks apart the triglycerides to be used as energy. Conversely, the lipoprotein lipase is found on the walls of the blood vessels and acts as a transporter, mopping up triglycerides in the blood and taking them to storage sites to be used as fuel later.

Exercise, especially when combined with reduced calorie intake through sensible eating, is the optimum approach to sustained weight loss, not only decreasing body fat but also enhancing cardiovascular profile, improving insulin sensitivity and lowering blood pressure.

The good news is that, surprisingly, weight loss of only 5% has been shown to have a positive effect on cardiovascular disease. Just 150 minutes of exercise per week typically leads to weight loss of around 2 kilograms and 420 minutes per week results in a considerable drop of 5 kilograms if combined with a sensible calorie restriction. Even something as simple as low-intensity walking can be of benefit to the overweight, if they are able to get their heart rate up to critical levels and prompt the positive responses we talked of earlier. However, obese persons have been known to sometimes suffer pain in the lower limbs when walking so cycling swimming, aqua exercise and rowing are strongly recommended.

Losing weight through exercise can be somewhat confusing, as cardio machines in the gym recommend in-built "fat-burning" programs at around 60–70% of maximum working heart rate, which you will remember from earlier in this series, we calculate from taking your age from 220, although this is a fairly low intensity, is probably a brisk walk for most of us.

This is based on the premise that at lower intensities, the majority of the calories burned are from fat stores rather than carbohydrate that is stored in the muscles and the liver. It is indeed true that as the intensity increases, a lower proportion of the fuel will be provided by fat, but the important factor to take into consideration here is the total number of calories expended.

So a vigorous workout may burn a lesser percentage of calories from fat stores but the total amount could be greater than working out for the same length of time at a lower intensity. So, as your fitness level starts to improve through regular activity, your ability to achieve and maintain higher intensities will also improve and therefore your capacity to burn fat during exercise will increase.

It's important to begin exercise gently, particularly if you have not done it for a while, but accelerated results will come from increasing the intensity of exercise, so you should try to do that as soon as possible. Of course, I strongly recommended that you consult your physician before embarking on a new exercise regime, particularly if you have any concerns about your current health status.

Now, there's another common misconception in this area, that fat burning during exercise only begins after a set period, usually quoted as being around 20 minutes, although sometimes 30 minutes is the magic threshold. Certainly, fat metabolism is a slow starter with transport to and utilization in the muscles requiring time to work effectively but after a while, the switch takes place from carbohydrate to fat for fuel. Interestingly, this switch occurs sooner for fitter people, again supporting my previous statement that the fitter you are the more fat you will be able to burn during exercise.

Studies have shown there are a number of physiological adaptations as a result of cardio exercise that help to shift body fat. Let's have a look at these. They include oxygen supplies increasing with regular exercise helping to burn fat more efficiently. Enhanced sensitivity to epinephrine results in greater release of fat stores. The amount of fat that enters the muscle to fuel movement can increase. The mitochondria, where fat burning actually takes place in the muscle cells, they increase in number and size. The combined result of these, then, supports the earlier hypothesis that regular exercise helps us to become better at using up our fat stores.

An exercise for fat loss program will depend upon 2 things. Now, we've encountered these several times in other presentations in this series, namely frequency and duration. Since the aim is to burn as many calories as possible, ultimately, exercising more often and for longer will help to tip the energy balance equation in our favor—that is, towards a negative calorie deficit. Here are 2 examples of how important these variables are when applied to 2 different exercise regimes: Let's consider 30 minutes brisk walk, 3 times per week, that will result in a burn of 600 calories. However, a 45 minutes brisk walk, 5 times per week will result in a calorie burn of 1500 calories. Although exact numbers will be dependent upon peoples' specific body weight and walking technique, we can calculate from this, that the first example, it will take us approximately 13 weeks to burn off 1 kilogram of body fat, whereas the second approach cuts this down to only around 5 weeks.

When considering exercise for weight loss, thought should be given to the influence of what exercise physiologists refer to as excess post-exercise oxygen consumption, or EPOC, which is calorie consumption immediately after exercise has ceased—the after-burn if you like. This is due to the increased metabolic effect of your body removing waste products from the cells and then refueling. Clearly, if this can be maximized it will lead to a boost in calories burned, even though you could actually be relaxing back at home after your sweaty endeavors.

It will probably come as no surprise to learn that EPOC is dependent upon the intensity of the workout, so the tougher the workout then the greater the after-burn, with 70% of your maximum working heart rate being an absolute minimum. This allows us to now summarize exercise for weight loss as follows. Fat can be burned at any exercise intensity, and low intensity exercise is recommended for those with a low fitness level as this is more likely to encourage you to stick at it.

Whilst the percentage of fat compared to carbohydrate being used as a fuel source varies with intensity, the most important figure is the total number of calories consumed. Frequency and duration need to be high enough to have a significant impact on reducing body fat. And remember that EPOC contributes significantly to calorie expenditure and is greater for higher intensity exercise sessions.

Importantly, remember fat loss involves creating a negative energy balance and although exercise can make a big difference to the calories used up, clearly weight loss will only be achieved if we don't eat too much, so putting too much energy in. Whilst people will often equate weight loss exercise to cardio options, such as cycling, running, swimming, it's fair to say that regular resistance training results in a short term boost in fat burning after exercise, but a long term increase in muscle tissue, which then has an associated raise in resting metabolic rate.

This implies then, that you'll burn even more calories just when you're sleeping. For this reason, the best exercise prescription is to combine intense cardio and resistance training modes. Since low calorie diets lead to slowing the metabolism, resistance training is actually vital as a tool to counter this, and so it's highly valuable to help you maintain weight loss progress, if you're combining exercise and food restriction.

To try to quantify the value of resistance training, it's useful to know that a kilogram of extra lean tissue will lead to an additional 100 calories being burned every single day. If you consider that a resistance training program can reasonably be expected to add 3–5 kilograms of muscle mass, this equates to using up an extra 300–500 calories per day, just in doing everyday activity. This can even add up—think about this—to a considerable 9–15 kilograms of fat loss over a year. The important thing to remember here is that you get out of exercise what you put in, so resistance training, like the cardio, needs to be intense and progressive. Weights should be selected to produce momentary muscular fatigue at around 12–15 repetitions and then increased once it becomes too easy.

At this point, having discussed exercise in some detail, I wish to address a myth you may well have encountered regarding the suggestion that exercising in the morning on an empty stomach is a great way to shed fat. Research at the University of Leuven in Belgium confirmed this will actually work, as fasting (which is essentially what happens overnight as we sleep) leads to an increased adrenalin and reduced insulin levels, creating an environment that is more conducive to the breakdown of fat for energy.

The study revealed that those who exercise without eating beforehand do burn significantly more fat than those who had a pre-workout snack. However, be warned, the fasters were not able to perform intense training as well as their counterparts who were fuelled up, according to another study in the *Medicine & Science in Sports & Exercise* journal.

Before you set your alarm for an early morning jog before breakfast, be aware that not everybody is in agreement about this area. And some experts would suggest that exercising with low blood sugar could lead to you becoming dizzy, uncoordinated, and could even increase the risk of injury. You'll certainly feel somewhat uncomfortable exercising when you're feeling hungry and may lead to you subconsciously eating more afterwards than you actually need. So, beware.

Now we've established the impact of exercise upon weight loss, let's consider a few specific approaches that will produce results. High Intensity Interval Training requires 10 sets of 4 minutes at 95% of maximum working heart rate with 2 minutes rest between, an absolutely vital tool in your armory. A resistance training circuit performing perhaps 20 repetitions at each of 12 weight training stations with little or no rest, and the stations ideally should alternate between upper and lower body for a good calorie burn. We could try Sprint Interval Training which involves full-on effort for 30 seconds followed by 4 minutes of light exercise, repeated 6 times. Another technique is Fartlek Training, interspersing continuous steady pace with quicker bursts of varying duration, for example 2, 4, 6 minutes in sort of an unstructured format.

Metabolic conditioning is the idea of working continuous cardio at a moderate intensity of around 70% of your maximum working heart rate for around 40–60 minutes, and then Step-Up Interval Training starting at an easy cardio pace and speed increasing perhaps every 4 minutes by around 15%

until you reach the set target of between 20–60 minutes, depending upon your current fitness level. As we start to get a little fitter, another technique is Near Maximal Training, 5 sets of 5 minutes at 95% of your maximum working heart rate followed by 5 minutes at just 50%. So there are a few different formats there we can use to achieve our weight loss goals.

Encouragingly, both research and anecdotal evidence suggest that most of us are capable of successfully losing weight, with the bigger challenge being to maintain our new weight. A study in 2009 revealed that regular exercise can be linked to sustained weight after a reduction, proposing that more is better and a target of 40 minutes per day will prevent weight gain.

Using a common sense approach, it's not too difficult to identify critical times for relapse, enabling tactics to be developed to avoid such. The triggers to weight regain can be divided into 3 distinct categories that can then be subdivided, as follows. Let's think about lifestyle first of all. Taking part in sport, especially team games, can be a great motivator to remaining regularly active, so hanging up your cleats, spikes, sneakers, gloves or whatever can lead to a dramatic reduction in activity. Instead of ceasing sport, a sensible approach is to think instead about switching from one sport to a more gentle option.

Believe it or not, marriage can be a problem, particularly for men, as it is commonly accompanied by a reduction in exercise levels and an increase in food intake. The key is to be conscious of these 2 factors, retaining your current commitment to activity and keeping a food diary to help avoid more regular eating and increased portion sizes.

Those who give up smoking may find that weight increases as nicotine speeds up metabolic rate so withdrawing it causes a slowing. Regular exercise and 5–6 small meals rather than 2–3 larger meals each day are both tactics that will help to give the metabolism a boost.

It goes without saying the festive season is fraught with danger in terms of the risk of putting back lost weight, but it doesn't have to be. On nights out alternate between an alcoholic and a soft drink, at parties stand away from the buffet table to avoid constant grazing, take the skin off your turkey, steam the vegetables at Christmas, these are all simple tactics that will allow you to get through yuletide without storing your saddlebags with enough fuel to keep you going until Easter.

After lifestyle, let's look at stress. Restrained eaters can sometimes worry less about their weight when under stress and then throw caution the wind regarding food intake, so efforts should be made to try to adhere to regular patterns. Bereavement can lead to comfort eating and a lack of motivation to exercise. At this time it's important to remember that exercise brings an endorphin release that can lift your mood, so is actually a great coping mechanism.

Having mentioned marriage previously, divorce, now, can be associated with feelings of depression and a break in routine that affects both eating and activity patterns. There is a school of thought that suggests women cope better than men with this, either way, commitment to maintaining routine is vital here.

So after lifestyle and stress, our third category is Hormones. Changes linked to menopause are known to generally lead to a shift in body composition, so resistance training exercises, as we mentioned earlier, are particularly useful at this time to both elevate your metabolism but also to help increase your bone mineral density, so reducing the risk of osteoporosis.

Pregnancy will obviously lead to an increase in body weight but it's important to try to restrict this to around 10 kilograms. Specific exercise guidelines can be found in a separate lecture in this series, addressing both ante and post natal periods.

Fat cells are known to multiply during growth spurts and are then retained for life, early puberty being one of these periods. It's important to remain active and avoid a diet that includes too much junk food at this time. At the other end of the spectrum, girls who crash diet risk slowing their metabolic rate resulting in the same outcome.

It's well documented that a recurring problem is not only regaining lost weight after a concentrated effort, but actually putting on more than was lost and ending up heavier than before the campaign began. Those who successfully keep the weight off are noted to exhibit a number of common characteristics supported by the National Weight Control Registry study of 784 people who had lost at least 60 pounds and then kept it off for 5 years. So, what were these characteristics? Exercising for 250 minutes per week (but, remember we can break that down to piecemeal fashion); frequently stepping on the scales; they never skipped breakfast; they maintained a written record of their weight loss progress and a food diary.

No examination of weight loss issues would be complete without a mention of cellulite, so here's a brief explanation of what it is, why we get it and a summary of what we can do about it. Although rarely seen in males, it is estimated that 85% of females exhibit the dreaded dimple effect somewhere on their body. Cellulite is the result of fat protruding from the subcutaneous layer into the dermis, or skin, due to laxity in the connective tissue within the skin. Liposuction, creams, injected products, massage, and suction treatments produce varying results, from some anecdotal reports of amazing improvements to sadly others declaring that they made the appearance even worse. Newer treatments, such as laser and low energy shock-wave therapies have produced very encouraging results. The good news is that exercise, there it is again, can help to tackle cellulite in 2 ways, by helping to reduce the presence of body fat but also toning the muscles, as slack tone in the muscles around the hips and thighs particularly add to the unwanted visual appearance associated with cellulite.

Helping the nation to reclaim its waist is not an easy task and requires the combined efforts of politicians defining public health strategy, the medical fraternity treating weight related conditions, and the fitness industry in providing both a preventive and reactive exercise prescription.

Ultimately, though, a pandemic such as obesity can be broken down to the decisions of individuals. I hope you now feel confident that you have the requisite knowledge of exercise for weight loss to make the right choices, for you, today, tomorrow, and for the rest of your life.

Mobilizers and Stabilizers—Managing Your Abs
Lecture 24

T he perfect stomach remains the most significant aesthetic indicator of fitness and continues to be the focus of advertising campaigns for well-known brands and a multitude of products and services. In this lecture, you will learn about the abdominal muscles, and you will discover whether your expectations for your abs are realistic. In addition, you will explore a range of exercises that target both the mobilizers and stabilizers and feature varying levels of difficulty so that you can work your way up to more demanding exercises.

The Abdominal Muscles
- There are 2 types of abdominal muscles: mobilizers and stabilizers. **Mobilizer muscles** bring about movement, and **stabilizer muscles** work to fix body parts in place.

- The **rectus abdominis** is the most visible mobilizer, stretching from the **xiphoid process**, where the ribs meet at the sternum, and ribs 5 to 7 down to the pelvis through a sheath, or **aponeurosis**, that joins to the symphysis pubis. The aponeurosis is divided by tendon insertions that run across it and, more noticeably, centrally to give the appearance of separate blocks.

- Interestingly, these divisions are not uniform, so you may see an 8-pack rather than a 6-pack in some people. This is purely due to genetics rather than a response to working out. When contracted, the rectus abdominis, like any other, draws its ends closer together so that the ribs move closer to the hips.

- The oblique muscles are located on the sides of the abdominal region. The external oblique muscles are larger than the internal oblique muscles and run from ribs 5 to 12 down to the iliac crest, the highest point of the hip, and partly into the linea alba, the tendinous line at the center. The internal oblique muscles are positioned between ribs 8 to 12 and the linea alba. These muscles work in tandem to assist the rectus abdominis in drawing the ribs and hips closer together, but they also serve to rotate the trunk and to laterally flex.

- When you bend sideways, the 2 oblique muscles on the same side work together, but due to their diagonal alignment, the external oblique on one side works in harmony with the internal oblique on the other side when engaging in a rotating movement.

- The stabilizer muscles are located beneath the mobilizers. The **transversus abdominis** runs from the thoracolumbar fascia of the back and the iliac crest through the lower 6 ribs and into the linea alba. The transversus abdominis is responsible for pulling in, compressing the abdominal cavity, and creating pressure that splints the lumbar spine as a result. The internal oblique muscle can assist in creating this intra-abdominal pressure.

Exercises to Tone Your Mobilizer Muscles
- Because there are 2 different groups of muscles involved in the abdominals, you need 2 different sets of exercises to tone them. Selecting the wrong exercises might lead to not achieving your goals.

- The mobilizers require movement to train them while the stabilizers require static, or isometric, contractions that challenge you to hold a position.

- To join in on the exercises, you just need enough space to lie down on the floor and perhaps a mat if you'd like. You will start with exercises for your mobilizers by engaging in a sit-up and a reverse curl.

- With the following exercises, your goal is to do between 12 and 15 repetitions, but you can build up to that goal. If you find any of the exercises easy, you can add a couple of extra repetitions. After you start to reach the point of momentary muscular fatigue, take a short rest.

- For the sit-up, make sure you keep your elbows back and rest your head in your hands so that you can support the weight of your head. Also, be aware of having a neutral, or comfortable, spine position. Then, bring your feet up and bend your knees, which helps to keep a relaxed lower spine position.

- Start by doing single sit-ups with a comfortable rhythm. Use visualization to imagine your abdominal muscles as a spring that you're squeezing together, trying to bring your ribs closer to your hips. Breathe out as you go up and in as you go down—don't hold your breath. Take a short rest when you start to experience fatigue.

- Then, sit up and down at 1/2 the speed you were just going—2 counts up and 2 counts down. Focus on sitting up, getting a maximal contraction. Relax your head and neck, and try not to hold your breath. Take a short rest.

- Next, sit up for 3 counts and down for 1. Rest. Hopefully, you're beginning to feel that these are becoming more difficult as you go slower.

- Finally, sit up for 7 counts and down for 1. To start, take a deep breath. Take a quick rest.

- By slowing down the count, you are forcing to recruit all the muscle fibers in the abdominals. The slow-twitch fibers will work first, and then they'll start to exhaust, so you'll have to recruit some of the fast-twitch fibers. As they begin to exhaust, you'll recruit the rest of the fast-twitch fibers, reaching the point of momentary muscular fatigue, which is what you need—overload for all the muscles.

- With sit-ups, you're working predominantly the upper part of your abdominals, but with reverse curls, you'll switch to working on the lower part of your abdominals. However, the same timing is used when doing reverse curls.

- Start by lying down, putting your hands down by your sides and bringing your knees up to your chest. In the air, cross your feet over each other. It is important to drop your heels down; you don't want to be swinging your legs.

- This exercise involves a very small movement: Bring your knees a little closer to your chest, lift your hips off the floor, and lower them back down—but don't swing your legs. It's a squeeze in the lower abdominals that lifts your hips off the floor.

- Start with a single count up and down at a comfortable pace. With this exercise, you may notice a little bit of strain in your neck; try to keep your neck relaxed by drawing your shoulders down. You can use your hands, placed at each side on the floor, for a little bit of balance. Take a short rest.

- Then, as you did with the sit-ups, move on to taking 2 counts up and 2 counts down. Rest. Next, take 3 counts up and 1 count down. Rest. Finally, take 7 counts up and 1 count down. Rest.

- To work the oblique muscles, you will do a modified version of the exercise that involves sitting up with a twisting motion, bringing your elbow across to your opposite knee. As you bring your knee to your elbow, you will actually bring the same knee to the same elbow.

- Start by lying down with your hands behind your head and do 4 movements: sit up, twist, back, and down. As you sit up, tilt to the side a little. The work of the rotation comes from the oblique muscles—not from the arm and leg. If you find this movement easy, you can always add a few repetitions at the end.

- To work all 3 of these muscles—the upper and lower abdominals and the oblique muscles—take a dumbbell or any weight in either one of your hands and sit up, twisting the dumbbell across to the other side of your body. Then, switch sides. Rest.

Exercises to Tone Your Stabilizer Muscles

- The stabilizers are the muscles that work to hold your posture in place, particularly your neutral alignment—that comfortable position for the spine, particularly for the lower spine. By definition, these muscles require isometric contractions that don't move. These muscles are involved in holding a particular position.

- First, you will do a plank, which you might have done by resting on the forearms. The challenge is to go into the full position, which will cause some bone loading through the wrists, strengthening the bones in the wrist.

- Start by lying on your stomach and slowly lifting your body off the floor with your hands, which should be located directly under your shoulders. Then, drop your hips just a little bit so that you are in a neutral spine position—with a gentle lordotic curve. Don't stick your backside in the air or drop your hips down. Gravity is trying to pull you down, so you have to fight against it by pulling in tight through the abdominals but also at your sides.

A typical plank position involves resting on your forearms, but the full position brings you up onto your hands.

Take a little rest. To release the pressure that you might experience, you can rest into the child's pose if you're familiar with yoga poses.

- Your challenge is to progress through variations of this exercise that become more difficult as you go along. You should find the exercise

111

that you can do comfortably, and then try to hold that position for as long as you can—increasing with practice.

- Begin in your plank position. A tip is to lock into the middle first, engaging your core muscles and pulling in through your stomach, waist, and pelvic floor. Keep the energy fixed in the middle, and lift one foot off the floor. The challenge is to hold the position, against the force of gravity, for as long as you can. It's important to take a rest when you get to the point where you start to shake—if not before.

- For the next level, after you assume your plank position, drop your hips down slightly so that there is a natural curve in your lower spine. Use a mirror, if you can, to check your position. Then, lift one leg off the floor and slightly out to the side. This position is tricky because you're trying to maintain your neutral alignment. Take a brief rest.

- Having targeted the lower body, now try a variation that involves the upper body. Again, start in the plank position. The challenge is to stay fixed in the middle and then lift one hand up toward your shoulder without rotating. When you start to reach the point of overload, take a rest.

- Taking this one step further, start in your plank position—keeping your abs in tight and your hips in a neutral position—and lift one arm and the opposite leg. After you can no longer hold the position, rest down onto your knees. This is a tricky exercise, but it should give you something to aim for.

- Another exercise that will strengthen your stabilizers involves kneeling on the floor, sitting up nice and tall. Start with a simple lateral flexion—bending to the side. Hold that position, and then return to the center. Rest.

- A variation of this exercise involves starting in the same position but lifting your hands up above your head with your shoulders down. Engage your core muscles before you move, and then lean to one side. Don't twist—just lean. You can do this on both sides, resting in between changes in position.

Exercising Your Abs

- All of these abdominal exercises will, over time, help to firm the muscles and possibly create a slimmer outline through improved posture, leading you to pull in your stomach. However, we all have a great natural 6-pack, but for many of us, it's hidden in a corpulent cover-up.

- Don't be fooled by advertisers' claims that exercising your abdominals will remove body fat from your problem area. A crucial factor in any plan to redefine your body shape is to strip away the body fat that covers your abdominal muscles, which can only be achieved by creating a negative calorie balance. The best way to achieve this is through a combination of cardio exercise and sensible eating.

Important Terms

aponeurosis: A sheath in the abdomen that is divided by tendon insertions that run across it and, more noticeably, centrally to give the appearance of separate blocks.

mobilizer muscle: An abdominal muscle that brings about movement.

rectus abdominis: The most visible mobilizer that stretches from the xiphoid process, where the ribs meet at the sternum, and ribs 5 to 7 down to the pelvis through a sheath, or aponeurosis, that joins to the symphysis pubis.

stabilizer muscle: An abdominal muscle that works to fix body parts in place.

transversus abdominis: A stabilizer muscle that runs from the thoracolumbar fascia of the back and the iliac crest through the lower 6 ribs and into the linea alba. It is responsible for pulling in, compressing the abdominal cavity, and creating pressure that splints the lumbar spine as a result.

xiphoid process: The point at which the ribs meet at the sternum.

Mobilizers and Stabilizers—Managing Your Abs
Lecture 24—Transcript

A short spell of surfing the shopping channels and you'd be forgiven for drawing the conclusion the whole world has gone ab-crazy. This is supported by the cover stories on many of the mainstream health, fitness, and lifestyle magazines on the shelves of the newsagents. The truth is that in my 30 years of teaching fitness in clubs, hotels, gyms, spas, corporate facilities, with sports teams, the question I'm most often asked is how to achieve a flat tummy by females or how to get a rippling 6-pack by the guys.

The perfect stomach remains the most significant aesthetic indicator of fitness and continues to be the focus of advertising campaigns for well-known brands and a multitude of products and services. In this lecture we will look closely at the abdominal muscles, whether our expectations are realistic, and explore a range of exercises to target this most important area.

The starting point then when looking at the trunk is to establish the difference between mobilizer muscles that bring about movement and stabilizer muscles that work to fix body parts in place. Here is a practical way for you to understand this; you can actually do this with me:

I'm going to stand with my feet about hip width apart, you can even do this sitting, what we're going to do is put one hand here just where your ribs meet, one hand just below the belly button, and the trick here is can you get your hands closer together without leaning forwards? And what were actually doing there is squeezing the abdominal muscles together, bringing your rips down to your hips. That's one exercise.

Secondly, I'm going to stand on one leg, and catch the ball. Now, what I had to do there was to use my stabilizer muscles to lock on in the center, to hold my trunk steady, so that when the ball hit me, I didn't fall over, fortunately.

Now, let's look at these 2 muscle groups in a little bit more detail. Firstly, the mobilizers we spoke about. The rectus abdominis is the most visible, stretching from what we call the xiphoid process where the ribs meet and the sternum and the ribs 5–7 down to the pelvis via a sheath, or aponeurosis that joins to the symphysis pubis. That aponeurosis we talked about in the lecture on muscles. It is divided by tendon insertions that run across it but also more noticeably, centrally from top to bottom the linea alba, to give the appearance of separate blocks.

Interestingly, these divisions are not uniform so you may see in some people an 8-pack rather than 6-pack, or perhaps blocks that do not line up but are actually staggered, that is purely down to genetics rather than a response to working out. When contracted, this muscle like any other draws its ends closer together so the ribs will move closer to the hips.

Moving to the side, the oblique muscles, the external obliques being larger and running from ribs 5–12 down to the iliac crest or the highest point of the hip and also partly into the linea alba at the center, and also then there's the internal oblique muscles, positioned between ribs 8–12 and the linea alba itself. And these work in tandem to assist the rectus abdominis in drawing the ribs and hips closer together, but also they have 2 other functions, to rotate the trunk and also to laterally flex.

Interestingly, when bending sideways the 2 obliques on the same side work together. But due to their diagonal alignment, this way and this way, the external oblique on one side works in harmony with the internal oblique on the other side when we're doing that rotating movement.

Let's look at the key stabilizer, muscles, and these we have to go a little bit deeper to find. So beneath the above 3 muscles we've just talked about, we have the transversus abdominis, running like a cummerbund from the thoracolumbar fascia of the back, and the iliac crest through the lower 6 ribs and into the linea alba, this tendinous line at the center. It has only got one action, and that action is to pull in compressing the abdominal cavity and so it creates pressure that effectively, as we pull in, splints the lumbar spine. The internal oblique muscle, that smaller of the oblique muscles, can actually assist in creating this intra-abdominal pressure, through its attachment also to the thoracolumbar fascia, it's not directly attached through something called a lateral raphe, but it still has that effect of helping to pull in. And more detail on this when we'll talk about in the lecture on the spine.

Clearly, then, if we have 2 different groups of muscles, we're going to need 2 distinctly different sets of exercises to tone them, and this is often where the confusion arises, as selecting the wrong exercises will mean you may not achieve your goals.

You won't be surprised to learn that the mobilizers require movement to train them whilst the stabilizers require static or isometric contractions, no movement, that challenge you to hold a position. Let's look at examples of the 2 and you can join me here, you just need enough space to lie down on the floor, so ensure you can get in a position so that you can turn your head to the side and still see what we're doing, and you can join in trying these exercises.

So we've reached an important part of the series, now, because this is where we begin to get into our actual exercise. And you'll notice that what I'm going to do throughout the workout is continually refer back to the knowledge that you've just acquired. So look out for little references back to lectures we did earlier, but also little graphics to help you understand, to help you visualize the muscles you are working. Talking of working muscles, let's get started with our abdominals.

We've got 2 different muscle groups, remember, we're working here: the mobilizers and the stabilizers. So, let's start with our mobilizers. These are the muscles that move you. I'm going to start with a couple of very basic exercises, the sit up, and the reverse curl. But, I'm going to work with some different timing. So, hopefully you are ready to go with this, just a couple of tips on the sit up technique, make sure you're keeping your elbows back, not pulling with the arms, rest the head into the hands so that you can support the weight of your head, and also be aware of having a neutral or comfortable spine position, and you'll notice that Jenn has brought her feet up here, knees bent, and that helps to keep that nice relaxed lower spine position. So, hands behind your head for me please.

We're looking for our single sit ups, first of all, so I'm going to ask you to just do those little sit ups, and back down for me, in a nice comfortable rhythm. Beautiful. So a little visualization helps here when we're working the moving muscles, the mobilizers, try to imagine your abdominal muscles like a spring and think about squeezing that spring together so you're trying to bring your ribs closer to your hips. Can I get a couple more please? Fabulous. Then take a rest there. You'll notice that Jenn is breathing out as she comes up, and in as she goes down. It's not absolutely crucial, but it does help to exhale on the exertion, and the hardest part is actually lifting. But whatever you do, don't hold your breath.

So what I'm going to do now is change the timing. I'm going to ask you to sit up and down at half that speed. So what we're going to do is sit up and up, and down, and down. And again, sit up, and up, and down, so you're going much slower, keep going. Up, and up, and down, really focus on sit up, and up, getting that maximal contraction. Squeeze, and squeeze, and down, and down. Relax your head and neck. And up, and down, and down, keep the elbows back. Up, and up, and down, try not to hold your breath, sit up, and up, and take a little rest there, well done, have a quick rest.

Let's take this one step further, and I'll explain in a minute why we're doing this. I'm going to ask you this time to sit up for 3 counts and down for 1, so you'll go up, up, up, and then down for 1. Okay, get ready, here we go. Sit up, and up, and up, and down, and again, sit up, and up, and up, and down, sit up, and up, and up, and down, and again, sit up, and up, and up, and down, take a quick rest there. Hopefully you're beginning to feel that get a little bit more difficult as we go along. Just to be sure, we're going to slow it down even further.

I'm going to ask you to sit up for 7 counts, and down for 1. So take a deep breath first, get ready to go, here we go. We go up, and up, and up, and up, and 5, and 6, and 7, and down. And again sit 1, and 2, and 3, and 4, and 5, and 6, and 7, can we do 2 more of those please? Sit up, and up, and up, and 4, and 5, and 6, and 7, just 1 more, let's go, you can do it, sit up, and 2, and 3, and 4, and 5, 6, 7, and take a quick rest there, have a little rest.

So what we're doing there is by slowing down the count, I'm actually forcing you to recruit all the muscle fibers in the abdominals, the slow at which fibers will work first, and then they'll start to exhaust, so then you have to recruit some of the fast twitch fibers, and then as they begin to exhaust, as we slow down again, you'll recruit the rest of the fast twitch fibers, so we get to that point of momentary muscular fatigue which is what we need, we need overload for all the muscles. We can use that same timing on the reverse curl. You may have noticed on that exercise you're working predominantly the upper part of the abdominals.

What we're going to do now is switch this to the lower part, so if we can take the hands down by the side, bring the knees up to the chest, and cross your feet over for me please. Important point here, drop the heels down. What I don't want you to do is swing with the legs. Now, this is only a very small movement. All that's going to happen is you're going to bring your knees a little closer to your chest, lift your hips off the mat, and lower it back down, but don't swing the legs. So when you come back down, don't let this drop too low. So it's a squeeze in the lower abdominals that lifts your hips off the floor. So we'll do the same thing, let's work with our single count first of all. So we'll lift up, and down. And up, and down. Fabulous, now you may find in this one, keep going, up, and down, and you keep going, up and down, you may notice a little bit of strain in the neck. Try to keep the neck relaxed on this one; try consciously to think about that, by drawing your shoulders down. You may use your hands at the side for a little bit of balance, but the important thing is, don't squeeze with the feet upwards. Up, and down, and up, and take a little rest.

So we'll move straight on to what we did before, 2 counts up, 2 counts down. So we'll go up, and up, and down, and down. We go up, and up, and down, and down. And again, sit up, and up, and down, 1 more of those please, we go up, and up, and down, hopefully you're feeling that in the abdominals.

We're going to move straight on now, 3 counts up, 1 count down. We sit up, up, up, and down, and again, go up, up, up, how you doing at home? We go up, up, up, I hope you're still with me. We go up, up, up, and hold it there.

Next one hopefully you remember now, we're onto 7s. Seven counts up, 1 count down, come on, be strong, we can do this. Let's go up, 2, 3, 4, come on 5, 6, 7, and down. One more go up, 2, get those hips off the floor, and 4, and 5, and 6, and 7, 2 more of those. Let's go sit up, 2, 3, 4, 5, 6, 7, can we do just 1 more? Let's go up, 2, 3, 4, 5, 6, 7, and take a quick rest there. Well done, well done.

Okay, now remember, I'm doing a certain number of repetitions here but you might need to build up to those, if you found that easy you can always throw in a couple of extra repetitions. But the secret there is taking 2 very common exercises, the sit up and the reverse curl, that will target the upper part and then the lower part of the abdominals but to vary the timing, and what that will do is force us to recruit all the muscle fibers so we'll get that improved tone.

Okay, we're going to move on now; we're going to shift from the upper and lower abdominals, into the obliques at the side. Now the important thing here is you may have seen this exercise bringing your elbow across to your opposite knee, this sort of twisting motion which indeed, will get a little bit of rotation through the spine. However, what generally happens is most of the movement comes from the arm and from the leg, and so we end up not getting much benefit through the waist. So what we're going to do with this is I'm going to change it slightly, so when we do knee to elbow, I'm going to ask you to do the same side, the same knee to the same elbow. So this is what I mean. Hands behind.

So it's 4 movements, again, so we're going to sit up, twist, back, and down. Sit up, and twist, and back, and down. Beautiful. Up, and twist, the same elbow to knee. Sit up, and twist, and what I also want you to do is a little tilt. Up, and tilt to the side as you do it. Sit up, tilt with that. Back, and down. Fabulous. Up, and tilt, and back. Now we're getting a little bit more rotation, and that work has got to come from the oblique muscles. It's not coming now from the arm and the leg. We go, sit up, and tilt, and back, we're looking at those oblique muscles. Keep going, sit up, and tilt, keep breathing, keep the head in the hands to support the weight. Up, and tilt, can we feel something going on in the waist? Sit up, and tilt, and back, and down. And again sit up, and tilt, would I be pushing our relationship too far to ask for 2 more? Sit up, and tilt, and back, 1 more at home please, sit up, and tilt, and back, and take a rest there. If you're finding that easy, you can always do a few more repetitions after we've done.

So we've got a little bit of work for the obliques there. What I'm going to do now is combine those exercises together. So, we've just done our sitting up, we've also just worked with a rotation movement, so what if we can put those together for the ultimate exercise? This is what I'm going to do. I'm going to take a dumbbell, it doesn't have to be a dumbbell, it could be a tin of beans, it could be anything that's a little bit of weight. I'm going to ask you to take down your right hand, please. This is what we're going to do, we're going to do a sit up and a reach twist, so we're going to sit up, and twist this dumbbell across so lift your left hand for me please, so the movement here is to sit up, and reach the dumbbell across to this side.

Okay so sit up, and reach, and back, and keep going for me please. Sit up, and reach, if you've got a dumbbell great, if not any weight, sit up, and reach, and back. You'll know if it's too heavy. Sit up, now ideally, we're looking for 12–15 repetitions on each side please. Sit up, and twist, beautiful. So now we're getting that work through the upper abdominals, and the lower abdominals as we're picking up, but then also through the obliques at the side, as we get that twisting movement. Is that about 12 yet? Must be there or thereabouts.

And take a quick rest there and we'll switch over to the other side, just have a quick rest for a second. So we're putting this arm out as a marker to see where we want to be, and twisting across. When we come back down, also add the twist so we're just going down onto this shoulder, so that we're really maximizing that rotation through the waist to combine with that sit up movement. So shall we try it on the other side? Beautiful. Dumbbell by the shoulder, and up we go, and twist, now when you go down, just put your left shoulder down. Good. See how the right shoulder stays up? Just the left shoulder goes down, and away we go.

Sit up, beautiful, and down. Sit up, so look for that twist, look for that reach, good. Sit up, a real combination, a compound exercise using lots of different muscle groups here. And the benefit of this as well, by extending the arm we're getting a little bit of work for the triceps, for the back of the arms, beautiful. So you'll have fabulous arms as well as an hourglass waist. Up we go, not that you've not already got that of course. How are you doing at home? And reach; can I get a couple more please? Our target, remember, 12–15 repetitions is what we're after. You might need to build up to that, if you find it too easy, you could take a slightly heavier weight. One more, and take a little rest there. Beautiful. I'll take the dumbbell, thank you, that is heavy! Pull your knees into your chest, and just have a little bit of a rest there.

So those are your mobilizer muscles. As you can see there in all of those exercises, we're moving. We're going to move on now to the stabilizers. These are the muscles that really work to hold your posture in place. And the exercises, as such, then, are slightly different. Let's have a look at those. Let's move onto the stabilizer muscles, so by definition these are holding your position, particularly your neutral alignment, that comfortable position for the spine, particularly the lower spine. So, by definition they will be isometric muscles, they're not moving, they're just holding the position. And, what I'm going to ask you to do first of all is a plank. Now, before we do this, you may have seen the plank done resting onto the forearms. What I'm actually going to ask you to do this time is to go for the full plank; I'm going to challenge you to go into the full position. The reason for this is that what this will do is cause some bone loading. It will overload through the wrists, which is a good thing, because, remember we talked about how fitness works, this theory of progressive overload.

What we'll do here is start to strengthen the bones in the wrist. Now bear in mind that the wrist is a common fracture site, as the result of falls. It's important for us to get some kind of exercise that gives us that bone loading that will develop the bone density. So we're going to go into our plank position first of all please, Jenn.

Hands are under the shoulders, and then drop the hips just a little bit for me please, so we're into that neutral, neutral spine or comfortable spine position, where we've got that gentle lordotic curve, we're not sticking the backside in the air, we're not dropping the hips down. Gravity, here, is trying to pull you down. So what we're doing is pulling in tight through the abdominals, particularly the transversus, the muscle across the middle. But we're also pulling in at the side, through the waist. And take a little rest there. You can rest into child's pose, like so, to release the pressure. Fabulous.

So our challenge here, or your challenge here, is I'm going to take Jenn through a progression here, and they'll get a little bit more difficult as we go along each of the exercises. You've got to find the exercise you can do comfortably, and what you'll then trying to do is hold the position for as long as you can. It will increase with practice. So we're going to go into our plank position please, let's set ourselves up first, and the key here, and this is a really good tip, is to lock on in the middle first of all, engage those core muscles, pull in through the tummy, pull in through the waist, excellent, we're pulling up through the pelvic floor also.

So we've created this energy in the middle, keep it fixed, and we'll lift one foot off the floor please. So the challenge here is can we hold that position, you'll see now gravity is really trying to pull you down, you're in a disadvantaged position, but we're keeping the abdominals pulled in tight, well done, well done, do you want to take a rest there, and drop down onto your knees. So it's important to have a little rest in between. When you get to the point where you start to shake, that's where, really, we need to have that rest.

Okay, so, shall we move onto the next level? But remember, you just work to the level you're comfortable with, I'm showing you these exercises so you've got some room for progression, somewhere to go. Okay, shall we move onto the next one? When I say we, obviously I mean you, because I'm not doing anything at all. Okay, so we're going to drop the hips down slightly, so you've got that natural curve in your lower spine, perhaps you can use a mirror, if you have one handy, just to check your position. Can we lift one leg off the floor, please? Could we now lift it slightly out to the side? Now it's getting a little bit tricky, because we're trying to keep that pelvis fixed, we're trying to keep this lower spine, this lumbar-pelvic region, in our natural, neutral alignment. And put it back down, and take a little rest.

So again, looking to just hold the position and then over time, can we gradually build that up. So that should have felt a little more difficult than the one before, okay? So having done the lower body, shall we try something with the upper body? We're back into the plank position, please. And you may be beginning to feel this, which is good, because that means we're getting to that point of overload. So our challenge now, again, is can we stay fixed in the middle, so stay strong in the middle, can we lift one hand up towards the shoulder without rotating please? We can do this. Oh that's a tricky one. And back down, and take a little rest there, well done. Drop onto your knees, well done.

So the challenge here is can you fix yourself in position first, can we really get locked on, and then can we lift the hand? It's not an easy exercise to do, it really isn't very easy. Okay, so shall we take that 1 step further, please? Now this is a tough exercise, I'll warn you. So we go into our plank position, we're fixing in the middle, keeping the abs in tight, so this is what we're going to do. I'll let you choose. Can we lift one arm, and the opposite leg? Ooh stay fixed in the middle, 1 more time. That's a really good effort. Go on, 1 more, third time lucky. Brilliant. And rest down onto the knees, excellent stuff, well done well done, have a little rest there. It's a tricky exercise, but it's giving you something to aim for further down the road. And the challenge is there, can you keep the abdominals pulled in really, really tight, the hips in your neutral position, when you lift into that difficult lift? So something to aim for, there.

Let's change things slightly, we're going to go onto our knees, please, but sitting up nice and tall. So you're sitting up tall, through the knees. What I'm looking for here is a simple lateral flexion, so we're going to bend to the side, that's all I'm going to ask you to, take a bend to the side. Brilliant. So we're getting a little bit of work through here. Now, there's a possibility that you'll start to feel an arching through the lower spine, a little rotation. This is where our core muscles are beginning to work, because I want you to keep that position fixed. And then come back up to the center. Shouldn't feel too difficult.

What I'm going to ask you to do now is to take one leg out to the side, so if I could turn you so that you're on the mat, that way around. Brilliant. So if you pull your, that will do, one leg out to the side, this is what I'm going to ask you to do. You're going to bend to the right for me please, let the top of your head drop. And hold that position there. Now, what we're doing here is working on keeping the abdominals pulled in really tight. We're stopping ourselves from rotating, we can hopefully feel something going on in our middle, and also what you'll feel particularly in this position is that as the abdominals pull in, they're pulling on what's called the thoracolumbar fascia, it's this structure at the back that's supporting the lower spine. And, bring yourself back up to the top please. Fabulous, just have a quick rest for a second.

Now obviously, we do this on both sides, but just for the purpose of today, I'm just going to go through one side. So, can we go back to that position for me please, only this time what I'm going to ask you to do, lift your hands up above your head, okay. So, hands are up, shoulders are back down, brilliant. Okay, so, this is where we go. Stay fixed in the center, engage the core muscles before we move, and then we'll take the lean, please. Lean times, brilliant. We're not twisting through the hips, we're keeping the abs pulled in tight, drawing the tummy button in. We're pulling in through the waist, lifting up through the pelvic floor; can we feel something going on at the back here?

What's happening is those internal obliques and this muscle at the front, the transversus, attach to this sheath at the back and it's now splinting, supporting the lower spine. That's great, that's what we want. And back up to the top, have a rest for a quick second, only a quick rest. I feel really cruel doing this to you, but could we take that please?

Same position, same exercise, this is not easy. Now, remember, hold it there just for 1 second. The problem with these exercises is they look easy. That just means they're easy to do wrong. So lift the hands up, abdominals are in tight, and we lean to the side, and hold it, we're trying to fight the rotation, there should be no rotation, no arching through the lower spine, keep the abdominals pulled in really tight, back up to the top, take a rest, and I'll take that dumbbell you'll be pleased to hear. You're going to be lying down on your back. Well done, well done.

So the aim with all of these exercises is can we get into the position, they're stabilizers, we're challenging them to hold it in that position, these are postural muscles. So what we're going to do here is lift the hands directly up to the ceiling, and the feet directly up as well, please. To start with, I'm going to take the knees bent, so if we can have the knees bent. Fabulous. So all I'm doing here in your lying down position is I'm going to challenge you to maintain your neutral or comfortable spine. Once you start to feel that pulling to the arch, that's the point to stop and go back a level, in an easy movement first of all. Be aware of your position in space. Could we just take one hand down behind your head to the floor please? Just slow lower it down. Beautiful. And then slowly bring it back up to the top. And can we do the same on the other side? And back up to the top.

So what we're doing here, that's a simple exercise, it's challenging. You might begin to feel a little bit of an arching going on already. I want you to keep abdominals in really tight. Also try to keep the neck relaxed. That's fabulous. And take a little rest there at the top, okay. Can we make this slightly more difficult? Could we do the same thing, one foot and then the other? All I'm asking you to do is lower it down to the floor, touch, and back up. You're making this look really easy. So the challenge is can we keep a neutral, comfortable spine by keeping pulled in, keeping that engagement through the core muscles. And relax.

We could make that slightly more difficult; can we take the leg straight up please? Brilliant. Okay so we're looking for our neutral comfortable spine, there should be a little bit of an arch, could I ask you to lower slowly the right leg down towards the floor please, nice and slow, and hold it, and then back up. So now, then the other leg, we're getting a little bit more of a challenge, and back up, on those core muscles. Nice and slow, and then back up. Beautiful. Hold it there for me please. All the time I'm trying to pull you into this position, you've got to work to pull it in.

Could we make it slightly more difficult? Remember, I'm giving you levels you can aim for. So if you're having a go at these, and finding them difficult right now, stick with the easier level. This gives you something to aim for. The challenge now is can we do the opposite arm and leg? Nice and slowly please. Slower is better. Try and keep your breathing relaxed, and slowly back up. And across to the other side. Again, we're feeling that your back wants to arch. But, we're fighting against it, we're keeping the abdominals in tight, we're pulling in through the waist, really working through those core muscles. One more, and then a rest at the top there. Brilliant. Hold it there for me for a second please. The idea here, what I'm trying to do is challenge you in a position that you'd never be in, and it's like elite sportsmen will always train harder than they'll perform on the day. What I'm doing here is making you work harder than you would normally need to in your everyday tasks, and that'll ensure you'll be able to accommodate those tasks.

Final version: Can we take opposite arm and leg out to the diagonal please? Brilliant. She's been dying to kick me, that was deliberate. And back up to the top. Beautiful, slow is better. And trust me, Jenn is making this look a lot easier than it is. Out to the other side, it's a great exercise. Your challenge, keep your abdominals in tight. Work those core muscles to maintain that natural normal curve in your lower spine. Take a rest now, pull your knees into your chest and give them a hug. Well done, well done.

There's a range of exercises that will work your stabilizers, and the idea being that we're really challenging ourselves to hold a position by doing some other exercises. You have a range of exercises for the mobilizers, for your 6-pack muscles, and those obliques at the side, and now you have a range of exercises that will work your core muscles on that spinal alignment. So remember, we've got different levels so you can work your way up, and practice makes perfect.

Now if you found those exercises difficult, don't worry, you can build up gradually in terms of the number of repetitions and on those stabilizer exercises, in terms of holding the time. Start at a comfortable level, but aim to progress; you'll find as you get stronger you'll be able to do that.

Whilst these exercises will, over time, help to firm the muscles and possibly create a slimmer outline through improved posture leading to you pulling in the tummy, a point worth mentioning here is that we all have a great 6-pack, naturally, but for a lot of us it's actually hidden in a corpulent cover-up.

So don't be fooled by the advertisers' claims of spot-reduction, the myth that exercising your abdominals will remove body fat from your problem area, it's not true. A crucial factor in any plan to redefine your body shape is to strip away the body fat that covers your abdominal muscles, which can only be achieved by creating a negative calorie balance. As we've learned, the best way to achieve this is through a combination of cardio exercise and sensible eating.

However, there's an important question here that's very rarely discussed: What use is a 6-pack? As we saw earlier, the 6-pack is achieved by targeting the rectus abdominis muscle with sit up type exercises, but think about it. How often you actually need this movement in your everyday tasks? I'm going to guess twice, when you get out of bed in the morning and when you get back into bed to go to sleep at the end of the day.

It's fair to say, then, the 6-pack muscle is not the most important of muscles to get you through the day, it's primarily cosmetic, so I wonder why it has become the omnipresent symbol of fitness that it is. The transversus abdominis, on the other hand, serves to brace your lower spine in essential movements such as pushing, pulling, twisting, lifting, and carrying, protecting it from injury and allowing you to generate force in these activities.

In conclusion, I'm not suggesting you avoid training the rectus abdominis entirely, but to support my argument that you should devote more time to the core stability exercises, think function rather than fashion. Let me put it this way, our bodies are not a lot different than our primeval ancestors who, to survive as hunter-gatherers needed very strong core muscles to throw spears and then to drag their spoils home to feast, and I'm pretty sure they didn't spend much time in the cave doing sit ups!

Body Weight Workout
Lecture 25

The great thing about a body weight workout is that it simply involves using the weight of your body against gravity. You don't need any expensive equipment, and you can do it anywhere—indoors or outside. You can take it on vacation with you, and you can use it if you're working away from home. Furthermore, because you'll be working with your whole body, you'll be engaging in functional fitness, working on balance and core strength, which can help you in your day-to-day life.

Guidelines
- Before you start, it's important to warm up with gentle, mobilizing movements from your head to your toe that start to work through the dynamic range of movement through your joints, to get the synovial fluid working, and to raise your body temperature. Start gently with a walk and perhaps slowly build up into a jog.

- With each of the following exercises in this workout, your goal is to complete 1 set of 15 repetitions. If you regularly exercise, you might want to try to complete 2 sets of each exercise, and if you are an advanced exerciser, you can try to aim for completing 3 sets. Regardless of how many sets you choose to do, make sure you take a brief rest in between exercises.

Side Lunge: Reach Right
- Starting with your feet about hip-width apart, take a lunge out to the right with your right leg pointing outward and slightly to the side. Your left leg remains straight. Hinge at the hip, and reach your right hands down and out to the right. Return to your starting position.

- Make sure that you're not rounding your spine.

- Keep your abdominals pulled in tight, working your core strength.

- You should start feeling a little warmer now.

Hindu Press-Up

- Start in a downward dog position—a yoga pose. You should be forming an upside-down V with your body, with your backside sticking up in the air. Then, take your chin down to the floor, go through your hands, and up into the cobra pose. Keep your legs and pelvis on the floor, but your stomach and upper body are hoisted up by your arms. Return to downward dog by dropping your chin down and lifting yourself back into an upside-down V position.

- This exercise involves both dynamic flexibility and strength.

- You're working through the range of motion of your shoulders, into the lower back, and into the hamstrings as you come back up from the cobra into the downward dog.

- You'll feel a stretch through your calf and Achilles' heel in the back and another stretch in your chest and shoulders in the front.

- Remember to keep breathing; don't hold your breath during strength exercises.

- Be careful not to lock your arms, and make sure the whole movement is under control.

Side Lunge: Reach Left

- From a standing position, lunge to your left side, working your left leg.

- When you step out, remember to point your knee and toe slightly out so that you can follow the natural hinge movement.

- When you're bending, don't round your shoulders and lower back; instead, hinge from your hip.

- Keep your abdominals in tight.

- In this exercise, you're working through your core muscles as well as the front and back of your left thigh and gluteus. The bonus is that you're also working the dynamic flexibility of your right leg.

Gecko Row

- The gecko row involves challenging the position of your postural muscles; you're going to try to keep your body in a fixed position. Start by getting down into a press-up position, but keep your feet wide for stability. The goal of the exercise is to bring your left knee up to your right elbow at the same time, briefly holding the position. This challenges the muscles around the lumbopelvic region. Pull your abs and obliques in tight. Try not to twist or stick your backside up in the air. Then, switch legs and arms.

- Do this exercise slowly.

- The challenge is to keep the natural alignment in your lower spine.

- Don't round your shoulders.

- Let the top of your head drop forward.

- Don't worry if you lose your balance a couple of times—that's going to happen. Just reset yourself if you do.

Single-Leg Squat: Right

- Imagine you're picking something up from the floor. Start by lifting your right leg in front of you. Bend over, and reach your left hand down to the floor. You can use your right arm for balance by holding it out straight to the right side. Keep your abdominals in tight as you go down. This motion involves hinging your hip—not bending or rounding it. Then, stand up onto your right foot, lift your left leg, and bend down.

- You might start to wobble a little, but just reset yourself.

- A single-leg squat is the most effective exercise you can do to tone your glutei.

- You're trying to fight any rotation through the knees or hips, working your stabilizer muscles.

Lying Triceps Press: Right
- Start by lying down on your left side, with a little bend in your knees to make them comfortable. Bring your right hand over the front of your body and keep your left hand down on the floor. Your right elbow should be pointed upward. Press up straight through your right triceps, and then bring it back down.

- Try to keep your body in a comfortable position, and make sure you're not lifting through your waist.

- Try to relax your head and neck.

- Naturally, you'll feel your abs trying to work, but try to concentrate on the muscles that should be doing the work—the triceps at the back of the arm.

Single-Left Squat: Left
- This time, you'll do some single-leg squats by lifting your left leg.

- Again, you can hold your left arm out for balance.

- Don't let your shoulder drop forward.

- Keep your abdominals in tight.

- In this exercise, you're challenging your core muscles and your stabilizers around the hip and knee to help keep your balance.

- This is also a great toning exercise for your thigh and buttocks.

Lying Triceps Press: Left

- This time, you'll start by lying down on your right side and pressing your left arm up, working your left triceps.

- Keep your right hand out of the way so that you can press up and down with your left arm.

- Keep your breathing relaxed.

- This is an isolation exercise that is targeting only your left triceps.

Plank Up and Down

- When doing planks, the challenge is to keep your hips fixed—with your lower back in a neutral, comfortable spine—while you're changing your position. From the plank position—starting on your hands and toes with your arms straight—lock your abs in tight and try to avoid too much rotation as you go down onto one elbow and then the next. Then, raise back up onto your hands from your elbows.

When doing a side plank, the key is to engage your core muscles, which will help stabilize your body.

- Keep your backside down so that you have a natural bend in your lower back—a lordotic lumbar curve.

- When you start to get a little fatigued, don't stick your backside up in the air.

- The challenge is to work particularly on the transversus muscle across the middle of the abs, so keep your belly button pulled in tight.

- Your inner obliques and pelvic floor are also being worked, and all of these muscles are working to keep your lower spine in place.

Diagonal Lift: Right

- This exercise offers a variation on the single-leg squat, turning it into a diagonal lift by adding some rotation. Start by lifting your right leg behind you, keeping your left arm out for balance. As you go down toward the floor, reach to the right side. As you come up, reach to the left side. You're going from a low diagonal to an upper diagonal.

- As you come up, extend through the position; instead of coming straight up, you're extending to the opposite side.

- There is some balance work involved with this exercise.

Diagonal Lift: Left

- This time, start on your right foot and lift your left leg, keeping your right arm out for balance. Again, reach down and come up to the opposite diagonal.

- Your balance will improve with practice.

- The spine flexes and extends, but you should be hyperextending it with this exercise.

- It's important to work through your full range of motion.

Single-Leg Bridge

- Start by lying with your back on the floor. Bend your left knee so that your left leg is propped up, and lift your right leg straight out in a comfortable position. Press into your right heel, and lift your whole body as one. Make sure your shoulders stay on the floor, and keep your abs in tight. Then, lower back down, and try not to put too much stress on your neck.

- Keep the movement under control by doing this exercise slowly.

- Don't swing your leg. The lift should be coming from pressing the heel down on your right foot so that you feel the work of the hamstring at the back of the thigh and into the gluteus.

- The challenge is for your core strength to stabilize you in the middle.

- Then, do the same exercise, but lift your left leg.

- Be aware if you notice any difference from one side to the other; perhaps one leg needs a little extra work.

V Sit-Up
- Normally, a sit-up works only the upper part of your abdominals, and a reverse curl only works the lower parts, but this exercise combines the 2 to work both. Start in a sitting position and lift both legs in front of you, bending at the knee. Then, raise your arms out to each side. Do a sit-up in this position, lowering your body down without having your feet touch the floor. Then, come back up to the original position and bring your knees to your chest.

- This exercises the top and bottom of the rectus abdominis.

- When exercising your abdominals, picture the abdominal muscles as being a spring. As you're sitting up, try to squeeze that spring together.

Turkish Stand-Up
- The goal of this exercise is simply to stand up without using one of your hands. Start by sitting on the floor, and raise either one of your hands toward the ceiling—and keep it there throughout the exercise. Once you are standing up, keep your hand in the air and

try to sit back down again. It doesn't matter which hand you use in the beginning; switch to the other hand after 7 repetitions.

- This is a whole-body exercise. You're using your abs on the first part of that movement, and you really need to use your legs. The thoracolumbar fascia, the sheath at the back of the core muscles, helps transfer the strength from your upper to your lower body—it's what gets you up and down.

Cooldown
- Start with some gentle movements to get your joints moving—similar to the types of exercises you did in the warm-up.

- Let your pulse rate and temperature drop slightly.

- Then, do some stretches—perhaps 1 set of 15 for each exercise, building up to 2 sets and then 3 sets.

Body Weight Workout
Lecture 25—Transcript

Welcome to your body weight workout. Now, the great thing about this is all we're going to do is use the weight of your body against gravity; the clue is in the title. We really don't need any expensive equipment, we can do this anywhere, hopefully you're doing it with us now at home, you can do this indoors or out, you can take it on holiday with you, you can do this if you're working away from home.

You might question whether this actually works. Well, you can join me with this simple exercise. If we do a little squat, down, hopefully you can feel a little bit of work into the front of the thighs, back of the thighs. If I ask you now to do that on a single leg, it starts to get a little tougher. If I now ask you to do it on a single leg but do it really slowly, and you'll begin to see that this can really have some effect in terms of building up our strength. Also, working with your whole body, we're starting to do functional fitness. We're working on balance, and you'll remember this from our balance lecture, we're working on our core strength, you'll remember from our lecture on the spine.

Now, before we start, it's important to have a warm up like the guys are doing now. Gentle mobilizing movements from head to toe that start to work through the dynamic range of movement through your joints, start to get the synovial fluid working, start to get your body temperature up, that's important.

Start gently, maybe you start with a walk, maybe you begin to build up into a jog like the guys are doing now, there you go. Fabulous. You'll start to get your core temperature up a little bit. We're aiming for 1 set of 15 repetitions in this workout. Those of you who are already doing some exercise, you might want to go for 2 sets of each exercise, and those of you who are exercising really regularly, maybe even 3 sets, you have the choice with a brief rest in between. Be aware, I'm deliberately alternating here between floor and standing, we'll constantly be changing, getting up, getting down, getting up, may be a little bit annoying but the great thing is, it's going to increase the energy burnt through this, we're going to burn a few more calories. Also, it's practicing an essential functional movement that we need every day.

Shall we get started? Starting with your feet about hip-width apart, are we ready, guys? What we're going to do here is take a lunge out to the right, with your right leg. Take a look at it first. We're stepping out, we're lunging down, there's a slight point outwards on this leg, we're hinging at the hip, reaching the hands down. This leg is staying straight, and back to the side. We're looking for 15 repetitions you can begin nice and easy, are we set?

Let's go guys, 15 repetitions. Reach out, to the right leg, and back, right leg. Out, and down we go. You're pointing the knee and the toe slightly outwards, as we go down, and you're hinging from the hip, not rounding your spine. Keep going for me. So you're keeping your abdominals pulled in really tight, working that core strength. Really getting down onto that leg, really getting nice and deep, get a good range of motion, we should be a little bit warmer now. Look how this knee and toe on John is pointing out, slightly to the side, so that we follow the natural hinge through the knee, bending down, pressing the weight through the heel, abdominal are in tight, hopefully we're starting to feel a little bit of work getting into that right leg, into the thigh. We're looking for 15 repetitions. Keep your breathing nice and relaxed, excellent. I'm going to trust you guys to count to 15. No cheating, stopping yourself from cheating. Beautiful. Excellent work. Are we nearly there yet? Just joining for the last couple, that's me. Fabulous. Good work, good work.

We're moving on, we're moving on, to our Hindu press up. I'm going to show you this from the sideways on so you can see what we're doing. We're going to start in a downward dog position. The feet are up, the backside is up, we take the chin down to the floor, we go through the hands, up to the cobra, back up to that position. The chin is down, along the floor, up we go, and back to that position. Beautiful work through the mobility of the shoulders and the lower back. Down we go, guys, are you ready at home, I'm looking for 15 repetitions, and away we go. Chin down to the floor, up we go into that upward dog, and then back up to the downward dog, down we go. Beautiful, fabulous work. Keep it moving, continuous all the way through; I'm after 15 reps please. Good, pushing it up.

So the great thing about this is it comes with dynamic flexibility exercise as well as a little bit of strength. We're working through the range of motion in the shoulders, into the lower back, also into the hamstrings as we come back up from that upward dog into the downward dog, a little bit of a stretch maybe through the calf and Achilles at the back, as we push back into that downward dog. Little bit of stretch through the chest and shoulders at the front. How are we doing? Hang in there. Fifteen repetitions at home please. Beautiful. Get into a nice rhythm and go with that pace. Remember to keep breathing, don't hold your breath on these strength exercises. Excellent work; keep it going keep it going. Beautiful. Be careful not to lock out your arms, make sure the whole movement is under control. Good. How many is that, about 3, is it? Four? I'm losing, I'll take that. Go on, 1 more will do me.

Fabulous, and we're back up, quick up, we get up we get up. We go straight over to our side lunge, but on the other side now. So we're working your left leg. Remember when you step out, to point the knee and toe slightly out so that we can follow that natural hinge movement. Are we ready? Stepping out with the side lunge, and down we go, and back, can I get 15 of those please? It's not really a question, let's go. Now, remember when you're bending, don't let the shoulders round, don't round through the lower back, but hinge from the hip. Away we go, 15 reps, make sure you're hinging from the hip, keeping the abdominals in tight, we're not rounding through the spine. Okay, fabulous work. And again, he says quickly getting out of the way.

Look how we point out slightly on this toe, which allows the knee to point out slightly, and follow a natural hinge. What we don't want is too much lateral motion through here. The abdominals are staying in tight, we're working through your core muscles as well as hopefully you can feel some work getting into this left thigh, into the front of the thigh, into the back of the thigh, and hopefully as well a little bit of work into the glutes. Beautiful bonus here is we're also working dynamic flexibility through that other leg.

We're going to move onto a gecko row. This is about challenging the position of our postural muscles. We're going to try and keep our body in a fixed position. So, take a look at it first. We're down in a press up position, but the feet are wide for stability. The aim of the exercise is to bring the knee up to the elbow; at the same time I'm going to lift the opposite hand. What

I'm trying to do is fix myself here, so this is really challenging the muscles around the lumbo-pelvic region. Abs are pulled in tight, obliques are pulled in, pelvic floor is lifted, we're trying not to twist, and we're certainly trying not to stick your backside up in the air. The aim is to just lift one hand up to the shoulder, the opposite knee up to the elbow, okay?

Take your time on this one; we're looking for 15 repetitions so pick your good leg first. Down we go, excellent. Get yourself fixed first of all, backside down, no backside sticking up in the air, and away we go. Slow is better on this one. Good, lifting the hand up to the shoulder, and the knee up to the elbow. Beautiful. So the challenge here is can we stay locked on in center to keep your natural alignment in your lower spine. See how gentle this little curve in the lower spine there. That's what we're looking for. Beautiful, don't be rounding the shoulders. We're really pulling in through the tummy, keeping your abdominals pulled in tight, pulling in through your waist.

Good, let the top of your head drop forwards; you don't want any nasty creases in the back of your neck there. Good. Abdominals are in tight, good. Challenging those core muscles, remember those postural muscles that work isometrically, which means they're not changing their length, they're just trying to fix you in the center, so don't worry if you lose your balance a couple of times, that's going to happen. Just reset yourself if you do. And when we're done, we're done. Beautiful. You get a few extra ones in there, John? Excellent.

I'm moving on now to the single leg squat. So the single leg squat, again I'm using a functional movement. I want you to imagine you're picking something up from the floor, so you'll get a little bit of a hinge through the hip as well. Let's pick our right leg first, all I'm going to ask you to do is bend, reach that hand down to the floor. What we're going to do here, this hand you can use for balance, put it on your hip if you're feeling okay, but what I'm asking you to do is hinge your hip, keep your abdominals in tight as you go down, you're hinging, that's not bending or rounding, but hinging from the hip as we reach the fingers down to the ground. Sit yourself up onto the right foot, left leg lifted, and we're going to go down please. Can I get 15 of those, let's go.

Remember, you might get a slight wobble and you might need to reset yourself. That's okay. Challenge yourself; can we get that left hand down to the floor? Beautiful. See how that knee is bending? Now remember, we've mentioned this in a couple of the other workouts, single leg squat is the most effective exercise you can do to tone the glute muscles. That's your buttocks, in other words. Fabulous. Down we go. Excellent. See how we're hinging from the hip, but that's challenging you to keep abdominals in tight; don't let the tummy drop down. What we're trying to fight here is any rotation through the knee, any rotation through the hip. So, really working those stabilizer muscles. Remember when we talked about mobilizers and stabilizers in one of the earlier lectures. Fabulous. Good, well done!

And remember, we're going up and down, up and down, so I'm going to show you this one sideways on. Going to do a little bit of work for the triceps. So we're both going to be facing that way, guys. This is what we're going to do for your right arm, first of all. You're going to be lying sideways down, a little bend in the knees to make them comfortable. You're actually going to put your right hand over the front, and take the left hand down. See how this elbow is high? All I'm going to ask you to do is to press up straight through here and work into that tricep. That's all we're doing working into that right tricep. Okay, let's go, down we go.

Heads that way. That's it, beautiful. Bring that arm across. We're pressing up from there, press up, and back down. Beautiful. Try and keep your body in a nice comfortable position, a little bend through the knees, and make sure that we're not lifting through the waist, but it's all coming from that press, isolating onto the outside head of the tricep. Super. Make sure you stay sideways on through this exercise. Excellent. Try to relax your head and neck, try not to build too much stress through the neck as we do this. Now you can't help but cheat slightly, trust me, naturally you'll feel a little bit going around the waist, but try to focus your mind in muscle, try to concentrate on the muscles that should be doing the work, the triceps at the back of the arm. Excellent, we're just looking for 15 of those. It's looking really good. Excellent. I do feel guilty not doing anything, honestly. You're doing really well, guys. How are we doing at home? I hope you're still with us. Once you've done your 15 repetitions annoyingly we're back up again. Well done, well done.

We're moving on to the other leg; you're on your left leg now for your single-leg squats. Remember this arm is out for balance, this leg is out of the way, when we bend we're hinging at the hip, reaching towards the floor, and then back up, and don't let the shoulder drop forwards. Set yourself up, left foot down, right foot lifted, are we ready, let's drop that right hand down to the floor, can I get those 15 single-leg squats please? Beautiful. Let's reach this hand down to the floor. Good. Reset your balance if you need to, excellent. Excellent, there we go, keep the abdominals in tight.

Remember in our balance lecture we talked about how important the core muscles are in maintaining that balance. So what we're doing here is challenging those core muscles. We're also challenging those stabilizers around the hip, around the knee, to help keep your balance on this exercise. But also it's a great toning exercise for the thigh, for the buttocks. Super exercise. And probably one of the most functional movements we can do. How often each day do we bend down to pick something up? But you know what, you don't want to be bending down to pick something up and injuring your back, so that's why it's good to practice this movement. Excellent, excellent, excellent. About time to do a couple with you, or are you done? Oh, is that it? Okay, we're going to move on.

We're on our lying tricep, but this time we're onto your left hand. So let's turn and face that way, laying yourself sideways on, down we go, bring that hand across, fabulous stuff and away we go. Pressing. Remember, keep this hand out of the way so that you can press up, and all the way back down, working into that tricep at the back of the arm. And press, good, how we doing? Keep your breathing relaxed, super. Press in, excellent. You're making that look really easy. Good. We're looking for 15 at home, remember, 15 is our magic figure. Good. Really important area, and this is an isolation exercise. Remember we talked about compound exercises and isolation exercises; this is really targeting those triceps alone. Fabulous. And look at this; we don't need to use anything more than our body weight. Beautiful, well done, well done, well done, well done. Excellent.

We're moving onto some plank work, and again the challenge here is can you keep your hips fixed, your lower back in your neutral or comfortable spine, while we're actually changing our position, so that's the challenge.

I'm going to show it front on and then side on. From the plank position, all I'm going to ask you to do is lock on in the middle, try to avoid too much rotation as you go down onto the elbow, onto the elbow, back up, and back up. So what we're trying to avoid here is either this happening, or this happening. Keep the abdominals in tight, lock on in the middle as we go down, keep it locked on as we go up. Are we set? Are you ready at home? And away we go.

Onto the elbow, and then up to the hands. Keep the backside down a little bit so you've just got that natural little bend in the lower back, that natural lordotic lumbar curve. Down we go. So sometimes change which hand you lead with, now when you start to get a little fatigued, don't stick your backside up in the air, remember the challenge here is to work particularly on this transversus muscle across the middle, so you're pulling your tummy button in tight all the time. You're also getting some work for the inner obliques here, you're also getting a little bit of work in the pelvic floor pulling up, everything is fixing the lower spine in place on these exercises. Good, how are we doing? Looking good, guys. Excellent. Onto the elbows and back up, try to avoid too much rotation if you can, you're doing really well. How are you doing at home? I hope you're still with us. Good, looking good. Well done. Well done. Well done. We're back up.

We're taking a little variation now on that single leg squat and turning this into a diagonal lift, so now we're adding a little bit of rotation, a little bit of extra plane of movement. So we're starting on our right leg again. This time, the leg is behind, but as we go down, I want you to reach over to there. When you come up, I want the foot forwards and reach over to there. So we're going down from the low diagonal, to the upper diagonal. But look now how we're getting much more movement through here, so this is more of a challenge, because now I'm reaching down, but then as we come up, look how I'm extending through this position. Down, and now instead of straight up, we're extending. So a little bit of balance work as well.

So let's get onto our right foot, guys, lift the left, this arm's out for balance, let's reach it down to there, and bring it up to the opposite diagonal, we're off to our 15 repetitions, nice and slowly. Remember if you lose your balance, that's okay just reset yourself. That's one of those things we talked about, flexibility, with strength of your cardio, it will get better with practice. Beautiful. How are we doing? Reach it down, excellent, and back up. Really good stuff. Well done. Really extend through that position. Beautiful. Remember we said that the spine flexes, extends, but it also hyperextends, so we're getting that little bit of hyperextension. Remember that it's important to work through your full range of motion, if we're only working through a restricted range, we'll only develop the strength through that restricted range. So what we're trying to do here is work through our full range of motion. Excellent stuff. I think I'll get a couple as well, beautiful. Down we go. And reach it up. Good balance, everybody. How are you doing at home? You see I said that and then completely lost it; that was bound to happen.

We're shifting on now, we're going to go onto a single leg bridge exercise, and I'll show you this sideways on. You'll have your head at this hand when you do this, guys. So what I'm going to do is going to the right leg first. I'm going to put the left leg straight out, comfortable position, and pressing into the heel, lifting your whole body as one, keeping the abs in tight, and then lowering back down, try not to put too much stress on the neck, make sure the shoulders stay on the floor, okay let's try it.

This is a really good exercise again for the glutes, but also getting into the hamstrings. So let's get that leg up, there you go, perfect. Are we set? Are you ready at home? And away we go. Just a little tip if you're doing this at home, make sure that leg comes up as well at the same time. Up you go. Beautiful. You weren't cheating there John, I hope? And up we go, he's taking it really easy over here. And up we go, beautiful, I'm looking for 15 repetitions, keep it under control. Don't swing the leg. The lift is coming from pressing the heel down on your right foot; you'll feel the work into the hamstring at the back of the thigh, into the glutes.

But again, we've got that challenge for your core strength in stabilizing you in the middle, great exercise. Getting 3 benefits from this single exercise. Beautiful stuff. And again, we don't need any equipment, just working with your own body weight. Slow is better, keep it under control. Now make sure you're in a comfortable position when you're doing this. You want to ideally be sideways on, so you can just tilt your head and see what you're doing. That's of course, assuming you're not sitting on the sofa eating cookies. You should be doing this with us. Excellent. When I say us, obviously I mean you, because I'm not doing anything, but it's time to get back up and we're onto the other leg.

So we're into our diagonal lift, but we're on the left foot now, okay? So sit yourself up the left, be aware if you've got any difference from one side to the other, does one side need a little bit of extra work? We're onto our left foot, the right foot is lifted, we're going to reach down to the low, up to the high diagonal, with that slight leaning backwards, remember. Down, and then really work it through the hyperextension. Let's go, 15 repetitions. Does it feel any different to the other leg? Maybe better maybe not. Who knows? Beautiful. So what we're looking for here is to be locking on in the middle, pulling your tummy in tight, if you start to lose your balance, that's okay, you can reset yourself.

We're getting some really good work on this supporting leg, working through the front of the thigh, the quadriceps, working through the hamstrings at the back, remember we said we're working the glutes here. So this is what we're talking about in terms of total body exercises. Great thing about that is it burns lots of calories. We're doing really well. Good. Was there a wobble there? Actually it's really windy here. That's it—if it looks like we're wobbling it is the wind. Excellent. Well done guys, locking on in the middle. Make sure you can feel this energy by pulling in here and lifting up through the pelvic floor, you'll feel that abdominal balloon we talked about when we talked about our spine and our core strength. Brilliant stuff.

We're straight back down onto the single leg bridge on the other leg, so down we go. Beautiful, that's it. Straight out, are you with us? You should be ready now for your left foot to press down for your single leg bridge, and away we go. Up, excellent. So remember, we're looking to lift here the whole body up, that nice long line, keep going for me. That nice long line that goes from your heel all the way down, so when I'm pressing here into the heel, look at that line that goes from there all the way down here. That's what we're looking for. Great work for the glutes and the hamstrings. Slow is better. Good, excellent.

Just the job, keeping the abdominals pulled in tight. Super. Hopefully we can feel something going on there at the back of the thigh, maybe into the glutes. Excellent. Keep your breathing nice and relaxed, try and keep your neck relaxed in this position. Good. I hope you're still with us at home. Good work. Well done. We there? Excellent, we're moving straight on.

You know, we've got to do some abdominals, I'm sorry. It's only fair. You can stay down for this one, only because I'm going to really make you get up on the last one. So for this one, we're going to do a little bit of a V-sit up, so the great thing about this exercise, normally your sit ups will work just the upper part of the abdominals, the reverse curl will work the lower parts, so we're going to do the 2 together. So let me show you sideways on what this looks like.

I'm going to start with feet in this position, I'm going to start with the hands out like so. All I'm looking to do here is sit up there, both together. Both together. If you're feeling particularly fresh though, put them on the floor when you go back down. So we're bringing the knees to the chest, and sitting up at the same time, so for the rectus abdominis down the middle here, we're getting to the top and the bottom at the same time.

Okay, are we set? Hands out, beautiful. I'll take 15 of those please. Away we go, beautiful. Knees to the chest at the same time, and you'll see there's a little bit of balance influence here as well. Super. Remember we talked about when we're doing our abdominals, so this kind of exercise; picture the abdominal muscles, the rectus, like a spring. As you're sitting up, try to squeeze that spring together, get your mind into the muscle. That will help you with this exercise. Don't worry; I can give you a pull if you need. How are we doing at home? Fifteen is our target. If you're finding that too easy, remember what we said, you can always take a quick rest, do another set. If you're feeling particularly strong, you could always do 3 sets, but that gives us something to aim for. Brilliant. Make sure you're breathing. Excellent. You'll be pleased to know there's only 1 exercise after this. You're doing really well. Fabulous, well done, good little work for the abs, hopefully you felt that.

So, our last exercise—just take a rest for a second, guys—is the Turkish stand up. The aim here is simply to stand up. That's it. So what I want you to do is take one hand, doesn't matter which hand because you're going to swap over after 7 repetitions, and point to the ceiling. The aim is to stand up, ideally, without using the other hand. So, what I'm going to do is lay myself down, point one hand straight to the ceiling. This hand stays pointing to the ceiling all the way through. So I come up, stand up, keep it pointing to the ceiling, and then guess what? Do exactly the same thing; keep it pointed to the ceiling on the way down. If you find that a little bit difficult, you can use the other hand when you get to here, to push yourself up, but ideally what we're aiming for is not using that other hand. Let the abs do the sit up; let the legs do the work. There we go.

You can pick whichever hand you like, with your head at that end and your feet at this end, point whichever hand you like to the ceiling, because you're going to change after 7 reps, legs straight out to start with, okay, are we set? Let's go. Legs in, keep the finger pointing to the ceiling, both of you are cheating, I hope you're doing better than this at home. Have we got the receipt for these 2; I might need to take them back. Point to the ceiling, keep it pointing to the ceiling, keep it pointed to the ceiling, and up we go. And down, you see you're lucky, you can't see their faces, they're pulling faces at me here. Come up, up we go, excellent, and down.

How are we doing at home? Probably better than these 2. Good, up we go, up, up, up, good, and back down. You can see why I only demonstrate the first 2 and then don't do any more afterwards. Come on, up we go, how many is this? I should have brought a book with me or something. Up we go, point to the ceiling, good, you're doing really well. That's 6 already, and only an hour or so gone. Good. Are you changing arms now? Good, well done. Are we changing arms yet? I'd change the legs; use somebody else's if I were you. You're doing really well. How are we doing at home? Remember 15 is our target, it shouldn't feel easy, if it feels easy there's no point in doing it. You're doing really well, guys. It's easy for me; I'm not actually doing anything, as you've probably noticed. Good. You're doing well. I think we've only got a few more to do.

So the great thing about this is that it's a whole-body exercise. You're using your abs on the first part of that movement, you've really got to use the legs, and remember we talked about, when we talked about our core strength, about this thoracolumbar fascia, this sheath at the back, and the whole point of that is that's what helps transfer the strength from your upper to your lower body, that's the link that gets your whole body working together, and you're really having to use that here, you're having to brace yourself in that movement, that gets you up and down. Are we done? Fabulous work. How did you do at home? Hopefully you did really well.

What we're going to do now is a little bit of a cool down, with some gentle movements to get the joints moving, just similar to how we did in the warm up. Let your pulse rate come down a little bit, let your temperature come down a little bit, and then we're going to go into a few stretches. So let's just get ourselves moving, guys, just a few gentle mobilizing moves, you know the kind of thing that we do for the warm up. Remember if you're not sure on the stretches to use, we've got that flexibility workout for you where you can go straight into that now and use those stretches.

Don't forget how important progression is, so maybe we're looking at 1 set of 15 for each exercise to start with, we could build that up to 2 sets, and then 3 sets. You can either do that by doing 3 sets of each exercise, then onto the next one, and then onto the next one, and what you could do is the whole routine, and then do the whole routine again, it's your choice. But certainly to start with, it's about the quality, not quantity. Get the technique right; that's the most important thing. Because these whole body movements are really focusing on those core muscles, and they are vital.

The beauty of what we've just done, all of those movements are functional, we use those movements every day. So this workout, with no equipment, is something that you can take into your everyday activities. Benefit of that is it's going to really help to protect your lower back from injury.

Medicine Ball Workout
Lecture 26

While both speed of movement and pure strength are important criteria for many athletes, the vital ingredient is the marriage of these, which results in power. A medicine ball serves as a great tool for developing power and lends itself to a plethora of both individual and partner drills that will enhance performance in most sports. Furthermore, medicine balls are relatively cheap and require very little storage space, so you can easily adopt the workouts in this lecture to ensure your home workouts are fun and always keep you moving closer to your goals.

Guidelines

- Always warm up first, taking about 5 minutes to raise your core body temperature with light cardio, and mobilize your joints by gently moving your limbs through various planes of motion.

- You will need space for a couple of these exercises. It won't be a problem if you're working out at the gym, but you may need to move outside if you're working out at home.

- Choose a weight of ball that is challenging but does not slow down your movements too much.

- Do 12 to 15 repetitions for each exercise.

- Never sacrifice correct technique for speed of movement in the search for more power.

- Workouts like these that concentrate on power are best done when you're ready to do them—not after an intense cardio workout or heavy resistance session, for example.

Squat and Throw

- For this exercise, make sure your feet are a little wider than hip-width apart.

- When squatting, press into your heels, keep your abs in tight, and keep your shoulders back.

- Don't let the ball pull you forward.

- This is a plyometric, or explosive, exercise, so you will be making an explosive movement as you come up from your squat.

- Because it is a medicine ball, it'll go up and bounce practically right in front of you, so you can grab it immediately and continue doing more repetitions.

- Don't throw the ball with your arms; instead, your arms should be almost straight, and you should use your abs and legs as sources of power.

- Work within your full, comfortable range of motion.

Lunge and Twist

- Focus on your core, pull your abdominals in tight, pull in through your waist, and lift up through the pelvic floor.

- Keep your feet hip-width apart—even when you step out into your lunge—because if you don't, you'll lose your balance.

- Keep your arms slightly bent throughout the movement.

- Try to rotate your hips—and upper body—as much as you can to execute a deep lunge and twist.

- By rotating your spine, you're also working your obliques.

Chop

- In this exercise, you experience movement through the lower spine, working your core muscles and obliques, which are working contralaterally.

- This is a great exercise for anyone who plays golf or tennis.

- When doing a chop, keep your arms almost straight—but not quite.

- Slow is better on these kinds of exercises.

- This exercise involves some rotation, but there's also a mix of flexion and extension through the lower spine because you're flexing at the hip to reach the ball down to the floor.

- Keep your chin back and your head lifted. Try not to drop your head particularly as you move toward the floor.

- Try to keep a neutral, comfortable position in your lower spine.

- When you switch to the other side, you may notice that one side is a little more flexible or stronger that the other. Be aware of those weaknesses so that you can work to improve any muscular imbalances.

- The weight of the ball you select shouldn't feel too easy; it should be beginning to feel difficult as you approach 12 to 15 repetitions.

- If you have any shoulder mobility issues, you might want to drop the ball for this exercise because you can just as well do it with your hands.

Sprint Pass

- This exercise is designed to be done with a partner, but you can also throw the medicine ball against the wall instead.

- Make sure that you are standing up straight and tall.

- This is a true power exercise; it works your entire body.

- This exercise starts with the power in your legs and transfers it into your arms. To get that power to move from your legs to your upper body, you need a strong core, so there is an emphasis on your abdominals.

- Be aware of keeping your abdominals in really tight to protect your lower spine.

- This exercise works the thoracolumbar fascia, which is the key to transferring the load from the upper body to the lower, and vice versa.

Lean
- Make sure to start in a wide kneeling position, which will help keep your hips square to the front.

- If you have any shoulder or lower back problems, start by trying this exercise without the resistance.

- When you lean out to the side, hold it for 3 seconds and then return to your starting position, using smooth movements throughout.

- It is important to keep your hips, chest, and shoulders square to the front. Don't let yourself twist—even though you are going to feel the inclination to do so.

- Focus on pulling your abdominals and obliques in tight, reinforcing the thoracolumbar fascia.

- Take a quick rest as you switch to the other side.

- It is best to move slowly through the movements of this exercise.

- Drop the top of your head so that you have a nice, long alignment of the spine.

- Avoid rotating your hips and exaggerating your lumbar curve.

- Focus on pulling in your transversus muscle, across the front of your abdominal region, to prevent you from arching your lower back too much.

- Try to keep your breathing relaxed throughout this exercise.

Press-Up
- The target areas for this exercise are the chest, the front of the shoulders, and the triceps.

- For this exercise, an extra challenge for the core muscles can be attained by making sure that you keep your abdominals in tight and your hips in a comfortable position.

- When you're in your press-up position—whether you're in a full press-up position or on your knees—the important thing is to not drop your hips down.

- Don't stick your backside up in the air; you want to maintain a comfortable alignment in your lower spine.

- To find your neutral spine, drop it and lift it until you find the position that feels most comfortable.

- By adding the medicine ball to this press-up exercise, it puts a challenge on the muscles around the shoulder girdle. You have to focus on maintaining stability through the shoulder girdle as you work on an unstable surface.

- Try not to twist your hips, even though you're fighting the feeling to drop them.

V Sit-Up
- You have 2 options for this exercise: You can keep your feet down on the floor if you want to try the easier version, or you can lift them

up to the ceiling if you think you can handle it. For both positions, you can either use the ball or have no resistance.

- Slow is better for this exercise because you want your abdominals to have more time under tension.

Adding a medicine ball to your workout is a great way to develop power and enhance fitness.

- For any abdominal exercise, try to think of your abdominals as being a spring, and really try to squeeze it as you pull up.

- Keep your breathing relaxed, and exhale on the exertion—breathe out on your way up.

Chest Press
- The triceps can be a problem area, so make sure that you're in a comfortable spine position and that you have some space to do this exercise.

- To begin, don't push the ball up too high. Take a couple of practice throws, which will allow you to determine where you need to throw it, and then you can start to make the movement more dynamic.

- This chest press is similar to a basketball chest pass, and it's similar to a press-up, but you are using the muscle fibers in a different way for this exercise.

- The goal is to incorporate plyometrics, so you want to exhibit an explosive movement.

- The challenge is to keep yourself in a neutral spine position throughout the exercise.

- As you push the ball up, exhale.

Cooldown
- Finish your workout with some stretches that will work the major muscle groups, including the hamstrings, quads, abdominals, lower spine, and inner and outer thigh.

- For static stretching, take your muscles past their normal length, and hold the position for about 15 seconds.

- If you start this workout and progress through all the exercises, then you might want to run through the exercises with no weight at first. Then, progress to a very light ball. Obviously, increasing the weight of the ball makes the exercises more difficult.

- Additionally, you can do 1 set of each exercise, take a quick rest, and then do another set. However, you can also do these exercises as a circuit, which involves doing the whole routine straight through and then doing the whole routine again.

- Don't do too much too soon. Only increase the resistance of the ball or add extra circuits if you find that these exercises are easy and that there is room for progression.

- One way to progress is to generate more power, which is where plyometric exercises come in. For example, with the squat and throw, you can throw the ball higher; with the sprint pass, you can make the movement more explosive.

- If you're struggling for balance, you can try grabbing one of your ears to stay upright. This is probably an effect of the vestibular balance system.

- Toward the end of your cooldown, your pulse rate should be decreasing, and you can take a few deep breaths to complete your workout.

Medicine Ball Workout
Lecture 26—Transcript

Whilst both speed of movement and pure strength are important criteria for just about any sportsman, the vital ingredient and often the deciding factor that gives you that winning edge, is the marriage of the 2—namely power.

The ability to quickly generate force, from whatever body part, is a useful skill to help to get us through our daily tasks. But for the sportsman, it's vital; it can be the difference between being the MVP or warming the bench, being on the medal rostrum or standing in the crowd, shattering records or shattered dreams.

A medicine ball is ideal for use at home as it's relatively cheap and takes very little storage space. It's great to develop power and lends itself to a plethora of both individual and partner drills that will enhance performance in most sports, but you can also adopt these to ensure your home workouts are fun and always keep you moving closer to your goals.

The medicine ball has been around for an incredibly long time, with the first reference to wrestlers training with sand filled bladders appearing in Persia, around 3000 years ago. Hippocrates had them sewn out of animal skins and stuffed with sand, and used to challenge his patients to throw them back and forth for injury prevention and rehabilitation.

So, get your ball out and get ready to take your medicine! First of all, here are a few guidelines to make sure you train smart. Always, like the guys are doing now, make sure you warm up first, take around 5 minutes to raise your core body temperature with some light cardio some mobilizing gentle movements, moving your limbs through various planes of motion, and that will get you in the position ready to go. You will need space for a couple of these drills which won't be a problem if you're at the gym, but you're at home you might want to take a couple of these exercises into the garden. Choose a weight of ball that is challenging but does not slow down your movements too much; remember we're trying to generate power.

Our target is going to be 12–15 repetitions, that's what I'm asking you to do, 12–15 repetitions of each exercise, and some of them will flip over to both sides. Never sacrifice good technique for speed of movement. Remember workouts like this that concentrate on power, are best done when you're fresh, so these are not something you'd do after a heavy cardio or heavy resistance session. All right then, let's get started.

So our first exercise, we're going to take the feet about a little bit wider than hip width apart. Take a hold of the ball; we're holding it low. Let's just get a little practice first of all. We're going to squat down, pressing into the heels, keep the abs in tight, your shoulders are back. Don't let the ball pull you forwards. This is a plyometric, an explosive exercise, we're going to press through the heels, extend the legs, lift the ball, and actually throw the ball. Now, with it being a medicine ball, it'll go up and bounce pretty much right in front of you so we can grab it again, ready for the next exercise. This is a plyometric; we talked about that in Lecture 3 in our energy systems about explosive movements.

This is what we're going to do, bend the knees, are we ready for our 12–15 repetitions? And away we go. Throw it up, and away we go. Twelve repetitions please. We're pressing through the legs, and you're going to keep going and I'm going to keep talking, so we're looking for an explosive movement as we come up. See how the ball bounces in front of you, so it's easy to grab it again, keep the abdominals tight all the time, we're not throwing with the arms, importantly, we're lifting an almost straight arm, lift, abs are in tight, make sure we get a good bend. How low do we go? We go as low as is comfortable for you. Work to your full, comfortable range of motion. Did that one nearly go bouncing, then? And up, you can see why I said you might want to take some of these exercises into the garden. I'm looking for 12 repetitions, done? Well done. I trust you. Excellent, and we're moving on.

The next exercise is a lunge and twist, going to put a little bit more work into the core muscles, here, which we talk about in our lecture on the spine. A great exercise, working both sides. Important things here: Focusing on your core, pulling your abdominals in tight, pulling in through your waist, lifting up through the pelvic floor. We're generating that abdominal balloon we talked about.

We're starting with the feet hip width apart, an important balance one here. Now the ball is actually going to start up high, it's up in front of you but the arms are slightly bent. We're going to step forwards, with your right leg, nice and long. We're going to go down into our lunge position, and we're going to twist the ball down. Come back, lift, and step up to the top at the same time. We're going to swap over to the other leg. Down it goes, lunge down, knee down towards the floor and rotate, and back up. So like the first exercise, the arms are staying just slightly bent, all the way through. We're looking for as much rotation as we can, and that deep lunge and twist.

Are we set? 12 of these, please. Abdominals in tight, and away we go. Right leg, lunge down, and back up. And to the other side, beautiful. And keep going for me guys. Excellent stuff. Be aware when you're stepping out into that lunge, see how the guys are keeping the feet about hip width apart, otherwise what will happen is if you step onto a tram line, you'll find that you'll start to lose your balance, so keep those feet hip width apart. Keeping the abdominals in tight, trying to get a little more rotation if we can through the upper body. Beautiful. Remember we talked about the spine and its movements, we talked about flexion and extension, but we also talked about this rotation, and that's what we're doing here, we're getting a little bit of work into the obliques as well. Fabulous. You're doing really well. Hope you're still with me at home, there. Oh, didn't lose our balance there, did we? Blame it on the matt. Fabulous. And that will happen, if you need to reset yourself, that's fine. Is there 1 more, there? Beautiful. Excellent stuff. Okay, well done. Should have felt a little bit of work going into the legs there, as well as working through the waist.

And we're going to isolate that one a little bit more now, really getting into the muscles that protect the lower back, so what I'm going to ask you to do this time, and this will be a great exercise for any of you who play golf or tennis, a perfect exercise. So what we're going to do here is start with the ball high again, but this time, take a look at the feet. I want you to take your right foot and turn it onto the ball of the foot, here, like so. We're lifting up, and we've actually turned our hips over towards your left side now. What's going to happen is a simple chop, keeping the arms almost straight, we come down through that semi-circle, reach down, and there's a little bit of flexion at the hip, here. So we're reaching down to the floor, and then back up. And again we're looking for 12 of those please, away we go. Nice and slow, slow is better on these kinds of exercises.

And away we go. Beautiful. And up. Okay so we're looking for that rotation, there's also that little mix of flexion and extension through the lower spine as well, because we're flexing here at the hip, to reach the ball down to the floor, that's great. Now really go for that big movement, trying to get a big semicircle. Keep your chin back, keep your head lifted. Try not to drop your head particularly as we come down here, see how Cameron is keeping his head lifted there? Try and keep that neutral, comfortable position in your lower spine. See how we're getting that twist through the movement, and no surprise that this exercise clearly, as I said, is going to help you with your goal for your tennis swing. We're looking for 12 repetitions and then we'll swap sides and do it the other way around, remember I said right at the top there that we will do some exercises on both sides. Beautiful. Over on the other side yet? Step over. Set yourself up, excellent. That's it. And up to the top, fabulous. And for obvious reasons, this exercise is called the Chop. Great.

One thing you may notice, switching from side to side, you might have already seen this on the last exercise, when we're on the lunge, you may have difference from one side to the other, maybe one side's a little more flexible, one side is a little stronger, don't worry, that will happen, but be aware of those weaknesses, we do need to try and iron out those muscular imbalances. And the weight of the ball, you need to select for yourself, remember what we're saying is it shouldn't feel too easy, we should be getting to somewhere between those 12 and 15 repetitions, that's your target, it should be beginning to feel difficult when we get there.

Now just something to be aware of here, as well, if you do have any shoulder injuries, any shoulder mobility problems, and Cameron is working through one at the moment, you might want to drop the ball for this exercise, because you can just as well do this with the hands, the important thing is getting that rotation, getting that flexion, as we are doing now. As you can see here, we're still getting that movement through the lower spine; we're still getting that work for the core muscles, particularly here, getting a bit of work into the obliques. Remember we talked about the obliques working contralaterally. So you're working your external and internal this way, or external and internal the other way. Fabulous, great stuff.

Okay, you'll be pleased to know we're going to hit the floor. You might not be pleased to know that we're doing the sprint pass. I'm going to set this up and use the guys as partners. You can do this with the ball, and throw it against the wall. So we're going to use 1 ball and take just your ball there into the sprint position for me please.

This is actually called a sprint pass. The ball is on the floor, you're in your sprint position, if you stand up nice and tall for me, Cameron, all that's going to happen is in 1 movement as we step up, we're going to throw the ball at the same time, we're going to catch it, then you're going to take your step back, and you'll get ready to sprint. So let's have a couple of examples. Pick it up, throw the ball, and up you go, and we swap over, down you go, ball on the floor, knee on the floor, up you get, and push the ball all in 1 movement. Fabulous. Down we go. Can you keep that going for me please, guys? So this is a true power exercise. Great thing about it is we're working through your whole body.

Now the key is that you stand up and throw the ball at the same time, so we try and get the whole body working together, working through the legs as if you're driving out of that sprint position, we're also then transferring that power through into the arm. To get that power to move from your legs to your upper body, really relies on a strong core, so this is putting some emphasis on the abdominals as well. It might not look like an obvious abdominal exercise, but be aware of keeping your abdominals in really tight on this exercise, protect your lower spine. And this will work, as we talked about in our lecture about the spine, we talked about the thoracolumbar fascia. This is the key to transferring that power, transferring the load from the upper body to lower, or lower to upper, as we're doing here. Using that power through the legs to transfer into that movement through the ball. How many have we done? One more? I don't want you both throwing the ball at the same time, that would be a tough one. Beautiful stuff.

Okay, so, that's your sprint pass, again if you haven't got somebody to work with, you can do that by throwing the ball against the wall. What we're going to do now is take the ball and get down onto the floor for a little leaning exercise really get into the obliques. What I'm going to ask you to do here is set yourself in a kneeling position, nice and wide, and if you take my ball, because I'm going to take the easier option on this one, this is what I'm going to ask you to do. Set yourself up nice and wide to keep your hips square to the front. Take your left leg out to the side like so, for balance. The important thing here is you're going to keep your hips, chest, and shoulders to the front. We're going to take the ball and lift the ball up to the top, and I'm showing you the easier version, without the resistance. Again, if you have any shoulder problems, or particularly any lower back pathology, we want to make this slightly easier, first.

Our aim here is to take a lean, we hold it just for 3 seconds, and then we come back to the top. Smooth movements. And away we go, take it down, get a nice long lean, challenge yourself, and then back up, and away we go. Can I get 12 of those please guys?

So the important things here, he says, trying not to trip over anybody, it's to keep your hips, chest, shoulders square to the front. Don't let yourself twist, and there will be a feeling like you want to twist, but you really need to work through pulling your abdominals in tight, pulling in through the obliques, you should begin to feel something at the back, as we begin to brace ourselves on that thoracolumbar fascia. So either let your whole body move as one, and particularly 'til you're lower down, and lift up, excellent well done. And again as we said, if you have any issues with your shoulders, we can always do this, and you'll still feel, just nod at me; tell me you can still feel that exercise, Cameron? Brilliant. Excellent stuff. We're looking for 12 repetitions. Again I'm trusting you guys to count for me. Can we feel something going on in the middle, there? Brilliant, excellent stuff.

Keeping your hips square, keeping a long spine. So this is that, remember we talked about those spine movements; we talked about that lateral flexion. You're at 12? Take a quick rest as we swap over to the other side. Well done guys. Towel down. You know, we're famous, there should be someone to towel you down, you know? That's where we should be on this.

Are we set guys? Left leg out for me please Cameron? Brilliant, so get yourself a nice stable base, first of all, slow is better on these exercises, and away we go. And you see how we're dropping the top of the head this way, so that you get this nice long line down through the spine, nice alignment, keeping the abs in tight. So the things to look out for here, we're trying to avoid that rotation of the hips, we're trying to avoid any exaggerated lumbar curve. So you should really feel like this transversus muscle across the front, well done take a rest, and that's a great little tip there, what Cameron is doing is working with the resistance for as long as he can, but then instead of sacrificing his technique to stick with the resistance, puts the resistance down and makes sure he gets the technique right. We said that right at the top; don't sacrifice your technique to get a little extra speed, power, or resistance. It's all about getting the technique right.

So this transversus muscle that wraps across the middle here, you're really pulling that in to prevent you from arching the lower back too much. Excellent. Good work. Try and keep your breathing relaxed. Again I'm trusting you guys to give me 12 repetitions. Although we just say 12–15, so if you want to throw in an extra 3, I don't mind, really, you know, it's your choice. For you at home, get your money's worth. Excellent stuff, well done guys. Take a quick rest for a second.

So we're moving on now, little bit of a press-up work for the chest, for the front of the shoulders, for the triceps, but we're going to vary things slightly by using the ball here for this exercise, we can get an extra challenge, certainly for the core muscles by making sure that we keep the abdominals in tight, keeping your hips in that comfortable position. When you're in that press up position, whether you're in the full press up position, or on your knees, the important thing is that we've not got the hips dropping down. And also that we're not sticking the backside up in the air, we want that nice comfortable alignment in your lower spine. A tip to find your neutral spine is to drop it, and lift it, until you find the position that feels most comfortable, and that's really your neutral spine there.

What I'm going to do for this exercise is make things a little bit more difficult by using the ball. What this does, now, is put a challenge on the muscles around the shoulder girdle here, we've got to really work to try and keep that stability through the shoulder girdle as we work on an unstable surface. So the press-up is going to be one on the ball, then roll it to the other side, and down. Okay? Roll it, and down. We're looking for 12 repetitions all together, there's the ball. I'm going to give you the choice, you can either do the full press-up, if you're feeling strong, or you could start on the full press-up and then go down to your knees. But if you're doing it on your knees, I don't want you in a box position, I want your feet lifted. Obviously I'm going to have somebody in the full press-up position and somebody on their knees. Did anybody guess the right answer to that? Okay let's get 12 repetitions, please. Look at this, fabulous.

Roll it across, and down you go, excellent work; we're looking for 12. Try not to twist through the hips, keep your abdominals in tight, again guys I know it looks like I'm doing nothing, but I do feel your pain. You're doing really well. Little bit of work into the chest, into the front of the shoulders, into the triceps. Great work. Excellent. Keep those abs in tight; remember we're fighting this feeling for your hips to drop down. Great work. I did mine earlier, honestly, I did. That's my excuse. So as well as feeling this in those target muscles, there's a little bit of extra work around the shoulder girdle there, hopefully you felt that as we're trying to really stabilize that position there. Excellent stuff. Well done. That's a great exercise.

We're going to flip over now and really get into a problem area for a lot of us, with our V sit-ups. So for this position, I'm going to ask you to sit yourself down. I'm going to give you 2 options, actually, for this one. So we're sideways on, the first position is just having the feet down, like so. And we're going to take the ball here, and we're going to lift. That's all it is to get the shoulders off the floor. Our easier version, which I'm going to do, is like this. Or, as the guys are going to do, can we lift the feet up to the ceiling please? We've got a hold of the ball, so you've got my easy version, which is—I've planned this well, haven't I? I've got no weight, and I've got the feet down—or this version, that the guys are doing. Can I get 12 repetitions please? Up we go. Remember the target is 12–15, so we're really looking to work into the abdominals here. Slow is better, more time under tension, and a little tip here on any of your abdominal exercises, try to think of your ab muscles like a spring, really try and squeeze them together.

That's what we're trying to do on this reach, really squeeze those abdominal muscles as we pull up. Fabulous.

Keep your breathing relaxed, a little tip is to exhale on the exertion, so breathe out, as Renee's doing there on the way up. Is that 12? You could have done 15 there I'm sure, go on, there you go. And that's a good point; you get out of it what you put into it, so push yourself a little bit. Well done. Brilliant stuff.

Excellent, just take a quick rest for a second, and I'll steal your ball, and then our last exercise, you'll be pleased to know, working into the chest and triceps again, triceps can be a problem area, so make sure you've got yourself in a comfortable position on this one, and make sure you've got a bit of space.

I'm going to have the feet close to the backside, I'm going to find that neutral comfortable spine position again, okay, and I'm going to ask you to go very easy on this one, first of all, so we're resting the head down, the chest press is literally pushing the ball up. So go small at first, don't go too far with the height of the ball. It's a chest press, like a basketball chest pass, and what we're looking to do here is to work, again, into that idea of plyometrics, that idea of working the muscles a little bit more explosively. So, it's a similar movement to the press up, but we are using the muscle fibers in a different way here.

So let's set ourselves up, guys, for this one. Brilliant, sorry, I just need a bit of space there. Excellent. So start nice and easy, get a couple of practice ones, don't throw it too high, beautiful. So the challenge here, also, is to keep ourselves in that neutral spine, that comfortable spine position. And we're looking for that little bit of an explosive movement. So drop it down to the chest, and then give it a good push and blow out at the same time. Let's make it a bit more dynamic. Fabulous. And just a little tip, make sure you catch it on the way down. But a few practice ones first of all will allow you to get the feeling of where you need to throw it, and then we can start to get a little bit more dynamic with this movement. So again, as opposed to our normal press-ups, we're working, as we talked about in Lecture 13 in our energy systems, we're working a little bit more plyometrically, here, on this exercise. Great stuff. And push. Brilliant. Feel that? Only just caught that one. And take a little rest there. And if you sit yourselves up.

And there you go; you've got yourselves there a full top-to-toe workout. Now what we're going to do is finish off with a little stretch, which I'll advise you to do. We'll pick the major muscle groups to do that, so since we're in that position, shall we just start with a little hamstring stretch?

Remember for our static stretching we're looking to take the muscles to a little bit of length, past their normal length and hold that position for about 15 seconds, let's just hold that and I'll keep talking. A couple of things here, in terms of progression for the exercises, if you're really starting out right at the start, shall we swap that over? Then I would advise you to perhaps run through the exercises with no weight at first. Don't use the ball, and then maybe to go with a very light ball to start with. Obviously increasing the weight to the ball makes it a little bit more difficult. Let's get a little bit of work into the lower spine. Bring one foot across to the others side. One hand behind, and let's get that little twist around.

And then also, in terms of progression, we only did 1 set of each exercise there. So you've got 2 options here, you can either do a set of the exercise, take a quick rest and then do it again—let's swap over to the other side—or do it as a circuit, you could do the whole routine, and then do the whole routine again. My advice to you is don't do too much too soon, you should only be doing that if you're finding that it's easy, then you've got that room for progression. So either increasing the resistance of the ball, or adding extra circuits, maybe 2, as we go to intermediate and maybe 3 as we move to advanced. But also—and come back to the center, let's get a little bit for the inner thigh, take the soles of the feet together, take a hold, sit up tall, and a little press down at the side will give you that stretch on the inner thighs— but also bear in mind that one way to progress it is to generate more power, and that's what we're doing here with these plyometric exercises. So with the squat and throw, we'll throw it higher. With the sprint pass, we'll be a little bit more explosive. So the actual technique itself can improve through your progression as well. Beautiful.

And let's turn it over; we're onto all fours. Little bit of work for the lower spine, pull up to the ceiling, now we've done a lot of work through the middle here, and release that, and put one foot forwards, hands on the knee to help you get up, beautiful, we're up to the top, let's get just a little bit of work for the quads, they did their bit. Take a hold of the left, you're struggling for balance, I still haven't quite figured this out, why, but apparently if you grab a hold of your ear like that, you'll stay upright. I think it's probably got something to do with the vestibular balance system. And swap it over to the other side. Stretching through the quads, front of the thigh. Beautiful. Pulse rate should be coming down now, and just to finish off shall we take a deep breath in, up to the top, and back down, and 1 more, and believe it or not, stick a fork in you, you're cooked.

That's your medicine ball workout. I hope you enjoyed it. Well done.

Step and Interval Workout
Lecture 27

For this step workout, you're going to use some interval training techniques to improve the capabilities of your cardiovascular system. You're also going to alternate between cardio and strength exercises, which will allow you to burn a lot of calories and tone your body at the same time. You're going to do 1 minute of cardio exercises, 30 seconds of rest, and then 1 minute of strength exercises. Within each 1-minute session, spend the first 15 seconds making sure you have the correct technique, and then begin to increase your rate of exercise.

Guidelines
- For the following exercises, you'll need a step platform—a great tool to have. If you don't have one, they're easy to find, and they're not too expensive.

- Start with a warm-up that involves a few mobilizing exercises, working through all the major joints. You can do some basic stepping up and down on the step.

- The following exercises alternate between cardio and strength exercises.

- Do each exercise for 1 minute with a 30-second rest between exercises, which results in a 2:1 work-to-rest ratio.

- Take some water breaks whenever you need them.

Shuffle
- When using a step platform, try not to stomp on it—just keep your feet nice and light.

- Find a good pace, and keep moving.

- Use your arms as well, and keep your abs in tight.

- After 1 minute, take a deep breath, and rest for 30 seconds. Keep your feet moving at a slow pace.

- You might have to straighten your step because it might move a little during this exercise.

Press-Up Walk
- Start in a full press-up position, but if you start to fatigue, then you can drop your knees down, resting your knees on the floor.

- Throughout the exercise, keep your abs in tight and keep breathing.

- This is a strength exercise that works your chest, the front of your shoulders, and your triceps.

Over the Top
- In dancing terms, this exercise involves doing a chassé, or sashay, across the top of the step.

- Try to control your lateral motion while stepping over the step.

- Keep your feet light so that there is less impact, and try to make your movements quick.

- Because you're working on your aerobic fitness, the goal is to increase your heart rate during this exercise.

- This exercise focuses on the large muscle groups.

- Try to increase your pace for the last 15 seconds.

3-Direction Lunge: Right
- This exercise focuses on the hips and thighs.

- Make sure that your lunges are deep to maximize your workout.

- Increase your pace if you can throughout the exercise.

- This is a strength exercise, but because you're using large muscle groups, you'll also need to make sure enough oxygen is being passed through to your lungs and heart.

- Make sure you're on the ball of your foot when doing lunges.

Jumping Jacks
- Throughout this exercise, you want to keep moving—even if you need to stop and take a few deep breaths—because of the effects of blood pooling.

- When doing jumping jacks, remain light on your feet; you should be on your toes.

- Get into a good rhythm and then keep that pace up.

If it's too difficult for you to do jumping jacks using a step, you can start by doing them on the ground.

- Use your hands for balance if you need to.

- Keep your abs in tight.

3-Direction Lunge: Left
- Keep your abdominals in tight throughout this exercise.

- Start with a strong forward stride for the lunge, and try to sink down low into it. Pick up the pace when you can.

- This exercise works to tone the hips and thighs, moving those large muscle groups.

- Although this is a strength exercise, some cardio work is still involved.

- When lunging, you'll get a forward hinge from the hip, but don't round your spine. Keep your chest lifted.

Across the Top
- This exercise is similar to the exercise you did that involved going over the top of the step, but it is a little more difficult.

- Don't worry about the height; keep your feet moving quickly across the step.

- For the last 5 seconds, try to speed up your pace.

Triceps Dips
- For this exercise, start with your hands slightly wider than your hips on either side and with your fingers pointing in the same direction you're facing. Lift your backside off the step, keeping your knees and elbows slightly bent.

- Keep your abdominals in tight; keep your chest and head lifted.

- This exercise shouldn't be too difficult, so get a good pace going.

- This exercise focuses on the triceps, but you are also working on your core, keeping your abs in tight.

- When you're about halfway through, increase your pace.

- During the last 15 seconds, you should start to feel a burn, which is the lactic acid buildup.

Knee Repeater: Right
- Make sure your right foot remains on the step throughout this exercise.

- Move as quickly as you can for the entire minute.

- Use your arms. Make sure to keep your trunk fixed, which will improve the efficiency of the speed and power in your arms and legs.

- Your body temperature should start increasing, getting your heart and lungs working.

Twist and Reach Up
- The goal for this exercise is to get your blood moving from one area of your body to another—namely, from your upper body to your lower body.

- You're mainly working the rectus abdominis, but you're also working the obliques when you twist.

- You can pick either arm to reach with because you're going to reach with the other one for the next set.

- Keep your feet flat and your knees bent.

- Find your comfortable, neutral spine position—a position where the lower back has a bit of an arch.

- As you do this exercise, you should begin to reach a little bit higher than the last time, making sure that you're also getting a good twist.

- At the end, take a quick walk around to keep your blood from pooling. Take some deep breaths because taking oxygen in helps to clear the lactic acid that is building up.

Knee Repeater: Left
- The goal is to move your feet as quickly as possible and to increase your speed as you can.

- Keep your left foot on the step throughout this exercise.

- Your heart rate should be increasing. Burning calories and improving your fitness level should be the focus of this exercise. The fitter you are, the sooner you start to burn fat as an energy source.

Twist and Reach Up
- For this exercise, reach up with the opposite hand that you chose for the first twist.

- You're working your abdominals and obliques as you sit up and reach across.

- Get into a good pace, and continue that pace unless you feel as though you can move faster.

- Exhale on the exertion—in this case, on the sit-up; breathe out as you come up, and breathe in as you go down.

- If you need to take a brief rest, you can, but start back up as soon as you can.

Speed Skating

- As you straddle the step and make a speed skating movement from side to side, make sure that your heel lifts up and over the step, focusing on your lateral motion.

- This exercise involves dynamic equilibrium and controlling your lateral movement by bending down on your knee and loading up the muscle, which results in a large force that propels you in the other direction.

- Move your arms side to side along with your feet, and increase your speed as you become comfortable with the movement. The bigger the movement, the more calories you're going to burn.

Side Plank Hip Hitch: Right

- This exercise focuses on the core muscles and the obliques.

- After you bring one of your legs out to the side, you can put your other leg wherever it is comfortable—in front or behind your body.

- Make sure to drop your hips and then lift them to create the hip hitch. Avoid rotating your hips.

- Keep a long position—from the top of your head down through your tailbone to your heel.

- Remain balanced throughout the exercise by keeping your abdominals pulled in tight.

- This exercise involves a much smaller movement than most of the other exercises, but it's a really good exercise to work your core muscles and obliques. These muscles work on stabilizing your lumbopelvic region.

- Try to keep your breathing relaxed and constant when doing this exercise.

Jump Up and Click Heels

- Whatever energy you have, you're going to squeeze it out for this exercise.

- When it comes to fitness, the more you put in, the more you're going to get out. Take about 10 seconds to get into the rhythm of the technique, and then increase your speed as much as you can.

- Don't rest in between jumps—unless you absolutely have to.

- Land quietly if you can. The softer the landings, the easier this exercise is on your joints.

Side Plank Hip Hitch: Left

- Again, this exercise focuses on your core and oblique muscles.

- You should be sweating at least a little bit. Remember that the waste products of exercise include carbon dioxide, water, and heat.

- As you become fitter, this exercise will get easier. Eventually, you might be able to build up from 1 minute to 1 minute and 30 seconds, or you might choose to do the entire routine in 2 circuits.

Cooldown

- At the end of your workout, you can sit down on your step and do a couple of easy stretches.

- Do a few mobilizing moves—just as you did at the beginning of the workout. Then, stretch the large muscle groups, including the quads and hamstrings.

Step and Interval Workout
Lecture 27—Transcript

Hi, and welcome to our little step workout where we're going to be mixing our training techniques. We'll use some interval training techniques; you may remember from our talk about the cardiovascular system, we'll talk about improving its capabilities through interval training. We also mentioned this when we talked about fuel in the energy systems lecture. So, we're going to get a mix of things here.

We're also going from cardio to strength, which is a great way to work out, we're going to burn a lot of calories and help us tone up at the same time. Importantly, as the guys are doing now, you need to get yourself a good warm up, and that's working through all the major joints, mobilizing some basic movements, you can do some basic stepping up and down on the step since you've got one, just to get you kind of warmed up a little bit. And then remember for the workout, what we're going to do here is work in intervals of cardio and strength, so we're actually going to do 1 minute of cardio, and then we'll take 30 seconds and we'll go into 1 minute of strength exercises, where your pulse will come down, it's going to be doing a lot of that. So with that 1 minute, what I'm suggesting is that we spend the first perhaps 15 seconds making sure we've got the technique right, and then we really start to ramp up the rate you're working at there. You want to be looking at getting to a 7, 8 out of 10 on your intensity scale there.

So, let's get ourselves warmed up, I'm assuming you guys are warmed up, if not press pause and make sure you get a few of these mobilizing exercises done first. And we're going to move onto our first exercise. We're going to run through the whole lot, and just do 1 set, you might want to do 2 sets, or you could always do a second set afterwards, second circuit if you're feeling fit enough, but for now let's get ourselves started. Thirty seconds resting between each, so since we're working for a minute, and then doing a 30 second rest, we've got a 2:1 work to rest ratio, remember we talked about that before in our cardio training.

The first exercise, don't do anything just yet with your little step platform, is one foot on, the shuffle is literally just a swap, side to side. Try not to stamp on it, just keep it nice and easy. Are we ready to go, guys? Let's get close to that step, one foot on it; I'm going to take a minute on, are you ready at home? Let's go.

Up we go. Let's go, get into a good pace. Oh, a little bit quicker than that. Come on. Beautiful. Try and keep the feet nice and light, keep yourselves moving. You'll be pleased to know that's 10 seconds already. Come on, keep going at home. Onto the toes. Beautiful. Using the arms as well, keeping the abs in tight, good. Foot on the board. Excellent. Yours is going for a walk, I think. How are we doing at home? We're halfway through already. Can we go a little bit quicker? It's not really a question. Come on, keep it moving, keep your arms moving. Up, up, up. Come on let's go. We've only got 15 to go. Let's go, with the arms as well. Come on. We're into our last 10 seconds. Come on, keep it going. You're not out for a country hike you know, come on. Last 2 seconds, and take a rest there.

Take a deep breath; straighten out that step for me. You might find like John's has just done, the step might move a little bit. Take a deep breath, keep your feet moving, taking our 30 seconds, I'm going to show you the next exercise.

We're moving onto a press-up walk, so this is what's going to happen: One hand is on the step, one is off. We're going to walk onto the step, press up, onto the step, press up. If you start to get fatigued, you can drop your knees down, but if not, start in the full press-up. Are we ready guys? Down we go. One hand on, one hand off. And 1 minute's worth, let's go.

We're away, beautiful, get into a good pace and go with it. Start with your full press-up position; if you start to fatigue then we'll take that down to resting your knees on the floor. Let's go, walk on, walk off, and press up, chest down. Oh is that a half-press up there, Jenn? I hope not. Keep your abs in tight, we're working into the chest here, we're working into the front of the shoulders, we're working into the triceps at the backs of the arms. Excellent work, looking good. We're halfway through already. Come on. Full press ups, this is excellent.

Come on, down we go, keep breathing. How are we doing at home? A little strength work here, getting into the chest, getting into the triceps, getting into the fronts of the shoulders. Looking good. Looking good. Looking good. Only about another 45 minutes to go I think I've pressed the clock wrong. No, keep going, we've only got 10 seconds, we can do this. How are we doing at home? Stay with me, do the last 10 seconds, come on. We can do this. And, couple more, there's 1 more rep there, Jenn. And take a rest there, well done, well done.

Get yourselves up, keep yourselves moving; when you're taking that deep breath just keep yourself moving on the spot. Get ready for our next exercise. That's strength, we're moving onto cardio again. So now we're doing an over the top, we're going all the way over, tapping, and then coming back. So start from one side, doesn't matter which side you are, we're going to go over the top, tap the feet, it's a little—actually, we're going to get into dancing terms, we're doing a sashay across the top of the board. Try not to go too far, what we're trying to do to control our lateral motion and the idea is light feet keeping quick, a little Billy Elliot on the board. Are we ready, guys? So if we're facing outwards please, facing that way for me, are we ready at home, you're going across the board and back, and let's go.

Over, good, quicker with the feet, quicker, quicker. That's it, quicker. Good, come on, let's go. So, over we go. And back. Come on. How we doing? Lovely. Come on, keep going with it. Over the top. Good, come on; let's get that heart rate going. Moving those big muscle groups. Fabulous, come on, we're working on that aerobic fitness now, come on, little bit quicker, straight over, straight over. Don't dilly-dally. Oh we're over halfway already, good. Keep the feet light, excellent. Preferably keep it quiet, then we're getting less impact. Beautiful, speed across the board, speed across the board, we're into the last 15 seconds. Can we increase the pace on the last 15 seconds? Apparently, we can. Up. Good, good. We're into the last 5. Good speed, good speed. Excellent. And take a little rest there, well done.

You've got 30 seconds, take a deep breath, keep your feet moving when you take that deep breath. We're going to move on now to a little bit of strength work again. Really getting into the hips and thighs in a 3-direction lunge. So what we're going to do here is put your right foot on the board, what you're going to do here is to take a lift with the knee, we're lunging forwards first of all. Take a long stride forwards, drop down with the knee. Lift it up, take it out to the side, squat down, take it round behind, and back up. So a 3-direction lunge. We're going to the front, we're lifting, going to the side, abs are in tight, lifting, and down behind.

Okay, let's get our right foot on the board, guys. Right foot on, okay, are we good to go? Let's lift that knee first of all. Okay, get ready for your 1 minute. Let's go. Lunge down, and up. To the side, and up, behind, and up. Let's go. Lunge, good, out to the front, to the side, behind. Excellent. To the front, come on, little bit quicker, up, beautiful, and down, good, let's make those lunges deep, can we go a little bit quicker? We've only got a minute. Come on, that's nearly halfway already. Come on, let's go. Really working into the hips and thighs, here. Fabulous exercise. Little bit of strength, but because we're using those big muscle groups now, it's beginning to get into the heart and lungs as well. We need to keep that oxygen getting through.

We're down to 45, come on, let's go. Deep lunge. Down for the side. Right the way behind. Excellent. Make sure you're on the ball of the foot on those lunges. We're into the last 5 seconds, let's keep going. Looking good guys, looking good. How are you doing at home? I'm hoping you're still with us. And take a little rest there. Well done.

Keep yourself walking around, keep your feet moving, get some deep breaths in, get yourself set ready for our next exercise. We've gone from strength, we're moving back onto cardio.

This time we're going with jumping jacks. So our jumping jacks, you'll know the move. You know this jumping jacks move. But all I'm going to do with this is to use the board as well. So we're going to be jumping up, and down. That's all we're going to be doing for our jumping jacks. Okay, you've got a couple more seconds, get your breath back, how are we doing? Keep yourself moving. Remember we talked about blood pooling when we talked about the cardiovascular systems. It's important to keep moving, you don't want to stop still. Even if you need a breather. I hope you're taking some sips of water along the way as well.

Okay, let's get ourselves ready. Feet either side, let's face outwards please. Get ready, feet straddle, and away we go. Let's go. Jumping jacks, up and down. Come on, let's go. Let's go. Light on your feet. How are we doing at home? Come on. Up, up, up. Come on; let's get that pace up. Let's get that pace up, that's 15 seconds. Come on, light on your feet, on the toes. Does he go a little quicker? Good. Looking good, John, looking good. Keep it going, guys. Use your hands if you need to. Good, get into a good rhythm. We're halfway through. Let's go. How are you doing at home? Fabulous. Keep it going, keep it going. Does it go a bit quicker? Excellent. Thank you for not cursing at me when I asked that question.

Come on. We're into 15 seconds, you're on your sprint for home, come on. Come on. Let's go, up. Abs are in tight. Look how we're bending the knees. Stopping in the ankle so we get nice soft landings. Beautiful, last few seconds, and take a rest there.

Keep yourself moving. Get a deep breath, well done. You didn't fall off the board then, did you? Fabulous. Keep the feet moving. You wouldn't be surprised to know that the next exercise, opposite of what we just did on the other side. So this time, we're doing our 3-direction lunge on this side, to the side, up and down behind. So get yourself ready, we're going to be over to this side of our step. And to get the left foot on. Get ready to lift your right knee up to the top. Oh we're nearly there, that's our 30 seconds. Remember that work to rest ratio, 2:1, and away we go.

Lift it up. Up. Up. Abdominals in tight all the time. Get a good stride forward for that lunge. Sink down. Sink low, keep going. Good. Beautiful. Beautiful, can we get a bit lower? Can we go a little bit quicker? Not really a question. Up, lift it up and out. Really working into toning the hips and thighs. Moving those large muscle groups. So although we're in our strength exercise, still a little bit of cardio work going on here. Fabulous. Up. Good. Good, we're halfway through, team, come on. Lift that knee up in between. Get it right up, lift it right up. Good, lift it right up. Keep the abs in tight. You'll get a little bit of a forward hinge from the hip, on those lunges, but don't be rounding your spine, keep the abs in tight, good. Chest is lifted. Fabulous. Last few seconds, how are we doing at home? And well take a rest there. Keep the feet moving, well done, good work.

Okay, we're going to move onto our next cardio exercise, cardio exercise now is across the top, so what we're going to do, just as we did when we went over the top, which was this way, we're just going to make it a little bit more difficult now, and do it long ways on the boards. So you're starting at the side of the board, you're going all the way over, and all the way back. I'm going to go with you, and let's go.

Up, all the way over, all the way back. Come on let's go. Up. Up. Up. How are you doing at home? All the way over the top, come on. Keep those feet moving. Good. Keep going, keep going. Fifteen seconds already. Come on, good let's go. Let's go. Fabulous. Quick feet. Don't worry about the height; get quick feet across the board. Let's get that shuffle moving, we're halfway through. Come on, guys, doing well. Is that a bead of sweat there, John? Absolutely brilliant. Well that's the warm up, finished. Come on, let's go. You're smiling too much, that worries me. We've only got 20 seconds to go, come on team, how are you doing at home? Hang in there in the across the top. You're doing well. Ten seconds, come on, we can do this. Keep going, don't rest. In fact, if anything, for the last 5 seconds speed it up, speed it up. Looking good, looking good. And take a rest there, well done.

Keep your feet moving. Get some deep breaths, how are we doing at home? So we're going to move onto our next strength exercise, keep yourselves moving for a second and just take a look at the next one.

So we're going into our tricep dip. You're going to come around the front of your step for this one. Okay, dead simple, all I'm going to ask you to do is put your hands either side of your hips, with the fingers pointing in the same direction you're facing. You're going to lift your backside off the bench, your knees are slightly bent, you're going down, and back up. See that bend in the elbow? And then pressing from there gets into the tricep. Keep your abdominals in tight; keep your chest lifted and your head up. Make sure there's nothing going on in the middle, just here for our tricep dips.

Okay, let's get ourselves in position, guys, at the front of the step; get yourself in position at the front of the step. Hands are just slightly wider than the hips; the fingers are pointing forwards, lift your backside off, and are we ready to go? One minute, let's go.

Now this isn't too difficult, so let's get a good pace going. Down we go, and back up. Backside down to the floor, and up we go. Come on, let's get into a good pace, and go with it. Come on. Yes, beautiful, working into the triceps, now. Getting into the back of the arm, here. But also a little bit of work on the core, keeping the abs in tight. Can we feel something going on in these triceps? That's what we're after. Into the triceps. Back of the arm. Look at those triceps? Wicked. Here's one I prepared early. Fabulous, keep it going. We're over halfway through now so come on, let's turn up the pace, turn it up. Come on, can we get a few more done, please? Keep it going.

You're into the last 15. We should be getting a little bit of burn, remember that lactate we talked about, the lactic acid system. Remember we talked about that in Lecture 13 in the energy systems? Come on, work with it. Remember if we can push that forwards. And take a rest there. Well done. We'll be able to burn more fat sooner. Good work, well done.

Get yourself a breather, keep yourself moving. We're going to move onto a knee repeater on your right leg. So you're going to put your right foot on the board, and you're going to be facing the corner. The right foot is going to stay on the board all the time, and your left knee is simply going to go up, touch the floor, up, touch the floor. But we're going to go as quickly as you can for your 1 minute. Are we ready, team? Let's get the right foot on the board, facing this way, get ready with your left knee to come up, and down. Keep that right foot on the board all the time. Are we set? One minute, I hope you're ready at home, let's go.

Up, up. Come on, use the arms. Use the arms. Come on; imagine we're sprinting now, let's go. Fabulous. Keeping those abs in tight, now any good sprint will tell you how important that core strength is. Remember, we define core strength as the ability to keep your trunk fixed. And because of that, it'll improve the efficiency of the speed, the power, in your arms and legs. Look how Jenn is staying fixed in the middle, really working those arms and legs. Come on John; let's get that knee up a bit quicker. We've only got 20 seconds to go, come on, we can do this. Knees up. Knees up. We should be getting that temperature up; we should be getting those heart and lungs working. We're doing well. We're into the last 10. Come on guys, let's go. How are we doing at home? Hang in there. Last 5, come on. Come on. Beautiful, and take a quick rest there, well done. Keep yourself moving.

Going to move on now to our next exercise. So we're going to change it now. Upper body, lower body. Let's get that vascular shunt we talked about in our cardiovascular lecture, that idea of moving the blood from one area to the other. So what I'm going to do now—I'll show you this one straight on—is a little sit up and reach. So I'm going to get myself down to the bench for this exercise, starting from our normal sit up position, but what I'm going to do is take one hand, reach it diagonally up and across, so I'm going to start with them down at my chest, but I'm reaching and getting that twist. So now, I'm really getting into here, but I'm also getting into the obliques with that twist.

So guys, if I can get you down on the bench facing outwards, brilliant. And you can pick which arm you want to reach with, because it doesn't matter, you know you're going to do the other one on the next set. So the aim here is the feet are flat, the knees are bent, we're looking for our neutral spine position. What that means is the comfortable spine position. That's what we're after. Looking for a position where the lower back has got that little bit of an arch. Okay, so the hands are up by the shoulders, you can decide which hand you're going with, but when you sit up, I want you to reach across to the diagonal. Okay, so, let's get ourselves set. One minute, away we go.

Sit up, and reach across, beautiful. And let's reach a little bit higher, up to there, up to here. Beautiful, that's it. Get a really good twist, fabulous. Up and twist. Good. And a little bit higher on that reach. Let's get it up here, reach up. Fabulous. And back down. Okay, let's go let's go. Working into the 6-pack, into the rectus, we're also working into the obliques. Great work, keep it going. We're doing well. Good work. Come on team, how are you doing at home? Fabulous. And reach. Beautiful, up we go. Yes. Up we go, we've only got 15 seconds.

How are you doing at home? Can we feel something going on in the abdominals? I'm going to take that deafening silence as a yes. Come on. We're doing well; we've only got 10. This is it, come on, let's go, get those last few reps. Let's work those abs, work those abs. And take a quick rest, well done, get yourself up, have a little walk around. We don't want any blood pooling. Get some deep breaths, get some oxygen in. Remember getting that oxygen in is going to help to clear away the lactic acid. And let me show you what our next exercise is going to be.

We're going on a side lunge. One foot is on, one foot is off the step. And all we're going to do here is literally switch them over on the top. Now what we're doing here is getting a little rotation through the waist as well, at the same time. How quick can we move those feet? Let's stand on the step, facing outwards please, team. One foot on, get ready, one foot on the board, are we ready to go? And let's go. One minute.

Come on, keep that foot on the board and let's go. These are our side lunges, come on. Little bit quicker, don't go up, go across. I feel the need for speed, looking good. There you go, come on. Does he go a little quicker? How are we doing at home? Come on. These are our side lunges, getting that heart rate up. Burning calories is what it's all about, improving our fitness level, and remember, we've already discovered that the fitter we are, the sooner we start to burn fat as an energy source. Let's get rid of that fat. Come on. Beautiful. Looking good. We've only got 20 seconds, guys. Let's turn it up. Come on. Excellent stuff. Doing well, how are you doing at home? I hope you're still with us. Good work. Come on. Looking good. Last 5. Can I get a couple more reps in there? And beautiful, hold it there, take a walk around, you've got your 30 seconds, remember we talked about that work to rest ratio, 2:1, we're working for a minute, 30 seconds to get ourselves set. Remember we talked about the benefits of interval training, great stuff.

We're back down for our sit up and reach, only this time whichever hand you went with last time; you're reaching the other way this time. Remember you're going to sit up, reach up, and across. Get yourselves ready to go. And you know what? I'll take it now. Let's go.

Sit up and reach up to that high diagonal. So we're getting this work for the 6-pack muscle, we're getting this work for the obliques as we sit up and reach across. Sit up and reach. Beautiful. Let's go, let's go. I'm trusting you to swap sides. Don't let me down. Fabulous. Get into a good pace, and go with it. Remember we talked about breathing in our respiration lecture, and we talked about exhale on the exertion. So you your exertion here is the sit up. So breath out as you come out, breathe in as you go down. Good work.

We've only got 20 seconds to go. When I say "we," obviously I mean you, because I'm just checking the clock. But somebody has got to do it; it may as well be me. Come on guys, hang in there, how are we doing at home? If you need to have a quick rest, you can, but please join back in. Don't forget, we've only got 10 more seconds and then you can have a rest. Good work. Come on. Fabulous, we're nearly there. And take a little rest. Well done, get yourselves walking about.

We're going to go for a little speed skate movement. So keep yourselves moving, but keep your eyes on me. We're straddling the step, and this time we're literally going to speed skate from side to side. Get that heel up, over the board, let's get some lateral motion. And this is, if you remember, our balance lecture; we talked about dynamic equilibrium. What we're doing here is controlling this movement. Remember, it's one of our skill-related fitness components. We talked about agility, we talked about dynamic balance. What we've got to control here is that whole lateral movement, that deceleration, and back into acceleration to the other side. Secret to that is bending down on the knee, loading up the muscle so that we can go back in the other direction. Guys, let's get straddled, that doesn't sound right, does it? But you know what I mean. Let's lift one leg, get ready, and let's go. Side to side.

Let's go, come on. Up. Like you're speed skating. Get those arms moving, side-to-side. Come on, get those arms moving. Can we go quicker? What's happening here? It seems to have gone in slow motion in the back. Come on, let's go. You've done 20 seconds already. Come on guys, beautiful. Shift the body right across, swing the arms across. Good, the bigger the movement, the more calories we're going to burn. So make it big make it big. You're halfway, come on. Looking good. And looking very graceful. I think we might be calling you the Torvill and Dean of the—did Torvill and Dean translate? I'm sure you know what I mean here. Looking good. Speed skating. Come on. Although I don't remember Ravel's Bolero looking quite like this. But it doesn't matter; we're nearly there. Five seconds keep going at home, 5 seconds. And take a rest, well done. Keep your feet moving, take some deep breaths.

I'm going to show you the next exercise. We're going to move on here and put a little bit of work into the core muscles, but also particularly into the obliques at the side. What I'm going to do is take one leg out, like so, the other leg you can put it wherever is comfortable, in front, behind, wherever works for you. I'm going to drop the hips, I'm going to do a hip hitch, lift it up, and drop it down. Lift it up, and drop it down.

I'm looking to avoid any rotation here, and really get some work into here. Stay long from the top of your head down through your tailbone, and down to your heel. Keep a nice long position. Drop the hip, lift it up, drop the hip, no rotation, just drop and lift. Let's face outwards, guys, beautiful. There you go. Are we set? Get yourselves balanced. And hang on, hang on, let's go.

Drop the hip, and lift. Drop the hip, and lift. Beautiful. Now this one is a much smaller movement than most of the other exercises you've been doing, but it's a really good exercise to work those core muscles, keep your abdominals pulled in tight all the time, but also really working into the obliques here. You can really feel now how they work on stabilizing your lumbo-pelvic region, keeping your hips in that position. How are we doing? We're halfway through. How are you doing at home? Great stuff, keep going. Try to keep your breathing relaxed. Try to keep your breathing constant while you're doing this. We've only got 20 seconds to go. Keep going. That's beautiful. How are you doing at home? Looking good. You'll be pleased to know that we've only got a couple more exercises to do, so hang in there you can do this. What a great way to spend 30 minutes. Fabulous. We've only got 10 more seconds. Was that a moan and a groan there I thought I heard? That's why they haven't got mics, so you can't hear them complaining. And take a rest there, well done. Walk about, get your feet moving. Well done. Can you feel that? Just nod. I'm going to take that as a yes. Beautiful.

We're going to move into our last little cardio, and this is, and we've saved the best until last, it has to be said. So we're going to do, is it the Wizard of Oz? It's the Wizard of Oz, clicking your heels together. And you might want to wish that you were somewhere else when we do this. Because what we're going to do is click the heels together over the step. So basically whatever energy you've got left, I think we're going to squeeze it out now. Remember we said when it comes to fitness, the more you put in, the more you're going to get out. So I'm going to let you probably have about 10 seconds of getting into the rhythm of the technique, and then we're just going to go like crazy. Okay, so facing outwards, straddle the step, please. Are we ready? Okay.

Now, bearing in mind this is the last little cardio one we're going to do, and then we're just doing that hip hitch on the other side, and we're done. So whatever you've got, I want it now. Let's go. Up, jump touch those heels together. Touch. Yeah I think in that rest in between there, did you want us to bring you a coffee or something? Just get straight on with the next one, no rest in between. Come on. How are we doing at home? Click those heels together. I'm sure the Wizard of Oz never looked like this, did it? I'm sure it didn't. Come on, up. Click those heels. You'll be pleased to know we are now halfway. Come on. Landing quietly if we can please. The softer the landings, the easier it is on the joints. Come on. Let's go. Little bit quicker. Come on, stop pretending you can't hear me, I know you can. A little bit quicker. Good, last 20 seconds. You'll never do this again, come on.

Actually, I hope you will. Just trying to make it sound easier. Let's go, we're into the last 10 seconds, come on guys. Come on, how are you doing at home? This should be getting close to, we should be on about 9.5 out of 10 here, definitely last couple, and take a rest there. Keep your feet moving. How did you do? I can feel that. I don't know why I'm saying that, I wasn't doing anything; they were doing all the work.

Okay, so, we're then onto the other side. So you guys are going to be facing inwards this time, while we go onto our last little exercise. The hip hitch, remember this time, drop it down. Lift it up, really getting into the core muscles, really getting into those oblique muscles, so let's set ourselves up; I think we're facing in this time. One hand down, you'll be pleased to know we're nearly there, guys. Okay. Hopefully I'm not stretching our relationship too much in asking you for 1 more minute, please. Let's go.

These guys will never speak to me again after this. Drop the hip down and lift it up. Beautiful. Was that a grimace or a smile? I think it's a smile, because we're nearly there, it's the last exercise. Good, well done. Well done. That's not real sweat, we just, that's makeup, that's how we made that look. Come on. But if you're getting a little bit of sweat on at home, that's good. Remember we talked about waste products being carbon dioxide, and water, being heat, this is what's happening. Come on, we're halfway through. You've got 30 seconds, and then you'll never have to listen to me ever again. Come on. But you will, because you're going to play this again, because as you get fitter, this is going to get easier. And who knows, you might build up from 1 minute to 1 minute and 1/2, or you might actually do the whole thing in 2 circuits. Who knows?

Come on, we've only got a few seconds, and literally I mean a few seconds. Guys you're doing really well. Really well. And take a rest there, well done. If you want to sit yourself on the step, and just have a couple of little stretches, you're done.

So what we're going to do now is go down into a little cool down and stretch. You'll see we're doing a couple of mobilizing moves, just like we did at the beginning, and then we're going to have that stretch of the major muscle groups, we're going to get into the quads, because the legs have done some work, we're getting into the hamstrings, we'll have those little stretches, and remember if you're not too sure on those stretch techniques, we've got that flexibility workout for you, you can do them then.

So we've got nothing more than a step, that's all it is a little step platform. You might have one gathering dust in the garage, you might have one sitting around in the cupboard under the stairs, it's going to be one of those places you don't often look for it. It will be covered in dust, but they're a great tool to use. If you haven't got one, they're easy to get a hold of, they're not too expensive, and as you can see, all those cardio, all those strength exercises, you're going to get some results with this. So get yourself a step, get sweating.

Dumbbell Workout
Lecture 28

A dumbbell workout is another great home workout. If you don't have dumbbells, they are relatively inexpensive to purchase, but you can also improvise with a few cans of beans or a couple bags of sugar. Weight training brings a number of health benefits, including reduced risk of osteoporosis, lowered blood pressure, and shorter gastrointestinal transit time. When it comes to changing your shape, weight training is the top choice due to its effect on raising your metabolic rate, which helps you burn more energy quickly. In addition, it can completely resculpt your silhouette.

Guidelines

- Before you begin this workout, remember that muscle training comes with a few common myths, including the myth that women will become big and bulky if they do weight training. In fact, the key to muscle growth is the testosterone hormone, and women don't naturally possess this in their bodies in high enough concentrations to produce bulky arms or shoulders.

- To ensure you get the most out of this workout, keep in mind that the longer a muscle is forced to work against resistance, the more damage there will be to the muscle fibers and, therefore, the greater the adaptations will be in their structure. Therefore, the harder you work, the better the results you will achieve.

- This workout involves a continuous rhythm pattern, and the following pattern of counts has been devised to enable you to exhaust all the muscle fibers. For each exercise, you're going to do 1 count up and 1 count down 8 times, 2 counts up and 2 counts down 4 times, 3 counts up and 1 count down 4 times, and 7 counts up and 1 count down 2 times.

- To help you with the rhythm, you'll need some music playing that's ideally in the medium range of beats per minute. If the music is too fast, the singles—1 count up and 1 count down—will be impossible to complete, ending up with short movements. If the music is too slow, the 7 counts up and 1 count down will take an eternity—probably leaving you in pain.

- Beginners should aim for 1 to 2 sets of each exercise, and advanced people can try to do 3 sets of each exercise.

- The amount of weight you should use when starting with dumbbells will typically be lighter than what you will be using once you master the techniques involved with weight lifting. Work with the heaviest weight that you can manage—while still maintaining good form. Switch to a lower weight if you reach a point of failure, which involves not being able to complete the repetition or maintain correct form. The best way to determine what weight you should be using for each exercise is simply trial and error. Start with a light weight, and make adjustments as necessary.

- The following exercises cover your whole body, alternating working the upper and lower body. This results in shifting the blood from one part of the body to the other, which will lead to a greater calorie burn. In addition, while one part of the body is resting, you can work another part of the body, so you won't need to rest in between exercises, allowing you to get more work done in a shorter amount of time.

- First, take about 5 minutes to warm up.

- The following exercises include sections that focus on the legs and back, shoulders and legs, and then chest and abdominals.

Squats
- When you pick up your weights, make sure to bend your knees, keeping your abdominals in tight.

- Keep your shoulders back and down.

- Your feet should be about hip-width apart, and your heels should be down on the floor.

- By the time you get to the last count—7 counts up and 1 count down—you should feel the muscles working hard in the legs and buttocks.

Bent-Over Row
- For this exercise, you're going to bring your dumbbells in front of your body, keeping your knees slightly bent.

- Keep your abdominals in tight, and hinge from the hip.

Always be sure to bend your knees when picking up your weights to begin your workout.

- You're going to lean forward and drop your dumbbells down to just below your knees.

- Don't let your back become rounded.

- Keep your elbows up and high.

- This exercise works the upper back—especially between the shoulder blades—when squeezing the rhomboids together. You're also working your biceps and the back of your shoulder.

- At the end of this exercise, straighten yourself up, roll your shoulders, and give your legs a little shake.

Lunge: Right
- Start with your right leg forward and your left leg behind your body, remaining on the ball of your left foot.

- Make sure your shoulders are back and down, and then drop your knee down.

- Keep your abs in tight.

- This exercise really works the front of your right thigh.

Prone Fly: Left
- For this exercise, you're going to drop the dumbbell in your right hand and rest your right elbow on your right knee.

- With a slight bend in your elbow, lift the dumbbell in your left hand, squeezing your shoulder blades together.

- Keep your hips, chest, and shoulders facing the front.

- This exercise really works the back of the shoulder and upper back.

- Keep your abs in tight, making sure not to twist your body.

Lunge: Left
- This exercise requires both dumbbells, so pick up the one you dropped for the last exercise.

- This time, start with your left leg forward and your right leg behind your body, remaining on the ball of your right foot.

- Remember to keep your shoulders back and down and to not twist your right leg on the lunge.

- Keep your chest and head lifted.

- Squeeze your buttocks for extra power.

Prone Fly: Right
- If you're starting to get fatigued, switch to a slightly lighter weight. It's important to get your form correct.

- This time, you're going to drop the dumbbell in your left hand and rest your left elbow on your left knee.

- With a slight bend in your elbow, lift the dumbbell in your right hand, squeezing your shoulder blades together.

- Don't let your body twist.

- This exercise really works the back of the shoulder.

- Remember to keep your hips square to the front and your abs in tight.

- At the end of this exercise, you can drop your dumbbell and take a short break. Dry your body off if you need to, and take a sip of water.

Plié

- Be careful when picking up your dumbbells.

- Your feet are going to be wide, and your knees and toes are going to point outward. You're going to rest the dumbbells on top of your thighs and push your knees out, following the line of the toes.

- In addition to working the front and back of your thighs, you're also starting to work the inner thighs—the adductors.

- Keep your abs in tight, chest up, and heels down.

Lateral Raise

- Your feet should be hip-width apart, and your knees and elbows should be slightly bent.

- When you lift your arms up to the sides, they should reach to about the level of your head.

- Keep your abs in tight.

- The exercise works your shoulders—specifically, your deltoids.

Plié

- Remember to keep your feet wide and to rest your dumbbells on top of your thighs, making sure your knees and toes are pointing outward.

- When you sit down, don't stick your backside out; try to keep it tucked underneath.

- Keep your abs in tight, and you'll start to feel this exercise in your inner thighs, the front and back of your thighs, and your buttocks.

- Dip your body as low as you can comfortably go.

- Do this exercise slowly; you don't have to come back up too soon.

Shoulder Press and Twist

- Start with slightly bent knees. This position protects you from swaying backward and forward, which puts a lot of strain on the lower back.

- Bring your dumbbells up—with your palms facing your body and your knuckles facing outward. As you press up, twist your palms to the front.

- Don't lock your elbows at the top of the movement.

- You should have a controlled momentum throughout this exercise.

- Use your knees to carefully put your dumbbells down.

- Dry your body off if you need to, and take a sip of water.

Press-Up

- Start by getting down onto the floor or a mat in an all-fours position.

- You're going to use your dumbbells as a rest for your press-up position, so both hands are going to be on your dumbbells.

- Begin on your knees or in the full press-up position—whichever you feel comfortable with. The full press-up position becomes difficult by the end of the exercise.

When doing a crunch, support the weight of your head with your hands, and keep your feet hip-width apart.

- Your slow counts should be on the way up.

- Keep your abdominals in tight throughout the exercise.

- Your elbows are out to the sides, but don't lock your arms when you reach the top of the movement.

Sit-Up
- From the press-up position, you're going to flip yourself over to work on your abdominals. Basically, you'll be doing a simple crunch.

- Put your hands behind your head to support the weight of your head—taking the stress off the neck—and keep your elbows back.

- Your feet should be about hip-width apart.

- Your slow counts should be on the way up.

- Squeeze your abdominals, lifting your shoulders off the floor or mat.

- Focus on the abdominal muscles, concentrating on squeezing your ribs closer to your hips.

Press-Up
- Turn yourself over from the sit-up position to set up for the press-up position.

- This time, your slow counts will be on the way down—rather than on the way up.

- Remember to keep your abdominals in tight.

- Maintain a comfortable curve in your lower spine.

- Remember not to lock your arms at the top of the movement.

Sit-Up
- Again, turn yourself over from the press-up position and put your hands behind your head. Keep your feet about hip-width apart, making sure you are in a comfortable lower spine position.

- This time, your slow counts will be on the way down—rather than on the way up.

- Focus on pulling your ribs to your hips. Imagine that your abdominals have a spring in them, and squeeze the 2 ends together.

Cooldown
- At the end of your last sit-up, pull your knees into your chest and rest.

- Then, take the time to do some stretching.

- At this point—when your body temperature is high—you should hold your stretches for about 15 to 30 seconds, which will help you to gradually cool down.

Dumbbell Workout
Lecture 28—Transcript

Hi, and welcome to your dumbbell workout. Now another home workout, the dumbbell workout, is great because you don't have to have dumbbells, you might have some sitting around in your garage gathering dust, although relatively cheap to get a hold of anyway, but if you don't have them, this workout you can improvise with a couple of tins of beans, couple of bags of sugar, something like that.

As we've already seen in other lectures in this series, weight training brings a number of health benefits, including reduced risk of osteoporosis, lowered blood pressure and shorter gastro-intestinal transit time, but when it comes to changing your shape it really is the number 1 choice due to its effect on raising your metabolic rate, so helping you to burn more energy quickly and also it can seriously re-sculpt your silhouette. Now who wouldn't want to drop some fat from here and maybe firm up a little more there?

It's important at this juncture, to remember that muscle training, comes with a few common myths, probably the most important one being that women will bulk up, become big and bulky if they do weight training. We've looked at this before, the key to muscle growth is the testosterone hormone and women simply don't naturally possess this in their bodies in high enough concentrations to produce Arnie's arms or Sly's shoulders.

However to ensure you get the best from this workout, we're going to work on a principle called Time Under Tension theory (TUT) the TUT theory. This states the longer a muscle is forced to work against resistance, the more damage will be caused to the muscle fibers and therefore the greater the adaptations in their structure. So, to put it plainly, the harder you work the better the results you will achieve, but if you've followed the other lectures in this series, you'll already know that.

Now what we're going to use here is a continuous rhythm pattern. So this following pattern of counts has been devised to enable that we exhaust all the muscle fibers. And so it's important to follow this count. Now I'm going to explain this to you very briefly but you'll get the hang of it as we go along.

We're going to do eight 1s, we're going to do four 2s, we're going to do four 3s, and then two 7s. If you kind of remember that, you'll get the hang of it as we go along.

To help you with the rhythm you'll need your MP3 player or some tracks playing, some music playing, that's ideally in the mid-range of beats per minute. If the music is too fast, the singles, the eight 1s we do will be impossible to complete, ending up with short movements. And if the music is too slow, when you come to the 7s, they'll take an eternity. Probably leaving you in tears.

Beginners should be aiming for 1–2 sets; advanced people to progress this, you can do these exercises 3 sets of each exercise. What we're going to do, are just 3 sets for you today that are going to cover your whole body, and the beauty of this is we're going to work upper and lower body alternating. The beauty of that is that we start to shift the blood from one part of the body to the other, and that will lead to a greater calorie burn, but also while one part of the body is resting, we can work another part of the body, and in that case, we won't need the resting between so we can get more work done in a shorter time. Sounds good, the high speed train.

Let's get some music and get started. Remember you need about a 5 minute warm up like the guys have hopefully done behind me right now, and we're going to start with a set of legs and back, so the music starts now.

Be careful how you pick up your weights, bend your knees please. Take a hold of them; keep your abdominals in really tight. Take them to the side. Shoulders are back and down, abdominals are pulled in. Feet about hip width. We're going to squat down, single count. There's down, and up. And again, let's go. Down, have we got the hang of that? Okay let's go with our single count. Down, and 2, beautiful, and 3, keep going, and 4, remember we want 8 of these, there's 5, abs in tight, 6, heels down, and 7, now we're going to slow the count. Two counts down. One, 2, and up. Down, sitting down, keep the abs in tight, 2 counts. One, 2, and 1 more of those please, 1, 2.

Now we get our 3s, 3 counts down. One, 2, and 1 up. One, 2, 3. How are you doing at home? Let's go. One, 2, 3, and again please, 1, 2. Now the

7s. Slowly, slowly, go 1, 2, shoulders back and down, 5, 6, 7, do that again please, let's go. One, 2, 3, can we feel that in the legs, can we feel that in the buttocks? And press up beautiful, hold it.

Give the legs a little shake. Bring the dumbbells round in front, the knees are slightly bent. Keep the abdominals tight, now we're going to hinge from the hip. You're going to take a lean forwards, drop the dumbbells down to just below the knees. Don't let the back round. Keep the abdominals in tight, tilt the top of the head towards me. Here we go, get ready to row.

Five, 6, 7 go lift, and down, elbows up and high, up, beautiful. Abs are in tight. Lift. Elbows high, make sure you're leaning forwards. Top of the head to me. Can we go for our 2 counts please? Up, 2, and down, now we're really working into the upper back. Two, and down. Between the shoulder blades, the rhomboids, squeeze them together. Up, 2, what about 3 counts? One, 2, 3, and down. How you doing? Up, 2, little bit of work into the bicep at the front of the arm, up, 2, 3, and also the rear of the shoulder, up, 2, 3, shall we try 7s? It's not really a question, up, 2, 3, 4, 5, 6, 7. One more time, let's go up, 2, 3, how you doing, 4, 5, 6, 7 down. Straighten yourself up; give your shoulders a little roll, give the legs a little shake.

Okay so we've done legs, back, let's go straight back to legs. Put your right leg forwards, left leg behind. On the ball of the foot. Shoulders are back and down, we're going to lunge, drop the knee down. We're going to lunge. Drop the knee down. Down, and lift, down, beautiful, keep going, down, fabulous, keep going, 4 more please, down, how you doing? Down, good, abs in tight. Two counts this time please, down, down and up, up, slow down. Down, down, and up, beautiful. And down, down, working into the front of the thigh, and again. Down, down, 3 counts down, 1, 2, 3, see how we're on the ball of the foot. Three, 2, 1, and up. Three, 2, 1, and up, beautiful. Three, 2, 1, can I take 7s? Seven, 6, 5, 4, 3, 2, 1, 1 more of those please. Seven, 6, can we feel anything in the legs yet? I hope so, down, down, up.

Beautiful, this is what we do, bring that foot up slightly. You're going to put this dumbbell down. You're going to rest your elbow on there, right on right. Keep your hips, chest, shoulders facing the front, drop it down, elbows slightly bent, get ready to prone fly. Lift it up. Lift, up, really working into the back of the shoulder, upper back, lift, how we doing? Lift. Lift, okay now it's getting tough, 2 counts. Up, 2, down, 2, up, abs are tight, press into this knee, make sure you're supporting your weight, don't twist your body. Up, 2, and down. Three counts up. One, 2, 3, and again, up, 2, 3, come on, you can do this. Up, 2, 3, 1 more, let's go. Up, 2, 3, you know what's after 3s, 7. Up, 2, 3, 4, I should have gone with a lighter weight, 6, 7, let's go, we can do this, up, 2, this is real sweat you know, and up, 5, 6, 7, beautiful, pick up the other dumbbell, up we get.

Swap over legs, your upper body can rest, because you're going on to legs. You've now got your left leg forwards, right foot on the ball of the foot, shoulders back and down. Remember not to twist this rear leg on the lunge. Chest lifted, head up, in 5, 6, 7 go single. Two, good, 3, looking good, give me 4 more of those please, 4, 3, and 2, shoulders back and down, 2 counts. Down, down, up, up. Down, working into the front of the thing, 2 counts, down, into the hamstrings at the back of the thigh, and down, down. Three counts down, 3, 2 1, and up. Beautiful. Three, 2, 1, squeezing into the buttocks as well. Three, 2, 1, and up, can we feel this in the legs? Three, 2, 1, 7 counts, come on. Down, 2, 3, 4, 5, 6, 7, you've got 1 more of those. Go down 1, 2, 3, 4, smile, 5, 6, 7. Well done, well done, good work for the legs.

Now we're going to move to the prone fly, on the other side. If you're starting to get fatigued, like the guys are doing here, this would be a good time to swap to slightly lighter weight. It's important to get your form dead right. Now to set this up, put the other 1 down, rest your left arm on the left leg, drop the right hand down, with a slight bend in the elbow, get ready to lift in 5 6 7, let's go. Single, and down, up, squeezing the shoulder blades together. Don't let your body twist. Four more please. And up, keep going, 2 more, up, 1 more. Two counts this time, we lift, up, up, and down, beautiful, don't let the body move. Up, up, and down, really working into the back of the shoulder. Up, and down, down, and into the center of the back, beautiful. Three counts, this time we squeeze up, 2, 3, and keep those hips square to the front. Up, 2, 3, beautiful, can we feel this working? Up, 2, 3, and down, don't twist. Up, 2, you know what comes next, 7 please. Up, 2, 3, come on, 4, 5, 6, 1 more, abs are tight. Up, 2, keep your chest facing the floor, don't twist, up, up, beautiful.

The good news is you can put that down, take a little rest, get yourself toweled down, get yourself a sip of water, now's a good time to have a quick break, that's legs and back. We're going to shift on now and do our second set which is going to be legs and shoulders. A little bit of extra work in the hips and thighs, why not?

Okay so let's grab those dumbbells please guys. Careful in how you pick them up. The feet are going to go wide, the knees and the toes are going to point outwards. We're going to rest the dumbbells on top of the thighs, right at the top. Get ready. For our plié, push the knees out, down, and 2, now the great thing about this, as well as working the front and back of the thigh, we're starting to get into the inner thigh as well, the adductors. Beautiful. Two counts please, 1, 2, and down. Abs are tight, heels down. Look how the knees follow the line of the toes. Down, and up, fabulous. Down, down, 3 counts down, slowly. One, 2, come on, get your money's worth, and up. Down, can we feel that in the legs? Let's go, down, chest lifted, and again, down, now you're probably getting the hang of this by now. After 3s, we've got 7, 6, 5, come on, 4, 3, grit your teeth, 2, 1, 1 more of those please. Let's go 1, 2, 3, 4, 5, 6, 7. Beautiful, walk your feet in slightly.

Hip width, knees are slightly bent, elbows slightly bent by the side, get ready for your lateral raise, we're going to lift the arms up to the side, just about to head level, and we're also going to tilt the little finger slightly higher. Get ready, in 4, and 3, abs are tight, let's lift. Up, and 2, how we doing? Working into those shoulders. The legs are getting a rest, give me 4 more. Four, and 3, keep it going, and 2, and 1. Two counts this time. Up, up, and down, down, knees are slightly bent. Up, up, and down, down. Let's go up, up, and down, down. Up, up, 3 counts up go. Up, 2, working into those deltoids, let's go, up, 2, 3. Two more of those, we can do it, up, 2, abs are tight, and again. Up, 2, 7s, we can do this. Up, 2, grit your teeth, 3, come on, 4, look at that shake, 5, 6, 7, 1 more of those. At this point, I'd normally say do you want fries with that shake, but I won't. And up, and up, and up, and up, back to the pliés.

Legs wide, please, rest the dumbbells on top of your thighs, make sure the knees and toes are pointing out, your shoulders can have a little bit of a rest while we work back into the legs. Now remember, when we sit down, don't stick the back side out, try and keep the back side down underneath, make sure the knees follow the line of the toes. In 4, in 3, in 2, let's see what you can do. Sit down, down, beautiful, abs tight, super, can we feel something in the inner thighs? Down, as well as the front and back of the thighs? As well as the buttocks? Two counts please, 1, 2, and up, 2, nice and low. As far as you can comfortably go. And again, 1, and 2, and up, last time. Now we're going to change things slightly, down for 1, up for 3. Down, 1, 2, 3, so the reverse of what we did last time. Up, 2, 3, hope I didn't startle anyone there when I just yelled. And up, down, 2, down for 1, up for 7, let's go. Down, slowly, don't get up there too soon. Up, no prizes for coming in first, 1 more time, down we go. Down, up 1, 2, 3, 4, 5, how you doing at home? Beautiful.

Walk them in. Slightly bent knees, and reason we bend the knees slightly is what that does is protect us from swaying backwards and forwards, which puts a lot of strain on the lower back. So the knees are always slightly bent. Bring the dumbbells up, palms facing you, knuckles facing me. Now all we're going to do on this press is to get a little twist. As we press up, we twist the palms to the front. Get ready, 4, 3, 2, shoulder press. Up, 2, how we doing? Three, don't lock the arms out at the top, keep going, 4 more, 4, 3, good, looking to not quite lock the elbows at the top. Two counts please. Up, 2, and down, beautiful, controlled momentum. Up, 2, see how the elbows, stay slightly soft at the end. Up, and 2, and down, and again. Up, 2, down, up for 3. One, 2, 3, and down. Up, 2, 3, come on we can do this. Up, 2, 3, 1 more of those. Up, you know what comes next. Seven, 7, 7 up, 2, 3, 4, 5, 6, 7, 1 more, 1 more.

Go up, 2, 3, come on 4, 5, 6, 7, and take it down, put the dumbbells down careful how you do it, use the knees. Get yourself a sip of water, towel yourself down, get ready for your last set. So that was your shoulders and legs, we've done back and legs, what should we work on next? What about chest and abdominals? A problem region for a lot of us. So we're going to get down onto the mat, onto an all-fours position please.

So what we're going to do here is use the dumbbells as a rest for our press up position. So the hands are going to be on the dumbbells. We're going to be on the knees or in the full press up position, whichever you feel confident with, I would warn you, full press up position does get tough. Either way, whether you're in the full position, or on the knees, abdominals are in tight, the elbows are going out to the side, press, and don't lock the arms when we get to the top. Are we ready? Set up your position, maybe a full position, don't know why I'm looking at you, or maybe on the knees, I'm definitely looking at you. In 5, 6, 7, go down, and press. Two, and 3, how we doing? Give me 4 more of those please. There's 4, up, 3, come on, 2, 2 counts down, 2 up. One, 2, up, 2, good. Down, 2, and up, for 2. Down, down, up, up, good. Down, keep the abdominals in tight all the time. Down for 3, down, down, down, and up. Down, down, down, and up. Come on, down, down, down, and up. Keep those abs in tight. Down, down, 7s. One, 2, 3, 4, 5, 6, 7, 1 more, let's go. One, 2, you can do this, 3, 4, 5, how are we doing at home? Seven, beautiful, we can take a little rest there.

You're going to flip yourself over, feet this end, head there. So we're going to work into the abdominals now, little bit of work, a simple crunch. All we're going to do is a simple crunch. But we're still going to use that timing, that count. So for this exercise, I want to make sure you've got your hands back, elbows back, the hands are there to support the weight of the head, take the stress off the neck. So lay yourselves back down please. Fabulous. Hands behind your head. Feet are about hip width apart. Now all we're looking for is a squeeze in the abdominals, to lift the shoulders off the mat, that's all we're going to do. Get ready.

Using the same count we've been using, focus on your muscles in the tummy, in 5, 6, 7 sit up, and down. Two, and down. Up we go. Up, and down. Up, 4 more. Four, concentrate on squeezing the ribs closer to the hips. Up, 2 counts now please. Up, up, and down, down, come on. Up, up, and down, looking good, let's go. Up, up, and down, keep your elbows back. Up, up, and down, 2 more. Up, up, and down, 1 more. Up, up, okay 3 counts. Three counts up, we go up, 2, 3, and down. Up, 2, 3, and down. Up, 2, 3, and down, last one. Up, 2, now you know what comes after 3s, let's go. Up, 2, 3, 4, 5, 6, 7, and down, 1 more. Up, 2, keep those elbows back, 4, 5, 6, 7, and down. Beautiful, turn yourselves over. We've only got 2 more things to do, that's 1 more set of the press ups, we're going to do the slow count in the other direction, 1 more set of sit ups, then we're done.

Looking good guys, looking good. This is not fake sweat, you know that. Set yourselves up for the press up position. Remember the tips, abdominals are in tight, nice little comfortable curve in the lower spine, remember not to lock the arms out at the top. Are we ready? In 4, and 3, and 2, press ups, let's go. Down, and press. And 2, good. Good form. Down, keep your abdominals in tight. One more, 2 counts please. Down, down, up, and up. Down, down, up, and again. We go down, down, and up, up. Down, down, down for 1 up for 3. Down, up 1, 2, I saw that. Down, up 1, 2, 3. Down, up 1, 2, 3. Down, up 1, 2, now it gets tough. Down, up 1, 2, 3, 4, 5, 6, come on 1 more of those. Down, up 1, 2, 3, 4, 5, 6, 7. Beautiful, turn yourselves over.

It's time for your sit ups, last set, this is the last exercise you're going to do. We're going to do exactly the same thing but this time, your slow counts will be on the way down, rather than on the way up. Just like we did with the press ups. Hands behind the head, beautiful, feet are about hip width apart, make sure you've got that comfortable position, neutral spine, that comfortable lower spine position, for 4, for 3, for 2, let's go. We sit up, and down. Two, and down. Beautiful. Focus on pulling the ribs to the hips. Really focus on a spring in the abdominals, squeeze it together. And down. Two counts, slowly. Up, up, down, down. Up, up, and down, and down. Up, and up, and down, and down. Last time, up, and up, and down, now hold it there, we're going up for 1 and down for 3. Okay get ready, get right up, up, down 1, 2, 3. Up, good, 1, 2, 3. Sit up, down 1, down 2, down 3. Sit up, 1, 2, up for 1 down for 7. Up, down 1, 2, 3, 4, 5, 6, 1 more, you can do it. Up, down 1, 2, don't die on me yet, 4, 5, 6, beautiful, and hold it there, pull your knees into your chest and have a little rest.

You'll be pleased to know you're done. Chest and abs, chest and abs, chest and abs. Great little exercise there, the press up, not just the chest, you're also getting into those trouble areas, into the triceps. So you've got a total body workout there. What we're going to do now is possibly fall asleep. We're going to have a little stretch, and remember it's a good idea if you can't remember any stretches, to look at that flexibility DVD. You've got that whole workout there with the range of stretches, you need to be holding your stretches at this point when you're nice and warm for about 15–30 seconds; that would be ideal. And that will help you gradually cool down, I hope you enjoyed the workout. Well done.

Combat Workout
Lecture 29

Whether you're a hardcore combat fanatic or have no boxing or martial arts experience, you can expect to get great results from this combat workout. Combining cardio, punching, and kicking rounds to burn calories with unique sculpting moves, this routine is guaranteed to reshape your whole body while helping you improve your suppleness, enhance your concentration skills, and give you extra confidence. In addition to the health-related fitness components associated with this workout—including cardio, endurance, and flexibility gains—you will also be honing various skill-related fitness components, including agility, balance, coordination, power, and reaction time.

Guidelines

- It's always important to do about a 5-minute warm-up before you start that includes some gentle movements—such as arm swings, knee lifts, and shoulder circles—to mobilize your joints. You should also march in place to get your heart rate up slightly and to begin to increase your core body temperature, which helps to reduce your risk of injury.

- If it's possible, check your technique in a mirror—particularly your posture.

- Be careful not to round your shoulders, and keep your abs pulled in at all times.

- When you're kicking, take a slight lean backward, but don't sink into your hips.

- Be careful to control your momentum.

- Don't lock your arms or knees on the kicks; keep them soft and control them.

The 3 Blocks

Rising Block
- Start with your right leg forward. Bring your hands up, in loose fists, to your face, and practice your mean face.

- Then, bounce in place. If you want to keep the intensity fairly moderate, just bounce a little using your legs. If you want to increase the intensity and burn more calories, bounce on your toes. Either way, keep your hands up to your face to defend it.

- Every technique that you will learn starts from the feet, so you will be working from the ground up.

- Each technique is a whole-body workout because for any technique to be effective, you have to use your whole body.

- To start, push your right foot forward, along with your hips, moving into a lunge. Then, add a rising block to defend your face. There should be some tension in your arms.

- Then, increase it to double time. Imagine someone is trying to take a swing at you, so you've got to defend your face.

- Keep your abs in tight throughout the movements.

- Take a short walk around. Get your breath back.

- Switch legs. Put your left leg forward, and repeat the same movements. Make sure your muscles are doing some work.

Cross
- To defend your body, move your arm across your chest. Start with one foot in front of the other, and push into a lunge using your hips.

- Then, increase the speed to double time. Push your arm across your chest with a little tension in your arm. Make sure you keep your arm in line with your chest. Don't bring your arm too high; remember, you're defending your chest.

- Keep your abs in tight throughout the movements. All the power is coming from the middle of your body.

- Switch legs, and repeat the movements. Regain your breath in between.

Down

- Start by pushing your right foot forward. Make sure your hips come with your foot, and go down with a little dip.

- Don't lock your arm; keep it slightly bent.

- Imagine that someone is taking a kick straight at you. You have to block it.

- You can keep your other hand anywhere you like—just keep it close.

- Increase your speed to double time.

- Switch legs, and repeat.

Combination

- Combine all 3 blocks: rise, cross, down. Once you have the moves down, increase the pace.

- Get on your toes if you aren't already.

- Double time.

- Switch legs, and repeat.

- Take a quick break, and go get a sip of water.

The 4 Punches

Jab

- To generate the power that's all in the middle of the body, you need to start from the ground up. Put your right foot forward, and bring your hands up to your face.

- Make sure you're taking your whole body with you; bring your rear hip forward. There's also some work going on in your glutei.

- Pretend that you are placing your right hand on your opponent's chin. Make sure your punch is accurate, directing it straight down the middle.

- Make sure your arm doesn't lock. Next, snap your arm back.

- Make sure there's some tension in your abs.

- Keep your shoulders down and relaxed.

- Double time.

- Switch legs, and repeat. Take a rest in between.

Cross

- The important thing is to get your body in the right position. Start by squatting down a little into your lunge.

- Twist your rear foot—your left foot to start—which allows you to twist your body with some power.

- Your left hand goes straight down the middle to the chin of your opponent. Add a little bit of a snap to your punch.

- This exercise works your core and your obliques.

- Double time.

- Switch legs, and repeat. Take a quick break.

Hook
- This time, twist your right leg on the ball of the right foot.

- As your body turns, you can put some power into a hook. Make a round movement with your elbow up high. You're aiming for the side of your opponent's head—the side of the jaw.

- Keep your shoulders down and your head up tall.

- Double time.

- Switch legs, and repeat.

Uppercut
- This punch is similar to the cross. Your left foot twists forward, but instead of just turning your body to the front, lift your body up, gaining power from your legs.

- Add the uppercut, which is aimed at the underside of your opponent's chin. You might want to picture someone in front of you that you really don't like.

- This exercise works your quads, hamstrings, and glutei.

- Double time.

- Switch legs, and repeat.

Combination
- Put all 4 punches together. Start with your right leg forward. Slowly bring your hands up and do the punches in order.

- This portion of the workout will help the skill-related fitness component of coordination.

- Remember that all your power comes from your toes.

- Don't get flustered if you get a few of the movements wrong. As long as you're moving, you'll be improving.

- After you have the movements down, speed up your pace.

- Switch legs, and repeat.

- Take a quick break, and get a drink of water.

The 3 Kicks

Front Kick

- Each technique is going to be set up with a step. You're going to start nice and slowly.

- Get your hips in the right position.

- Take a step with your left foot, and lift your right leg into the space in front of you. Then, bring your right leg down and back into the original position.

- When you step, make sure you point your toes to the front because your hips, chest, and shoulders need to be facing the front. The power is in your hips, so you want to push them forward.

© iStockphoto/Thinkstock.

When kicking, make sure that you don't lock your kicking knee or your standing knee.

- Tilt your head back slightly so that you maintain a long line through the spine.

- Next, add the front kick. You'll be kicking with the ball of your foot, so you pull the toes back. The kick should not only be going up in the air, but it should also be going forward. There should be a little bit of a snap as your leg comes back to you.

- Keep your hands up and your abs in tight. Keep your shoulders down.

- Double time.

- Take a deep breath, and switch legs. Repeat.

- Fighters and boxers normally have a stronger, more flexible, easier to coordinate side, so you may notice as you swap from side to side that one side is not as good as the other. That just means that you need more work on it.

Side Kick
- Turn your feet and body to the side, but keep your head and hands toward the front. Take a little squat down.

- This time, you're going to take a step forward with your back leg and then lift the front leg, pointing the knee toward the side.

- When you add the kick—nice and low at first—this position allows you to really push with the side of your foot and hips.

- Make sure your knee comes back after your kick in a controlled way.

- Act as if you're pushing somebody away with your kick.

- Keep your hands up and your shoulders down.

- Double time.

- Switch legs, and repeat.

Round Kick

- Start with your right leg forward, and add a little bounce to your lunge. Turn yourself sideways, keeping your head and hands facing the front. Step forward—just as you did for the side kick—but lift your leg into a hurdle position.

- Your knee should be slightly higher than your ankle, which sort of slopes a little bit.

- Keep your hips, chest, and shoulders stable. Keep your hands under control.

- As you lift your leg, lean away from your opponent, which allows you to lift your leg a little higher.

- When you kick, point your toes toward your opponent because that will allow you to kick with your laces on top. Add a flick to your kick, and control the momentum of your leg on its way back with your hamstrings.

- Keep your abs in tight and your shoulders down.

- Double time.

- Switch legs, and repeat.

Combination

- Link the 3 kicks together. Start with your hands up and your right leg forward. Add a little bounce. Slowly go from the front kick to the side kick and, finally, to the round kick.

- You're going to need to take small steps in between each kick and shuffle yourself backward at the end.

- Double time.

- Switch legs, and repeat.

- Get a quick sip of water, and take a short break.

Finale
- In the final round, you're going to put everything together, nice and slowly. Start on your toes with the blocks, adding the punches and then the kicks.

- Double time.

- Switch legs, and repeat.

Cooldown
- Do a few minutes of shadowboxing to cool you down, and then do some static stretches of the major muscle groups.

- If you still have any energy left, do a few more combinations of each side—just be careful, as you get tired, not to lock your arms and legs.

Combat Workout
Lecture 29—Transcript

Whether you're a hardcore combat fanatic or have no boxing or martial arts experience at all, you can expect to get great results from this combat workout. Combining cardio punching and kicking rounds to burn calories with unique sculpting moves, this routine is guaranteed to reshape your whole body at the same time as helping to improve your suppleness, enhance your concentration skills and give you extra confidence.

While some estimates of martial arts based classes have suggested calorie burning may reach as high as 500–800 calories each hour, the American Council on Exercise research suggests that only very large individuals working out at exceptionally high intensities are likely to burn that many. However, you can realistically expect to expend 350–450 calories during a typical workout, which is a significant amount if weight loss is your goal.

In addition to raising your heart rate, making this good for cardio gains, fatiguing the muscles, making it good for endurance gains and moving the limbs through a full range of motion, making it good for flexibility gains, a combat workout doesn't just benefit these health related fitness components.

You may remember from our very first presentation in this series, we talked about the components of fitness, we talked about health-related and also skill-related components of fitness, and this is where this workout really comes to the fore. We can work on agility, balance, co-ordination, power, reaction time. All things that really are quite unique to this type of workout.

As always, here are a few guidelines to ensure that you exercise safely, because you're going to get off the sofa and join us today. And this will make sure you get the maximum benefit from your blood, sweat and tears— metaphorically speaking, of course.

First of all, it's always important to have around a 5-minute warm up, as the guys are doing now, with some gentle movement such as arm swings, knee lifts, shoulder circles, et cetera, to mobilize your joints. Also add marching on the spot, just to get your heart rate up slightly, and begin to increase your core body temperature. Remember, that's all about reducing your risk of injury.

If it's possible, check your technique in the mirror, particularly your posture. You've got to be careful not to round your shoulders, try not to be a pseudo-boxer, and also keeping your tummy pulled in at all times, I'll allow you particularly when we're kicking to take a slight lean backwards, but not to sink into your hips, and you can see the difference there, in the alignment of my spine.

Be careful to control momentum, and I'll keep reminding you of this as we go through the workout. I don't want you to be locking out your arms, or locking out your knees on the kicks. It's about keeping them soft and controlling them. And then at the end, you'll probably cool down with about 2 minutes of light shadow something like that, and then we'll go into the stretches of the major muscles groups.

So, why don't we get started? Let's get a little bit of music, are we ready to go? Now I'm going to be putting the right leg forwards for your left, and my left for your right, so that you're mirroring what I'm doing, so what that means right now is put your right leg forwards, please. Okay, hands up, practice your mean face. This is what we're going to do, take a little bounce on the spot. I'm going to give you the choice how hard you want to work, you can choose, if you want to keep the intensity fairly moderate, we're just taking this little bounce on the legs, keep your hands up. If you want to increase that intensity, you'll be on your toes. Now I'll probably be shouting at you an awful lot for the next 30 minutes, to get on your toes, to make sure we burn more calories. But if you need to, take that little sit down and that's fine. We're going to learn first of all 3 blocks. We're going to learn to defend your face. Get ready.

The first thing we do is move our feet. Every technique goes from the feet first, we work from the ground up. Push that right foot to me, push that right foot forwards, push. The great thing about this, it's a whole body workout, because for any technique to be effective, you have to use your whole body. Push your hips forwards, push. So you're now moving in to a lunge. We're going to add a rising block. Are we ready? Up. To defend your face, push.

How are you doing? Push it up. And again. Give me a couple more. Lovely. Some tension in the arms. Double time please. Let's go. Up, up, time to do some work, push it up. Imagine someone is trying to take a swing for you, you've got to defend your face. Up, abs are tight, little tension in the arm, give me a couple more, 1 more, and hold it there. Take a little walk around. Change legs. Get your breath back. And sit it down. Are we ready to go on the other side? Your left leg forwards.

We start from the bottom, work our way up. Push. Push. Best form of defense is attack. So push forwards. Push, good, now the hips come with you. It's turning into a lunge. Beautiful. Rising block. Up, left with left, good. And push, how you doing? Hope you're doing this at home and not sitting on the sofa. Come on. Push, beautiful. Push, can we double-time that please? Go up, come on do some work, pull your abs in tight. Good, little tension in the arms, make sure those muscles are doing some work. Give me just 4, and 3 hold it, change legs. Beautiful.

Sit down, let's do some work. You can now defend your face, let's defend your body. Cross. That's the technique we're looking for. Across your chest. Okay let's start to build it up. Feet first, push, push, beautiful, push, now, into a little lunge, push, using your hips, good. We're going across your chest. Are you ready, right hand, cross, cross, cross. Give me 1 more. Should we double time? Speed it up, 1, 2, 3, come on, push it across, little tension in your arm. Tension in the arm. Make sure you keep it in line with your chest. Don't go too high, we're defending the chest. Good, give me 4 more, 4, and 3, abs are tight, 2, 1 more, hold it there, change legs, well done guys. Sit down, sit down.

Beautiful, get your breath back in between, how you doing at home? Let's push that foot forwards, push, and push, looking good, good. Hits come with it. Push, all the power is here. All the power is in the middle, good. Arm across. Chest. Left and left. Good, cross your chest. One more slow. Double time, let's do some work, push, come on, defend yourself. Push, and again, push, just give me 4 more, there's 4, there's 3, there's 2, change legs.

Beautiful, you can defend your face, you can defend your body, we're now going to defend low down. Okay, from the feet first, right foot to me. Push the right foot to me. Push, make sure the hips are coming with it, and we'll go down, down, give me a little sink, down. Be careful, remember I said at the top, don't lock out the arm. Keep it slightly bent. Down. Can we go double time? It's not really a question. Go, and down, and down, and down, give me 4, give me 3, 2, beautiful, change legs.

You've got to imagine someone is taking a kick straight at you, for 4, and 3, and 2, push that foot forwards. Left, come on, and push, how are you doing? Let's go. Now we're working in rounds, make sure your hips are coming, you'll get a rest soon, so stay with me. Down, down, left, careful not to lock. Beautiful. Give me 4 more of those. How we doing? Imagine that kick coming towards you, block it down, double time, let's work. One, 2, yes, down, your other hand anywhere you like. Like friends, have it up, or you can have it down there. Just keep it close. Last one, hold it there, change.

One more thing, you now have 3 blocks. Is there any chance we can put those 3 blocks together? Take a little sit. We can do this. Sit down. So, rising block. Rise, cross, down. On your toes. Five, 6, 7, up, across, down. Can we go a little quicker? You know you can, let's go. Up, cross, down. And again, up, cross, down, 2 more like that. Up, cross, down, just 1 more. Up, cross it, do some work, get on your toes, double time. One, 2, 3. One, 2, 3. How are you doing? Three different blocks, up, cross, down. Yes, come on, you can defend yourself. One more. Change legs. That's not fake sweat, that's not makeup, it really is getting warm in here.

Put those blocks together, up, cross, down. One more that slow, up, cross, down. Slightly quicker, up, cross, down. Get ready, up, cross down, beautiful. Let's go, up, cross, down. Come on, let's go, 1, 2, 3. Give me 4 more of those come on, 1, 2, 3. Up, cross, down. Can I get 2 more please, 1, 2, 3, last time, let's go. One, 2, now hold it there, take a quick time out, go get yourself a sip of water, quickly come back, you've got 3 blocks, we're going to move onto the punches next.

Hurry up. You've done your blocks, now we're going to move onto our punches. Now, there are 4 punches, as with everything, to generate the power that's all in the middle, we need to start from the ground up. Feet first, put your right foot to me, right, push it right, beautiful. Now make sure you're taking your whole body with you. Bring your hips forwards. Hips, beautiful. Now all we're going to do is place it, the right hand, on the chin. Place it. Nice and easy. Place. Beautiful, make sure the arm doesn't lock out. We can now add a little bit of snap to it. Snap it back. Can we go double time? Let's go. One, 2, come on, let's go, push, make sure you're not locking the arm out, make sure there's some tension in your abs. Give me 4 more, just 4, just 3, and 2, and change legs.

Get a breather in between, remember you can always squat down or stay on your toes. Hands up, look mean. Foot first, good. Good. Make sure you're bringing the rear hip forwards, push your hips. Some work going on in those glutes. Push, should we place the punch? On the chin. Just place it first, make sure you're accurate, straight down the middle, good, push. Don't lock it out, can we add a little bit of snap to it? Let's go. Snap it. Snap it back. Good, make sure it doesn't lock out. Good, couple more. Last couple. Abs in tight. Other hand ready, double time, let's go. Push, push, shoulders down, relaxed. Abs in tight, if there's something going on here, make sure you push in, give me 4, and 3, and 2, change legs, beautiful.

We're going to move onto the cross, or reverse punch. Give me a little squat down. Important thing here is to get your body in the right position. So your rear foot, your left foot, turn it around. Look how that twists. Twist, now that allows you to twist your body. Twist. Now we get some power where that left hand comes straight down the middle to the chin. How we doing? Push. Good, can we add a little bit of a snap to it? Pull, pull, pull, good, should we go double time? Come on, how you doing? Twist your body. All the power is just here. That's why we're getting this big twist. Look at that twist. And also, working through your core, working through your obliques, hourglass figures, come on. Give me 4 more, it's 4, 3, 2, change legs.

Get your breather, with just the right foot, twist it, twist the right foot. Twist. Now the hip, turn it to me, good. Now the right hand on the chin, how you doing? Hope you're still with us. Good, add the little snap, pull it back, pull it back, twist, let's go, double time, let's do some work. One, come on, come on, twist, twist, twist the body, go. Come on, give me 4, 3, 2, hold it there, beautiful, change legs.

We're back onto the front. This time, look for the twist on your right leg. Twist, twist, on the ball of the foot, turn it in. Now the body can turn, now you see how we can get some power into what's going to be round the corner with a hook. Round, elbow high, good. We're going round the side of the head, side of the jaw. Good, round, with the body, beautiful. Double time. Let's go. Push, how you doing, come on, hope you're still with us. You can do this. Give me 4, 3, 2, and change legs.

Left leg forwards, just the twist, twist. Twist. Make sure onto the ball of the foot, turn the knee, now we'll add the body, rotating through the core, twist, twist, beautiful, shoulders down, head up tall. Round the corner. Come on, your hands are lethal weapons. Double time. Come on, twist, how you doing? Let's go. Twist, elbow high. Give me 4 more, just 4, just 3, just 2, fabulous, change.

One more punch, I did promise you 4. This is like the second one, the left foot twists forwards, now instead of just turning your body to the front, this time I want you to lift it. Lift, lift, keep going where you are. The movement is like that, lift, lift, see it? Lift, beautiful. Because now we're going to add the upper cut. Up, under the chin. Under the chin, up, see how the legs are working now? You're going down and up. And up, beautiful, up. Okay, double time, come on speed it up. Up, up, come on do it like you mean it, you need to picture someone in front of you you really don't like. Not me, give me 4 more, 4, 3, 2, well done, well done. Change it.

Same thing as the second one, just the twist. How you doing? Good, twist, remember the body this time, down and up. Down and up, Good, work those legs. Getting into your quads, getting into your hamstrings and back. Getting into the glutes. Up, fabulous, right hand, chin, come on, up, twist your body into it, fabulous. How you doing? Come on up, up, up, super, up, okay, double time, you know it's coming. Let's go. Up, twist the foot, twist the body, down and up. Give me 4 more, 4, come on, 3, you can do this, 2, and 1. Change it over.

You may remember with the blocks we learned 3 blocks, then we put them together, same thing with the punches. Right leg forwards, take a little squat down. Get your breath back. So, nice and slowly. Hands up, punch, twist,

twist the front foot. Twist the back foot and up. Little bit of work, remember we talked about coordination in the skill-related fitness components? So, nice and slow, in 4, and 3, and 2, come on let's put it together.

Jab, cross, hook, and up. On your toes, remember all the power comes from here, if this isn't moving, then neither are you, so let's go. We push, 1, twist, twist, up, hold it. Are you ready, in 4, 3, 2, jab, cross, hook, up. On your toes. Last time slow, jab, cross, hook, up. Okay, it's the moment of truth. Speed it up, let's go, 1, 2, 3, 4, hold it, 1, 2, 3, up, let's go. One, 2, 3, up. We go jab, cross, hook, up. Four more, you can do it. One, 2, 3, up. Let's go. Beautiful, and again, go, look at the legs, look at the legs, 1 more. One, 2, beautiful, change legs.

Can we skip it on a little quicker now? Because you know what's coming. Left leg forwards, in 5, 6, 7, jab, cross, hook, up. Make sure the legs are moving, make sure the body is moving. Jab, cross, hook, up. In 4, this is your last time slow. Let's go. I sounded a bit mean then, sorry, come on, you can do this. Let's do this, in 5, 6, 7, go. One, 2, 3, up. And again, 1, 2, 3, up. We start with the jab, cross, hook, up, come on. One, 2, don't get flustered if you get it wrong, if you get 1 or 2 wrong, that's okay. As long as you're moving, you'll be improving. Just so long as it doesn't look like that. One, 2, 3, up. One more please, 1, 2, 3, and hold it there, take a breather. Quick time out, get yourself a quick drink, you now have 3 blocks, 4 punches. Quickly, come back and we'll add onto it, 3 kicks.

Welcome back guys, so now you've got 3 blocks, you've got 4 punches, and we need to finish it off. We're going to learn 3 kicks, a front kick, a sidekick, a round kick, all 3 quite different. Now, the beauty of this is I'm going to set up each technique with a step first. We're going to start nice and slowly, I want to get your hips in the right position, you're going to take your left foot and step it up. Nice and slow, step, we're going to lift the other leg, your right leg. We're going t put it down, we're going to take it back. Take a little bounce, so that generally where we're going, step, lift, down and back. Are we ready? Nice and slowly, we'll go. Step, right, back and down. Just working on that right leg. Take a step up first, when you step, make sure you point your toes to the front. Towards me. Because what I need you to do is keep your hips, chest, shoulders facing the front. Because the power, like we said, is in the hips, so I want to push them forwards.

Do we see that? Little step, and push. Keep going. When you step, push the hips in. This is where the power is, in the glutes. Push, good, but do you notice the head tilts back slightly so I still get a nice long line through the spine. We'll add the front kick to that. Step, flick, back. You'll actually be kicking here, with the ball of the foot, so in reality, you pull the toes back. But what I'm concerned about is just making sure it's not going up in the air, the kick is going forwards. Step, push it forwards, 1 more, step, beautiful. Can we go double time? Let's do some work. Step, kick. Step, kick. Beautiful, now I want you to keep your hands up, remember you're a lean, mean, fighting machine. We're not doing this, this is not the Charleston. Hands up. Push, good, push your hips forwards, abs are tight. Shoulders down. Good, and hold it there, turn it around, let's build it up nice and slow off the other side.

Remember first of all, step with the right, lift the left, down and back. Take a deep breath, be aware of abs in tight, shoulders back, let's go. Step, lift, down, back. How are you doing? Lift. You may notice fighters, boxers, will normally have either once side, or the other, they'll either be orthodox or southpaw. We'll all have a stronger more flexible, easier to coordinate side, so you may notice as you swap from side to side, one side is not as good as the other. That just means we need a little bit more work on it. Here we go. Step, lean back, good, step, lean back, push your hips to me, can we have the kick? Push, beautiful, 1 more.

Step, okay, I think we're ready. Let's go, double time. Step, push, come on with that front kick. Let's go. Come on, do it like you mean it. This could save your life one day. Come on, up, let's go. Push. Good. Abs in tight. Shoulders down, push your hips to me. Come on, up, 1 more, change legs, hold it there.

You've got your front kick, everything to the front. We're going to change it to the side kick, turn your feet and your body this way, but keep your head and your hands towards me. Take a little squat down, good. Now this time, you're going to step up with the back leg, you're going to lift the front leg, but you're going to lift the knee in that direction. Step, lift. Are we ready? Step, lift. So you have the knees over there. Step, lift, the beauty of that is it allows you, when we add the kick, nice and low, to push. Push, see that? Step, push. Now your toes should be pointing in that direction, you're pushing with the side of your foot, hips, push, should we get a couple of more? Make sure your knee comes back after the kick, control it. Should we go double time? Step, push. Step push. Step push. Come on, how you doing? Four more. Step push. Step push, 2 more, 1 more, beautiful. Change legs.

Feet are this way, chest is this way, hips this way, but the hands and the head are to the front. Good, so lets' set it up the same way. Step up first, knee, good, step, knee, fabulous. Up, knee, keep your hands up, shoulders down. Beautiful. Now we'll push. Push. See how you're pushing somebody away. Good. Push, push, good. Push, double time, let's go. Step push. Step push, give me 4 more. Come on. Side of the foot, toes are pointing that way. Come on, up, 1 more, and hold it there, change legs.

So you've now got a front kick, you've now got a side kick, we're now going to go for a round kick. Right leg forwards. Give me that little bounce. Hope you're getting warm, this is what we're going to do. Turn yourself sideways on again. Same beginning, step up, but now lift the leg into a hurdle position. You can do this, we go. Step, lift, see that hurdle position? And you see how the knee is slightly higher than the ankle? Don't be lifting this way. Keep the hips, chest, shoulders there. Lift, lean away from me, lean away, what that's going to allow you to do is lift that leg a little higher. Now when we kick, you're going to point your toes to me. Because that will allow you to kick with the laces on the top, let's add the flick. Step, flick, see how the toe is pointed, so the contact will be with the laces. Control it on the way back. Good, and again, step, flick, let's do some work, double time. Step kick, good. Step kick, good. How you doing? Control the momentum, abs are tight, lean back, shoulders down, 1 more. Change legs.

Beautiful. Turn yourself sideways on. Feet this way, chest this way, hips this way, the head and the hands are to the front. Give me a little bounce. We start by stepping up with the right, lift the left. Step. Lift. See how you're lifting into that position? Hurdle, but with the knee, a little higher. Keep going. Then the ankle, see that kind of slope, step, beautiful. What we're going to do now is take a lean back. Beautiful. Keep going. Step, lean. So you can lean away from the kick, lean. Beautiful, let's add the flick. Step, flick, point the toes to me. And again, keep your hands under control. Step, double time, let's go. Step, kick. Step kick, come on. Beautiful, point the toes, abs are tight, shoulders down. Beautiful. Really getting into the hamstrings to control that pull back on the kick. Come on, 3 more. Two more. One more. Hold it there.

Beautiful, 1 more thing to do. Can we, like we did with the blocks, and we did with the punches, can we link those 3 kicks together? Bear with me, hands up. Right leg forwards. Give me the little bounce. So, front kick, side kick, round. We go step, step, front, down, step, side, down, step, round. You're going to need to take small steps in between, then shuffle yourself backwards. Four, 3, 2, let's go.

Step, front, turn sideways, stay sideways, round, so you've got a little step in between each kick, shall we try that again? And 4, and 3, and 2, step kick, step, kick, down, step, side, down, step, round. How we doing? Can we go double time? Four, it's not really a question. In 4, 3, 2, step, front, step, side, step round. Get back get ready. In 5, 6, 7, step, front, step, side, step, round. Back you go, hold it, should we change legs?

Left leg forwards. Exactly the same thing, but we'll go slow first of all. In 5, 6, 7, step, front, down, step, side, down, step, round. How you doing? Should we do 1 more time—slow? In 4, and 3, and 2, to the front first. Step, front, down, to the side, push, round, beautiful, back we go. Any chance would I be stretching our relationship too far to ask you to do that double time? Five, 6, 7 go. Step front, step side, step round. Back you go. In 5, 6, 7, step front, step side, step round. Watch that one, in 5, 6, 7, go. I nearly lost an ear, then. And round, and hold it there, so you now have 3 blocks, 4 punches, and 3 kicks. Get a quick sip of water, and get ready for the finale, where we're going to put it all together.

Okay, if you're still with us, well done, because this is the final round. You've made it to the final round. We're going to put everything together, nice and slowly. Okay? On your toes. Come on, so, finishing straight, what we're going to do is add the blocks to the punches, to the kicks. We'll go slowly at first, get ready in 4, and 3, and 2, here we go slow. Block, block, block, punches, 1, 2, 3, step front kick, step side kick, step round kick, how did you do? Get ready. The whole thing, let's just call the first one a rehearsal, just in case. On your toes. Mean face. Float like a butterfly. Get ready. (I've stolen that quote.) In 5, 6, 7, go. Block, block, block, 1, 2, 3, 4, step front, step side, step round. Fabulous, change legs. Left leg forwards. Slow first, 5, 6, 7, block, block, block, get ready, punch, punch, remember to twist your body, front kick, turn for the side kick, flick for the round kick. Fabulous, back you go left leg still forwards. Double time. In 4, in 3, in 2, show me what you can do, 1, 2, 3, 1, 2, 3, 4, step front, step side, step round. And there you go.

What we're going to do on your toes is have a little cool down. A little bit of shadowboxing to cool us down, and then we're going into a static stretch. Remember if you can't figure out which stretches to do, you've got that flexibility workout, you can pinch some stretches from there. Although, if you've still got any energy left, I wouldn't mind you doing a couple more combinations off each side, just be careful as you get tired not to lock out your arms and legs. Stick with this workout and you'll soon be fighting fit.

Fitness Ball Workout
Lecture 30

F itness balls, also called Swiss balls and stability balls, are great tools for working whole-body strength. Because you're working on an unstable surface, you can start to put some stress on your core muscles, helping to develop them—which, in turn, can help you look slimmer and taller and can help you improve the health of your lower spine. Before you start a fitness ball workout, it is important to choose the right ball for your body because fitness balls come in many different sizes.

Guidelines
- When using exercise balls, you need to check regularly that they're fully inflated.

- Ideally, you'll use your exercise balls on a smooth surface. You may choose to use a mat for the following exercises.

- For the following exercises, be aware of keeping the natural curves in your spine at all times—particularly the normal, neutral curve in your lower back.

Figure 30.1

Fitness Ball Chart

Fitness Ball Size	Height of Individual
30–35 cm	< 4'10" (< 145 cm)
45 cm	4'8"–5'5" (140–165 cm)
55 cm	5'6"–6'0" (165–185 cm)
65 cm	6'0"–6'5" (185–195 cm)
75 cm	> 6'5" (> 195 cm)
85 cm	heavier or long-legged exercisers

© iStockphoto/Thinkstock.

- It's always important to warm up, which you can use the ball for. The main goal of your warm-up is to increase your body temperature by doing some mobilizing exercise for 3 to 5 minutes.

- Always exercise under control; remember that slower is better.

- It's useful to practice using a fitness ball if you've never used one before by sitting on the ball and getting a feeling for your natural alignment and the way it changes.

- As with most of the workouts, your target for each exercise is 12 to 15 repetitions.

- Beginners should probably aim to complete 1 set, but if you're already doing some exercise, you might want to aim for 2 sets. Advanced exercises should attempt to complete 3 sets of each exercise.

Wall Squat
- This is an exercise that you can do against a wall with your exercise ball.

- Make sure your feet are about hip-width apart.

- The benefit of doing this exercise against the wall is that it allows you to get a little deeper into the squat because you can use the wall for support.

- By going deeper into the squat, you are able to work through a greater range in the quadriceps and glutei as a result of the hip flexion and extension. In this way, your strength is angle specific.

- If you only work through a partial range, you'll only develop strength through that partial range. Instead, you're able to develop strength through a greater range of motion, which could be useful in sports performance and in everyday tasks.

Sideways Single-Leg Wall Squat

- This is a more difficult variation of the wall squat that involves a single-leg squat.

- You can lift your arm for balance, keeping your abdominals in tight.

- Be aware of your alignment. You want to have a nice lift through the top of your head, including a long neck and long spine.

- You need to make sure that you're keeping your hips square, which forces you to fight against the rotation of the hips.

- When you change legs, you can either turn around and face the other way or continue to do it in the same direction.

- When doing this exercise, you can either lean against the wall, or a partner can provide the balance. Once you've practiced this exercise, you and a partner can work together, but it's tricky because you need to work in unison.

Single-Leg Adduction

- This is an exercise that works the inner thigh but also works your core muscles—particularly the obliques.

- There are 2 positions for this exercise: resting on your elbow or resting your head on your hand, whichever is comfortable for you. The important thing is to make sure that you have a nice line through the body—from the heel through to the tailbone to the top of the head.

- Press down onto the ball with your top leg, lifting your hips. Make sure you are not twisting or rotating your hips.

- The knee of your top leg should be slightly bent—not locked. Your other leg is bent underneath for support.

- Try to keep your breathing nice and relaxed.

- Do this exercise slowly and under control, making sure you're not dropping your body with gravity.

- Exhale on the exertion; breathe out as you press onto the ball.

Leg Curl
- The leg curl, or hamstring curl, is a great exercise for the back of the thighs, but it also works the glutei.

- You have 2 options for this exercise: You can keep your hips down a little lower and curl your heel toward your backside, or as you curl, you can also lift your hips up, getting a full extension through the posterior chain.

- Keep your shoulders down on the floor so that you don't feel a strain through the back of your neck.

- You might find that you need your hands to help you with your balance.

- Don't worry if you lose the ball a few times—just reset yourself and continue with your repetitions.

Press-Up on Ball
- This exercise works on challenging not just the chest and the triceps with some shoulder work involved in the press-up, but there is also an extra challenge in terms of the instability that is presented by the ball.

- You have 2 options for this exercise: You can either do a full press-up, or you can go onto your knees for the press-up.

- The key is dropping your chest down to the ball and controlling that movement.

- This exercise works the smaller muscles, the stabilizers, that are located around the shoulder girdle. These are called the rotator cuff muscles and are a group of 4 muscles that attach to your shoulder blade to help stabilize the shoulder: the supraspinatous, the infraspintatous, the teres minor, and the subscapularis. For this exercise, these muscles are working to control the wobble that you probably feel.

Hyperextension
- Roll forward on the ball, making sure the ball is under your hips.

- There are 2 options for this exercise: You can put your hands on the ball to stabilize yourself, or you can make it slightly more difficult by putting your hands behind your head.

- Try to maintain a long spine as you lift yourself up backward. Your spine is designed to flex and extend, and if you extend past the center line, it's called hyperextension.

- If your hands are behind your head, you have to balance through your pelvis because otherwise, you'll wobble. You have to stabilize yourself through the lumbopelvic region as well as with the erector spinae muscles, which are the muscles in the lower back that help to give you a strong movement through the hyperextension.

- Try to keep your breathing relaxed, which can be more difficult for this exercise. You have to breathe consciously because of the pressure on your abdomen.

Reverse Prone Fly
- If you find this exercise easy, you can add extra weight to this exercise by using dumbbells.

- When resting the ball on your abdomen and chest area, your arms are lifted out to either side. Your elbows will be slightly bent, but if you straighten your elbows a little, the exercise is slightly more difficult. If you bend your elbows, creating a smaller lever, the exercise is slightly easier.

- You want to squeeze your shoulder blades together, working the rhomboid muscles that attach from the inside of your shoulder blades to the first 4 thoracic vertebrae. You're also working the middle part of the trapezius.

- This is a great exercise for toning your back muscles and helping you maintain your natural, neutral alignment.

Reverse Hyperextension

- This exercise works to stabilize your shoulders. You're working the triceps, and you're also getting some bone loading through the wrists, which is beneficial in terms of protecting against osteoporosis and fractures.

- Be careful when lifting your legs through your lower body. You want it to be a smooth, controlled movement.

- You're working through the erector spinae, the glutei, and the hamstrings. The core is working to maintain your balance so that you're not wobbling around on the ball.

- You can take a short break in between each set if you're feeling any stress to your muscles.

Press-Up on Floor

- You have 2 options for this exercise: You can either rest your feet on the ball, or you can rest your knees—or maybe even your hips— on the ball. The higher the ball is on the line of the body, the easier the exercise will be because the ball's taking more of the weight of your body.

- You want to maintain a natural curve through your lower spine. You have to fight the tendency for your hips to drop down in this position.

- Be careful not to lock your arms at the top of the movement, which can put an extra strain on your elbows. Make sure that your movement is controlled.

Crunch

- For this exercise, you have 2 options: You can do a normal crunch movement, or you can drop yourself further behind the ball. If you do this exercise on the floor, you can only go as far down as horizontal. However, the ball allows you to work through a greater range for the abdominal muscles.

- You need to stabilize yourself, so make sure your feet are planted wide. A smooth surface, such as a mat, helps to stabilize you.

- Your hips should be slightly lifted; don't let them drop down.

- As with any crunch-type exercise, try to picture your abdominal muscles squeezing together like a spring, moving your ribs closer to your hips to work the rectus abdominis.

The challenge when using an exercise ball in your workout is to control it by keeping your core muscles stabilized.

Side Crunch

- For this exercise, you're going to be positioned sideways on the ball—with one leg over the top and one leg straight out, which will prevent you from twisting your hips. Keep one hand behind your head.

- Stabilize yourself on the ball; get in a comfortable position.

- You don't want to twist your hips. Instead, your spine is moving in lateral flexion, working the obliques.

- Focus on your waist, pulling your ribs to your hips.

- Don't hold your breath.

- It's OK to wobble a little on the ball. Just reset yourself, and get ready for the next repetition.

Jacknife
- It doesn't matter whether you start with the ball in your hands or feet, but the key is to swap the ball from one to the other each time your body comes up.

- This exercise works the abdominals, but it also works the chest and inner thighs as you squeeze the ball.

- Slow is better with this exercise. Otherwise, you might spend much of your time chasing the ball that's rolling all over the floor.

Rollout on Knees
- The rest of the exercises in this workout are dynamic; they're all isotonic exercises that involve the shortening and lengthening of muscles. However, this exercise is an isometric exercise in which the deeper postural muscles are working to hold you in a position.

- For this exercise, the challenge is to hold a fairly awkward position. As you roll the ball forward, your hips begin to drop. Keep your abdominals in tight to stop your hips from dropping.

- It's vital to ensure that your technique is correct. Therefore, if your hips start to drop down, take a brief rest and reset yourself.

- Your goal is to do 3 to 5 repetitions of this exercise—not 12 to 15— because the challenge is to build up the amount of time that you can hold the position, training the endurance in your postural muscles.

Cooldown

- At the end of your workout, cool down and stretch.

- Hold static stretches for about 15 seconds.

- Stretch through the major muscle groups that you used during this workout.

- Your core body temperature should gradually drop, and your breathing should return to normal.

- Hopefully, as you stretch, you will feel a hint of the work you did in your muscles.

- Straighten up your body, and take a deep breath. Shake out your hands and legs.

Fitness Ball Workout
Lecture 30—Transcript

Welcome to the workout today. What we're going to do is work with our Swiss balls, fitness balls, stability balls. They're called different things, but the point is they're a great tool for working whole body strength, and because we're working on an unstable surface, we can start to put a little stress on the core muscles, helping to develop those core muscles, which in turn is then, well, first of all it can help you to look a little bit slimmer and taller almost immediately, but certainly will help to improve the health of our lower spine.

Now, these balls it's reckoned were first used in Italy in the early '60s, but since then we've come a long way, an awful lot of stuff we can do with them.

Now, importantly, you need to choose the right ball. You may have noticed that the balls are slightly different size, and if you take a look at the chart on your screen now, you can see roughly the right size ball to choose for you.

As with any exercise program, we need some safety tips. Firstly, particularly with these balls, you need to check regularly that they're fully inflated. Ideally you're going to use them on a smooth surface. We're using the mat today. And at all times be aware on these exercises of keeping the natural curves in your spine, particularly that normal neutral curve in the lower back.

So, you'll notice that it's always important to warm up. The guys are using the ball for the warm-up. Our warm-up is about getting our body temperature up, so some mobilizing exercises, and you can see a few of the things the guys are doing. Now, you need about 3–5 minutes to do that. Always exercise under control. Remember slower is better. And it's always worth getting a little bit of practice, if you've not used the balls before, just by sitting on the ball and get a feeling for your natural alignment and the way it changes. Our target, as with most of our workouts, is 12–15 repetitions. That's where we're aiming for. Beginners, you're probably looking at 1 set; if you're already doing a little bit of exercise, maybe 2 sets. Those of you who are advanced will be looking for 3 sets of each exercise.

Okay, so, the first exercise we're going to do is actually a wall squat, an exercise you do against the wall. We don't have the wall here, so I'm going to cheat this exercise and use the other wall for today, cameraman. Sorry about that.

This is what's going to happen. Imagine you're against the wall here. What Renee's going to do is take the feet about hip-width apart, so I hope you're ready for me, and we're going to start with our squatting exercise. The beauty of this—away we go, please. We're looking for our 12–15 repetitions please. The beauty of doing this against the wall using the ball is it actually allows you to get a little deeper into the squat because you've got that support. Without the ball there, that wouldn't be a possible position.

Now, the great thing is that by going a little deeper into here we're working through a greater range in the quadricep. We're working through a greater range through the gluteals, through that hip flexion, hip extension movement. The beauty of that is that our strength is angle-specific. If we only work through a partial range, we'll only develop strength through that partial range. The great thing about this is now we're developing that strength through a greater range of motion, which could be useful to us in sports performance and in everyday tasks.

How many have we done? Is that it? Beautiful. Now, the great thing about this is we can also vary it and move round to do our single-leg squat. So, this is a little tougher. One leg forwards. Notice how Renee's using the arm for balance as well, keeping your abdominals tight. Remember we said in the beginning about being aware of our alignment. We've got a nice lift through the top of the head, long neck, long spine, abdominals in tight.

Now, what we're working against here—Renee's making this look a little easier than perhaps you're finding this at home—making sure that we're keeping the hips square. She's actually having to fight against a little bit of rotation in this exercise as well. You can either, when you come to change legs, turn around and face the other way or we could do it the same way. Beautiful. Arm out for balance. Good work. Lean into the ball. Excellent.

So, if you do want to do it against the wall, you can do that way or as we're doing here, camera is providing the balance also. If you're feeling particularly fresh, if you've had a few goes at this exercise before, what you could do is both of you work together, but I'll warn you that is tricky. You do need to work in unison.

So, great exercise this. Little bit of research at University of San Diego found that the best exercise for your gluteals, for your buttocks, is actually the single-leg squat, so this is a fabulous exercise to do. Are we done? Brilliant. Well done. Thank you. If you'll grab your ball for me please.

We're down onto the floor now, so get yourself down, ready for some single-leg adduction. So, you guys are down. The ball is at this end. We're facing outwards. Brilliant. Now, this is an exercise that works into the inner thigh—beautiful exercise—but also works into your core muscles, particularly this obliques at the sides. So, you'll notice we've got 2 positions here. First of all I've got Cameron resting on his elbow. If you're comfortable that way, then that's fine, resting on the elbow. The important thing is here is making sure that we've got a nice line through the body from the heel through to the tailbone to the top of the head, or perhaps we might be resting the head down on the hand, as Renee is doing, whichever is comfortable for you.

Can we start, please, guys? We're pressing down with the top leg, pressing into the ball, lifting the hips from that position, and we'll start to get that work into the inner thigh, also into the obliques. Try and keep your breathing nice and relaxed. We're looking for those 12–15 repetitions. Remember we said all exercise we do slowly, under control, so making sure we're not dropping down with gravity.

A tip also is to exhale on the exertion. We always say that, so try to breathe out as you press onto the ball. Hopefully we're feeling this working into the inner thigh and then we're also feeling it into the obliques into the waist working into those core muscles. Looking for our 12–15 repetitions. Well done, and then we're flipping over to the other side. Great stuff.

So, this top leg you're going to keep the knee just slightly bent, not locked out for me please. You'll see the other leg is bent underneath the support, and away we go. Fabulous. And you've got that choice, remember, between working either, resting the head onto the hand or resting on the elbow—whichever works for you, as long as we're getting that lift of the hip, making sure we're not twisting, not rotating through the hips.

Focus a little bit on the muscles that are doing the work, little bit of mind and muscle. So, let's think about the inner thigh doing the work. Let's also think about this work through the obliques. Can we feel something in the waist? Yes? Concentrate on those muscles. We're going to take that as a yes. Fabulous stuff.

Okay, so we're changing exercises now. We're going to shift onto the leg curl, the hamstring curl. Great exercise for the back of the thighs, and for those of your sports guys out there, be aware that hamstring strains are a common problem and actually results from a muscular imbalance a lot of the time. Having very strong quads and weaker hamstrings is not a good position to be in. So, this is a great exercise.

So, what we're going to do here is let yourself down on the floor, heels on the ball. I'm going to give you 2 options here. You could keep the hips down a little lower, and we're looking to just curl the heel towards the backside. You also have the option to then, as Cameron is doing, as we curl in, we're lifting the hips up as well, getting a full extension through what we call the posterior chain. Fabulous. Working through those hamstrings and working through the glutes as well. Beautiful.

So, we're looking for our 12–15 repetitions, making sure it's nice and slow, it's under control. Try to be aware, particularly in this position, that you've got your shoulders down on the floor, that we're not getting any strain through the back of the neck. Excellent. You might find that you need your hands just to help you with that balance, and again, the guys are making it look perhaps a little easier than you're finding it at home. So, don't worry if you lose the ball a couple of times. Just reset yourself, as Cameron is doing there, and then get ready to go for your final few repetitions. Okay? It's a fabulous exercise to work the hamstrings at the back of the thighs. Brilliant.

We're going to change it over now. So, we've done some work for the hamstrings. What about a little bit of press-up work on the ball? So, let's flip ourselves over please, guys. What we're doing here is working on challenging not just the chest and the triceps, little bit of shoulder work, for the press-up itself, but we're also going to add an extra challenge here in terms of the instability. Remember, this is the whole point of the Swiss ball, of the stability ball: To work that extra challenge. So, we've got 2 options. We can either go full press-up or we can go onto the knees for the press-up. The key here is dropping the chest down to the ball. I want 12 repetitions please. Let's go. And controlling this movement. So, we're working the smaller muscles, those little stabilizers around the shoulder girdle. We're talking about your rotator cuff muscles, a group of 4 muscles there that are helping to stabilize the shoulder.

We're talking about the supraspinatous, the infraspintatous, the teres minor, and the subscapularis. These are the 4 muscles that attach to your shoulder blade that help to fix it in position, and they're doing the work here in controlling this little bit of wobbled that we might feel. There will be a little bit of wobble. Don't worry about that. Excellent. But also hopefully at the same time, as well as working that stability, you felt that little bit of work through the chest for the triceps.

We're moving on now to a little bit of hyperextension for the lower back. So, what I'm going to ask you to do now is to roll forwards on the ball. So, the ball is about under your hips. Excellent stuff. Feet are on the floor. The ball is under your hips. Excellent. So, we've got 2 options here. First of all, Cameron is going to put his hands on the ball to stabilize himself. Renee is going to make it slightly more difficult and put the hands behind the head. What we're looking to do here is simply lift yourself up backwards.

Now, try and maintain a nice, long spine as we do this. Remember, your spine is designed, as we talked about in our lecture about the spine, to flex and extend. Now, also, if you take that extend past the center line, it's actually called hyperextension, and this is the sort of movement, to put into a sports context, if you were to smash the tennis ball you'd probably be in a position where you would be in a hyper-extended position, first of all, perhaps on the serve even also.

So, the easier version is to support your weight there. What's happening here is what Renee is having to do is to balance through the pelvis because otherwise there's this little bit of wobble going on, so she's stabilizing herself through the lumbopelvic region as well as working these erector spinae muscles, the muscles in the lower back that are helping to give us that nice strong movement through the hyperextension. Excellent stuff. Try and keep your breathing relaxed. It can be a little bit more difficult here. You have to breathe consciously here because of the press on the abdomen.

So, I'm going to move up the back now to the prone fly. So, this time, if you can grab your dumbbells for this one so I can show you 2 alternatives. If you find this easy, we can add a little bit of extra weight to this exercise.

Now you're resting the ball probably abdomen/chest area. Arms are at the side of the ball, and our aim here, with the reverse fly, what we're trying to do is lift up and out to the side. Now, the elbows, if you have the elbows a little bit straighter, now, they'll never be straight. They'll always be slightly bent. This is a little bit more difficult. If you bend the elbows, that lever is smaller, so it makes it slightly easier. So, what I'm looking for—away we go please—I want 12 repetitions at least. If you're feeling flush we'll go for 15.

What we're looking to do here is don't change your upper body position on the ball. We're looking to squeeze the shoulder blades together, so we're really working into the rhomboid muscles that attach from the inside of your shoulder blades to the first 4 thoracic vertebrae. Then also we're working the middle part of the trapezius as well.

Now, this is a great exercise for those of you who spend much time sitting at the desk working or if you're driving a lot. This kind of rounded shoulder position, this kyphosis position, this is a great exercise for toning those muscles at the back and helping you to draw back, back to your natural neutral alignment. And remember, your spine works more efficiently when it's in that natural position with those normal curves.

Now, I'm going back to hyperextension again, but this time we're going to do the reverse hyperextension, so if we can bring the ball back a little bit please, guys. So, be careful how you get into the position for this one. It's a little bit more tricky. You're walking over the front of the ball. Always do that slowly. You're resting on your hands. So, the great thing is here we're going to get a little bit of work again to stabilize your shoulders. There's a little bit of work through the triceps here. You're getting some bone loading through the wrists. Now, this is important. In terms of our risk of osteoporosis, we need to try to get to that point where we're getting a little bit of stress through the wrists. Remember this is a common fracture site. So, I am leaving you in this position and it'll feel a little bit uncomfortable, but trust me, that's doing us some good.

So, what we're doing here is a reverse hyperextension, so we're lifting through the lower body. The legs are lifting up and back down. Now, be careful with this movement. Remember we said right at the top that we want controlled movement. So, while you're doing this, please make sure it's smooth; no jerking movement.

Now, we're working here through a little bit of work through the erector spinae, through the glutes and also into the hamstrings as well. So, nice and smooth with this exercise, and again, we're working through the core to maintain that balance. We're not wobbling around on the ball. And the whole purpose of this, again, we're working on an instable service, which is great for challenging those core muscles, but at the same time you can see we're really working into the glutes here—buns of steel. I feel I know you guys well enough to say that now. Away we go. Fabulous. I'm looking for those 12–15 repetitions on every exercise, please. Well done. Well done. Take a quick rest there.

So, what I'm going to do now, and again, you can take a little rest in between each set just in case we're getting a bit of stress here, but remember, that's what we're after. We're after this bone loading, and it's site-specific. Remember, particularly as we get older and that risk of falls, this is a common fracture site, and so it's important for us to get that extra bone density work if we can. Remember our bone mineral density begins to decrease with age, so we're going to try and do a little bit of work on that.

We're going down now into the press-ups. So, I'm going to give you an option on this one, so start from this end, feet on the ball. You weren't taking the easier option then, were you?

So, we've got 2 options here on this. You can either have your feet on the ball or you can rest the ball a little higher onto your knees or maybe even onto your hips. So, the higher the ball is on the line of the body, the easier the exercise will be because obviously that's taking more of the weight. The important point for this is we want to keep a nice natural curve through the lower spine. There'll be a tendency in this position for your hips to drop down. We've got to fight that, lowering the chest down, elbows out to the side for our push-up, press-up position.

So, remember what we said: If the ball is a little higher up the body line, it's a little bit easier. If the ball is further away, so you have perhaps just your feet on the ball, then you're taking more of the weight. It's a little tougher.

Well done, guys. You're doing really well. Be careful on this exercise not to lock your arms out at the top. That can put a little bit of strain on the elbow. So, try to keep them soft. And again, it gets back to that point we were saying about trying to make sure that the movement is controlled.

Well done. Well done. You're making this look too easy. Good work. We're moving on now from the chest. Let's move onto our abdominals, and we're going to do a little crunch this time, so this time you're on the ball for me. You're both taking the easy option. If I can get you sitting on the ball facing me, please. Fabulous stuff.

Okay, so, first of all you need to stabilize yourself. So, make sure you've got your feet nice and wide. Make sure you're planted. And again, this is why, remember, we said you want to be on a smooth surface, and the mat helps us for that.

So, we're looking into our normal sit-up, crunch type exercise, so away we go, please. What I want you to be aware of on this is that the hips are already slightly lifted. Don't let them drop down. And you've got options here because you've got your normal crunch movement, and again, with any of these crunch-type exercises, really try to picture the abdominal muscles squeezing together like a spring. In fact, what we're trying to do here is to move your ribs closer to your hips. That's how we work the rectus abdominis. That's what we're looking for.

What you could also do with this, as Renee is doing, you're dropping a little further behind the ball. So, if you were doing this on the floor, obviously you can only go down to horizontal. This allows us to work through a greater range for the abdominal muscles. Fabulous exercise. So, you've got the choice to be doing that. Maybe experiment with it. Can you go a little bit further back? That would be great if you could. Fabulous.

So, having worked through the rectus there at the front, all we're going to do now is same position, guys. We're just going to flip around to the side and work on the side crunch. So, you're turning yourself sideways on now. That's it. That's it. I want one leg over the top, one leg straight out. Doesn't matter which way first because you're going to do both. Beautiful stuff. One hand behind the head. Stabilize yourself on the ball.

So, get yourself in nice comfortable position, first of all. The aim of this exercise, again we're just doing a crunch, but we're on a side crunch now. So, you'll see how for this exercise we've got one leg out straight but then we've also got one leg over the front. What that will do also is prevent you from twisting your hips. We don't want to twist. Let's keep this because remember we talked about the spine moving in lateral flexion. We're working laterally here, little bit of work into the obliques giving you an hourglass figure, he says, or your money back.

Excellent stuff. Really feeling that into the obliques, really squeezing through the waist. Remember what we said? When you've done your 12 repetitions, we'll swap over to the other side. Remember we said on this, we want to get our mind in muscle, so really focus on the waist, really focus on pulling the ribs to the hips. That's what we're trying to do on this exercise. And again, don't hold your breath. Stabilize yourself, first of all. And remember, as we said, you might be finding while you're doing this at home that you're wobbling a little bit on the ball. That's okay. Just reset yourself and get ready to go with the next repetition. It will happen. If it was easy, it wouldn't be worth doing. The whole challenge here is we're taking some fairly common exercises you may have seen before, but we're doing them on an unstable surface, and that's the key. We're going to end up working a lot more muscles. Beautiful stuff. Just 1 more? Excellent stuff. Well done. Well done.

We're getting down now, still on our abdominals. We've only got 2 more exercises to go, so hang in there, guys. You can do this. We're going to be down now for the jackknife, so the ball is at this end. You're down on your backs, please. Fabulous.

Okay, so, little bit of a tricky one. Doesn't matter whether you start with the ball in the hands or the feet, but the key is each time you come up with the hands and feet, we're going to swap the ball over, so a little bit of work for the abdominals, but we're also working through the chest and squeezing the ball, and then you'll find the inner thighs as well as we squeeze the ball.

So, away we go. We're going to sit up, transfer the ball. I hope it's not going to go rolling away, and back down, and then back up. Beautiful. Sit up, then back down, then back up. Fabulous, and we're just going to do 143 of these, please. I'm only kidding. We're aiming for 12–15 repetitions. That's our target. Up we go. Sit up. Brilliant. And up. Excellent.

Slow is better with this. Otherwise you're going to find you'll spend half your time chasing around the ball that's rolling all over the place. And up. Brilliant. Hopefully beginning to feel this a little bit in the abdominals now. Again, I do feel guilty that I'm not doing it, but I just have got to check that we're all doing it right. Okay?

Fabulous work. Well done. Really getting into those abdominals. It's a target area for a lot of us. Brilliant stuff. Well done. Well done. How did you do at home?

So, we're going to change it over. You'll be please to know this is the last exercise, and it's a little easier than that one. We're going to flip it over for our rollout.

So, this one, rather than the rest of the exercises are all dynamic; they're all what we call isotonic. The muscle that we've targeted has been shortening and lengthening, shortening and lengthening. We're now going to work through an isometric exercise, and that's because the deeper postural muscles work that way. That's what they do. They hold us in position.

So, for this exercise I'm challenging you to get into a fairly awkward position but then to hold it. So, you'll see the guys are starting on the knees with the elbows hands on the ball, and all we're going to do for a rollout because I'm going to ask you to roll the ball forwards, so as we roll the ball forwards we get ourselves into a position where you'll see the hips are now starting to drop. So, the challenge now is can we keep the abdominals in really tight and stop that from dropping.

So, I'm going to ask you to take it out there and hold it please. Hold that position. When we get to the point where you feel, "Hang on, my hips are dropping down," or, "I'm beginning to shake," we can roll back and take a little bit of a rest. And our aim here is just can we begin to build up that time. We're training the endurance in those postural muscles. That's what they're designed to do.

Remember, as we said right at the top, it's absolutely vital to ensure we get the technique correct. So, if the hips start to drop down, we need to come back, take a little bit of a rest, and we'll try that again.

Now, you're only looking at about 3–5 of these repetitions. This is not one that we're doing for 12–15 because the challenge here is the time, can we hold the time on this exercise. Beautiful. Should we try just 1 more of those? When I say we, obviously I mean you and you. Holding it, fabulous. Try to keep your breathing relaxed. Do you want fries with that shake? Sorry, I have to get that line in somewhere. And beautiful. If you put the balls back on the stands for me, please, and get yourself up, we'll have a little bit of a stretch.

So, we're going to cool down with a little bit of a stretch now. So, the whole idea of that workout: targeting your whole body but also really getting into those core muscles as well. Let's take the hands up, interlock your hands chest level. Let's just press them out, spreading the shoulder blades apart. That prone fly really got into the upper back, so we'll open that out.

We're going to hold our static stretches for around 15 seconds. You can always press pause and hold them a little bit longer.

Lift the hands up. Keep the abdominals in tight. Press high. Press high. Press high, lifting up through the upper back, through the waist. Remember those side crunches we did? Really important to get that little stretch out.

Take them down behind. Remember the press-up work we did for the chest and shoulders? Lock them behind. Squeeze the shoulder blades together to feel that stretch. Try not to arch your back too much. So, we're just going to stretch through the key target muscles here that we've been using, the major muscle groups; although, remember in our lecture on flexibility we'll show you lots of other exercises as well.

Ease that off. The knees are slightly bent. We take one hand up and we take a stretch across to the side. Let's reach and take it back up to the center. You should feel like your core body temperature is dropping a little bit down. Your breathing is coming back to normal, but hopefully you can feel a little bit of a buzz in the muscles, like we've done some work.

And back over. Beautiful. We're going to take the left foot. Get a hold of it. Now, a little bit of balance work since what we've been doing here is working on our core strength. You're going to need it for this exercise.

Heel up to the backside. Should be feeling that stretch on the front of the thigh there. I'm going to take that foot and put it down in front on the heel with the toe lifted. Put your hands onto the right thigh and then take your chest forward so we can get that little stretch in the back of the thigh. Remember that hamstring curl, when you were pulling the ball towards yourself. Important to get that little stretch for the hamstring curl. Drop your chin onto your chest and slowly curl up. Your head is the last thing up.

We'll swap over to the other side. Let's take the right foot. Get a hold of it. Squeeze the heel towards the backside. Remember, for your balance, keep this knee slightly bent. You might want to put this hand out to the side or grab a hold of the ear, whichever works for you. Keeping the abs in tight, little bit of a core challenge here also. The heel goes down in front, the toes up, hands on the other thigh, so just the basic stretches of our key muscle groups.

Now, we've done a little bit of work for the inner thigh. Chin on the chest and slowly curl up. So, to get a bit of a stretch there we're going to take the feet out a little bit wider and point the toes out for a little plié position. See how the knees go out? Take the hands just above the knees and press backwards, keeping the abs in tight. Should start to get that little stretch on the inner thigh there as we press backwards. Good. Keep your breathing relaxed.

Straighten it up. Walk them in. Give yourselves a deep breath. Give your hands a shake. Give your legs a shake. Good work, team. Well done. I hope you enjoyed your fitness ball, stability ball, Swiss ball—whatever you call it—I hope you enjoyed your ball workout.

Balance Board Workout
Lecture 31

Balance boards, core boards, and Bosu balls provide an unstable surface, forcing you to engage your core muscles to control your balance. This workout is a great total-body workout, and it also works on proprioception. Within the joints, joint receptors—including the Golgi tendon organ and the stretch reflex—detect movement of the joints and cause contractions to control movement. If you strengthen these areas, you'll reduce your risk of injury. In addition, exercising on balance boards allows you to recruit 20% more muscle fiber, causing you to get an even better workout than you would on a flat surface.

A Bosu ball provides an unstable surface that adds the challenge of balancing to your workout.

Guidelines

- The following exercises are going to be done in a circuit, involving 1 minute of each exercise and then a rest of about 15 to 20 seconds in between exercises.

- During that minute, try to get a feel for the form of the exercise in the beginning, and then at least for the following 30 seconds, try to increase your pace.

- Before you do any workout, it's important to warm up—for example, making circles with your shoulders and wrists and marching in place—to increase your body temperature slightly.

- If at any time you need to rest and grab some water, you can do that during the breaks between exercises.

- You can purchase balance boards at a sports store; they are relatively inexpensive.

- Be careful when getting onto your balance board. If you're not used to it, take your time and practice a few times before you start your workout.

Run in Place: Right
- Start by placing your right leg forward.

- Get into a rhythm, and keep it going.

- Pump your arms forward and backward.

- Try to control your movement.

- If you lose your balance, it's OK to reset yourself.

- Be aware of pulling your abdominals in tight. You'll also feel some tension in the glutei. Focus on controlling your trunk, pulling in through the waist.

- By tilting forward and backward, you're working your legs and getting a cardio effect. You're also challenging the smaller muscles—the joint receptors—in your ankles to control that movement.

Run in Place: Left
- Reset yourself, and place your left leg forward this time. Start slowly.

- Be aware of any differences you might have from one side to the other so that you can work on any weaknesses.

- Remember to pump your arms. Keep them moving.

- Take some deep breaths. Keep your abdominals in tight and your chest lifted.

- You're training the joint receptors to get used to responding to different angles.

Squat

- Unlike the last exercise, which focused on cardio, this is a toning exercise.

- Try to stay balanced in the middle of the board, but you might drift from one side to the other. Pull in tight through the abdominals to keep your trunk strong.

- As you squat down, lift your arms forward to help you balance.

- When your muscles shake, they are trying to respond to the extra challenge of balancing.

- If you lose your balance, just reset yourself.

- You're working the front and back of the thigh and the glutei. This is a whole-body workout.

Lunge off Rear: Right

- The goal of this exercise is to try to keep your right leg balanced while your left leg lunges off the board. Don't let your right leg tilt to one side or the other.

- Your arms should be working as well when lunging.

- Try to place your left foot further back as a challenge.

- Make sure your left foot is on the ball of the foot when it reaches back and lands on the floor.

Lunge off Rear: Left

- Switch legs. This time, your left leg is in the center of the board and is the leg you're trying to keep balanced.

- Keep your hips square. Don't let your knee twist.

- Start nice and easy for the first few. Get used to the movement.

- Keep your chest lifted, and keep your abdominals in tight.

- Increase your pace if you can to burn more calories.

- Not only are you toning your hips and thighs, but you're also getting a cardio effect, burning calories. You're also working on the agility skill of proprioception, which is useful to develop if you're a sports performer but is also helpful in reducing the risk of injuries.

Lunge off Side: Right

- This exercise involves lunging off the side with the same setup as the last exercise. Start with your right foot in the center of the board.

- Point your left toe and bend your knee slightly outward as you lunge down.

- Try to keep your right foot balanced. Don't let the board tilt to one side or the other. The challenge is to keep it in the center.

- Use your arms in opposition.

- Pick up the pace when you can.

- Pull your abs in tight, and keep your chest lifted.

- The challenge is to try to sink lower into your lunge.

Lunge off Side: Left
- This time, start with your left foot on the board, making sure it's in the center. Try to get used to that balance point.

- Keep your head and chest lifted all the time.

- Keep your abs and waist pulled in tight.

- You should feel some work in the lower leg and the gluteus, but you will really feel your abdominals working hard if you keep them in tight.

- Sink lower into your lunge. The more you bend your right knee, the more work your quads, hamstrings, and gluteus will do.

Run in Place: Side to Side
- Instead of running forward and backward, this time you're running side to side, working through the range of motion in your ankles.

- Use your arms in opposition.

- The challenge is to keep your abdominals in tight and to keep the movement fluid.

- Pick up the pace so that you are running.

- You want to get some movement through the ankle, forcing the joint receptors to detect to and then causing the muscles to contract to control it. This movement helps to speed up the nerve messages that are traveling to and from the brain, reducing your risk of injury.

Twists
- This exercise focuses on your obliques, and it will help you understand how core strength is important for integrating the power and strength from your upper and lower body.

- The thoracolumbar fascia is the sheath in the lower back to which many different muscles attach—particularly, the transversus abdominis and the internal obliques, which are key core muscles. From below the hamstrings, the glutei indirectly attach to the thoracolumbar fascia, linking your upper and lower body.

- Try to use your upper and lower body to help you twist side to side.

- Use your arms and legs. To try to integrate the upper and lower parts; keep your abdominals in tight.

- You will lose your balance with this exercise; just keep resetting yourself.

- One of the principles of fitness is that you only begin to progress when you approach your limit. Therefore, if you're at the boundary where you're starting to lose your balance, that's good because that's where your balance begins to develop and improve.

Chop: Right
- You're going to put your right foot on the board and bring your left foot out to the side—not too wide.

- The key is to twist and control the movement of your midsection—while also controlling the tilt forward, backward, and side to side.

- Be careful of your knee; it is not designed to bend inward.

- Try to keep the board balanced; try not to let it touch the floor on the side.

- This is another exercise that links the upper body to the lower body. To do that effectively, you need to keep your core engaged.

- This is a whole-body workout—from the upper body, through the middle, and down to the legs. You're also doing some toning work with your legs as you squat and lift.

Chop: Left

- Switch legs, and set yourself up for the chop.

- While you're twisting on the board, you're also trying to balance it.

- Make sure you're twisting on the ball of your right foot so that your knee doesn't bend inward.

- This movement relates to playing golf and maybe even to tennis. You can't do either of those sports without a strong core.

Squat and Lift Knee: Right

- Start with your right foot on the board, and you're going to lift your left knee. Try to balance the board in the center.

- Bring your hands forward slightly.

- Keep your abdominals in tight and your chest lifted.

- When your upper body comes forward, don't round your spine. Instead, hinge your hip forward.

- You're working your abdominals, but you're also working your lower leg, focusing on balance and proprioception.

Squat and Lift Knee: Left

- This time, balance your left foot on the board.

- Keep your abs in tight.

- Your arms should work in opposition to your legs.

- Make sure you're focusing on keeping the board balanced in the center, and make sure you're getting low on the squats. The more you bend your knee, the more work you're doing through the legs and buttocks.

Kick Front and Touch Board: Right

- Start with your right foot on the board, and kick with your left leg.

- Try to keep the board balanced, but you might find that it tilts one way or the other. Your balance will improve with practice.

- Keep your chest up when you kick, and keep your abs in tight.

- When you touch the board, don't round your spine. Bend your knees, and hinge from the hip.

Kick Front and Touch Board: Left

- Start with your left foot on the board this time.

- The challenge is to try your hardest to keep the board balanced.

- You may have done this exercise on firm ground, but once you start doing it on an unstable surface, it becomes a whole different exercise.

- Bend your knees a little to get down to the board.

Press-Up with Twists

- You're going to get on your knees for this press-up exercise to make sure that you can do the full movement.

- Your normal press-up is not going to move, so you're just working the chest, the front of the shoulder, and the triceps. However, because this exercise involves a twist, there's extra work going on around your shoulder girdle that involves the rotator cuff muscles. The goal is to control the movement of the shoulder.

- Keep your abdominals pulled in tight. You don't want your backside sticking up or your hips dropping down. Maintain a natural, normal curve in your lower spine.

- It often works better to breathe in on the way down and breathe out on the way up.

- Don't lock your arms at the top of the press-up.

Triceps Dips
- You may have done this exercise before on a chair or on a step platform, but once you do it on a balance board, it's a much greater challenge because finding your balance point is not easy.

- Be careful not to lock your arms, and keep your abdominals in tight.

- Don't push your hips forward.

- In addition to working your triceps, this exercise works your shoulder girdle, which keeps you from wobbling.

Cooldown
- To cool down, do some mobilizing exercises just like you did for the warm-up.

- Then, move on to some static stretches, holding them for about 30 seconds each.

Balance Board Workout
Lecture 31—Transcript

Hi, and in our homework series today we're working with a balance board. Now, this could be a balance board that we have here, a simple one. One could be a core board or maybe a Bosu. The idea is we're working with an unstable surface. Now, the beauty of that is that it really forces you to engage the core muscles to control your balance.

Now, remember, that core strength we talked about before, the idea of that is if we develop the strength here, that will allow us to be more effective with our limbs, and you'll really see that in this kind of workout today. It's a great total body workout. It's also working on what we call proprioception.

Now, within the joints you have joint receptors. We have the Golgi tendon organ; we have the stretch reflex. We touched on those before when we talked about muscles and joints. Now, what they'll do is detect the movement, maybe the speed or the angle that the joints is moving through and cause contractions to control that movement. Now, the beauty of that is if we train for that then what we'll do is actually reduce our risk of injury as well as, at the same time, getting a cardio effect, getting a toning effect, which sounds pretty good to me; and the theory is that working on balance boards we actually end up recruiting 20% more muscle fiber, so we're getting an even better workout than you would do on a flat surface. However, if you're not used to this then take your time at first.

The way we're going to work today, a whole range of exercises. I'm fumbling around in my pocket for a stop watch because we're going to do this as circuit style today. So, the guys and I are going to work on 1 minute of each exercise, and then we're going to have a rest of about 15, 20 seconds—15, 20, we're still negotiating that—depending on how hard to work, but the idea is, for that minute, try and kind of get started, feel your way into the exercise, and then certainly for the next 30 seconds really try and pump it out a little bit. Okay?

Important before you do any workout: You've got to have a warm-up. I'm sure you know that now, so anything that involves circling the shoulders, the wrists, something like the guys are doing now, little bit of marching on the spot, just to get the temperature up slightly before we start.

Okay, so, are we ready with our first exercise? So, let's put one foot on the front of the board—careful how you get onto the board—and one foot towards the back. Now, our exercise, just get a little practice, is forwards and backwards. Let's just get a little feel for that. So, you're running on the spot, but we're tilting forwards and backwards on that board.

Are we set? Are we ready, guys? Can I get a minute? Go. Can I get a witness? And away we go. Get into the rhythm. Keep it going. Pump the arms forwards and backwards. Try and control that movement. If you lose your balance, that's okay if you have to reset yourself, but be aware now of pulling in the abdominals tight. There's a little bit of tension in the glutes. You're really trying to control what's going on in the trunk pulling through the waist. Keep going. Keep going. You'll be pleased to know we're nearly halfway there. Come on. Come on. Come on. You'll hear me panting in a minute. That's not special effects. That will be me panting. Keep going. Keep going. Keep going. We're halfway there. Keep it going. Keep it going. Keep going. Keep going. Keep going. If you lose your balance, that's okay. You can reset yourself.

We've got another 15 seconds. Keep it going. You weren't stopping then, were you? Keep it going. And you see this tilt forwards and backwards? You can see we're working through the legs. We're clearly getting a cardio effect—last 10 seconds—but what we're also doing here is really challenging the smaller muscles, these joint receptors in the ankles, to control that movement.

Take a quick rest there. Well done. Well done. Quick rest. Get a deep breath. Get off the board. Get back onto terra firma for a second. Get ready for your second exercise, which, guess what, is just the opposite of what you've just done.

Okay, I'm resetting. Other foot on the front. Are we ready? Now, be aware, you may have difference from one side to the other, so start off slowly. Let's go. We're running forwards and backwards. Oh, he says, struggling to get started. I think mine's just thawed.

Away we go, forwards and back, pumping one arm and the other, up we go. Forwards and back. Getting into that little running motion, running on the spot, forwards and back. You've got your left leg forwards this time, or if you had the left leg forwards, get the right one this time. Make sure it's opposite. And away we go. Get pumping. Get pumping. Get pumping.

Fabulous. Keep going. You're halfway there already. Take some deep breaths. Are you running? Keep your abdominals in tight. Try and keep it straightest in here. Fabulous form. Chest lifted. Here's one I prepared earlier. Fabulous form. Well done. Keep those arms moving. We're getting the heart rate going, but we're working into the legs, and also now we're challenging the small joint receptors here, training them to get used to responding to those different angles.

We've got 5 more seconds. Let's keep going, guys. Keep going. Keep going. Keep going at home there. And take a quick rest there. Well done. Well done. Step off your board.

We're moving onto a little bit more of a toning exercise now, not so much cardio. Get your breath back on this next exercise. We're going to squat, so be careful how you do this. One foot on the side, one foot on the other side. Now, ideally for the squat we're going to stay balanced. We're going to stay balanced in the middle, but you might find that you drift from one side to the other. If you can, try and set yourself in the center. Let's reset the clock. Can I get a minute? Let's go.

Now, what you might find when you're doing this is as you squat down, lifting the arms forwards will help with the balance. You see that little shake going on there? What's going on is the muscles are trying to respond to this extra challenge of balancing. Remember I said about a 20% extra muscle recruitment. Get into a good rhythm and keep going with it. If you lose your balance and it goes to one side or the other, that's okay. Just reset yourself. Try and stay in the center. Away you go.

So, fabulous exercise because clearly we're working into the front of the thigh, into the back of the thigh—the hamstrings—into the glutes. Are you sprinting on the spot? I think you've got a faulty one. Keep going and reset yourself. If it starts to shake, don't worry. But also what's happening here, really pulling in tight through the abdominals. If you don't keep the trunk strong, you are going to fall all over the place. There's only 10 seconds, you'll be pleased to hear.

Keep going. Keep going. And down you go, working into the front and back of the thighs into the glutes. It's a whole body workout. Step off and take a rest there. Well done. Well done. How are you doing at home? Remember, easy to get a hold of these little balance boards, so keep a lookout for them at the sports shop. You've got another few seconds.

We're going to change to another exercise now: Lunging off the board. So, you're going to put your right foot in the center of the board, and we're going to try and keep it balanced this time. Left foot is up close. All you're going to do is take it behind, put it on the ball of the foot, lunge down, and bring it back up. It's a real lunge, nice and deep. Are we set? Let's go. Step back, squat down, and up.

Now, try and keep this front foot, if you can, balanced. Don't let it tilt to one side or the other. The arms are working as well into this lunge. Keep it going. Keep it going. Beautiful. Take it right back. Bring it right up to the front. Down and then up to the front. Good. And down. Good. Further back. Good. And up, down. Good. Keep it going. Keep it going. See how we're having to work now on this balance here. Try not to let this tilt. We're halfway there, guys. Does that foot go further back? Apparently not. And back. Good. Put it on the ball of the foot at the back. Bend the knee down to the floor. Good. Come on, we've got 15 seconds. I'm going to join in and get my money's worth. And up. And up. Come on. Come on. Only 10. You can do this at home. Let's go. Up. Up. This is killing me. I only joined in halfway through. And take a little rest there. Well done. Well done.

Give the legs a shake. Get off the board. Just in case you haven't guess what's happening next, get a breather, and swap legs.

Left leg on the board. It's in the center because we're going to try and keep it balanced this time. Start with the foot by the side. What your right foot's going to do—just get a little practice—is go back onto the ball of the foot so you can drop down. Keep your hips square. Don't let this knee twist, and then step up.

Okay, let's go. Start nice and easy for the first few. Get used to the movement. Keep your chest lifted. Remember, it's all about your core strength. Keep your abdominals in tight. Down we go. Good. Keep it going. Good. Does it go further back? Reach that foot further back, chest lifted. Good. Reach the foot right back. Good. Keeping that foot balanced on the front of the board, try not to let it tilt. Come on, we're halfway there. Let's do some work. Come on. It's easy for me to say. I'm not doing anything. Come on. Lunge and up. Lunge and up. Take the pace up. Come on. Let's burn some calories, and down, and down. Let's tone the hips and the thighs. Good, come on. (I want to say buns of steel but that's because I'm a child of the '80s. I don't know if that means anything nowadays.) And down. Can I get just a couple more, please? Come on, we can do this, team. You can do this at home. And take a little rest there. Well done. Well done. Anyone else's legs burning? Good work. Good work. Good work.

So, remember, the beauty of this is not only are we getting that toning, we're getting a cardio effects—trust me—so we're burning some calories, but also we're working this proprioception, this agility skill, that's really useful in developing if you're a sports performer, but particularly for reducing risk of injuries.

So, we're going to lunge off the side now. So, same set up. Get your right foot on the board. Get it in the center. Ready? Start close, and now you're going to go for a side lunge, so you're going to step the foot out but point the toe and the knee slightly outwards when you go down. This kind of movement's not too good for us, and this certainly isn't. So, it's pointing slightly outwards, and the knee will go down that way as we lunge.

Step back in, out, and back in. Tall. Okay, are we good to go? Save yourselves. We're off. Come on, let's go, team. And down. Good. Get into the rhythm. Try and keep this foot balanced. Don't let the board tilt to one side or the other. Try and keep it in the center. That's the challenge. Good. Out and out. How are we doing? Lunge it out. Use the arms in opposition. Let's go. Out and back. Good. Beautiful. Nearly halfway there, and good. Perhaps not to wide. Just go a little lower. And down. Little bit quicker. Come on, let's pick up the pace now.

How are you doing at home? Pick up the pace. Good. Out. Out. Come on. You weren't slowing while I was over there, were you? I know that happens. Out. We've only 20 seconds to go. Come on, team. Give me that lunge. Bend the knee. Abs in tight. Pull in here. Pull in here. Chest lifted. We've only got 10 seconds. Come on, let's pick up the pace. Out, and out.

How are you doing at home? Hope you're still with us. Last couple of seconds. Last one, and take a rest there. Well done. Well done. Get a deep breath. Keep the feet moving. Anybody feeling anything yet? I do hope so.

Just in case you hadn't guessed, we're going to swap over to the other leg. So, you're going to put your left foot on the board. You're going to make sure it's in the center. Try and find that balance point right away. Just get used to that balance point. What we don't want on this is we don't want it tilted one way or the other. We're trying to control it. Keep it in the middle.

Start close. Just get a little practice, first of all. The left foot's on, so your right foot's going to step out. Remember the knee and the toe points slightly outwards for this so that we can get that lunge and then back in. We're trying to avoid this. We're trying to avoid going over on the ankle. So, point it slightly out. Out it goes and down. Step up, chest lifted all the time. Abs are in tight. Waist is pulled in. Are we set? Good to go? I think you had more than 20 seconds there, but I'll let you off that one. You can owe me some.

Okay, are we set? You ready at home? Let's go. Lunge and up. Right leg out and back. Come on. Keep that balance in the center, on your balance board, on your Bosu, core board—whatever it is, keep that foot in the center. Don't let it tilt to the side. That's the challenge. You should feel some work going on in the lower leg here. Should also feel some work going on here, here, in the glutes, but more than that, pull in here, abdominals tight. Keep going. Good. Fabulous. Keep the head up.

Can we sink a little lower into that lunge? Down. We're over halfway there, you'll be pleased to know. Let's pick up the pace. Good. Come on. Come on. Good. Nice and deep. The more bend we're going to get through this knee, the more work we're going to do through the quads, through the hamstrings, and through the glutes. That's what it's all about. Come on. Come on. Perfect pins. Yes, come on. Only 5 seconds. Five second. Stick with us at home. You can do this. Good. Come on. Come on. Come on. Smile. And take a quick rest there. Well done. Well done. Brilliant. How did you do on that?

Going to change things slightly. Let's go for a slightly easier exercise this time, give you a chance to get your breath back. So, what we're going to do this time is step either side of the board. Be careful how you get on. And all we're going to do here is run on the spot from side to side and literally let it touch down. So, we're working through that range of movement in the ankle. Okay. Are we good to go? Let's get running. Up. Side to side now. So, remember at the top we ran forwards and back. I'm running side to side now. Use your arms in opposition.

The challenge here is to keep your abdominals in tight and to keep it fluid. Can we keep going side to side? Can you prevent it from tilting you forwards and backwards? I did that deliberately, by the way. Up. Come on, let's go. Can we pick up the pace? We are supposed to be running. Come on. Come on. Pick up the pace. Let's go. Let's go. We're halfway there. Good. Side to side.

Let's get some movement through that ankle. See this work going on here? Forcing those little joint receptors to detect what's going on and then cause the muscles to contract to control it. It's speeding up those nerve messages that are going through what's called a neurolog. Actually it doesn't go right up to the brain. It just goes from here. It picks up that angle through the nerve fibers. It goes to the lower spine, to the spinal cord, which effectively obviously is to the brain, and then that message comes back down, quickly contract to get me out of that position. Keep going. Keep going. A few more seconds. And if we can increase the speed of those neuro messages, it's going to reduce our risk of injury. Take a rest there. Well done. Well done. Good work.

Okay, now this one you will be able to get your breath back because this is not so cardio, a little bit more about toning on this one, but if you can pick up the pace, that would be great. We're going to work for some twists. We're going to really get into some obliques now, and this will help you to understand how core strength is important for translating the power, the strength from your upper and lower body. It forms this integration, and the key to that is something we talked about in the lower spine lecture. We talked about the thoracolumbar fascia, the sheath at the lower back there, because so many different muscles attach to that, in particularly the transversus abdominis and the internal obliques. There our key core muscles. But also what happens is from below the hamstrings, the glutes indirectly will attach to it, and then also the last from above. So, actually, this link between your upper and lower body comes through here, which is controlled by here.

So, what we're going to do here is try and use the upper body and the lower body to help us twist side to side. We're trying to get that twist from side to side. You're going to have to use your arms. You're going to have to use your legs. But to try and integrate that, what you've got to do is keep the abdominals in really tight. You will lose your balance on this one. Just keep resetting yourself and do as best you can. That was definitely more than 20 seconds. Let's go.

Twist. Try and get into a rhythm if you can. Twist. Twist. Side to side. Good. And twist. You know what I was just thinking? If you've got this core board on a shag pile carpet, you're going to have a real job twisting, and I perhaps should've mentioned that. Twist. Come on. Twist. Side to side.

How are we doing? Keep going. Keep going. Keep going. Keep going. Both feet on. You weren't cheating then, were you? Beautiful. How is it every time I look they've stopped. I hope you're still going at home. Keep going, but don't worry, that will happen, particularly with this kind of training, balance training. Remember we talked about the principles of fitness. Keep going. You only begin to progress when you get near to your limit. So, if you're at that boundary where you're starting to lose your balance, that's good because that's where it begins to develop.

Keep going. You've only got another 14 minutes. I don't know what happened now. I must've counted that wrong. No, I'm just kidding. You've got about 5 more seconds. Keep going. Keep going. You're doing well. See, just as we get to the end, you've perfected it. I'll let it run a few more seconds because that looks good.

Fabulous. Take a quick rest there. Well done. Well done. Well done. Okay, you'll be pleased to know this: that's tough exercise but really good at getting that kind of integration from your upper to your lower body, and hopefully you can really feel like you're doing some work around your middle there, particularly the obliques at the side.

So, okay, we're going to change it slightly now. You're going to put your right foot on the board again for me, please, and we're just going to do a wood chop. So, we're going to take the left foot out to the side, not too wide for this one. Now, the key here is to get this twist and control the movement. Obviously we've got to control the tilt forwards, backwards, side to side, but also now we're going to get some rotation here. So, be careful of the knee. We don't want it to drop in. It's not designed to do that.

So, all we're going to do here is to lift the hands up and turn, and as we go down here, twist; come onto the ball of the foot on the left; drop down and back up, and down. So, the idea is we're chopping. Chop. And up and chop. So, see how we're getting the twist and the twist there? But what we're trying to do here is balance.

Okay, let's get into a good rhythm. Begin nice and easy, and then we'll take it from there. Okay, and let's go. Twist and lift. Twist and lift. Abs are in tight, and again, this is one of those exercises, now that you've just done that twist, where you're linking the upper body working with the lower body, and to do that effectively, like any tennis or golf player will tell you, you need to keep your core engaged, pulling the tummy button towards the lower spine, drawing in through the waist. Keep it going. And down. Beautiful. And twist.

Again, this is a whole body workout. Did yours slide like mine? Be careful of that. Twist. Beautiful. See this whole body working, upper body, through the middle through that twist, down to the legs. Fabulous. See how we're working on that balance. Try and keep that board balanced. Try not to let it touch down at the side. That's excellent. And down. Good. And also, we're getting that little toning work through the legs as we're squatting and lifting.

Hold it there. Well done. Well done. Quick rest. You won't be surprised to know the next exercise is we'll flip it across to the other side. Okay. Don't forget, if at any time you need to grab some water, you can always do that in these little breaks in between.

Okay, left foot is on now. Right foot out to the side. Okay, let's set ourselves up for the chop. Get ready, hands are up, and let's go. Down and lift, twist. So, you're getting this twist on the board. You're also trying to balance it. Don't let it top out. Good. Make sure you're getting that twist on your right foot. What we don't want is this knee to bend inwards.

About the first 20 seconds get used to the movement. Then can we start to take up the pace. Let's go. Down. Now, if you remember, a golfer or a tennis player will be using this movement quite dynamically, so we can pick up the pace a little bit. That's me trying to hint that you 2 should go faster, and you at home. Okay? Let's go. Of course, that's easy for me to say while I'm just watching. But come on, you can do this. Bend the knee. Good. Good. Beautiful. Look at that twist. You can see how this relates to playing golf, maybe to playing tennis. You can see this movement.

Five more seconds. You can't do either of those sports without a strong core, and in fact a lot of sports. And take a quick rest there. Well done. Well done. Good work. Tricky exercise but great because it's employing lots of muscle groups using your whole body, which gives us a good calorie burn.

Okay, we're going onto a squat and a knee lift, right foot on the board first. Okay, here we go. Again, we're trying to keep the balance in the center. You may find that it bottoms out on one side or the other, but try and keep that balance if we can.

Foot to the side, quite close. Now, remember, for your squat we decided we're going to bring the hands forward slightly. Lift the knee, squat. Lift the knee. Can we keep that balanced when we lift the knee? Try not to let it touch down on one side or the other. So, go a little slowly for the first 20 seconds and then see how you do.

Let's reset. 20 seconds, squat and lift the left knee. Let's go. Squat, lift, squat, lift. Abdominals tight. Let's get a good squat. If you're sitting down on a chair, push the backside out behind. Keep the abdominals in tight. Keep going. There's that little hinge of the hip. See how my upper body comes forwards, but it's not a rounding of the spine. It's a hinge from the hip forwards. Forwards. Down. Lift. Down. Let's go. Down and lift.

Oh, that's 30 seconds. I think it's time to pick up the pace. And down and lift. You did hear me say pick up the pace then, didn't you, team? And lift, down. Good. Beautiful. Beautiful. Keep the upper body chest lifted, tight here. Pull in. Pull in. Fabulous. Really working through those abdominals but also now really working into that lower limb here, really working on the balance, on that proprioception, remember. Last 2 seconds.

Take a rest there. Well done. Well done. You're not going to be surprised to know what comes next. If you need water, now's a good time, but make it quick. You still owe me a few seconds from that long rest.

Okay, we've got the left foot on. Remember, try and find the center. Make sure it's balanced. Get a couple of practice go's first. Squat, lift. Try and keep balanced. Don't let this bottom out.

Squat, abs in tight. Beautiful. So, I don't know about you, I think we're ready to go. Squat and lift. Squat. Up. Squat. Beautiful. Squat. Up. Fabulous. Abs in tight. Squat. Keep this balanced in the center. Try not to let it bottom out. Up. Arms can work in opposition to the legs if you wish. If you're feeling super comfortable—which I'm not; I don't know why I'm doing this—you can take your hands out of it, and lift. Keep going. We're halfway there. Down. Good, give me a good squat. Good. Out to the side on that squat. Beautiful. Good.

How are you doing at home? Keep going. Slightly different kind of workout, but you can see where we're going here. Come on. I can hear some puffing and panting. That's a good sign. How are you doing at home? Make sure you're keeping that balance in the center. Make sure you're getting nice and low on the squats. The more bend you get through that knee, the more work we're doing through the legs, through the buttocks. That's what it's all about. And take a quick rest there. Well done. Well done. Well done. That's your squats. Take a quick breath.

Okay, so, we're going to move on now and take that exercise slightly. We're getting close towards the end, so we're sort of getting into the home stretch, so it's going to get a little tougher now, but we need our sprint for home. So, we're going to go for a kick and a touch on the board here.

So, this is quite a toughie. You are again going to try and keep the board balanced, but you might find that you get a tilt one way or the other, but this is what's going to happen: You're going to take a kick, touch the board, kick, touch the board, kick. If we can, get to a rhythm of kicking and touching, and ideally, if we can, keep that elevated rather than bottomed out.

Get a few practice ones first. Where's the key to the balance? It's all just here. Are we ready? And away you go. Your right foot's on. Kick with your left. Touch with your left. Left. Left. Try, if you can, to keep the board in the center, not bottomed out. Don't let it tilt one way or the other. Fabulous. Let's go. And kick. Chest up when you kick. And down. Good. Touch the board. Good. Abs in tight, and remember that touch on the board. Can we pick up the pace?

When you touch the board, don't round the spine. Bend the knees. Hinge from the hip, from the hip. We're over halfway. Come on, let's pick up the pace, guys. Come on. It's not really a question. How are you doing at home? You should be feeling this now. Come on. Last 15. Touch. Try and keep that board balanced. And remember, it's tough. You will bottom out on one side or the other. You've just got to try and keep it in the center. It will get better. Good. Last few seconds. Last couple. Well done. Well done.

Take a quick rest there. Give your legs a shake. Get back on terra firma. We're onto the other side. Not far to go now. Not far to go now. Actually, I'm lying. We're not even halfway yet. No, no, no. Come on, let's switch over to the other side.

Okay, so, remember what we're doing here. Left foot on. You're going to take a little kick forwards with the right, touch down with the right. Kick with the right, touch down with the right. Kick and touch. Okay, I think we're good to go. Up, kick, touch. Kick and touch. Remember it's a challenge here. You've just got to try your hardest to keep that balance, if you can. Kick and down. Kick and down. Kick and down.

Now, some of you may have done this exercise—keep going—on terra firma, but once you start doing it on this unstable surface, certainly becomes a whole different exercise.

Kick and down. Good. Bend those knees a little bit to get down to the board. Kick and down. Give me a little kick. And down. That's it. Fight that balance. And that'd good. Remember, if you start to lose your balance, you're on the edge. You've got to your boundaries, and that's where you'll improve, so stick with it.

We've only got 20 seconds to go. Were you looking at the clock then, desperately? I'm keeping it hidden. Come on. Come on. You can do this at home. Keep going. Keep going. It's only a minute. What's a minute. Come on. In a New York minute. Come on, let's go. Beautiful. Kick. Give me that kick, and down. Kick like you mean it. Give me a martial arts kick. There's only 1 second to go. Quick, get one in.

Brilliant, and take a quick rest there. Well done. Well done. Well done. Okay, good work. You'll be pleased to know we're going to get down on the floor now for a little press-up work. So, if you want to take a moment to get a quick sip of water, that's okay. I'll show you the next exercise.

For the press-up exercise we're going to go on our knees for this one to be sure to make sure that we can get the full movement in on this exercise. I'll show you it, first of all, from the front so you can see what I'm doing here. What I'm going to do is take the hands wide on the board. I'm on the knees for the press-up, but as we go down I'm going to twist for the press-up, and back up, and then guess what? To the other side and then back up. So, you get that little twist as you go down, and again here, the difference, your normal press-up, it's not going to move, so you're just working the chest;

you're working through the front of the shoulder; you're working through the triceps. But now, because it's moving, you've got all this extra work going on around the shoulder girdle, those rotator cuff muscles we talked about in the earlier lectures. I've got to really control that movement on the shoulder. Okay?

Let me just show you sideways on. What we need to be aware of, even in this kneeling position, is your abdominals are pulled in tight. We don't want the backside sticking up. We don't want the hips dropping down. Keep that natural, normal curve in your lower spine, and as we go down we twist, and then on the next one we twist the other way. So, start nice and slow, and then we'll get the pace going.

So, are we ready? Abdominals in tight all the time. Away we go. Start at a nice easy pace, and up you go. Beautiful. Alternating side to side. You're on your knees for these press-ups because you've got a minute to go. And believe it or not, you've already done 10 seconds. That went quickly, didn't it? Didn't that go quickly? Come on, keep going. This is real sweat, you know. This is not makeup. Good work, and down. Keep it going. Good. 20 seconds. Come on.

Now, you're breathing. As long as you're breathing, that's fine. Truth is it often works better to breathe in on the way down and breathe out on the way up. So, and then blow it out and it makes it dynamic as you press up.

So, we've got value-added training here. We've got a little bit of work for your chest, shoulders, and triceps because we're doing press-ups, but what we've also got here is this work for your core muscles and also the muscles around the shoulder girdle, the rotator cuff, those 4 muscles that are vital. How are we doing? Keep it going, guys. Don't lock out your arms at the top of the press-up. There's only 5 seconds to go. Come on. Come on. You can do it. I'd love to join you.

Take a quick rest there. Well done. Well done. Well done. Were you looking at me for help then? I can't help you. That was fabulous.

Okay, so, press-ups. We've only got really 1 more exercise to do. So, we're going to do a little dip here, and you may have seen tricep dips. Beauty of this: it really gets into a problem area, backs of the arms. You may have done this before on a chair, on a step platform, but actually once you do it on here it's a much greater challenge. So, if you'll take yours behind you so that your feet are this way towards me, and I'll show you sideways on where we're going with this one.

So, we're going to sit in front of the board, hands on at the back. Find your balance point, which is not easy. You're going to bend the elbows to lower your backside down to the floor, and then press back up. It's only a small movement. Careful not the lock the arms out. Keep the abdominals in tight. Don't push the hips forwards. Just drop down and press up. So, it's only a small movement. So, we can get a pretty good pace going for that minute. All it is is bending the elbows and pressing back up, but we've got that extra challenge now, so as well as working the triceps, we're working again around the shoulder girdle.

Are we good to go? So, 1 minute. It's your last minute. Let's go. Okay, dip and press. Beautiful. Keeping that balance, don't let it bottom out one side or the other. Excellent stuff, and keep it going. Keep it going. Little bit quicker. So, working into the triceps, but also here what we've got to do is keep the abdominals pulled in tight. Good. And we've got that work going on around the shoulder girdle to stop it from wobbling. And let's go, like yours was there. Did you do that just to show them? That was good. That was good timing. Just as I said wobbling, we got a wobble. Perfect. We're halfway there. Come on. Come on. Just think how good your triceps are going to look. You'll be wearing t-shirts all through the winter as well as the summer to show off your fabulous arms. Keep going. We've only got seems to be 45 seconds. I must've got that wrong. I don't know, something wrong with this clock. Keep going. We've only got 10 seconds. Come on, you can do this. Last few seconds. Keep going, guys. And take a quick rest there.

Sit yourselves down. Well done. Or just fall down. Okay, we're going to have a little cool down now. I'd advise you to do some mobilizing exercises just like you did at the warm up, some little kind of mobilizing, some circles, little tilts, little rotations, nice and easy, and then we're going to move onto some stretches, some static stretches because now you're warm. This is the best time to do that work. So, we're going to look for holding those stretches for about 30 seconds. If you can't remember those basic stretches, take a quick look at the flexibility section in this series.

That was a great balance board workout. Hope you enjoyed it.

Kettlebell Workout

Lecture 32

Because kettlebells come in many different weights and there is a wide spectrum of exercises you can perform with them, a kettlebell is the perfect addition to anyone's fitness armory. Its unique design allows for swinging movements that incorporate momentum, which stimulates a different neuromuscular response than your body experiences with other resistance tools. Training with a kettlebell is founded on multijoint movements through different planes, creating a functional routine. This type of workout is a time-efficient way to improve your cardiorespiratory fitness, strength, and endurance. In addition, you can expect to improve your core strength, balance, posture, and coordination.

Kettlebell workouts can be used to increase your functional strength, making it easier to perform daily tasks.

Guidelines

- With kettlebell exercises—even more so than with other resistance tools—technique is vitally important because you have to work hard to control the momentum of the weight.

- Start with a light weight and only a small range of movement, and then you can increase both as you become comfortable with them. It is vital to observe the progressive overload maxim: If you want to avoid hitting a plateau, you need to keep increasing the weight as you become stronger.

- As with any workout, you need to start with a good warm-up; particularly, be aware of exercises that mobilize the lower spine because that's where you're going to be focusing.

- If you have any lower back injuries, this is probably not the ideal workout for you.

- Your target for each of the exercises is 12 repetitions on each side.

- Put your kettlebells down in between sets, and rotate through your lower spine, and do a few quick shoulder circles. Give yourself a brief posture break in between exercises.

Alternate Swing
- Start by dropping the weight down, making sure that your knees are slightly bent and that your abdominals are in really tight.

- You're going to alternate arms and do 12 repetitions on each side, so you can start with either arm. You might want to keep your other arm out for balance.

- Pressing through the heels, you will feel work being done through the hamstrings, glutei, and thighs.

- At all times, try to maintain a gentle curve in your lower spine.

- Let the weight swing naturally—up to about shoulder or face level—and then grab it with your other hand.

- The reason that this is such a time-efficient workout is because it works the whole body.

- The bending of your knee creates a contraction in the thighs, working the quadriceps and hamstrings. The whole posterior chain—including the glutei and the lower back—works to control the momentum that you don't get with other resistance tools. The rotator cuff muscles, located around the shoulder blades, work to stop the momentum, pulling you forward. You're also working the shoulder when you lift the weight.

- You should notice your heart rate increasing as you're doing this exercise.

Single-Leg Dead Lift
- This is a great exercise for the glutei and hamstrings.

- Be careful when picking up your weights. Make sure you bend your knees first and then pick it up, taking it in both hands.

- Keep your hips, chest, and shoulders square to the front because you're going to hinge from the hip.

- Start with your left leg behind you, and let yourself drop the weight down—but don't let it pull your shoulders down—until as far as it's comfortable, getting a stretch through the hamstring.

- Keep your abdominals in tight, and keep your shoulders back and down. Don't let your hip rotate up.

- Lift at your own comfortable pace. Slow is best.

- If you lose your balance, you can always reset yourself.

- Your front leg—your right leg—should be straight but not locked at the knee. There may be a slight bend to help with balance, but keep it almost straight.

- You're working on your dynamic range of motion through your hamstrings.

- Maintain a long line though your spine—from the top of your head to your tailbone down to your heel.

- Make sure you keep breathing at a normal, steady rate.

- Be aware that you may feel slightly different as you switch from one side to the other so that you can focus on the weaker or less flexible side.

Lunge Twist

- This exercise works the legs, quadriceps, hamstrings, and glutei—the big muscle groups. The more muscle groups you include, the greater the calorie burn will be. There's also some work going on in your arms and shoulders when holding the kettlebell in position, and the rotation is brought about by the oblique muscles, which are working through the waist.

- Step your left leg back, put it on the ball of the foot, drop your knee down to the ground, and rotate the kettlebell. It's all one movement.

- Keep your head lifted the whole time.

- Keep good posture by making sure your abdominals are pulled in all the time, working through those deeper core muscles, which can only help to protect the lower back if they're strong.

- Be careful of balance. When you step back, make sure to keep your feet about hip-width apart.

- Make sure you go as low as you can when lunging.

- Because you're working such large muscle groups, your heart rate may start to increase because you have to make sure that your heart is pumping enough blood to reach all of those muscles. Therefore, you may feel that you're getting a cardio effect from this workout, even though you might be going quite slowly.

One-Handed Plié Lift

- For the plié, you're going to take your feet wide, and point your knees and toes out.

- Keep your abdominals in tight, and make sure you're hinging from the hip—not bending from the back. Maintain a long spine.

- This exercise is going to put a lot of stress through your core muscles, so you might want to drop down to a slightly lighter weight—or at least start with a lighter weight, and then switch as needed.

- You'll start to notice a cardio effect because you're working the big muscle groups. You're working many muscles at once, but you're also creating a greater calorie burn at the same time, so 30 minutes is all you need with exercises like these.

- This is a plyometric, or explosive, exercise, so make sure you use some energy when you jump. However, at all times, you must protect your lower back with your core muscles during a movement like this.

Prone Row
- The challenge of this exercise is core strength protection for your lower back.

- Make sure you're in a comfortable, neutral spine position that allows your spine to be in its natural alignment.

- To make this exercise slightly easier, place your feet hip-width apart, but if you're feeling strong, you can keep them together.

- If you're new to this exercise, keep your knees on the floor, but if you are going to do that, place your feet slightly further back so that you're not in an all-fours position.

- Find the position that feels right for your lower spine, and then lock it in by keeping your abdominals in tight. Don't drop your backside down, and don't stick it up in the air.

- The row works your biceps, rear shoulder, and upper back.

- The challenge is to keep gravity from pulling your hips down. The glutei, hamstrings, obliques, and the transversus muscle—which runs across the center of the abdomen—are pulling in to try to keep the center locked.

- If you start to lose your neutral spine position, put your knees down. Take a rest if you've done 1 set.

- Make sure to keep your breathing constant, and keep your chest, hips, and shoulders square to the floor.

Turkish Stand-Up
- You might want to start with a lighter weight for this exercise. Because this is a difficult exercise, do 12 repetitions total—6 on either side.

- The challenge is to stand up without using the hand that is holding the weight, but if you get stuck, then use your free hand to help you up.

- You might need to keep your other hand out for balance.

- Your whole body is working during this exercise, but you really need to work hard with your core muscles to transfer strength from the lower to the upper body.

- Because you're using various muscles, you'll start to see a cardio effect because your heart has to work a little harder to get the blood around. You're also starting to use more calories.

- You might see differences from one side to the other, so take note of them.

- Go slowly on your way down, and remain under control.

Single Shoulder Press
- Be careful when you pick up your kettlebell. Bend your knees.

- For this exercise, you might want to keep your free hand out or on your hip for balance.

- Make sure that your elbow is slightly bent; don't lock it.

- Keep your abdominals in tight.

- As you take your very small squat, you're really working the shoulders.

- Keep your head tall, and keep your chin in.

- You're working your whole body—from your legs, through your core, and then through your upper body.

- Because your elbow is extended, you're working the triceps as well as the shoulder.

- As with all of these kettlebell exercises, you're focusing on your core. Having a strong core will enable you to perform better through your legs and arms.

Russian Twist
- This exercise focuses on working your core muscles, which help to strengthen the lower back.

- Start with your feet about hip-width apart, and make sure your abdominals are in tight.

- Make sure that you've got a long line from the top of your head down to your tailbone. You're sitting tall and then hinging backward— but not rounding—so that you can keep your abdominals in tight and keep the natural curve in your lower spine. The obliques are working at the waist to twist you from side to side.

- Try not to hold your breath.

- The challenge is to keep the transversus muscle, across the middle of the abs, pulled in really tight.

Cooldown

- In your cooldown, you should focus particularly on the lower back with some simple exercises.

- Drop yourself down onto your back, and pull your knees into your chest. Then, you can rock forward and backward slightly on the floor or a mat, massaging the lower spine.

- Next, bring your legs down to one side, and take your arms across to the other. Hold that position for about 15 to 30 seconds, and then switch to the other side.

- Also, you can get into a child's pose from yoga.

- Don't forget the lower body stretches because you've done a lot of work with your quads, hamstrings, and glutei.

Kettlebell Workout
Lecture 32—Transcript

Welcome to your kettlebell workout. Now, kettlebells are not a new innovation in fact their origins date back to military training in Russia in the early 18th century. The unique design with the inverted u-shaped handle allows for swinging movements and working with momentum, which stimulates a completely different neuromuscular response than your body experiences with other resistance tools. Training with a kettlebell is founded on multi-joint movements, through different planes, so this creates a truly functional routine. This workout is also a time-efficient way to improve your cardio-respiratory fitness, your strength and your endurance. And in addition, you can expect to improve your core strength, balance, posture and co-ordination. Now that's what I call value added training!

Now, since kettlebells come in many different weights and there is such a wide spectrum of exercises you can perform with them, a kettlebell is the perfect addition to anyone's fitness armory. As it can be used to increase your functional strength and so make it easier to perform daily tasks such as getting up off the sofa and putting your shopping in the boot of your car, clearly just about everyone can benefit from adding some form of kettlebell exercise to their regime. Now technique is vitally important here, even more so than with other resistance tools, as you have to work hard to control the momentum. Now, it's strongly recommended that you start with a really lightweight and only a small range of movement, and then you can increase both as you become comfortable with such. And remember it's important you'll remember from our lecture on muscles, it is vital to observe that progressive overload maxim, if you want to avoid hitting a plateau you do need to keep increasing the weight, as you get a little stronger.

Now as with any workout you need to ensure you have a good warm-up first. Make sure you are thoroughly warmed up before you begin as you can see the guys are doing now some shoulder rolls, some knee lifts, but particularly be aware of exercises that mobilize the lower spine because that's where we're going to be focusing, doing a lot of our work. And because of that, it's worth a mention that if you're carrying a lower back injury, this probably is not the ideal workout for you.

Now our target for all of the exercises is 12 repetitions and obviously on each side where necessary. So assuming you've had your 5-minute warm up and if you have not, press pause and do so now. Then we can begin. Let's take our weights guys. And remember that we are going to start with an exercise that uses your whole body. The guys are going to start with a slightly heavier weight, but there may be on some of the trickier exercises a point where there'll need to change. So you might need to have a little selection so you can choose the appropriate weight for each exercise.

Now our first exercise, the alternate swing, we're going to start nice and easy by dropping the weight down the knees are slightly bent and the abdominals are in really tight. Now just let it take a little swing for a second, get that feeling. It's an odd movement. You might want the other hand out for balance.

Now what we're doing here is pressing through the heels. There is work through the hamstrings at the back. Let's work through the glutes, work through the thighs keeping the abdominals in tight. We are going to let the weight swing up. Let it swing up to about shoulder level face level and then grab a hold of it with the other hand. It's not as tricky as it sounds. So let's drop it down, take a swing up. We will swap it over to the other side, and up it goes. Now let it swing naturally, okay, and away we go. Now we're looking for we said 12 reps, but obviously, you're swapping sides here, so I'm looking for 24 reps and I am going to trust you to count those 24 reps.

Now, the work here is, keep going for me, whole body this is the great thing about it and why it's such a time efficient workout. You can see that we're working through this bending the knee is bringing about some contraction in the thighs here front and back quadriceps and hamstrings. We're working through the gluts. We work the whole of what's called the posterior chain to control that momentum as we said we don't get that with other resistance tools, we've really got to work through the muscles in the glutes in the lower back. We're also working into the rotator cuff to stop it pulling us forwards and those rotator cuff muscles are around the shoulder blades. Yes, controlling that momentum, we're also working into the shoulder on the lift, so really getting total body. We're keeping the abdominals in tight and trying at all times to keep just a little gentle curve in the lower spine.

How are we doing? Is that 24 yet? We must be getting close. I would love to do them with you obviously. I'll joint you for the last couple. Fabulous. And you may start to feel as you're doing this your heart rate is increasing a little bit. I am really not counting. Please tell me we've got to 12 on each side by now. And gently take a rest. And I'd advise you to put them down in between sets. Give yourself a little rotation through the spine or a little side to side, a few shoulder circles. Give yourself that little posture break in between exercises.

We're going to move on now to the single leg dead lift and this is great for really getting into the glutes, hamstrings on this exercise. This is what we're going to do. Be careful how you pick up your weights, make sure you bend your knees first, pick it up, we're taking it in both hands. You're going to take your feet together. The important thing on this exercise, keep your hips, chest, shoulders square to the front facing me. Because what we're going to do is hinge from the hip so stay long in that position you're in now with your shoulders back and down. You are going to let the leg lift behind. Let's take your left leg first behind and let yourself drop the weight down, but don't let it pull your shoulders down. Just until we feel as far as it's comfortable getting that little stretch through the hamstring and then start to contract and pull that back up.

We'll stay on the same leg for 12 repetitions before we change to the other leg. So let's go nice and slowly. Abdominals are in tight, shoulders are back. Away you go guys, I want 12 repetitions please. Nice and smooth. Good, now make sure you're keeping your hips, chest, shoulders square to the ground. Don't be letting that hip rotate up. Let's go, keep it going at your own pace nice and comfortable. If you lose your balance, you can always reset yourself. Now we're looking for that front leg to be straight. Yes, your right leg is straight but not locked out at the knee. Yes, but it's straight. What we're doing here is working to your dynamic range of motion through those hamstrings as well, fabulous, keep it going.

Abdominals are tight. There is a nice long line though your spine from the top of the head to your tailbone down to your heel is that nice long line though the body. Maybe a slight bend, but only a very slight bend, on that knee if you need to for balance. Yes, working to your full comfortable range of motion. And clearly you can see how this is a functional exercise, picking stuff up off the floor every day is something that we do. Excellent, now this is really challenging you to keep your abdominals pulled in tight, otherwise what happens as you start to hinge down, the belly pulls. Yes, so you've got to really pulling tight through your tummy button in tight. Make sure you're still breathing. Is that 12 repetitions yet guys? If it is we'll swap over to the other leg.

Okay, so 12 on each side. It needs to be balanced. Now be aware you may feel slightly different from one side to the other. If you've had any history of injury or if you particularly did one sport that was one side dominant, you might find that one side the balance isn't as good, the strength isn't as good. The flexibility isn't as good, so that's important when you're doing your workout as we swap from side to side to make sure that we balance these things out. So concentrate on what you're doing. Slow is better, yes. There may be slight bend on that front knee just for your balance but ideally, we keep it almost straight. We're making sure that this hip stays twisted down towards the ground, abdominals are in tight and you're hinging from the hip. You're not rounding the spine, so make sure we know that difference between this and this. Yes, make sure we're hinging from the hip. Yes, it's all about there. That's what the guys are doing so you let your top of your head drop towards the screen while you're doing this exercise.

Fabulous. You should be really feeling this in that standing leg, particularly in the hamstring in the back of the thigh, but then also into the glutes at the back. Okay, fabulous exercise.

Okay, we're going to change things around slightly now. I'm going to ask you now to pick up the kettlebell, put the thumbs through the holes so you've got a hold of it now, slightly different exercise. Okay, take the feet about hip width apart. Now they're going to stay hip width apart when you take one leg back. Really going to get into the legs and into the waste here. What I'm going to ask you to do is step your left leg back, put it on the ball of the foot, drop the knee down to the ground and at the same time rotate the kettlebell to that side. I'm going to stay on the same leg for your 12 repetitions before we swap over.

Okay, are we set? Step your left leg back, drop, rotate and up. Down, twist. Beautiful. It's all one movement, let's go. Abdominals in tight. Head lifted all the time. Fabulous, down and twist. Beautiful, so you see how we're really getting some work now into the legs, working into the quadriceps at the front of the thigh, hamstrings at the back into the glutes. Working those big muscle groups. And the great thing about that the more muscle groups you include, the greater the calorie burn will be.

At the same time, you can see there's some work going on here in Frank's arms and shoulders holding that kettlebell in position, but also look at that rotation, and that's being brought about by those oblique muscles working through the waist. Also, what we need to be aware of is keeping good posture, so the abdominals are pulled in all the time, so we're really working through those deeper core muscles, which again can only help to protect the lower back if they're a little bit stronger. We're looking for 12 repetitions before we change legs.

Looks like we're done. Other leg, let's go. Looking good guys. And remember I might not be doing it but I feel your pain. Looking good. Step back and twist. Good. Now be careful of balance on this. We need to make sure that when you step back you're keeping your feet about that hip width apart. Beautiful. See how we're getting some work into the waist there. Fabulous with that twist on the kettlebell. Fabulous. Nice and low into that lunge. Low is better, get your money's worth. I feel guilty. I really should join you for a couple of repetitions.

And again because we're working such large muscle groups what you'll find is your heart rate may start to go up because what you've got to do is make sure the heart is pumping enough blood around to get to all those muscles. Yes, so you may feel that you're getting a cardio effect from this even though we might be going quite slowly. Yes, done. We'll take a quick rest.

In between each, give your shoulders a little rest. Don't forget to have that little rotation through the spine. You did a lot of work through those core muscles, muscles in the lower back particularly so. Let's make sure you get that little posture break in between each one.

Okay, we're moving on now to a one handed plié lift. Now we start to drift into we've talked about before perimetric exercises. We're going to drift into perimetric slightly here. So for the plié we're going to take the feet nice and wide, the knees and the toes are pointing out, yes. That kind of position. One hand out, let's take a hold of it. Left hand to start with. Abdominals are in tight and again be careful to make sure you're hinging from the hip not bending from the back.

Yes, nice long spine. Okay, now there's a little bit of a trick on this one, because what we're going to do here is as we lift it up, yes, we're going to turn onto the back like so. Okay, so there's a little rotation. Now it'll work a lot easier than that looks. So it rests on the back of the wrist, that's the movement we're looking for. Okay, what we're also going to do from there is then press up to the top without locking out the arm, but can we do all of that in one movement and add a jump, he says.

So, just to show you what it'll look like we'll pick it up and press, then just open the legs back out nice and wide and away we go again. Up and press. Good. Now this one is going to put a lot of stress through the core muscles. They've really got to work, so this is where you might want to drop down to a slightly lower weight or at least start and then you might need to switch. Let's go. Up, press. Keep it going, keep it going. I want 12 repetitions please. Beautiful and away we go.

So now hopefully as I'm panting already you'll start to notice you get a bit of a cardio effect now because we're working big muscle groups. And this is something we talked about at the top. We're working your whole body. That's the great thing about this, why it's so time efficient you're working so many muscles in one go, but what you're also doing then is creating a much greater calorie burn at the same time, so just half an hour this is all you need. How are we doing? Is that 12 repetitions? I hope you're counting. Take a quick rest and then swap it over to the other side.

Nice and wide with the plié. Feet wide, knees and toes pointing out. Let's go. Drop it down, pick it up, and it's all one movement. A plyometric is an explosive exercise, yes. So make sure we get a little bit of a jump here and push. Yes, so you've got to work quite niftily on that hand to make sure you roll it around and then press it up. Beautiful. And as you can see, we're going into here a little bit of work for the shoulder, on that shoulder press. Beautiful, some real work on the abdominals, pulling in tight.

At all times we've got to protect the lower spine. What we're doing here is basically challenging this movement. You wouldn't get this kind of stress in your normal day-to-day activities, but that's the point. If we can train our bodies, particularly the muscles in the core, to protect the lower back in a movement like this, then when it comes to your day-to-day activities—put them down have a quick rest guys well done—then you'll find that it's a little bit easier to do those exercises.

Okay, so we're going to head for the floor now and a little prone row exercise. Again, the challenge here is your core strength protection, your lower back. You'll remember that from the earlier lecture in this series. What we need to do is get ourselves in the position where we've got neutral spine. Neutral spine we talked about before. Another phrase for that is a comfortable spine, your natural alignment. So I'm going to show you what I mean by that.

So we're going to go down guys for the prone row. So you're going to be essentially in a press-up position yes, is where you're going to be. Let's put the kettlebell into your left hand. So to make things slightly easier, you can have the feet hip width apart. Yes, if you're feeling strong you can have them together. If not, slightly apart. If you're new to this exercise, I'd have your knees down on the floor, but if you are going to do that, I want them slightly further back so you're not in an all fours position, but the feet are further back there, so you can still rest on the knees.

Now the important point about this is your abdominals are in tight and you've got to find your neutral spine position so we don't want to be too dropped down, we don't want the backside in the air. So if you just have a little move around there, you'll find the position that's about right, and that works if you're on your knees as well. You've got to find that position that feels about right for your lower spine, where it's comfortable, and then lock it on by keeping your abdominals in tight.

Okay, so the challenge of this exercise, can we keep everything else still and then just lift it up to the shoulder and back down. Don't twist, stay locked in the center, lift it up, back down. Can we get 12 of those please? Let's go. Fabulous. So see how the challenge here is what's trying to happen is gravity is trying to pull your hips down, yes. So this is not just a case of the row, although the row is clearly working into the biceps, working into the rear shoulder, working into the upper back. Actually, that's only half the challenge. It's really what's going on in the middle, the glutes are working, the hamstrings are working pulling in the abdominal, this transversus muscle that runs across the center there. The obliques are pulling in. Everything is pulling in to try to keep the center locked still, yes.

Now, if you do start to lose that position I'd advise you to put your knees down. Take a quick rest if you've done 1 set. You're making this look way too easy. And onto the other side, into the full breast up position or on the knees, whichever. Find your neutral spine first, find your comfortable spine position and away we go. Lift up, fabulous. Excellent. So we're keeping that natural little curve in the lower spine, the lumbar curve there, yes. Making sure the backside is not sticking up in the air. Make sure you keep your breathing constant, keep your chest, hip, shoulders square to the floor, abdominals are in tight.

And again, should be able to feel this all over the body, yes. Real value-added training. You should feel the whole body working on each of these exercises. Yes. Don't let the body twist. How are we doing, is that 12 yet? I've only done 3. And take a quick rest there. Okay, give yourself a little stretch, a little mobilization. We can have a little lift at the arms, whatever you feel comfortable with. Just have that little posture break, and particularly do something through the lower spine.

Okay, we've only got 2 exercises to go, but I've got to say this next one is fairly tough, yes. A fairly tough exercise. So the Turkish stand up. You might want to already go for the lighter weight on this ne. So the Turkish stand up is just that. All you're going to do is stand up and then get back down again. Now, because this is a tough exercise, I said 12 of everything. Actually, this is just 12 total, I just want you to do 6 on either side.

So the challenge is—don't do anything yet, just yet guys, just take a quick rest. You've earned your rest. What I'm going to ask you to do is lie down and hold the kettlebell directly above the center of your chest. The challenge is can I keep it up, up there while I stand up without using the other hand, he says. And then can I get back down again. Again, ideally without using this hand, but don't let it go anywhere other than there.

Now, if you get to this point and get stuck, then use that free hand to help you up. Now to make this work, your whole body is working but particularly this is where you really need to work hard for your core muscles. And you'll remember when we talked in the lecture about the lower spine and we looked at the core muscles, one thing we said was that this is absolutely vital to transfer strength from the lower to the upper body, to integrate your strength you've got to be strong in the center and this really puts that to the test.

Okay, so we're going to do 6 on the left and then 6 on the right hand. So down we go. Fabulous, up in the air, legs are straight. Whenever you're ready, put one leg back and up we go. Up, up, up. If you need to use the hand, that's good. And then back down again. Beautiful. If you need to use the hand that's okay. You don't need to use the hand do you. And up, abdominals are in tight. And trust me this is one if you're doing this with us at home, which you should be you won't need me to tell you this is working your whole body. Up you get. Good, fabulous great work. Fabulous exercise.

And again, because we're using lots of muscles, you'll start to get a bit more of a cardio effect because the heart has got to work a little harder to get the blood around. But again, also we're starting to use more calories. Yes, so don't be fooled into thinking that the only way to burn calories is to do cardio. This kind of resistance work will really work if you're—have we done 6. Take a quick rest and then swap over to the other hand.

Fabulous. And be aware like we said earlier, that you might have differences from one side to the other. This time make sure you swap to the other leg so you should be pulling the other leg back first this time. Let's go. Use the hand if you need to. Of course you don't need to. And down we go. Great work. Abdominals in tight making sure we're keeping that dumbbell lifted, lifted, lifted all the time. Good, abs in tight. Under control, don't let gravity throw you back down to the floor, that's what we're working against. Up, up, up keep it up. Slowly on the way down, be under control. Fabulous.

How are you doing at home? I hope you're still with us. Up. I mean it's not that tough, all you got to do is stand up, surely. And back down. How many more have we got? Is it 2 more? And up. Good lift it up, lift it up, lift it up, lift it up, lift it up. Fabulous, just 1 more. Abdominals in tight. You might need that other hand out for balance. Is this it? Last one. Up, up, up. Okay, so that's a pretty tough exercise, the turkey standup, so just take a couple of moments here, maybe a little longer than the other breaks you've had to have that little posture break, to work through your lower spine. A good little exercise you can do there is to rest on hands on the knees and to pull the lower back up to the ceiling and down. Just hunch up and then let it release down, don't press down too low. It's just a great exercise to release your lower back. And it's important to have those little stretches in between each exercise, particularly something as tough as that Turkish stand up.

So we've got 1 more exercise before we get down on the floor. So this exercise is the single shoulder press, but slightly different than you might have done a shoulder press normally. Because what we're going to do here is actually sort of cheat a little bit. But what that would do is allow us to lift a little bit more weight and to use the whole body. So careful how you pick up your kettlebell, bend the knees please. And we're going to turn this around now. Remember resting it on the back of the wrist yes. Okay, so the beauty of this exercise, you might need the other hand out for balance, is we're going to use the legs with a slight squat and then press.

Now, we're making sure that the elbow is slightly bent. We don't lock out and the abdominals are in tight. Back down it comes. And up we go, I'm after 12 repetitions please. So this hand you can have on the hip or out for balance. And we're looking for those 12 repetitions really working into the shoulder. Keep going please, keep counting. Abdominals are in tight. Now as you take that very small, it's only a small squat there, yes, and we're really getting into the shoulders.

See Eric is keeping the head tall, chin in, abdominals tight. Beautiful. And again working through your whole body. See how we're linking. And remember we talked about your core strength helps you to transfer that weight. And look at it here, we're working through the legs, through that core and then through the upper body as well. Really working into that shoulder, but also what's great, swapping it over, fabulous. Whenever you're ready. You weren't taking a rest then were you?

But then also what you'll find is because of this elbow extension, we're really working into the triceps as well, often a problem area, so that's great to get into the triceps as well as the shoulder. But don't be fooled, it looks like the work is going on here in the shoulder, or maybe you can see a little bit of work going on here, but as with all of these exercises, kettlebell exercises, you're really working in the middle in the core. And remember, our definition of core strength is having the strength here to be able to maximize the strength out here. Yes, that's what it's about. Having a strong core will enable you to perform better through your legs and through your arms. Fabulous.

And we'll lose that one. So we're going to move on now down to the floor to really get into our very last exercise, getting into the abdominals particularly into the waist. Let's work on that hourglass figure. So you need to get yourself sitting down for this one. We're really getting into the abs now, particularly into the waist, Russian twist. Really going to work on those core muscles again, which can only help to strengthen the lower back.

So you're going to take your feet about hip width apart, nice and easy, pick it up. It's just in front of the chest. All I'm going to ask you to do on this one is to rotate side to side, drop it down and across to the other side. So if we're looking for 12 it'll be 12 each side, so that's 24 all together please. Or whatever, 12 each side. Just make sure we get those repetitions.

And keep going please. Make sure your abdominals are in tight. Make sure you've got a nice long line from the top of your head down to your tailbone. You're sitting tall and then hinging backwards, but not rounding. Remember that difference, this hip hinge. There, so that we keep the abdominals in tight and keep the natural curve in the lower spine. And what's bringing this about is that work through the obliques, the muscles at the waist that are really beginning to twist you from side to side.

Yes, fabulous. Try not to hold your breath. But again, as a real challenge here on keeping the transversus across the middle pulled in really tight, abdominals are pulled in really tight. Well done, well done. If you want to lose that kettlebell to the side. And what we're going to do now is slip into a little bit of a cool down, so I would advise you to particularly look at the lower back. So some simple exercises.

So should we just drop ourselves down onto the back and pull your knees into your chest for me. So a great exercise is just to pull the knees into the chest to start with. And you can maybe rock forwards and backwards slightly, slightly on the mat. Get a little massage for the lower spine. And then also what I do from there is then take the legs down to one side and take your arms across to the other. Beautiful. And hold that position. So your stretches you're going to hold there for about 30 seconds, 15–30 seconds, and then we'll swap it over to the other side. Also, a little child's pose that you'll know from yoga, so a few little stretches for your lower back.

Then also don't forget the stretches. You've done a lot of work for your quads, for your hamstrings, for your glutes, so those lower body stretches remember they're all on the flexibility DVD as well. So there's your kettlebell workout. Well done.

Plyometrics Workout
Lecture 33

Plyometrics, also known as jump training, involves stretching the muscles prior to contracting them. This type of training, when used safely and effectively, strengthens muscles and decreases impact forces on the joints. Plyometrics mimics the motions used in sports—such as skiing, tennis, and volleyball. These exercises are designed to increase muscular power and explosiveness. However, because this type of training is so intense, it results in a considerable calorie expenditure, so it's valuable in weight management and not purely for the elite sportsperson.

Guidelines

- Plyometrics is a beneficial training practice for those trying to increase their explosiveness, but you shouldn't incorporate it into every workout. It's intense, so your body needs time to recover.

- If you incorporate a plyometric workout into your training routine 1 day per week, it'll add variety and give an intensity boost that will improve the effects of your routine.

- A safe and effective plyometric program stresses quality of jumps— not quantity of jumps—so safe landing techniques are important because you want to reduce impact forces. Stop and reset yourself if you feel your form beginning to falter.

- Stretching a muscle prior to contracting it recruits the stretch reflex of the muscle to enhance the power of the second jump. This prestretching of the muscle occurs when you perform one jump after the other.

- Use visualization techniques to promote low-impact landings. For example, try to imagine yourself landing as light as a feather, and then think of recoiling like a spring after the impact.

- When landing, try to avoid excessive side-to-side movements, even when you're performing lateral movements.

- Landing forces can be absorbed from the knee musculature, which includes the quadriceps, hamstrings, and gastrocnemius. These work more effectively when the knee is bent, primarily at the inner hinge joint.

- In addition to jumping-based drills used to develop power in the legs, you can also use explosive exercises to target the upper body.

- Unlike traditional toning and body-sculpting exercises—where the focus is on slow, controlled, isolated movements—plyometric exercises focus on being explosive, including full-body movements that are great for burning a large number of calories, toning the major muscle groups in the body, and helping to improve core strength.

- For the following exercises, do 30 seconds of each exercise, and then take a 30-second rest. If you're a beginner, you might want to do 12 repetitions and then take a 30-second rest. Either way, do 2 sets of each exercise.

- Before you start the second set, take some deep breaths, and get a sip of water if you need to.

- If you find that you are mostly working on your technique for many of the exercises, do 1 more set of each exercise at the end of the workout. Do only 15 seconds, but really push yourself.

- As always, you need to warm up with gentle movements to mobilize your joints and to raise your body temperature, including marching in place and building up to a jog, lifting your knees, pointing your toes, and making circles with your arms.

- Suitable footwear with good cushioning and lateral support is ideal when doing these exercises.

- Concentrate on soft landing by flexing your joints. The quieter you land, the better your technique and results will be.

- Ensure that you are well hydrated before and during this workout.

Power Squat Press
- Be careful how you pick up your dumbbell—or other resistance tool, such as a medicine ball or a few cans of beans.

- The goal of this exercise is to squat, pressing into the heels.

- The feet are about hip-width apart.

- Keep your abdominals pulled in tight.

- Hold your resistance tool at chest level.

- You can take the first set nice and easy, focusing on getting used to the technique. For the second set, increase your pace.

- Try to land softly by bending through your knees, hips, and ankles.

- You should roll from toe to heel upon landing.

- You'll begin to feel that you're working several muscle groups during this exercise, which is going to contribute to increased calorie burn.

- The challenge for the second set is to squat deeper, jump higher, and go faster.

- Work at your own pace, but keep a quick rhythm. However, don't sacrifice technique for speed.

Squat Jumps

- For this exercise, be careful jumping on and off your step. You've got to make sure that you land straight into your squats. Ideally, there will be no noise on your landings.

- For the first set, jump on the step, and get used to stepping back down by just walking down. Also adjust to jumping up onto the step.

- For the second set, you should be able to jump both on and off. The secret is quiet landings going up and quiet landings going down.

- Don't jump forward; focus on jumping up.

- Make sure you land with your whole foot on the step—toe down to heel—bending straight into the squat to keep it soft.

- You're bending straight into your knees, ankles, and hips, and you're working through your core muscles, keeping the abs tight at all times.

Power Lunge

- Start with one foot on the board and one foot off—it doesn't matter which one you start with. The foot that is off the board should be on the ball of the foot.

- You're not shuffling side to side during this exercise; instead, you're jumping.

- Use your arms to throw yourself up in the air.

- You can use your first set just to get comfortable with the technique.

- Make sure you're getting some good height and landing quietly. Make sure your whole foot lands on the board.

- Sink down into your lunge. Try not to look down too much.

- Work at your own pace, and get a good rhythm going.

- For the second set, challenge yourself to see how high you can jump and how fast you can go.

- By the end of the second set, you should feel that the muscles in your legs did some work.

Lateral Jump
- For this exercise, you're going to move laterally over the step.

- There are 2 options for the first set. You could just step over the step to begin with and then maybe progress a little. In other words, take a step, hold it for a second, and then maybe bounce a little before you go back over—building up to a full jump over without a rest in between. First, get used to the lateral technique of getting up and over the step.

- The other option is to jump with both feet, but take a little hop before you go back over.

- Either way, make sure you're clearing the step by lifting up. Try to control your lateral movement by sinking down and getting yourself ready to jump.

- For the second set, increase your pace. If you can, try to jump straight over and straight back. It's OK if you need to take a hop before you go back over or if you need to take a rest to regain your balance. You can even lower your step if that will help you. This exercise is about quality—not quantity.

Lateral Power Lunge
- For this exercise, you're still moving from side to side on the step, but this time, keep one foot on the step. However, just as with the power lunge, you're not shuffling from side to side.

- The goal of this exercise involves shortening the muscles first and then allowing them to contract. Therefore, it's about height and landing straight into the lunge.

- Land with your foot flat on the step—toe to heel.

- Take a really good squat down, keeping your abs in tight.

- Use your arms to bring you up.

- Get the feel of the exercise during the first set.

- Even though you're traveling laterally, think about getting some height.

- Bend the knee to preload the muscles—using the elasticity in them to give you power—and then land quietly.

- For the second set, increase your height and pace.

When lunging off the side of a step, be careful that you are aware of how far away the step is.

- Hopefully, you can feel that your hips and thighs are doing some work during this exercise.

- Land quietly by bending straight into your hips, knees, and ankles. You want a cushioned, quiet landing. The quieter it is, the safer it is because it's less impact for your hips, knees, and ankles to absorb.

- You should feel this workout in your heart, lungs, and legs, involving the cardiovascular, energy, and lactate systems.

Power Push-Up
- The plyometric technique can be used for upper body work; a power push-up is an example.

- Start with your hands on the step, and set up for a normal push-up, but on the push, your hands should leave the step for just a second.

- As soon as your hands land on the step, bend into your elbows and through your shoulders.

- If you start to get tired, your knees can drop down to the floor.

- Keep your abdominals in tight.

- For the first set, take a nice and easy pace.

- This exercise works the chest, the front of the shoulders, and the triceps at the back of the arm. Hopefully, it's also working your heart and lungs.

- If you need a quick breather between push-ups, take one, but then keep going. Work at your own level.

Cooldown
- Get up and walk around a little, cooling down in the process.

- Do some simple, gentle, rhythmic movements just like you did for the warm-up.

- Take a few deep breaths.

- Do some arm circles, rotations, and knee lifts to gradually bring your heart rate down.

- Plyometric training is not easy, so you shouldn't do it every day of the week, but you can throw it in to vary your training.

- Plyometric exercises are great if you're involved in sports because explosiveness and power are vital in sports.

- These types of exercises burn a lot of calories because they are demanding and they use the big muscle groups.

- While isolation exercises usually focus on just one muscle, plyometric exercises are compound exercises, which involve many muscles working together. This results in a huge calorie burn, which earns you a calorie deficit at the end of the day.

- One of the barriers to fitness is time, and another benefit of a plyometric workout is that you don't need much time to do it because it's intense. The more you put into an exercise, the more you get out of it, so if it's intense, you're going to get great results.

Plyometrics Workout
Lecture 33—Transcript

Welcome to our plyometric workout, also known as jump training. Plyometrics involve stretching the muscles prior to contracting them. This type of training, when used safely and effectively, strengthens muscles and decreases impact forces on the joints. Plyometrics mimic the motions used in sports, such as skiing, tennis, and also volleyball.

If you enjoy dodging moguls or chasing down ground strokes or charging the net, plyometrics might be an appropriate training option as these exercises are designed to increase muscular power and also your explosiveness. However, because this type of training is so intensive, it results in a considerable calorie expenditure, so it's really valuable in weight management and not purely for the elite sportsperson.

Now, the eastern Europeans first used plyometrics in the early '70s to develop greater strength and power in their Olympic athletes and based their programs on scientific evidence that stretching a muscle prior to contracting it recruits the stretch reflex of the muscle to enhance the power of the second jump. You may remember talking about the stretch reflex in our flexibility lecture.

This pre-stretching of the muscles occurs when you perform jumps one after the other. For example, when you land from a jump, what will happen is the quadriceps muscle at the front of the thigh will begin to stretch as the knee bends, and then it'll quickly contract into the next leap, and it's this pre-stretch that enhances the power of that second jump.

Now, plyometrics is a very beneficial training practice for those trying to increase their explosiveness, but it isn't something you really want to do every workout. It's quite intense, so your body is going to need some time to recover, but having said that, if you incorporate this perhaps one day a week into your training regime, it'll add variety and also give an intensity boost that'll improve the effects of your routine.

Now, a safe and effective plyometric program stresses quality, not quantity of jumps, so safe landing—and I'll keep reminding you of this—safe landing techniques, such as landing from your toe down to your heel from a vertical jump and using the entire foot as a rocker to dissipate the landing force over a greater surface area is a really important technique because we want to reduce those impact forces. So, I'll remind you of that as we go along. But also, using visualization techniques—try to imagine yourself landing as light as a feather, and then think of recoiling like a spring after the impact to promote a low impact landing in that next jump. Also, when you're landing, try to avoid excessive side to side movements, even when we're actually performing lateral movements.

Landing forces can be absorbed from the knee musculature, which is the quadriceps at the front, the hamstrings at the back, the gastrocnemius just below. Now, these work more effectively when the knee is bending, primarily in the warm plain of motion that's designed to bend, the inner hinge joint.

In addition to jumping-based drills used to develop power in the legs, we can also use these explosive exercises to target the upper body, so we'll have a look as well at that in this routine you're about to do with me.

Now, since correct execution of these exercises requires and therefore promotes good core strength, our plyometric workout gives you a good 2-for-the-price-of-1 deal. So, what I'm offering you here is a modified version. It's rather advanced sport training techniques. So, it's vital to understand the what, when, where, and why associated with it. So, for that reason, here are a few important guidelines.

Unlike traditional toning exercises, body sculpting exercises, the focus there will be on slow, controlled, isolated movements. Not so in plyometrics. Really we focus on being explosive; full body movements that are great for burning huge amounts of calories as well as toning the major muscle groups on the body and also helping to improve that core strength.

You have a choice. Today what I'm going to ask you to do is 30 seconds on, 30 seconds off. If you're a beginner you might want to do 12 repetitions and then your 30 seconds rest. See how we go. We're going to do 2 sets of every exercise, but I'll tell you a little more about that when we get started.

Now, remember they're explosive movements, but they end in cushioned landings, so therefore you've got to concentrate on the whole exercise, not just the pushing off phase but also particularly the recoil.

Always, like the guys are doing now, you need to warm up first, and gentle movements to mobilize the joints, to get your body temperature up a little bit. That's what we're doing here. Marching on the spot, building up to a jog, and knee lifting, toe pointing—all these kind of rotational movements, arm circles, will all begin to work.

Think about your footwear on this one. Suitable footwear with good cushioning and a little bit of lateral support would be ideal, and remember the focus is on quality, not quantity. So, stop if you feel your form beginning to falter.

And again, once more to remind: Concentrate on soft landing by flexing your joints. As a rule of thumb here, the quieter you land, the better your technique and the better your results will be. So, ensure you're well hydrated before and during the workout, and we're going to get started.

So, I'm going to show you the first exercise. Ready, guys? We're going to take the dumbbell, so be careful how you pick it up. We're using a dumbbell here for our power squat press. You could be using a dumbbell or any kind of resistance tool, anything—a medicine ball or if you have a couple of tins of beans—something that we can use to do this. The aim of this exercise is to squat. So, we're squatting first, pressing into the heels. Keep the abdominals pulled in tight. We're holding this at chest level. We're coming up. We're going to continue into a leap and lift up to the top as well. Okay? So, this is how we're going to do this. We're going to take 30 seconds on, 30 seconds off. You know, the sad thing is you're going to have to do all the work because I'm going to have to keep the time. I'm really sorry about that.

So, this is what we're going to do. I'm going to ask you to do 30 seconds on and 30 seconds off. He's resetting his clock. So, the first set you can take it nice and easy and just get used to the technique. So, are we ready? 30 seconds, and away we go.

Down and press, down and press, down and press. Get into a nice easy rhythm to start with. Keep going for me please. So, remember the important points. We're trying to land softly. We're doing well, guys. Keep going. Halfway through. Beautiful. We are reaching up, keeping your abdominals in tight. Heels are down. We're rolling from toe to heel on that landing. We've only got 5 more seconds. Brilliant work. And we're going to take a very quick rest there. Well done. Well done. How did you do?

Now, hopefully you perfected the technique. What we're going to do for our second set is to turn up the pace. So, get yourselves ready. Get a few deep breaths. Hopefully you can begin to feel we're working lots of muscle groups in this exercise, and that's great because that's where the calorie burn comes from. Okay.

Get yourselves ready. The feet are about hip width apart. About 10 more seconds. Take some deep breaths. Hold your resistance too, whatever you've got there, at chest level. I'm going to challenge you this time to squat a bit deeper, jump a bit higher, and go a lot faster. Are we ready? Let's go guys.

Up, push, up, push. Come on, let's get into a little bit of a quicker rhythm now. Get a nice, deep squat and push it up. Let's go, let's go, let's go. Keep going. Keep going. Landing quietly. Deep squat. Reach. Come on, let's go. Let's go. Work at your pace but keep it going. Remember, never sacrifice technique. We've got 10 seconds left. We're doing well. We're doing well. Keep it going. Keep it going. Quiet landing. See how we're bending through the knees, hips, ankles, to soften those landings, and take a quick rest. We can put that dumbbell on the outside. Get some deep breaths. Have a little walk around. Keep your feet moving. I'll show you our next exercise. You've got another 20 seconds rest. You're doing really well.

So, our next exercise this is what we're doing. One foot is away from the step, so you've got a little bit of distance. We're doing a little depth jump here, so we're going to squat, jump onto the board and off. Now, be careful. Maybe in the first set we jump on and just get used to stepping back down.

Just get used to stepping back down. The second set I want you jumping on and off, and the secret here is quiet landings going up and quiet landings going down. So, let's get ready. Reset the clock. Are we ready? 30 seconds. Let's go, guys.

Up. You can walk down on the first set. Just get used to jumping up onto the step. Now, the feeling is landing up and on. Don't jump forwards. We're after some height. Some height. Let's go. And up. And up. Squat first. Squat first and up. Beautiful. You've got 10 seconds. Squat and up. Get some deep breaths. Make sure you land with the whole of the foot on the board. Remember, we're landing toe down to heel, bending straight into the squat to keep it soft, and a quick rest there. Well done. Well done. Get a deep breath.

So, for our second set this is what we're going to do. Take a quick rest. We're going on and jump off. On. Be careful on the jump off. You've really got to make sure you land straight into your squats, so ideally no noise at all. Okay? Are we set? Come on, guys. Get ready. Take a deep breath. We can do this. Think of all the calories we're burning. Let's go.

Up. Just 30 seconds. Jump up. Jump down. Squat. Squat. Squat. It's all about height. This is jump training. Jump. Good. Get up there. Get up there. Let's make those landings quiet. See how we're bending straight into the knees, into the ankle, into the hip, and at all times working through the core muscles, keeping the abs tight. We've only got 5 more seconds, team. Let's go. You can do it. You can do it. And take a little rest there. Well done. Well done. Great work. Get a deep breath. Keep yourself moving. If you need a sip of water, now is a good time.

We're going to change. We're moving onto a power lunge, a power lunge. I'm going to put one foot on the board, one foot off. The foot that is off I want really on the ball of the foot. Now, I'm not shuffling. We're not shuffling side to side. Remember what we're doing is jump training. So, we've talked about the muscle shortening first. That will only happen if we lunge down first of all. So, we go down and then change. Down and then change. It's about height. Up.

Use your arms. Again, quiet landings, but let's get on the ball of the foot at the back. Let's get a little down first, then up, straight back, down, swapping over the legs in between. You can use your first set just to get comfortable with the technique. Okay, pick a foot, any foot you like. Just put one on the board, one behind on the ball of your foot. Squat down and get ready for your 30 seconds. Here we go.

And up. Good. Make sure you're getting some good height and landing quietly. Up. Up. Good. Up. We're looking for height. Down into that lunge. Look how we go straight back down into the lunge. Work at your own pace. Work at your own pace. Get to a good rhythm.

We've got 10 seconds. Come on, team. And up and up. Get the whole of your foot on the board, landing quietly. Try not to look down too much. And take a little rest there. You've got 30 seconds. Get a deep breath. Get ready to do some work. How are we doing? Give me a thumbs up. Are we okay? Brilliant. Doing well, guys. Doing well.

Okay, 10 more seconds. Get a deep breath and get ready for your second set. This is when we do some work. Okay, 5 seconds. Let's get our foot on the board. Get yourself ready. How high can we jump? Challenge yourself. We're going to do the whole 30 seconds now. Here we go, team.

Up. Come on, let's go. Jump. Jump. Good. Can we get some height, please? Height. Up. Come on, can we jump a little bit higher? Can we go a little bit faster? Come on. Come on. Good. Use the arms. Throw yourself up in the air. You've only got 10 seconds to go. Come on. Up. Can we feel those muscles in the legs doing some work? Come on. Come on. Five. We can do this. Come on. And take a little rest there. Whoa. Take a walk around. Get a deep breath. Can I just say, we're not faking this? This is not meant to be easy.

The next exercise you stay where you are. I'm just going to show you how this exercise works. Keep yourself moving on the spot, guys. We're going to move laterally now. So, I'm going to turn this around for you just so that you can see what exercise I'm doing. A lateral jump—trying to catch his breath—is simply going over the step. Now, I'm going to give you options.

In the first set you could just step over the board to begin with. Maybe we can progress that a little bit. Take a step, but hold it for a second, maybe a bounce before you come back. But what we're going to try to build that up to is a full over, over, over without a rest in between it.

Okay, so maybe just hop first of all, get used to that lateral technique getting up and over the board. Okay, are we set? 30 seconds team. Let's go. So, you've got the option to start easy going over, just a little hop. Or maybe we can take it a little bit further. Jump with both feet but take a little hop before you come back. Little hop before you come back. Beautiful. That's 15. You're halfway there. Make sure you're clearing that step, lifting up, and we're trying to control that lateral movement, and that comes by sinking down, setting yourself—a little bit of skill-related fitness here—and take a little rest there. Deep breath. Get some air in. Get your feet moving. If you need a sip of water, now is a good time. Get ready for your second set, and remember, for this second set we're going to do some work.

Can we feel anything in the legs? Yes? I'm going to take that as a yes. I'm sure you can feel something in your legs. Okay, are we ready? This time, if we can, we're going to try and jump straight over and straight back. If you need to have a hop before you come back, that's okay. Are we ready? Let's go, team. Up. If you can, come straight back. If not, take a little hop first, but if you can, let's go straight over, straight back. Come on, let's go, team. Good. Both feet. Feet together. Both feet. Good. There you go. There you go. Come on. We're halfway through, team. Yes. Come on. Come on. If you need to take a breather, that's okay. Take a knee. Remember, it's quality, not quantity. Beautiful. Excellent. Oh, I saw that one. Lovely.

See how we've lowered the level there. So, I took it down a little bit to get a rest because it's about good quality. Last few seconds. Nice one, pumping it up, and take a little rest there. Well done. Well done. Well done. Get a walk. Keep your feet moving. Don't stop still. Remember in our cardiovascular lecture we talked about blood pooling. So, keep yourself on the move. Get some deep breaths, and get ready to go.

We're on our lateral power lunge. Now, the difference here: We're still going side to side on the step, but what I want to do this time is to keep one foot on the step. So, we're essentially going side to side, but again, like the power lunge, it's not a shuffle. We're not shuffling side to side. That's not the aim of this exercise. The aim of the exercise, remember we talked about muscle shortening. So, we stretch the muscles first, and then they contract. So, it's about height and it's about landing straight into it, and this time, even though it's a lunge, you're landing flat foot. So, you're landing down toe to heel so the foot is flat. Toe to heel so the foot is flat. Get a really good squat down. Keep your abs in tight.

So, first set get the feel of the exercise. Let's get one foot on the board. Get ready to go over and back, but even though you're traveling laterally, think about some height. 30 seconds. Let's go. Up. Up. You know the secrets now. We're bending the knee to pre-load the muscles, and we're also landing quietly. Up. Use the arms to take you up. Beautiful. Look at that lovely squat there at each side. Beautiful. Loading up the muscles, using that elasticity in them to give you the power. We've got 5 seconds guys for that second jump. Fabulous. Last couple. And you can take a rest there. Get a deep breath. Keep your feet moving.

Are we ready for that second set? Because now we're going to do some work. Keep the feet moving. Hopefully you can feel this is doing some work, particularly hips and thighs. Please know this is the last one you're doing for your legs. Are we set?

Okay, let's get ourselves loaded. So, remember the tips here. Land quietly by bending straight into your hips, knees and ankles. As soon as you land, you want a nice, cushioned, quiet landing. That's what we're after: Nice cushioned, quiet landing, going straight back down into your lunge. Remember, the quieter it is, the safer it is because that's the less amount of impact you're taking through the hips, knees, and ankles.

Okay, so, are we set? 30 seconds, team. Let's go. Come on, give me some height. Give me some height. Up. Up. Up. Up. Come up. Up the pace. Come on, let's go. Let's go. We're halfway through. Good. Good. Up. Give me some height. Give me some height. Up we go. Up we go. You're on your last 10. Come on, team. We can do this. Up we go. Looking good. Are we feeling this in the heart? Are we feeling this in the lungs? Are we feeling this in the legs? I'll take that one as a yes. And take a rest there. You can half a walk around.

Did you feel that at home? Remember when we talked about tour cardiovascular system, how the heart has to work? And we talked about our energy systems, talked about the lactate system. You might be feeling that a little bit in the legs now. I'm going to show you the next exercise.

We're moving onto, as I said right at the top, that we can also use this technique for upper body work. So, let's have a little look at a power push-up. So, what we're going to do here, I'm going to set it up first of all. Hands on the board for my push-up. Normal push-up. Keep the abdominals in tight. Down to the board, but on the push I want the hands to come away. If you start to get tired, the knees can go down. But the secret is to get your hands off the board on that push-up.

So, first set, nice easy pace. Let's go, team. Nice and easy pace to begin with. Okay, so, are we set? And away we go. Down and press. And we just need that little bit of distance, just as the hands leave the step just for a second. The same rules apply though. As soon as we land we bend into the elbow; we bend through the shoulder. Go straight back down into the next repetition. That's halfway. Keep it going. And we'll warn you: This is a little bit tougher than the legs, if you thought that was hard. Let's go. Five seconds, guys. Come on, we can do this. You can do this. And take a rest there. Well done, a well-earned rest. You've got 30 seconds before your second set. Take a deep breath. If you need some water, now is a good time.

Hopefully you're feeling this a little bit. You'll be pleased to know this is your last exercise in the routine, although we've not quite finished the work yet, so don't panic. Okay, are we set? Let's get ourselves in position. Get ready for that press-up. You've got 30 more seconds.

And here we go, and press. Up. Beautiful. Come on, just 30 seconds. You can do this. Working through the chest. Working through the front of the shoulders. Working into those triceps at the back of the arm. Come on, let's go. Hopefully also working your heart and lungs. Let's go. We need 15 more. Come on, we can do this. We can do this. If you need a quick breather, take a quick breather and then get started. Work to your own level. Come on. Although in time you'll be doing more than 30 seconds, trust me. Come on, last couple of repetitions. And take a rest there. Just get yourselves up. Get yourselves walking about. Please, come on up. We get up. We get up. We get. Have a little walk around. Keep your feet moving. Fabulous.

Now, there is a possibility that this being the first time that you've tried this kind of workout that maybe you need to work on the technique a little bit, and so perhaps you weren't working as hard as you could. So, I just want to be sure that we've driven home the technique for each exercise. So, what about we do 1 more set of everything. I hope I'm not pushing our relationship too far, but I'm only going to ask you for 15 seconds. What can you do in 15 seconds? Not an awful lot. 15 seconds on each exercise, but here's the deal: 15 seconds full out. Put your hand on your heart and tell me you're going to do 15 seconds full out. That's all I'm asking, and then we'll have a stretch and cool down. We can do this.

So, our first exercise, remember, was the squat and press. Let's grab those dumbbells, please. The squat and press, remember, was squat and press and squat and press. 15 seconds is all I'm going to ask you for, so get your tins of beans, medicine ball, dumbbell, whatever it is. If you've got a small dog, no, don't do that. Are we set? 15 seconds. Let's go. Come on. Up. Come on now. Let's get some work. It's only 15 seconds. That's no time at all.

Come on. Come on. Give me a good squat. And leap. Quiet landings, particularly when you're getting tired. Come on. We only need 4 more seconds—3, 2, 1. Take a quick rest. Well done. Well done. Let's lose that dumbbell on the outside.

Squat jumps were next. Remember the secret here is to squat, land on the step, land off the step, but straight into cushioning the landing. 15 seconds. Are we ready? Go. Come on, up, and down, and up, and down. Come on, come on. 15 seconds. Jump onto the step, jump off the step. Jump onto the step and off the step. Come on, let's go. Few more seconds. Come on, and take a little rest there. Well done. Well done. How are you doing? Take a deep breath. Take a sip of water.

The next exercise, just to remind you, was the power lunge. Up and up. Up and up. That's all we're going on the power lung. Get yourselves ready. One foot on the board. Take a deep breath. Remember, we're looking for height. We're looking for soft landings. We're looking to get started. Let's go. Up. Good. Up. Up. Come on, we only need 15 seconds. You can do this. This is our power lunge. You're halfway there already. Come on. Beautiful. Good work, team. Yes. Yes. And take a rest there. Well done. Well done. See how easy this is? 15 seconds goes by in no time.

Lateral jump. Remember that's either hop or take a little bounce before you come back, or since we're only doing 15 seconds, perhaps we can go straight from one side to the other. Get yourself ready to go side to side over your board, and let's go; 15 seconds. Come on. Come on. This is no time to drop out on me now. You can do this. But remember, quality not quantity. If you're beginning to lose your technique, take a rest. Come on. Come on. We're nearly there, guys. Last couple of seconds, and rest. Beautiful.

One foot is on the board; one foot is off. This is our lateral power lunge. There's only 2 more to go. Hang in. We can do this. So, one foot on, one foot off. It's about height. It's about cushioned landings. Are we ready? Let's go. Up. Come on. Up. It's not side to side. This one is up and down. Come on. Soft landings. How are we doing? Come on, guys, 5 seconds. Give me some height. Give me some height. Yes. Up. Up. You'll be dunking the basketball. And take a rest there. We've only got 1 more to go. Awesome work. I hope you're feeling this.

Power push-ups. It's the last exercise. We'll have a little stretch straight after, so come on, come on. Here we go. 15 seconds. Get yourself down. Remember the aim here. You'll press. Hands off the board. Hands off the board. Think about your core muscles. Keep your abdominals in tight when we're doing this. 15 seconds. Come on, team. Let's go. Beautiful. Come on. Come on. 15 seconds. That's all I need. Come on. Come on. Last few seconds. Hang in there. Hang in there. And take a little rest there. Well done. Well done. Well done.

Okay, up we get. Little bit of a walk, and if you guys can give me a little bit of a cool down, so we're going to cool down. Watch what the guys are doing: Some very simple, gentle, rhythmic movements just like we did in the beginning. A few deep breaths is a really good idea. I'm going to talk while the guys are doing a little bit of a cool down for you. You can join in with some arm circles, same as you did at the beginning, some rotations, some knee lifts, just some very gentle movements to bring your heart rate back down to gradually begin to bring your pulse down a little bit. And while they're doing that, I'll just talk to you about a couple of things.

Plyometric training, hopefully now you'll agree, is not easy. That's why I said right at the top this is something we're not going to do every day of the week, but you can throw this in to vary your training. It's great if you're doing any kind of sport because that explosiveness, that power, is vital. These are modified sports drills you're using. But then also remember that what we're doing here is burning a lot of calories. We are burning a huge amount of calories because, firstly, it's a demanding exercise, but we're using big muscle groups, compound exercises.

Now, remember, in our muscles lecture we talked about isolation and compound exercises, and isolation exercises is usually just one muscle, but here we're using here and here and here. Everything is working together, and that's where we get that huge calorie burn, which at the end of the day, remember in our weight loss lecture we were talking about trying to get that calorie deficit at the end of the day.

So, it's really effective, but also, in Lecture Three in this series we talked about barriers to fitness. One of those barriers was time. Now, hopefully you can see these guys regularly exercising, but like you, they have time problems, time issues. We all have to work against work, kids, all sorts of pressures. The beauty of a plyometric workout—hopefully you'll agree from that little section there—is that you don't need a lot of time. It's intense. And also when we talked in our energy systems lecture about getting fit, about burning calories, we said that the way exercise works is the more you put into it the more you get out. So, if it's intense, you're going to get really good results.

I hope you enjoyed your plyometric workout.

Resistance Band Workout
Lecture 34

Resistance bands have different thicknesses, so you can vary the amount of resistance you want for any exercise. Resistance band workouts are perfect for the home environment, but the bands are also portable. You can take them with you whenever you go on vacation—just in case there isn't a gym—and they don't take up much space, so you can easily pack them into your suitcase. You may have seen resistance bands without handles, but use the ones with handles for this workout. It can be uncomfortable to wrap the ones without handles around your hand.

Guidelines
- As with any workout, it's important to warm up with aerobic-type movements that involve large muscle groups.

- For each exercise, do 1 set of 15 repetitions on each side, when applicable. Regular exercisers should do 2 sets of each exercise, and advanced exercisers should do 3 sets of each exercise.

- Particularly as you start to progress and become stronger, you'll need to get a thicker band to work with as exercises become easier for you.

Squat
- Sit down into your squat as low as you comfortably can, pressing into the heels.

- Bend your knees slightly; don't lock them. Keep your heels down.

- Make sure to keep your abdominals in tight so that you're not sticking your backside out too far and so that you're not getting too much of an arch in your lower spine.

- Keep your chest lifted and your head up.

- You're working against the resistance in the band as you press up.

- This exercise works the front of the thighs, the back of the thighs, and the glutei.

Lunge

- Start with your right leg forward and your left leg back, but make sure your 2 feet are slightly spread out to help you balance.

- Keep your hips, chest, and shoulders square to the front.

- Slow is better with these exercises because you want to make sure that your movements are under control.

- Keep your abdominals pulled in tight to create a long spine.

- Be careful not to twist the rear foot; make sure it faces the front and is resting on the ball of the foot.

- Keep your breathing relaxed and constant.

- When switching your legs, be careful. You don't want the bands to suddenly spring up and hit you.

- Your hands should come up to shoulder level. Keep your head up.

- Try to focus your mind on the muscles that are doing the work—the thighs, quadriceps, hamstrings, and glutei.

Hip Abduction

- This exercise targets the hips and the side of the buttocks.

- Keep your abs in tight, and stand up tall. A slight lean is OK, but try not to lean too much.

- The benefit of doing this exercise standing rather than lying down is that on the other side of the hip, you have to work to support your structure and to remain balanced, so your supporting leg is working as well.

- Make sure that most of the work is coming from lifting your leg out to the side, working against the resistance.

- The further you lift your leg, the more the band is stretching and the more resistance it will give you, so it will be more difficult.

Plié

- Start by stepping out wide, pointing the toes and knees out slightly. When you sit down into your plié, your knees follow the line of the toes.

- This exercise focuses on the gluteus and hip adductors, which work the inner thigh.

- Keep your abdominals in tight so that your backside doesn't stick out when you go down.

Bent-Over Row

- For this exercise, you're going to lean forward with your knees bent, keeping your abs in tight to protect your lower back.

- Your hips are fixed as you row backward, lifting your elbows up to the ceiling.

- This exercise focuses on the upper back, but you're also working the biceps, shoulder blades, and core muscles. You're also working the legs isometrically.

- Focus your mind on squeezing your shoulder blades together as you row backward.

- By putting only one foot on the band, you can change this exercise slightly to make it more difficult.

- Rather than working the upper back, this change shifts the focus onto the rhomboids in between the shoulder blades, which are great for helping to improve your posture.

- Keep both knees bent, and place your other foot behind you for balance.

- This bent-over position allows you to work against gravity.

- You can make this exercise slightly easier by keeping your elbows bent, or you can make it more difficult by bringing your arms further up.

Pull-Down

- Start with your feet about hip-width apart and with your abdominals in tight.

- Fold your resistance band in half, and lift it up just above your head.

- Don't let the band pull you into an arched position. Keeping your knees slightly bent—not locking them—will help.

- Keep your breathing relaxed.

- Work against the resistance on your way back up. Don't let it spring back; control it.

- You're working the upper back as well as the lower part of the trapezius.

Chest Fly

- Wrap your resistance band around your hands a few times to shorten it. If the band still feels too light, wrap it around again.

- Your arms should be almost straight—but not quite—and at chest level. Your knees should also be slightly bent to give you a balanced position.

- Keep your abdominals in tight.

- This exercise works the pectoral muscles of the chest. Make sure you're not working your arms; instead, concentrate on working the chest.

Lateral Raise
- Choose one foot to start with, and place it on the resistance band, making sure that it is stable. You don't want it jumping up. Keep your other foot behind you.

- Make sure your knees are slightly bent for balance.

- You're targeting the middle part of the deltoid, the shoulder muscle.

- Lift up to the side—just above shoulder level. Be careful to keep your elbows slightly bent; don't lock them.

- Keep your abs in tight, and be careful not to arch your back. Keep your head up.

- Slow is better, particularly on the way down.

- Work against the natural elasticity of the band.

- Your body position stays fixed; just your arms are working.

- You have a choice: If you start to fatigue, you can bend your arms a little more, or if you're feeling strong, keep your arms almost straight as you lift up.

Shoulder Press
- Slightly bending your knees helps you to maintain your stability. It helps you to keep your hips fixed and your lower spine in place so that you can focus on just the shoulders doing the work.

- Keep your abdominals in tight.

- When you press up, make sure your hands are slightly in front—not behind, which is uncomfortable on the shoulders.

- Don't lock your elbows when you press up because that can put a lot of strain on the tendons around the elbows.

- This exercise works the middle and front parts of the shoulder.

Front Raise

- This exercise works the anterior part of the deltoid. The shoulder muscle splits into 3 parts, and this exercise enables you to work all of them.

- Start by lifting your arms up to face level, keeping your head up.

- If you have any concerns about your lower back, you might find it easier to alternate sides. If not, you can pull your abs in really tight to work both sides at once.

- Your arms should be slightly bent, lifting out to the front in a semicircular movement.

- Concentrate on working against the resistance on the way back down.

- Keep your knees slightly bent with your feet apart for stability.

Upright Row

- Place both feet on the resistance band for this exercise. Turn your palms toward your body.

- Keep your knees slightly bent and your abdominals in tight.

- The goal for this exercise is to lift your elbows up high.

- Try to keep your shoulders down so that you're not pinching the neck.

- The work is coming from lifting the elbows up and out, working the deltoid and the upper part of the trapezius.

- Don't hold your breath. Exhale on the exertion; breathe out as you lift, and breathe in as you go back down.

Biceps Curl

- In addition to flexing at the elbow, the biceps are responsible for twisting.

- Start with your palms facing your sides, and then as you lift up, turn your palms toward your body.

Resistance bands require you to work against the resistance of the band while maintaining control of your movements.

- It is vital not to lean back; you don't want to put any strain on your lower back.

- Keep your abs in tight. The only thing that's moving is your arms.

- Keep your elbows fixed to your side as you lift up—don't swing your arms.

- Keep your knees slightly bent to give you stability.

Concentration Curl

- Even though you're bent over and supporting yourself, you still need to keep your abdominals in tight to fix your position so that the biceps can do the work. Your abs are fixator muscles.

- Keep your breathing relaxed, and make sure you're not twisting your spine.

- Your head should drop forward so that your neck is relaxed.

- The shoulder muscles are also fixator muscles that work to fix the position of your elbows so that they don't move.

Triceps Extension

- This exercise works the back of the arms. Pull down on the band to give you the tension to work against. The more you pull down, the tougher it is, and the better your results will be.

- Your goal is to achieve muscular fatigue by the final repetition. If it feels too easy, you won't experience overload, so be tough on yourself.

- Keep your knees slightly bent to give you better stability.

- Pull your abs—fixator muscles—in tight so that nothing else moves.

- Try not to push your head forward; your neck should be in a comfortable position.

- Try not to lock your arm at the top; keep it a little soft.

- Try not to rush your movements. Slow is better.

Waist Twist

- The best way to work your abs with a resistance band is to loop it around a door handle or banister. Just make sure that one end is fixed.

- Stabilize yourself by pulling your abs in tight.

- Bend your knees, and point your toes slightly out. Your arms should also be slightly bent.

- The abdominals work contralaterally by working the external obliques on one side and the internal obliques on the other side.

- This exercise focuses on the waist by targeting the oblique muscles on the sides.

Chop

- This exercise makes the waist twist more challenging by still including rotation but adding flexion by involving the abdominals.

- Keep your knees bent.

- Your legs will move a little bit for this exercise, but that's OK.

- Slower is better.

- Focus on the abdominals and the obliques that are doing the work. Don't think about the arms.

- Keep your breathing relaxed and your head up.

- Make sure you stabilize yourself with a wide base, and rotate through the lower spine.

- Make sure you stay far enough away from the fixed end of your band so that there is always enough tension.

- Keep your arms only slightly bent, and don't push with your arms. This exercise is all about rotating through the middle.

Cooldown

- Your cooldown should be similar to your warm-up, including a few mobilizing exercises that move through large muscle groups.

- Then, do some stretches for the major muscle groups.

Resistance Band Workout
Lecture 34—Transcript

Now, you may have heard pumping iron, but today we're going to be pumping rubber. We're doing resistance band workout, which is absolutely perfect for the home environment.

Now, I've got 2 tools here you can have a look at. You may have seen resistance bands—you may even have one already—without handles, which are great; although sometimes wrapping them around the hand for some of the exercises can get a little bit uncomfortable. So, I prefer and we're going to use the ones today with handles. So, nothing wrong with it but no thanks, not today.

So, first of all, important to think about the tool we're using. The great thing about resistance bands, they variable in terms of you can get different thicknesses, so you'll get a different resistance when you're doing the exercises. They're so portable. You can take them anywhere. I actually take them whenever I go on holiday, just in case there's not a gym. And look how much space they take up; hardly anything. You can keep them in a drawer somewhere, and like I say, they can fit easily into your suitcase.

Now, what I'm going to show you today, a whole range of exercises so versatile. Always, as you know by now with any of our warm-ups, with any of our exercises, it's important to warm up. Aerobic-type movements that involve large muscle groups like the guys are doing now, little bit of rotation through your lower spine, some wrist, arm, shoulder circles—all those guys are things are actual workouts.

We're going to do today—you're going to do with me—1 set of 15 repetitions. Now, if you're already exercising a little bit, you might want to take that to 2 sets of each exercise. Those of you that are more advanced might want to take that to 3 sets of each exercise.

So, what I'm going to do here is take a journey around the body, starting with the legs, and show you how many different exercises we can do. So, 1 set of 15 repetitions on every exercise. Are you ready to go? So, let's first of all take the band, and be careful how you do this. Step onto the band with your feet about hip-width apart.

Okay, first exercise we're going to do is a squat. So, you're going to bend the knees just a little bit. Take the lock off the knees. We're going to take the band up. Hold it by the side there, ready to go.

Okay, abdominals are in tight. We're going to sit down for our squat. Press into the heels, and then press up. That's all I'm going to ask you to do. Let's go, guys. 15 repetitions in your own time. Keep going.

The important thing is here: Make sure we're keeping your abdominals in tight so that we're not sticking the backside out too far so that we're not getting too much of an arch in the lower spine. Keep the abdominals in tight as we come up. Keep your chest lifted and keep your head up.

Now, how far do we go down? We're looking for as far as is comfortable. Some of us will have different range of motion through the knees, but importantly, we need to keep those heels down. Look how Brent is pressing into the heels there, keeping the chest lifted, and we're working against that resistance in the band as we press up. Little bit of work here for the front of the thighs, for the back of the thighs, also getting into the glutes as well.

Okay, so, we're moving on now. Let's again stick with the legs, but let's change this to the lunge. So, if we can get your right leg forwards for this one, the left leg is back, but make sure it's slightly out to the side to help you with your balance. The feet are on tram lines rather than on a tight rope. And the same feeling. Lift the band up. Okay, so get a good distance back on that leg.

For our lunge, keeping your hips, chest, shoulders square to the screen, I'm going to ask you to take your knee down to the floor and then press back up again. Away we go. We're after our 15 repetitions, please. Slow is better with these exercises. I want to make sure that it's under control. Okay? Beautiful.

Now, look here. Emma is keeping her abdominals pulled in tight. Nice, long spine, nice and slowly, dropping the knee down, and be careful not to twist the rear foot. See how it stays facing the front on the ball of the foot. If we get that twist, that's really too good for the knee. How are you doing? Make sure you're doing 15 repetitions. I'm going to trust you to count 15 repetitions. Slower is better. It's all about technique. Hopefully you're beginning to feel this now in the front of the thigh, in the back of the thigh, maybe also getting into the glutes.

Keep your breathing nice and relaxed. When you've done your 15 repetitions you're going to swap over legs. So, put one foot on and be careful how you do that transition. We don't want the bands suddenly springing up and pinging you.

Set yourself up. The hands come up to shoulder level, remember. You've got the other foot behind this time. Abs in tight. Let's go for our 15 repetitions on those lunges, please. Beautiful.

Now, let's use our mind and muscle here. Try to focus on the muscles that are doing the work. So, try to think about the front of the thigh, the quadriceps. Think about the hamstrings at the back. Think about the glutes. At all times we're working our core strength, keeping the abdominals pulled in tight. You're working against that resistance on the band as you lift up on that lunge. How are you doing? Keep going. Keep your breathing relaxed and constant. 15 repetitions, please. Really getting into toning those legs. Keep your head up. Make sure you've got it under control all the time. And when you're done, you're going to take the feet again about hip width, resting the hands down by the side.

So, we're going to move on now. Let's really get into a target area into the hips, and we'll really get into working the side of the buttocks here. So, what we're going to do is sink the knees down slightly. We're going to work onto your left leg, first of all. All I'm going to ask you to do is keep your abs in tight. You might get a slight lean, but try not to lean too much. I'm lifting out to the side working against the resistance.

So, let's go with your left leg, first of all. Lift out to this side, working against that resistance, keeping the hands there. Beautiful. How are you doing? I'm looking for 15 repetitions on that left leg. This is our hip abduction, lifting it out to the side. Beautiful. Try not to lean too much, if you can.

Make sure the work is coming from, we're actually working through the gluteus medius here, really getting into the smaller buttock muscle, but you'll also be feeling this a little bit down the outside of the leg, but also, the great thing about this, doing these kinds of exercises standing rather than lying down is you're really getting into the supporting leg as well because on the other side of the hip you've got to work to support this whole structure to keep this balance. So, actually you're getting twice as much work. Once you've done one leg, set yourself, and we go over to the other side.

Now, again, this is only going to be possible if you're keeping your abdominals in tight, staying up tall. So, you might get a slight lean like Frank is doing there, but try not to lean too much. Make sure most of that work is coming from lifting that leg out to the side. This is what I talked about right at the top when we talked about variable resistance, because now the further you lift your leg the more the band is stretching, the more resistance it will give you, so the harder it will be. But that's for you to work with.

Again, as I said, if you find that, particularly as you start to progress and get a little stronger, as you find that it becomes a little easy, you'll need to get a thicker band then to work with. Fabulous. Just 15 repetitions, guys.

Then we're going to change onto a plié. So, this time we're going to step much wider. We're also going to point the toes out slightly and the knees out. Beautiful. We're taking the band up. Get a hold of it.

Okay, so for our pliés, when we sit down, the knees follow the line of the toes. Now, this time we're putting a little bit more work into the glutes, but also now you just worked the hip abductors that lift the leg out to the side. We're now working into the hip adductors into the inner thigh. Okay? I'm looking for 15 repetitions, working into the inner thigh now.

Important things here: Keep the abdominals in tight. Keep going for me, guys. What I don't want is the backside sticking out when you go down. So, keep the abs in tight. See how the knees are going out to follow the line of the toes. Toes are pointing slightly out, knees out, and that'll put that work into the inner thighs. How are we doing? Looking good? Looking good.

We're going to move on. There are your leg exercises. We're moving onto the back. Now, for this one what we need to do is have a little bit of slack in the middle. So, we're stepping down nearer to the handles on this one. The abs are in really tight. The knees are bent. You're going to lean forwards. So, for this I really need you to get a nice, long position, but your abs are in tight. Your hips are fixed because we're going to row backwards, lifting those elbows up to the ceiling. Let's go, team. Elbows to the ceiling. Look how your position doesn't change. Don't raise up with it. Stay bent over. It's a bent-over row, so those elbows have to go up to the ceiling. Up they go. 15 repetitions, please.

Now, we're really working into the last here, getting into the upper back. We're also getting a little bit of work for the biceps. So, think about those muscles doing the work. You're squeezing your shoulder blades together on this exercise as well. Also working those core muscles. You'll feel a little bit of strength because isometrically we've got to work the legs. Hold your position. How are we doing? Excellent stuff.

Now, just changing that slightly we can make that a little bit more difficult, and rather than working through the last at the back of the armpit, we can shift into the rhomboids in between the shoulder blades, and these are great for helping to improve your posture.

So, this time what we're going to do is just put one foot on. You can pick a foot, whichever foot, on the band. Again, both knees are bent. The other foot behind for a little bit of balance. Again we need to be in this bent-over position so that we can work against gravity, so leaning forwards but keeping the abdominals in tight. This time we're lifting with the arms.

Now, you've got a choice. We can do it slightly easier and keep the elbows bent, as Emma is doing, or taking the arms further out, like Frank is doing, is a little tougher. So, let's go for those 15 repetitions. You could go with elbows bent or you could go with the arms nearly straight, but your focus here is on squeezing your shoulder blades together. You're really trying to get that feeling of squeezing the shoulder blades together as we row backwards. That's your focus. Make sure you're bent over but the abdominals are in tight to hold that position and protect your lower back, so a good bit of core training there, but really focusing on seeing those shoulder blades squeeze together. Feeling that in the upper back. Great exercise for your posture. Lifting the arms up, pull the elbows up to the ceiling—whichever. 15 repetitions is all I'm asking you to do. You can do this. Brilliant. Well done. Well done.

Okay, so, should we move on? We'll be moving on to a pull-down now. Feet about hip-width apart. And you'll have seen this, the lat pull-down machine at the gym. I'm going to ask you to fold it in half. Take a hold of the ends like so. The knees are slightly bent. The abdominals are in tight. You're going to lift it up just above your head. Now, the aim here is you're going to draw it down just behind the neck, but at the same time you're going to pull it out to the side. So, we're dropping it down and pulling it out at the same time. And again, that's going to get into the last at the back here. 15 repetitions please, guys. Let's go.

Down we go. Abdominals in tight. Don't let it pull you into that arched position. And again you'll find that knees slightly bent, at least taking the lock off, will help you with this. Keep your breathing nice and relaxed. Don't let it ping back. Work against the resistance on the way back up. You're in control in every sense. Beautiful. And there's a little bit of work there into the lower part of the trapezius at the back as well. Take a little look at it so you can see what we're doing. Down it goes, and back up. Working into the upper back, and back up. Just our 15 repetitions. How are we doing? Excellent. Oh, I can see that one working.

That will cover you for the back. We're going to move on now to chest. So, for the chest press we're going to take it around, and we're going to do a little chest fly actually. Now, the problem here for this movement is it's a little bit slack. So, what we're going to do is have a little wrap around the hands. Let's shorten the bands slightly for this one. Okay, so we're out to the side. The arms are almost straight. Not quite. At chest level we're squeezing in and back out.

If the band is still feeling too light, we could always wrap it around again. And away you go. We're looking for our 15 repetitions, really working into the pecs here. The feeling here is squeezing the chest together. The chest muscle attaches from here into that bicipital groove, it's called, here. So, it's drawing the arm in, keeping the arm slightly bent. Let's not work the arms when we're doing this. Let's really focus, remember, on mind and muscle. Concentrate on the chest. That's what's doing the work. Abdominals are tight. Your knees are slightly bent to give you a good balance the position. Fabulous. How are you doing at home? I hope you're still with me. Oh, I can feel that one. Good work. Good work. Good work.

We're going to move on to your shoulders. Going to move on to, first of all, a lateral raise. I'm just going to put one foot on it. Again, you can pick which foot. I don't mind. But make sure always that when you're putting one foot on it you've got it stable. We don't want it pinging out. So, the other foot behind. Make sure the knees are slightly bent for your balance. We're really going to target the middle part of the deltoid, the shoulder muscle, here.

We're lifting up to the side, but this time be careful to keep your elbows slightly bent. Locking out the elbows is not good. Okay? So, we're lifting up to just above shoulder level and then back down. 15 of those please. Keep your abs in tight and be careful, again, not to arch your back as we get up there. Make sure all the work is coming into the middle part of your deltoid. Slow is better, particularly on the way down. Let's work against the natural elasticity of the band. 15 repetitions, please. Fabulous.

See how the body position stays fixed, remember, here. It's just the arms doing that work, and you've got that choice. If you start to fatigue you can bend your arms a little more. If you're feeling strong, like Frank is today, we're keeping the arms almost straight as we lift up. Need a little bit of tension in the wrist as well. Really working into those deltoids. Keeping your head up, keeping your abs in tight. Nothing else moves. Brilliant exercise. Well done. Well done.

Keeping one foot on, we're going to change that into the shoulder press now. This time we're bringing it up. This is a little bit tougher. So, you might just want to bend the knees slightly. Get yourself down a little. Okay. Again, abdominals are in tight. When you press up, make sure the hands are slightly in front, not behind, because that's really uncomfortable on the shoulders.

So, when we press up, they go slightly forwards. We don't lock out the elbows because that can put a lot of strain on the tendons around the elbows. Some of you may already be familiar with tennis elbow. So, keeping the elbows slightly bent, we're pressing up, again, really getting into the shoulders. You're getting into the middle and also into the front part of the shoulder on this one as well. Excellent. Beautiful. Keeping those abdominals in tight. And you see with that knee-bent position, that helps you maintain your stability. It helps you to keep your hips fixed and your lower spine in the position it needs to be, so you can really focus on just the shoulders doing the work. Can we show that in the shoulders, guys? Excellent. Was there a bit of shaking going on there? I've got to say we've been a bit cruel. We've given Frank the thick band to work with today.

Okay, well done. Well done. Hope you did 15 repetitions. We're moving on to the front raise. Really going to get into the anterior part of the deltoid now. The shoulder muscle splits into 3 parts, and so, this enables us to really get to all of them. So, one foot on please, one foot behind. Doesn't matter which foot it is, as long as you're balanced.

A front raise, abdominals in tight, lifting up to face level and back down. Now, if you've got any concerns about your lower back, you might find it easier to do alternating sides here. If not, if we can really pull the tummy in tight, pull in through the waist, I'll have those 15 repetitions like so, please. Remember the arms again are slightly bent. We don't want them straight but lifting out to the front in that nice big semi-circle movement. Up they go. And again, really work against the resistance on the way back down. Fabulous.

See how we're fixing this position? That's because we've got a nice bend on the knee here, nice and stable, feet are a little bit apart. Abdominals are pulled in tight so we can really focus. This is about isolating it to the target muscle we're trying to get to. Excellent stuff. Beautiful. Beautiful. Really working into those shoulders, keeping your head up. That looks great.

Going to change it slightly. We're moving on now to the upright rows. So, for this one I want both feet on. We want to take a little bit more slack from the band. Turn the palms to face you. The knees are slightly bent. As always, abdominals in tight. The aim on this exercise is to lift your elbows up high. So, can I get 15 of those, please? Elbows up and out. Try to keep your shoulders down so that we're not pinching into the neck, but the work is coming from lifting the elbows up and out, really getting into the deltoid and also the upper part of the traps. Great exercise. Up. Hopefully you can feel that. Abs are in tight. Whatever you do, don't hold your breath.

Remember when we talked about, in our muscle lecture, we talked about exhale on the exertion, the idea of breathing out on the toughest part of the exercise, so you'll breathe out as you lift and in as you go back down. Up. Good. 15 of those will do me nicely.

We're going to move on. We're moving onto the biceps, and we'll start with a bicep curl. So, fortunately we're in the same positions. Now, this is what I'm going to do. The biceps, and you may remember, when we looked at the muscle movement, the biceps as well as flexing at the elbow there are also responsible for twisting this way and twisting this way. So, we need to add a bit of a twist to get the best for the bicep. So, we'll start with the palms facing into your side, and then as you lift up you're going to turn the palms this way in towards you.

So, let's go. I'll have 15 of those. Get that little twist on the biceps. When they come down, they turn in. When they come up, turn that little pinky towards you. 15 of those please. Absolutely vital not to lean back. We're not cheating. We don't want to put any strain on the lower back. Keep your abs in tight. The only thing that's moving: The arms.

Away we go. Beautiful. Check out those biceps. Did you bring those with you or have you just got those now, doing this? Excellent stuff. Keeping your elbows fixed to your side, what we don't want is any swinging of the arm. So, keep that elbow fixed to the side as we lift up. Brilliant. Got biceps to go. Knees are slightly bent to give you that stability. Abdominals are in tight. You'll notice how important the core muscles are, working them all the time there. Fabulous. Fabulous.

Now, we're going to move on slightly to a concentration curl. So, for this one we're going to put the band down and step really close to one handle there. Now, for this, I'm going to take one foot back. I'm going to keep my abs in tight, and I'm going to lean down onto this leg, support your weight, because what we're doing here is lifting across to the opposite shoulder, across to your opposite shoulder. Can we see how that's getting into the bicep? 15 of those please. Keep your abs in tight. Lean the hand onto the knee to support your weight. Squeeze it across. That's our concentration curl. Beautiful. See how we're not swinging here. This is staying fixed.

Remember when we talked about how the muscles worked. We talk about fixator muscles. This is fixed in place so that the bicep can do its work. Now, even though we're bent over and supporting ourselves here, we still need to keep the abdominals in tight, and you'll see how the body is fixed. There's no twisting going on here. Really good isolation movement. See how this elbow is not moving. It stays where it is. And we can see the work into the biceps. 15 on this arm and we'll swap over to your right arm as well.

Having just seen your biceps, I think I better do some, to be honest. I'm going to join in on this one. Okay, set your position, and let's go. Squeeze it up. Fabulous. Keeping your breathing relaxed, making sure there's no twisting through the spine, supporting your weight with the other hand. Your head will drop forward so that you've got a nice relaxed neck. Try not to be in this position if you can. Beautiful. The elbow is not moving. The shoulder are working to fix that position. That's the fixator. How are you doing? I'm after 15 reps. I've done about 35 here already, I'm sure. And when you're done we'll take a quick rest there.

Now, remember we talked about the muscles working in opposing groups. So, we've worked our biceps there. So, what we're going to do now is work into the triceps. So, with the tricep extension, you're just going to take one hand. Let's take it in the left hand. You're going to take it round behind you. What's going to happen then is you're going to use the other hand to grab the band and then pull it down so that you've got some really good tension on the band already. Knees are slightly bent. Abs are pulled in tight because the exercise now is can we press up to the ceiling and back down.

So, you need a really good pull down with your right hand so that you've got some tension in the band as we work into the triceps. So, we're working into the back of the arms here, but see how I've pulled down on the band to give me that tension to work against. Don't be kind. Be tough on yourself. The more you pull down, the tougher it is, the better it will be. Remember what we're looking for is to achieve that muscular fatigue by the 15th repetition. If it feels too easy, you won't get that overload and it won't be doing you any good. 15 reps, then let's swap over to the other arm, please.

Again, look how important the fixator muscles are. Abs pulled in tight so nothing else is moving. The knees are slightly soft to give you that better stability. Try not to push your head forwards. See how the guys are keeping the head in a relaxed position? The neck is in a comfortable position pressing up on that tricep.

When you've done one side we'll swap over to the other side. Remember, take the hand behind the head. Get a hold of the band. Pull the band down, first of all, and then away we go pressing up. And that little extension, try not to lock out your arm at the top. Just press it up. Keep it a little bit soft at the top, working into the triceps into the back of the arm. Fabulous. Pressing up. Just the job. Excellent. Try not to rush it. Slow is better.

Muscular development relies on something called the time and attention, the TUT principle. So, the slower it is, the better it is for you because the more muscular fibers you'll engage in the exercise, and therefore you're more likely to get to that point at the end where we get that momentary muscular fatigue, the overload, that then stimulates all those responses we talked about in our muscle lecture that lead to the improvement in muscle tone. Fabulous exercise. Well done. Well done.

We'll do another one for the triceps. Triceps are a fairly important muscle group. For this one, really this is about working against your own resistance. So, we're going to turn sideways on here. So, if we all turn our feet this way, what's going to happen here is you're going to hold it there by your hip, and really, let's drop one end so that you can see. We're going to hold it here quite tight, and we're going to keep that position fixed. So, you're going to really sort of put this arm against yourself there to splint it, and then what we're going to do here is lift the elbow, the left elbow, and point it behind, because all you're going to do is press out and bring it back, so extend the arm behind. So, lift it up a little bit higher as it comes up. Beautiful.

So, again, we're working those fixators, fixing ourselves in position here, but now this isolation exercise. Remember we talked about isolation and compound exercises? So, those compound exercises use a combination of muscle groups. So, like the squats, remember I said we were using here and here and here, whereas this is an isolation exercise because we're really getting down to just this muscle here. There's not much else going on here. Looking for those 15 repetitions. Great exercise. Really working into the back of the arm here.

We'll swap it over to the other side. Again, remember: If you're in any bent-over positions, that puts a focus on the core muscles. So, keep the abs in really tight. Take a hold of it there. Take a hold of it there, the palms facing backwards. Let your arm rest against your tummy there, and all we're going to do is press back. The elbow stays high. Don't let the elbow drop down. Otherwise it becomes a rowing exercise, and that's into your back. We want to isolate this—just the triceps at the back of the arm. Excellent stuff.

See how it's just that small move really targeting into here, and you're keeping that elbow up high all the time. Brilliant stuff. That's it. Pressing back into the triceps. Abs are tight. Fix that position. Try not to let yourself rotate through your lower spine. Make sure it's just the arm that's doing the work. It's a great exercise for the triceps. A real isolation one. So, even though we're only working one muscle group here, it's still a fairly taxing exercise. I think you'll agree. Brilliant.

Now, we're going to have to get a little bit creative here because the next couple of exercises are to show you how we can use the bands to work your abdominals. So, the best way to do this would be to take a hold like so and to loop this around a door handle or around the banister or something like that. Now, we just don't happen to have—I'm going to take that from you—a door handle or a banister, but we've got Frank who's looking very strong and fit and able today. So, Frank is going to be our—sorry—door handle, banister. That's the deal today.

So, if I can take that, and you're going to take a hold of the handles for me. Okay, you're going to take a hold of that end, both hands. Hold it strong. So, you're going to do this for me, please. And back. Okay, so, little bit of work into the waist. So, you want to be there, nice plié position. Get yourself stable. Abs are in tight. Knees are bent, toes pointing slightly out. The arms are almost straight but not quite, and then we're moving in that rotation around. Beautiful.

Now, I don't know if you remember but in the muscle lecture we talked about the abdominals working contralaterally. So, what's actually happening here is you're working the external obliques on one side and the internal obliques on the other. Away we go. Beautiful. You're the perfect door handle, balustrade, whatever it is, on this one. Excellent. And can we feel that working into your abs? Beautiful. Little bit of rotation. Really targeting those oblique muscles at the sides. Excellent. Is that 15 yet? You're doing really well. Slow is better. Brilliant.

So, you just need to make sure that this end is fixed. That's all we need to do. Now, don't move. So, on the same side what we're going to do here is to just make that a little bit more of a challenge by including rotation, but also, remember the abdominals at the front bring in this flexion. So, what I'm going to do now is ask you to lift it up a little bit higher. So, what you're going to do is the same position, facing the front, but this time when you bring it across, you're looking to chop down. So, we're still rotating, but now we're adding a little bit of flexion into it as well. Fabulous.

So, you see how we're going from a high down to a low? So, still the rotation, but now what's happening, as well as turning here, we're now pulling down, adding that little bit of flexion as well, so making it just a little bit tougher on this side. Brilliant exercise. The knees are staying bent.

Now, you will get a little bit of movement through the legs on this one, but that's okay. I'm after 15 repetitions again. Slower is better. And again, think about that mind and muscle. Really focus on what's going on here. Let's not think about the arms. This is not an arm exercise. They're just there for show. This is really coming from here. Abdominals here, through the obliques at the waist, drawing down. Excellent stuff.

Looking good. Looking good. Looking good. Beautiful. Should we swap sides? So, if you can go that side, you can go that side, and I'll go back here, and away we go again.

So, exactly the same thing on the other side. You know what you're doing now? Fix that one end. Get ready to go. Knees bent, and away we go. Beautiful. Keeping your breathing relaxed, keeping your head up. Fabulous. Make sure this end is fixed. Make sure you've stabilized yourself with a wide base, looking at getting that little bit of rotation through the lower spine. Beautiful. I think you've been a bit kind. Pull it a little bit.

Keep the tension on the band. Make sure you stay far enough away so that you've got a little bit of tension on the band all the time. Beautiful. That should feel a little bit tougher. And remember, the arms are only slightly bent all the way through. Don't be pushing with the arms. This is not an exercise for the arms. This is all about rotating through the middle. I'm going to take it that we've done 15 now, and we're going to lift it a little bit higher, and this time you're doing the same thing but taking it down slightly.

So, remember, this time there might be a little bit of movement through the legs. That's okay, as long as we're focusing on the rotation and that little bit of flexion as we take it down to the side there. Let the waist do the work, not the arms. Keep your breathing nice and relaxed. Fabulous. Make sure that it's fixed and it's stable at that end, and this is called the chop for obvious reasons. Feel as though we're going from high to low in that chopping motion. 15 repetitions. Slow is better. Brilliant stuff. Are we there yet? I wish I could count. Brilliant stuff. Excellent. Super. Take a little rest there. We can drop that band.

So, what we're going to do now is go into our cool down, which we'll do similar to our warm-up, a few mobilizing exercises, guys, just as we did for the warm up, moving through those large muscle groups, some rotations, some knee lifts, heels to the backside, a few of those mobilizing movements, and then we'll go into a stretch for the major muscle groups. If you know how to do that from the other workouts, then away you go. If not, remember we've got that flexibility workout for you, so perhaps you can pop that on and do it now instead.

Training Bar Workout
Lecture 35

Training bars come in different weights and can be used for a variety of exercises. If you don't have a training bar, you can easily buy one from a decent sports retailer. For this workout, you should use an 8- to 12-pound bar. Ideally, beginners will work with a training bar that weighs around 3 to 6 pounds. The intermediate level is between 9 and 18, and the advanced level is anywhere from 24 up to 36. If you don't have a training bar, you can use a broom handle to get used to the exercises until you get one.

Guidelines

- Before this workout, as with any workout, you need to have a good warm-up—perhaps including practicing some of the moves you're going to do in your workout, such as squats and biceps curls.

- Do 1 set of 15 repetitions of each exercise. If you're already exercising regularly, do 2 sets of each exercise, and if you're more advanced, do 3 sets of each exercise.

- Your core strength helps you integrate the strength in your upper and lower body. The following exercises set you up with an upper body exercise followed by a lower body exercise, and then you're going to combine the 2 together, repeating for several sets.

When picking up your training bar, be careful not to lift with your back; instead, lift with your knees.

© iStockphoto/Thinkstock.

Squat

- Rest the bar across the top of your back, grabbing it lightly. Never squeeze it.

- Keep your feet about hip-width apart, press down into the heels.

- Keep your abdominals in tight. Resist the temptation to let your stomach or shoulders drop forward.

- This exercise works the quadriceps, hamstrings, and glutei. It is a great exercise for your entire lower body.

Shoulder Press Front

- Bring the bar over to the front of your body.

- Keep your abs in tight, and keep your knees slightly bent for balance, which takes the strain off the lower back. There should be some tension through the legs, stopping you from swaying backward and forward, which puts stress on the back.

- You should press straight up but slightly forward because if you push directly upward, it's an uncomfortable position for the shoulder complex. Ideally, you should be able to look straight ahead but use your peripherals to see the bar slightly.

- Don't hold your breath. Exhale on the exertion; breathe out as you press.

- Your elbow should be straight, but don't lock it. Control the momentum of your arm.

Squat and Press

- Lock your middle, pulling in through the stomach and waist.

- Start with the bar at chest level. Squat down and press up at the same time.

- You should notice that much more work is required to pull your abs in when you go down. There will be a tendency for your stomach to want to drop forward. Keep it in tight so that you maintain a comfortable, neutral spine.

- Make sure you keep breathing.

- This exercise works the legs and the shoulders—the upper and lower body.

- The great thing about combining exercises is that you use more muscle groups. The more muscle groups you use, the more demanding in terms of energy, so you're burning more calories.

Rear Lunge: Right

- Rest the bar on top of your shoulders.

- Keep your feet hip-width apart.

- When you step back with your right foot, place it on the ball of the foot.

- Make sure you don't twist your rear knee.

- Don't let your body drop forward. Keep your abs in tight as you step back.

- Working through a greater range of motion requires more muscular effort, so stepping further back makes it more demanding through the legs.

Rear Lunge: Left

- Be aware if there's any difference from one side to the other; if one side is a little weaker, it might need some extra work.

- Start with your feet hip-width apart.

- Keep your abs in tight, and stand up tall with your chest lifted.

- Make sure you're stepping onto the ball of the foot with your rear leg and that your rear knee drops straight down.

- This exercise works the front of the thigh, the back of the thigh, and the gluteus. You're using many large muscle groups, which use a lot of energy, so you're toning and burning calories at the same time.

Rowing Side to Side
- To maintain stability, keep your feet hip-width apart and your knees slightly bent. If you find that you start to wobble through the lower spine, do a split lunge—one foot in front of the other—because that's even more stable.

- This exercise challenges your core strength. The rotation tries to throw your lower spine around, so you have to pull in tight through the transversus abdominis—across the middle—and the internal obliques—the smaller oblique muscles—pulling the thoracolumbar fascia at the back that splits the lower spine to keep you stable.

- Core strength involves having strength in the middle that allows you to generate strength and power through the limbs.

Rear Lunge (Right) and Row
- You're going to row in opposition to the lunge so that you get some rotation, which causes your core muscles to work harder.

- You should feel the hip flexors on your side working as you're rotating.

- Don't sacrifice your technique on the lunge—keep it nice and deep. Make your legs do some work.

- Your arms and shoulders are doing some work by moving the bar, but you're using your obliques to turn, and you're keeping your abdominals pulled in tight to maintain your position.

Rear Lunge (Left) and Row

- Switch sides, noticing any differences between the sides.

- Keep your head up and your chest lifted. Keep breathing.

- When dealing with core strength, you're keeping your spine fixed in a central column, and all the movement of the arms and legs is going on around the outside.

Plié

- Keep your feet out wide. The wider you go, the more muscular energy is involved and the greater the toning effect will be.

- Your knees should follow the line of the toes, and resist the temptation for your knees to drop in toward the center.

- This exercise works the front and back of the thigh, and it even works the adductor muscles in the inner thigh.

- Keep your abdominals in tight as you go down. Be careful not to stick your backside out

- You should be staying a little more upright than you do for a normal squat, letting the legs do the work.

- Slow is better for these exercises.

Biceps Curl

- Make sure that you fix your elbows by your side, really getting into just your bicep.

- Keep your feet about hip-width apart. Avoid any swinging movement by keeping your knees just slightly bent, which will engage your core muscles, locking on your lower body and keeping you fixed.

- Exhale on the way up, and inhale on the way down—don't hold your breath.

- Focus your mind on the feeling of the muscle that's doing the work—your bicep. Try to imagine your bicep muscle shortening and lengthening, performing concentric and eccentric contractions.

Plié and Biceps Curl
- For this exercise, you're combining your upper and lower body, and that integration relies on your core strength, so keep your abdominals in tight.

- Keep your legs nice and wide, and keep your elbows fixed to your sides.

- Keep your chest lifted and your head up.

- Make sure your knees don't collapse into the center—keep them out.

- Control the momentum on the bar on the way down.

- You should start to feel the inner thigh working as you do some deep pliés.

Front Lunge: Right
- The front lunge is a little trickier than the rear lunge because of stability issues.

- If you have had knee injuries, this is a great exercise to do, but take your time with it because it builds up the muscles around the knee that help control your motion.

- Start with your feet about hip-width apart, and rest the bar on your back.

- If you're not careful, you could have some stability issue when you lunge, but your knee might also shoot forward too far, which would put a strain under the patella tendon. You don't want your knee to go past the line of your toe when you're moving.

- Keep your abs in tight, shoulders back, and chest lifted.

- Work at your own pace.

- The longer the lunge, the more muscular energy and muscle fibers you're using, and the better the toning effects will be.

- Control your movements; don't allow your body to wobble from side to side.

- You should feel some work in the front or back of the thigh as you lower down, but as you come back, you should start to feel it in the gluteus.

Front Lunge: Left
- Switch sides, making sure your feet are hip-width apart.

- As you step out, press off your front heel to get you back to where you start.

- You're working your gluteus by pushing your heel off the floor. This movement involves hip extension.

Lateral Raise: Right
- Make sure you hold the bar in the middle. It doesn't matter if the bar wobbles a little bit—just try to reset it.

- In terms of stability, this exercise challenges the core strength, so try to keep your feet hip-width apart with your knees slightly bent.

- Keep your elbows slightly bent, and lift the bar to about shoulder level.

- This is an isolation exercise, so nothing but the deltoids should be moving.

- You should feel your abs working because there is a balance issue. If you're not locking your abs in the center as you slowly lift, you're going to fall over.

- Concentrate on your shoulder. If you focus on the muscle that's doing the work, you're more likely to get the technique right.

Lateral Raise: Left
- When switching sides, be aware that you might have imbalances from one side to the other.

- Think about your technique. You're in a braced position with your abs in tight and your knees slightly bent.

- All the work is coming from the shoulder. Particularly, some of the work is coming from the front and back of the shoulder—the anterior and posterior deltoid—but most of the work is coming from the middle part of the shoulder, the medial deltoid.

- Slowly lower the bar down; don't swing it or let it drop quickly. You're working against gravity.

Front Lunge (Right) and Lateral Raise (Left)
- You're going to lunge in opposition to the lateral raise so that you remain balanced.

- When you step forward, there are some stability issues, so make sure your knee doesn't wobble and make sure it doesn't go too far forward when lifting the bar.

- Keep your feet about hip-width apart. You can also put your other arm out or on your hip for balance.

- Lunge deep, and lift the bar up to shoulder level.

- Keep your abs in tight.

- This is a whole-body exercise. You're working your calves, hamstrings, quads, glutei, abdominals, obliques, and shoulders.

Front Lunge (Left) and Lateral Raise (Right)
- Take your feet out wide again, and start on your other side.

- Control your forward lunge, which should be as deep as possible.

- Make sure your body stays upright in the center.

- Keep your head and chest lifted.

- This exercise relies on your core strength.

Sit-Up and Reach
- This exercise works your rectus abdominis by trying to draw your ribs close to your hips.

- Start with your feet about hip-width apart. Press the bar up, sitting up straight and tall.

- Make sure that the movement is initiated by your abdominals by thinking about your abdominals as a spring that you are squeezing together.

- Breathe out on the way up and in on the way down.

- Try to keep your heels down if you can. Your feet might wobble a little, but that doesn't matter as long as you're working your abdominals.

- When you were standing, you were working the deeper postural muscles that pull in and fix you. For this exercise, you're working the rectus, which is a mobilizer—responsible for moving you.

Sit-Up and Twist

- For this exercise, you're still using the rectus, but you're also adding work for the internal and external obliques.

- The internal obliques are deeper, and they work on your core strength. The external obliques are what help you with rotation. They work together but sort of in opposition because of the angle at which the muscle fibers run.

Sit-Up and Reach and Twist

- Adding the previous 2 exercises together, you are going to sit up—using your rectus—and then use your obliques as you reach the bar up and over to the side. There is also some coordination movement involved.

- Keep your movements smooth. Don't let yourself fall back down; instead, slowly lower yourself down.

- You might be getting tired, but don't sacrifice your form.

- Make your obliques do some work by really twisting your body.

Cooldown

- As always, cool down after your workout.

- Because your core has done a lot of work, do some stretches for the lower back and spine.

- Hold your stretches for about 30 seconds because you're warm, which is the perfect time to stretch.

Training Bar Workout
Lecture 35—Transcript

Hi, and today, next in your homework series, the workout is going to be with a training bar. Now, this is a great bar, comes in different weights, easy to get a hold of from decent sports retailers. We're using 12s. We've also got an 8. Not easy to improvise with this because you do need a little bit of weight on the bar, and ideally, beginners, you're working around 3–6 pounds. Intermediate is somewhere in 9–18. Advanced, you'll be working 24 even up to 36.

Got to remember before this workout, as with any workout, you need to get a good warm up, like the guys are doing now, a little bit of mobilizing and maybe even practicing some of the moves you're going to go through, the little squats, the bicep curls—those sort of movements.

Usual targets for this workout, we're looking at 1 set of 15 repetitions of each exercise. If you're already a little fitter, doing exercise already, possibly 2 sets, and those of you who are more advanced, you want to be looking at 3 sets of each exercise.

So, a little tip here. What we're going to be doing, and this kind of flipped back to our lecture on the spine when we talked about core strength, and we've touched on this a few times. The idea of our core strength is it helps us to integrate the strength in the upper and lower body. So, what we're doing here is we're going to set ourselves up with an upper body exercise, a lower body exercise, and then we're going to combine the 2 together, and we're going to repeat that on several sets. So, hopefully you've got your bar and you're ready to go. Take a hold, and we're going to start. Careful how you pick it up. Well done, guys.

We're going to start with simple squats. Now, you could hold it in front if you wish, or you might want to take it over the tip. Careful how you do it. Rest it across the top of the back, and hands lightly. Never squeeze on it. Feet are about hip width apart for the squats, and all I'm going to ask you to do is press down into the heels, keep the tummy in tight, and then straighten back up. So, should we go?

Down we go, and press. Away you go, please. I'm looking for 15 repetitions, and I'm going to trust you to count them. So, keep going, please, but keep your eyes on me while you're doing that.

What I want you to do is sit down. Press the heels back. Keep the abdominals in tight. Resist the temptation to let your belly drop forwards. Don't let the shoulders drop forwards. Fabulous. 15 repetitions, please.

Now, what we're doing here is really getting into the quadriceps, the front of the thighs. We're getting into the hamstrings at the back of the thighs, and we're getting into the glutes. Absolutely fantastic exercise for whole of the lower body. 15 repetitions, please. Well done, guys.

We're going to change that slightly now. Bring the bar over to the front. Keeping the abs in tight, keeping the knees slightly bent for your balance—takes the strain off the lower back—I'm looking for a shoulder press. We're going straight up but slightly forwards, and the reason for that is if you push directly upwards, that's a really uncomfortable position for the shoulder complex. So, actually, the ideal position would be to use your peripheral vision. You will push upwards. Keep looking forwards at me, but you still should be able to see the bar slightly.

Let's go for our 15 repetitions, please. Press up and back down. Now, ideally I don't want you to be holding your breath. The tip is to exhale on the exertion. So, breathe out as you press. Beautiful. Away we go. 15 repetitions. No cheating. The thing to look out for here: Abs are in tight to protect your lower back. The knees are slightly bent. There's a little bit of tension through the legs, and what that will do is stop you swaying backwards and forwards, again which stresses the back. Also worth looking out for: we're not locking out the elbow. Yes, we're going straight, but don't lock it out. Control that momentum. 15 repetitions, just 15, not 115. Fabulous. Well done.

What we're going to do now is put those 2 together. Now, this is harder than it looks because what we really need to do now is lock on in the middle, pull in through the tummy, pull in through the waist. Let's get set to go. We're starting at chest level. So, you're going to squat down and press up at the same time. Let's go. Squat and press and down. Squat and press. Now you should begin to feel. Keep going. You should begin to feel a lot more work is required here in pulling the abdominals in when you go down. There will be a tendency for your belly to want to drop forwards. That's not going to happen. Keep it in tight so that we maintain neutral spine. Talked about that before. That's a comfortable curve in your lower spine.

How are we doing? Fabulous. 15 reps, making sure we're breathing. Good. Looking deadly serious. Fabulous. Working through the legs; working through the shoulders. So, we're working upper and lower body, and the great thing about combining our exercises is that we're using more muscle groups. The more muscle groups we're using, it's more demanding in terms of energy. So, what that means is we're burning more calories.

Okay, we're going to skip on to our next exercise. Again we're going to take the bar over the top, rest it on the top. There you go. We're going for a real lunge. Now, careful with this. Your feet are hip width apart. When you step back with your right foot—remember I'm mirroring you—when you step back with your right foot, place it on the ball of the foot. Drop the knee straight down to the floor, and then we come back up. Make sure there's no twisting of that rear knee. Also, don't let your body drop forwards. Keep your abs in tight as you step back.

Okay, are we ready? I'll take 15 repetitions on your right leg. Let's go. Drop it back, knee down to the floor, and up. Down. Beautiful. How are you doing? Hope you're still with me. Good. Keep going. Remember, if you haven't got your training bar yet, you could be using just a broom handle to get used to the exercises until you've got one. Excellent stuff. And the best bit about this is working through a greater range of motion actually requires more muscular effort. So, stepping a long way back—what we're doing here—fabulous example. Long step back. Great range of movement. Little bit more demanding through the legs. That's what we're after. Great stuff. Abs are in tight all the time. 15 reps. Perfect. Guess what? Let's swap over to the other leg.

Now, be aware if there's any difference from one side to the other, if one side is a little weaker and maybe needs a bit of extra work. Start with your feet hip width. Abs are in tight. You're nice and tall, chest lifted, and away we go.

Drop down the left leg, your left leg. Knee down to the floor. Good. Down you go. Excellent work. Keep it going. Make sure you're stepping onto the ball of the foot and that knee drops straight down at the back.

Now, what you're also doing here is getting some work front of the thigh, back of the thigh, gluteals. Great exercise, but because of that, we're using lots of what are called large muscle groups. Compare those to the muscles in your wrist. They're large muscle groups, so they take a lot of energy. It's what we're after. We want that calorie burn, so we're getting some toning and we're burning up some calories at the same time. Fabulous stuff. Well done, guys. How are you doing at home?

So, we're going to get a little bit innovative with this now, and we're going to do a little rowing exercise. So, I really want you to be stable on this, and so I want your feet hip width apart and your knees slightly bent. Now, if you find that you still start to rock about through the lower spine, what I'm going to ask you to do is a split lunge, one foot in front of the other because that's even more stable.

So, all we're doing here, anyone who can remember Hawaii Five-0—I've just shown my age there, haven't I—we're going to do a little bit of rowing, so a little bit wider than chest width. All we're going to do is take it down to this side and then take it down to that side. Good. Now, if we go there and there, that's one. There and there is 2. Keep it going, please. So, what we're doing here is you're challenging your core strength. Because of this rotation, it's actually trying to throw your lower spine all over the place. So, what we've got to do is pull in tight through that transverses abdominis, across the middle, pulling tight through those internal obliques, the smaller oblique muscles, and what that will do is then pull this thoracolumbar fascia at the back that then splits the lower spine and keeps you stable. Remember we talked about what core strength means to us. It's having strength in the middle that allows us to generate that strength and power through the limbs.

How are we doing? I've completely lost count. I'm trusting you all to do 15. Beautiful. Okay, so, let's put those 2 together now, then. What we're going to do is our real lunge and our row at the same time. Now, the row is going to go in opposition so that you get some rotation, which again works those core muscles a little bit harder. So, what we're going to do, as you take your right leg back, you're going to row down to the left. Down then up. Down. Beautiful. Row down. Get a little rotation in the body now. Fabulous. You should really start to feel—keep it going—a little bit of work here on the hip flexors on your right side as you're getting that rotation there.

Don't sacrifice the technique on the lunge. Keep that good technique on the lunge, nice and deep. Make those legs do some work. Fabulous stuff, and getting that body rotating. So, clearly your arms and shoulders are doing some work moving the bar here, but really what's going on is that rotation in the middle is coming from your core strength. We're using those obliques to get that little turn, and to maintain that position, you're keeping your abdominals pulled in really tight.

Good work, guys, should we swap to the other side? So, you're lunging back with your left leg and rowing down to the right side. So, as the leg goes back, we row down and row, and row. Beautiful. Keep your head up. Keep your chest lifted. Keep breathing. Sorry, they told me not to yell. I shouldn't have done that. And down. Good. How are we doing? Keep it going. Fabulous. Great example. Keeping your head up.

Remember when we're talking about our core strength we're talking about keeping that spine fixed. So, we've got a nice central column, and all the work, the arms and legs, all that movement is going on around the outside. You've got this constant dance between mobility of the arms and legs and stability in the center, keeping it strong. That's really what we mean by core strength. You look like you thought I might do another one there, but I won't bother. That's okay.

What we're going to do now is move on to the next exercise. Now, if at any time between the exercises you want to stop and get yourself a quick sip of water, that's okay, but get back to me very quickly. Let's move on to the plié. Now, just a tip: If you find this position uncomfortable behind, for these leg exercises you can keep it down here as well, but it's just sometimes a little easier to get it out of the way there. For the plié, I want the feet wide, wide, wide, wide, wide. However wide you just put them, go a little bit wider. Point the knees and toes out slightly. They're pointing out at this angle because when you plié, the knees follow the line of the toes. What that will do is as well as working into the front and the back of the thigh, we now start getting into the adductor muscles in the inner thigh.

Okay, so, plié. We're looking for 15 repetitions. Be careful. Abdominals are in tight as we go down and down. Beautiful. Knees following the line of the toes, and be careful not to stick your backside out. That's not what we're doing. You're staying a little more upright than the normal squat here, and let the legs to the work. And again, that range of motion, the wider we go, more muscular energy being involved, greater the toning effect. So, look out for these knees. Slow is better on these exercises to make sure that they follow the line of the toes and resist that temptation for your knees to drop in towards the center. Okay, bring the feet back in slightly, and we're moving on to the bicep curl.

Fix your elbows by your side. Make sure they're fixed in. We lift up and then slowly down. Nothing else moves. Really getting into just that bicep, into the bicep. So, feet are about hip width apart, and again, we want to avoid that swinging movement, so keep the knees just slightly bent. Just bending the knees slightly will start to engage these muscles, which will lock on your lower body and keep you fixed.

Okay, are we ready? 15 repetitions. Up we go, and back down. Remember our tip on the breathing: Exhale on the way up, inhale on the way down. Failing that? Just keep inhaling and exhaling. Whatever you do, don't hold your breath. Good.

Now, a little tip here while we're doing this is to put your mind in muscle. Focus on the feeling of the muscle that's going the work. Really think about your bicep, and think back to our lecture on muscles—how they work. Try to imagine that bicep muscle just shortening and lengthening and shortening and lengthening. Remember we said a concentric contraction and an eccentric contraction, the muscle at work.

How are we doing, guys? Look at those arms. Fabulous. Oh, I got there just in time. So, just in case you haven't picked up the swing of what we're doing here, we're going to put those 2 exercises together. Nice and wide with the legs, and again, because we're combining upper and lower body together here, that integration relies upon your core strength, so abdominals in tight.

Okay, are we set? As you squat down, it comes up. Let's go. Keep the elbows fixed to your side. Keep your chest lifted. Head up. Keep smiling. Just think what this is doing for you. Knees out. Make sure the knees don't collapse into the center. Beautiful work. Control the momentum on the bar. When you're lowering this down—this goes for any weight training exercise—you must control the momentum on the way down. The exercise is not simply lifting the bar up. It's lifting it up and slowly lowering it down. Fabulous. Nice deep plies. Should really begin to feel that getting into the inner thigh as well. Well done, guys. Well done at home.

So, let's move on. Front lunge now. Now, the front lunge is a little more tricky than the rear lunge, reason being the stability issues now. So, this is great work. If anyone has had knee injuries, this is a great exercise to do, but take your time with it because it really builds up the muscles around the knee that help control your motion.

So, what we're going to do, again, you can rest it here. We'll get it out of the way. Rest it on the back there. So, feet are about hip width apart. For the front lunge, right leg you're stepping forwards, dropping the knee down, and then in one movement coming back to where you started on that right leg again, but be careful here because 2 things can happen. One, if we're not careful, we've got a stability issue here, but 2, what might also happen is your knee shoots forwards; and the problem with that is if the knee shoots forwards too far here, that puts a real strain under the patella tendon there, which is not a good idea. So, what we're looking for is only going as far as there so that it goes straight down. Really you don't want your knee to go further than the line of your toe while you're moving, so just look out for that.

Okay, are we set? Start hip width. Make sure you step hip width. Don't step onto a tight rope. Away we go. Right leg. Step, lunge down, and back. Abs in tight, shoulders back, chest lifted. Work at your own pace. You don't have to work in time with us. It's down to you. Good. Remember what we said: the longer lunge—and these are great lunges—the more muscular energy we're using, the more of the muscle fibers, the better the toning effects. Fabulous. Nice and long. Down onto the knee. Good.

Remember, we've got to control that motion. Don't let it wobble side to side. Don't let the knee overshoot the toe. So, you've got to take a nice, long stride. You should really feel some work in the front or back of the thigh as you lower down, but then as you kick back you should really start to feel that in the glutes, and to really exaggerate that, let's try this on the other side now. Think about pushing off with your heel from foot.

So, let's swap over sides. Set yourself up. Make sure you're hip width apart again. As you step out this time what I'm going to ask you to do when you lunge: really press off that front heel. Really get that feeling that you're pressing back off the front heel to get you back to where we start.

Okay, are we ready? Your left leg. Here we go, lunging down, and push, and down, and push from that front lunge. Let's go. Excellent. So, really getting into the glutes by work on that push off the floor there. So, what we're doing there is working into, if you remember when we talked about the joints and we talked about the hip joint, the movements about the hip joint, and we talked about hip extension, and that's what this is: returning from that forwards position from flexed back to that hip extension movement, and that's brought about by the gluteal muscles. So, we get a really good push off the floor to get us back. Really toning into the buttocks. Excellent work. How are you doing at home? I hope you're still with us. Remember, all of these exercises you can try just with a broom handle at first before you get your training bar.

Okay, so, we're going to add to that now. Let's move onto the upper body. Should we go with some work for your shoulders? Let's try our lateral raises. Little bit of a balance issue here. Make sure you get the bar in the middle. Doesn't matter if it wobbles too much. Again, in terms of stability, we'll challenge the core strength, so let's try and keep the feet hip width apart, knees slightly bent. If you find that you're starting to sway a little bit, remember we can split the feet, and that goes for any exercise you're doing where you're lifting the weights upper body. If you start to find that it's difficult to maintain that strong center, then if you split your feet into what we'd call a split lunge, a tiny distance there, that'll help you with the stability issues.

Okay, so, here we go. Knees are slightly bent. We're going to lift to the side but keep the elbows slightly bent as well, and we're just lifting to about head height, so the bar is up to shoulder level. Your hand is up to head height. There we go. Okay, are we set? We're looking for 15 repetitions. Now, this is an isolation. Nothing else moves. We're just getting into the deltoids. Up and down. Abs are in tight. You should really feel now because we've got a balance issue. If you're not locking on in the center, clearly you're going to fall over. So, you've got to lock on in the center there as you slowly lift. How are you doing? Really focus mind and muscle. Just concentrate on that shoulder. If you focus on the muscle that's doing the work, you're more likely to get the technique right.

How are we doing? I'll do a couple more. Up. Doesn't matter if the bar wobbles a little bit. Try and reset it. Abs are in tight, and if we're done, should we swap over to the other side? Again, be aware that you might have imbalances from one side to the other. How many of you carry your bag in one hand all the time, in the same arm, on the same shoulder. Okay, so, we're lifting up and back down. Think about the technique. Abs in tight, knees slightly bent, so we're in that braced position.

All the work is coming from the shoulder here. Particularly there's a little bit of work from the front and from the back of the shoulder, the anterior and the posterior deltoid, but most of the work is coming through there, the medial deltoid, the middle part of the shoulder. Abs in tight, and don't swing. Remember what we said. We're working eccentrically against gravity. We're slowly lowering it down. Don't let it just fall. Get your money's worth. Get the whole exercise.

Okay, so, it starts to get tricky now because we're going to combine these 2. So, you've got those stability issues when we step forwards, making sure the knee doesn't wobble in or out and making sure it doesn't go too far forwards at the same time as lifting the bar. Now, we're going to go in opposition here. So, what's going to happen here is you're going to lunge forwards with your right leg, but you're going to lift the lateral raise on the left side so that it keeps you balanced.

Okay, so, set yourself up. Feet are hip width apart. We're going to step forwards there with that leg and lift up at the same time, and back down. Not an easy exercise. Up and down. You can see I put this other arm out for balance. And down. Beautiful. Get a good, deep lunge. 15 reps, please. How are we doing? Excellent. Nice, deep lunge. Lifting up to shoulder level. Excellent.

Good work. These guys are super fit. They're only sweating because of the lights. Trust me. Good work. Keep going. Abs are in tight. Beautiful. Nice, deep lunges. So, don't sacrifice it. You've got a lot to think about here, and this is taxing because it's a whole body exercise. Trust me. We've got some calves; we've got some hamstrings; we've got some quads, glutes, abdominals, obliques, the shoulder. There's a lot of work going on here. It's fabulous. Swap it over to the other side. Fabulous for me because I'm not doing it. I'm just watching them do it.

Take the feet out wide again. We're onto the other side now. So, you're going to lunge forwards and control this lunge. We're lunging forwards with your left leg, and we're lifting the bar on the right side. Get a couple of breaths, and away we go. Nice deep lunge and lift. Fabulous. Boom. If you need the other hand out for balance or if you want it on the hip, that's fine. Make sure your body is staying upright in the center. Excellent. Head is lifted. The chest lifted. Fabulous. Don't sacrifice those lunges. Good. Don't rush. Don't rush. Always about getting good quality. Super. Tricky exercise.

Really relies on the core strength, what we call the inner unit, the diaphragm that pushes down, transverses, pulling in, the internal obliques at the side, and that motipitus muscle at the back, gives us that inner unit, which gives us what we call the abdominal balloon that pulls in and helps us stabilize the spine. Great work. Great exercise.

So, you'll be pleased to know that we're going to make it a little bit easier. Should we get down on the mat, take a little rest, guys. You deserve it. We're going to get down for some—no workout is going to be complete without some abdominal work, is it? So, let's work into our rectus abdominals, the 6-pack now.

Now, remember, the key with this exercise is you're trying to draw your ribs close to your hips. That is all the 6-pack muscle does. Really you only use it couple of times a day—getting out of bed in the morning and going back again at night.

So, for this exercise what we're going to do is take the bar across the chest when you lie yourself down. The feet are about hip width apart. As you sit up, you're going to press the bar up. So, make sure that the movement is initiated by the abdominals, and the way to do that, getting back to our mind in muscle, is to think about your abdominals as a spring and squeeze it together. That's what you're going to do. Think about the spring. Squeeze together and then lift the bar, sitting up nice and tall.

Are we ready? I'm going to take 15 repetitions, guys. Let's go. Remember your breathing. Breathe out on the way up and in on the way down. Try and keep your heels down if you can. You might find your feet wobble a little bit, but that doesn't matter as long as you're getting that work from the abdominals. So, think about initiating the movement by squeezing the ribs down towards the hips and reaching the bar, that extra resistance we're working against. Fabulous. Can we feel something going on in the center?

Now, this is slightly different because what we're working on in terms of abdominals here are not the abdominals I was talking about earlier when we were standing. They were the deeper postural muscles that just pull in and fix us. We're now talking about the rectus, which is a mobilizer. It's responsible for moving you. Different abdominal muscle group. Excellent. 15? Super, and a quick rest there.

Going to vary things slightly because what we're going to do is still use the rectus, but what I'm going to do now is then change it slightly and add some more oblique work. And again, remember the obliques. We have 2 different muscles here—the external obliques, that if you just were to put your hand on your waist, the direction of your fingers, really that's this sort of angle that the obliques run at. Whereas your internal obliques, if you turn your hand over, they run in that direction.

The internal obliques are deeper, and they're the ones that work on your core strength. The external obliques, just here, are what help us with rotation. But interestingly, and if you think about this, if you've got external obliques running this way and internal obliques this way, can you see how they work at opposite sides? So, if I want to go that way, it's this action—internal here and external there. If I want to go that way, it's actually going to be internal here and external there. So, they work together but sort of in opposition, if you see what I mean. So, it's internal and external that way, internal and external that way, and that's because of the angle the muscle fibers run at. We're going to add them together now and get that twist, but also we're getting a little sit-up, so we're getting some rectus work as well.

Let me just show you first of all. For this one you can continue to rest guys for a second, a well earned rest. You're going to sit up—so, this is where your rectus comes in—and then use the obliques as you reach the bar up and over to that side. We're just going to go to that one side first of all. Sit up and reach it across. So, a little bit of coordination movement here as well.

I'm after 15 repetitions, please. Are you set? Go. Up and twist. Beautiful. Up and twist. So, reach that bar up nice and high, a little bit higher up there. Fabulous. Good. And reach. Excellent. So, getting into that rectus abdominis, getting into the obliques with that twist, keep it nice and smooth, and don't let yourself fall back down. Remember to slowly lower yourself down. Get the full value for each exercise. Up and reach. Beautiful. Excellent work. Just 15 and then you can have a quick rest. Good work. Really working into those abdominals, problem area for a lot of us. We all want to work on this. This is a great exercise you can do.

Well done. When you've done your 15 you can have a quick rest. Excellent. Good work. Well done. So, all we've got to do, you'll be pleased to know, you've only got 1 more exercise to do, and that is the same thing, that sit up and twist, but we're doing it on the other side now.

Now, you might be getting a little bit tired, but don't sacrifice your form. We're nearly there. This is your last exercise. So, are we set? Let's go with it. Sit up and twist. Beautiful. Twist and reach upwards. Reach up. Just a little bit higher with that bar. Reach up to the corner. Fabulous. And up and twist. Beautiful. Beautiful. Up and twist. Good. Get a little bit more rotation if you can. Twist the body. Good. Really get into those obliques. Get a little bit more rotation if you can. Really make them do some work. Excellent stuff. Sit up and twist. Good.

I do feel guilty watching you guys do all the work, but you're doing such a great job. I don't look half as good as them doing this. Hopefully you're looking good at home. We done? You can have a quick rest. In fact, why don't you just lay the bar down and pull your knees into your chest and have a rest there.

What we're going to do now is go into a little cool down. Importantly, because we've done a lot of work through the core strength there, we need to do some stretches for the lower back.

What the guys are doing here is that little pulling your knees into your chest, and you can rock forwards and backwards and side to side. That'll really get into there because you've really worked around the center there on a lot of these exercises. Although we were isolating, like the bicep curl, when we combined upper and lower body, as I said, to get that integration you've really got to work your core strength.

What I'm going to ask you to do now is to drop both knees down to our side over here and then take your arms across to the other side. So, that little stretch there again, great stretch for getting through your lower back into the obliques and muscles that have just done some work. Try and just relax yourself down into that position.

You know the usual rule for our stretching exercises at the end there. We're looking for about 30 seconds because you're nice and warm now, so this is a good time to get that stretch, and if you're short of any ideas, don't forget you've got your little flexibility workout DVD in this series that gives you lots of stretching exercises you can use.

Shall we flip over to the other side? Particularly for this one and any exercises that are really using your core strength, so on our medicine ball, on our kettle bells, those kind of exercises—this training bar as well—what I want you to do is get a good little stretch and mobility work through your lower spine at the end there.

So, that is your training bar workout. Great tool. So many exercises you can do with it, so many different things you can do with it. Like I say, if you haven't got one to start with, you can still do that workout with us with a broom handle. Remember the guidelines. We're looking at 1 set of 15 if you're just setting out; 2 sets of 15 if you're already exercising; more advanced, 3 sets; and then also remember you've got the opportunity to go slightly heavier with these training bars.

It's a great workout. Have fun with it.

Stretching Routine
Lecture 36

The following stretching routine is designed to introduce you to a range of stretches that will help improve your flexibility. All you need is some space around you, some loose clothing to wear, and the thermostat set to a comfortably warm temperature. This routine can be used at the end of any workout that you do to ensure that your muscles will be prepared for the next time you need to use them. By the end of this routine, you will appreciate the many reasons that stretching is beneficial for both your body and mind.

The Benefits of Stretching

- Flexibility refers to the range of motion around a joint or group of joints. It varies from person to person and from joint to joint. It is primarily dependent upon the specific joint structure and is significantly influenced by the connective tissues around each of the joints. Because joint health is related to activity levels, age, and gender, these are key considerations in determining flexibility.

- In addition to the 3 fundamental determinants, there are 3 less influential items.

  o Body temperature affects range of motion, which is known to improve along with increasing heat. This is why exercise always begins with a warm-up period.

  o Contrary to common belief, rather than shortening your muscles and making them stiffer, weight training exercises that work through your full range of motion will improve your flexibility.

  o During pregnancy, the joints and ligaments in the lumbopelvic region are relaxed to allow for growth and movement of the fetus, making delivery a little easier in the process.

- Regular stretching has been shown to produce the following positive adaptations.

  o Enhanced range of motion.

  o Reduced risk of injury and degree of such if injury does occur.

  o Increased sports performance in terms of endurance and skill.

  o Improved posture, leading to reduced risk of lower back malady.

  o Increased positive impact on mental health by providing a vehicle for physical relaxation.

- Static stretching is the most common method of stretching that involves a gentle movement toward the end position to slowly lengthen the muscle and then holding at the point of mild tension for between 15 and 30 seconds.

- The idea of collagen creep is that after you hold a static stretch for about 6 or 8 seconds, the connective tissues around the muscle begin to stretch to align themselves in the same direction. After you start

Your calf muscles are most likely used in any workout, so you should take the time to stretch them.

© Michael Blann/Thinkstock.

to feel some mild tension, the tension will subside, and then you'll be able to ease a little further into the stretch. Breathe out as you stretch further into the position.

Warm-Up

- Make sure that you have some space to stretch, and make sure it's quiet.

- Start with some mobility work—from the top of the body to the bottom—to get the synovial fluid into the joints, and then move into stretching.

- Start with your feet about hip-width apart. Bend your knees slightly.

- Tilt your head from side to side at your own relaxed pace.

- Be aware if there's any differences from one side to the other.

- Next, drop your head down and lift it up. Don't flick your head back; just lift from the chin and look up at the ceiling.

- Then, make a half circle, starting with your head to one side and slowly rolling over to the other. Avoid squeezing at the back and impinging the blood vessels.

- Gently roll your shoulders forward. Then, roll them backward.

- Bring your arms up to chest level, and open them out, keeping your abs in tight, hips fixed, and knees slightly bent.

- Then, bring your arms forward and make some big circles. The shoulder is the only joint in the body that can do this movement of circumduction. Then, reverse your circles, bringing your arms backward. Try to do one forward and one backward as a mental challenge.

- Bring your knee up to about waist height, working through the hip flexors.

- Bring your heel up to your backside to do a leg curl, working the hamstring muscles at the back of the thigh.

- Try to get a good range of motion through the ball-and-socket joint at your hip by doing a hip circle on both sides.

- Starting with either leg, do a heel dig: Put one foot in front of your body and then the other, bringing your heel down and lifting your toe up. This stretches your calf and your Achilles tendon.

- Starting with your knees slightly bent, work on the flexion and extension of your spine. Take a deep breath, and be aware of lengthening your spine. When you exhale, try to blow all of the air out, which will start to draw the ribs down toward the hips. As you get toward the end of the breath, you'll start to feel your abdominals engaging deeper and pulling you down into that flex position. Then, take a deep breath in, lifting your face up and forward.

- Then, add an arm swing. Lift your arms up when you breathe in, and when you exhale, let them drop down. Let this pull you down slightly. Feel the back rounding, and then open it up.

Standing Stretches
- Drop one of your ears to your shoulder. Take your palm out to the opposite side, and press it down to the ground. You should feel a stretch coming through the neck and down into the shoulder. Try to keep your breathing relaxed. Switch to the other side, making sure to center yourself.

- Stretch your shoulders by lifting your head up, and bringing one of your arms across your chest. Hold your arm just above the elbow, squeezing it a little so that it goes further across. Don't let your body twist. Ease into your stretch position—to the point where you feel mild tension, and then hold it. Keep your breathing relaxed, and enjoy being at peace for a moment. When you're ready, switch to the other side.

- Bring your hands behind your back, and put your palms together. Lift away slightly from your backside, squeezing your shoulder blades together. Try not to arch your back; try not to stick your chin out. This is a great stretch for the pectoral muscles but also for the front of your shoulders and chest. Try to picture the elastic fibers of the chest muscles stretching gently.

- Then, bring your hands up to the front of your body. You can either interlock your fingers or put one on top of the other. Your arms should stay slightly bent while you stretch forward. The goal is to reach your hands forward and to round the back, stretching through the muscles in the upper back by pulling your shoulder blades apart. Drop your chin down onto your chest.

- To stretch your triceps, take one arm, and drop it down behind your body. Place your hand with your fingers pointing down onto the back of your spine. Put your other hand on top of the elbow and encourage your hand to walk further down the spine by pressing down onto it. Keep your abdominals in tight.

- Put your hands on top of your knees, which should be bent. To stretch your lower back, pull your belly button in tight, trying to lift your lower back up to the ceiling by rounding through your lower spine. This exercise works the erector spinae muscles. You're supporting the weight of your back by putting your hands on your thighs. Slowly, curl back up.

- To stretch your hip flexors, bring your left foot back, and rest it on the ball of the foot. Your hips, chest, and shoulders should face the front. Bend both knees. Tilt your pelvis up and forward, which will flex the iliopsoas muscles of the hip flexors. Switch feet, and repeat.

- To stretch your quadriceps, start by holding your left foot. Squeeze your heel close to your backside without squeezing it directly into your backside because that would put a lot of pressure under the patella tendon of the knee. Then, push your hip forward.

- Switch legs. For balance, you can bend your supporting knee. If you're struggling with your balance, you can hold onto something, or you can just reset yourself if you wobble.

- Because they are opposing muscle groups, you need to stretch the hamstring at the back of the thigh after stretching the quadriceps at the front. Start with your left foot out, keeping your heel down. Bend your right leg, and put your hands on your right thigh. Trying not to round your spine, bring your chest forward. As you drop your chest, you'll feel a stretch in the hamstring. Let the top of your head drop forward to maintain the natural curve in your lower spine. Switch legs, and repeat.

- To stretch your inner thigh, take a wide stance on the floor or on a mat. Point your toes out, and point your knees out along the line of your toes. Place your hands just above your knees, and push backward as if you are getting ready to sit down. You're opening your inner thigh, stretching the adductor muscles. Keep your shoulders and breathing relaxed.

- To stretch your outer thigh, bring your left foot over your right foot. With your left hand, you are going to displace your hip by leaning and pushing your hip at the same time. This stretches the lateral complex of the hip and your smaller gluteus muscles, but also the iliotibial band down the side of your leg. This is an important stretch for runners. Switch legs, and repeat.

- There are 2 muscles in the calf: the gastrocnemius and the soleus. You can stretch these muscles by bringing your left foot back, making sure your feet are facing forward, and sinking onto your front leg. Keep your back heel down, but shift your weight forward to feel the calf stretching. You might need to support your weight on your front leg. Switch legs, and repeat.

- As you ease out of that stretch, bend your knee to sink a little lower down in order to stretch the soleus and the Achilles tendon. Make sure your feet are about hip-width apart for balance. Shift your weight forward, keeping your heel down and leg straight. For runners, this is a particularly important stretch. Switch legs, and repeat.

- The great thing about standing stretches is that you can do them anywhere and at any time.

Floor Stretches
- Start by stretching your lower back by getting down onto all fours, placing your hands directly under your shoulders and your knees directly under your hips. Drop your chin down, and pull your belly button in as much as you can so that you're pulling your lower back up toward the ceiling. Try to round your spine.

- Take your left arm, and reach it down. Drop down onto your shoulder if you can—keep your hips over your knees—to feel a stretch across the shoulder and into the upper back. Try to keep your breathing relaxed. Switch arms, and repeat. You can turn your head into that position.

- Reset yourself with your hands under your shoulders and your knees under your hips. Take your left hand—this time, keep looking at your hand—and lift it up to the point at which you can feel a rotation through your lower spine. Try not to sit backward; keep your weight forward. You're stretching the lower back and the shoulders, releasing through the chest. Switch arms, and repeat.

- Next, go into an upward dog position—a yoga pose. Start by lying down on the floor or on a mat and lifting your hips and chest up off the floor. Lift your face up and forward. You're trying to extend up and forward—not backward—through the spine. Keep your shoulders back and down. This is a position of hyperextension, where you go slightly beyond the normal range.

- Sit back into a child's pose. This is a great pose because it can affect different people in different ways; experiment with it to see how it works for you.

- Return onto all fours and into a swan position. Bring your left foot forward. Bring your knee up, and turn it slightly to the side. Then, sit back. This pose also has many benefits; it's a great combination stretch. Focus on bringing your hips down, and try to keep your upper body relaxed. Switch to the other side, and repeat.

- Then, walk your hands back out of that position, and turn your feet to the back with your head down, and lie down in the corpse pose. Enjoy the moment, and be aware of how loose you feel throughout your body.

Guidelines for Stretching
- Try to stretch regularly, daily if possible.

- Hold static stretches at the point of mild tension for 15 seconds to maintain flexibility and for 30 seconds to improve it.

- Ensure that you are warm before stretching—either after some cardio exercises or after bathing.

- Be aware of your posture, ensuring that you are in a comfortable position to stretch that allows you to focus on the target muscle.

- Perform stretches that target the joints in which you feel particularly stiff or that replicate movements you need for your chosen sport or daily life.

- Use deep breathing, gentle music, and suitable visualization to enhance your efforts by helping to relax the muscles.

- If at any time you feel a sharp or stabbing pain, release the stretch immediately.

Stretching Routine
Lecture 36—Transcript

Earlier in this series we looked at the topic of flexibility—why it's important to us, what factors influence it, and finally how we can work to improve it. This workout is to do just that, taking you through a range of stretches. So, all you need for this is a bit of space around you, some loose clothing, and a thermostat set to a comfortably warm temperature. Before we begin, let's review the key knowledge we learnt from the flexibility lecture.

Now, flexibility refers to the range of motion around a joint or group of joints and not only varies from person to person but for each individual it also differs from joint to joint. It's primarily dependent upon the specific joint structure and is significantly influenced by the connective tissues around each of the joints. So, since joint health is related to activity levels, age and gender, then it's no surprise these are key considerations in determining our flexibility.

In general, it's fair to say that females tend to have better flexibility than males at most joints, and that can be attributed to small differences in the joints and the associated connective tissues. The effect of age on flexibility, however, is considerably greater than gender.

In addition to the 3 fundamental determinants of activity, age and sex there are 3 other less influential items that are, nonetheless, worth considering. Firstly, body temperature can affect your range of motion. It's known to improve along with increasing heat, hence the reason in all our other workouts before we exercise we have a warm up period.

Now, contrary to common belief, rather than shortening your muscles and making them stiffer, weight training exercises that actually work through your full range of motion will improve your flexibility.

During pregnancy, the joints and the ligaments, particularly in the lumbo-pelvic area, are relaxed to allow for growth and movement of the fetus, plus the actual delivery of the baby itself.

Now, regular stretching has been shown to produce lots positive benefits: enhanced range of motion, reduced risk of injury and the degree of injury when it occurs, increased sports performance, also improved posture, leading to reduced risk of back problems, and a positive impact on mental health through the vehicle of physical relaxation. So, a lot of benefits there.

Static stretching is the most common method of practice, requiring a gentle movement toward the end position. It slowly lengthens the muscle and then we hold at that point of mild tension for somewhere between 15 and 30 seconds. Now, although you may remember we looked at 2 other techniques involving partner work, this static method is the most easily accessible, and that's the one we're going to do today.

So, first of all let's make sure it's nice and quiet. Make sure you've got some space. Switch your phone to silent. Lock the kids in the bedroom if you need to. It's a bit of met time. This is just for you now. And we're going to start with a little mobility work just to get the synovial fluid into the joints, and then we'll move into our stretches. So, we're going to start by taking your feet about hip width apart. Knees are slightly bent.

First of all, all I'm going to do is work from the top and work down. So, we'll take a little tilt of the head from side to side. Tilt it one way and the other at your own pace, nice and relaxed. Keep it moving. You don't have to be in time with me, just as long as we're working through a little bit of dynamic mobility work, first of all, just a few more of those.

We'll rest that, working through our rotation as well. Let's get a little tilt from one side to the other. Doesn't matter which side you go first. And just enjoy that movement. Try to be aware if there's any difference from one side to the other. Fabulous.

We're going to drop it down and lift it up, but don't flick the head back. Just lift the eyes up to the ceiling, repeatedly squeezing back and cause a little impingement on the blood vessels at the back. So, we just lift from the chin up to look up to the ceiling.

Then the circle. We're going to half circle to one side; drop down to the other. Again, we're going to avoid that movement where we squeeze at the back. So, just rolling from side to side. Hopefully you're beginning to release that tension through your neck, and hold it there.

Let's take the shoulders and just roll them forward nice and gently, little roll of the shoulders. Just enjoy that freedom of movement. Let's take them backwards. This is all just about mobilizing those joints. We're also beginning to increase our core body temperature a little as we go along. We're going to bring the arms up to chest level, and we're going to open them out. Again, nothing stressful; at your own pace. Keep your abs in tight. The hips are fixed. The knees are slightly bent. Good. Let's hold it there.

Can we take the arms forwards. Nice, big circles. Remember in our lecture on movement in the muscles we talked about circumduction. The shoulder is the only joint in the body that can actually do this. We'll go backwards. That means we're getting a full circle. Doesn't happen around the hip. Beautiful.

Now, just a little tricky one for those of you who remember our mental fitness lecture. Can we do one forwards and one backwards? I'm not even going to look at you guys to check whether you're doing it right.

Swap it over. One forwards, one backwards. You weren't ready for that. I didn't tell them we were going to do that. Hold that there. Have a little rest.

We're going to go to knee lift. I'm just going to ask you to bring it up to about waist height. That's all. Just a little knee lift. Working through the hip flexors, little bit of movement through the hip, little bit of bend through the knee, nice and easy just up to about waist height will do, as long as you're not sticking to the yoga mat. Beautiful.

Going to change that slightly to a leg curl. Heel up to your backside. That's all we need to do. Heel up, getting into those hamstring muscles at the back of the thigh. Fabulous. Lift it up. Take a little rest there.

We're going to hip circle. It'll go in and it'll go out, and in and out. Get that little circle through the hip. Beautiful. One more on this side. Doesn't matter which side you're on, as long as you now swap over to the other side to circle it. In and out. Beautiful. Try to get a good range of motion through this ball and socket joint at the hip. Hold it there.

We're going to change for a little heel dig. Doesn't matter which leg you do first. I just want you to put one in front and then the other. All you're doing is bringing the heel down and lifting the toe up. Getting a little bit of a stretch there through the calf into your Achilles. Fabulous. A couple more, and hold it there.

This is what I'm going to do. Take the knees slightly bent. All we're going to do here is take a little work through the spine, get through that flexion and extension that we know we've got in the spine. So, first of all what I'm going to ask you to do is take a deep breath and be aware of lengthening the spine. When you exhale I want you to try and blow all the air out. Keep blowing. Keep blowing. Keep blowing, and what you'll find is it'll start to draw the ribs down towards the hips.

Taking a deep breath in, make sure you're extending through and lifting the face up and forwards. When you exhale, try to blow it all out. Keep blowing. Keep blowing. Keep blowing, and as you blow, as you get towards the end of the breath, you'll start to feel the abdominals engaging deeper and pulling you down into that flex position. Let's make more of that. Take a deep breath in and down.

What I'm going to ask you to do is add the arm swing to that now. Let the arms lift up when you breathe in, and when you exhale let them drop down. Blow all the air out. Let it pull you down slightly. Feel the back rounding, and then open it up.

So, we're trying to be aware of the spine now flexing and extending. Keep breathing. I'll turn sideways. As we go down, exhale. Let it roll forwards. Knees are slightly bent. Lift up. Remember when we talked about the movement through the spine. We talked about that extension and we talked about the flexion. Let it round. Let it round. Let the head come down. Again, couple more. Deep breath in. Just mobilizing through your lower spine particularly, and down. Relax yourself back to the center. Well done. Well done.

We're going to work through our static stretches now. So, you'll remember from our lecture on flexibility we talked about collagen creep, and I'll remind you about that once we get started. We're going to arrange your stretches standing, and then we're going to get down to do some on the floor. You know what? This is really pretty boring TV, so I hope you're not watching. You need to get up and join in on this one.

So, this is what we're going to do. Let's take one ear down to the shoulder. Shall we go this side first? Drop the ear to the shoulder. Take the palm out to the opposite side and press it down to the ground. Now, hopefully when you do that we can start to feel the stretch coming through the neck and down into the shoulder.

We're looking to hold it for around 15 seconds is our target for maintenance work to develop our stretch. Then we'll take it a little closer to 30 seconds. Try and keep your breathing nice and relaxed. We'll ease that off and come up to the other side.

Center yourself. Take it across to the other side. Ear to the shoulder first. Feel the stretch through the neck. Take the palm out and push it down to the floor, and feel that stretch come a little deeper down through the neck and into the shoulder. Beautiful feeling, particularly if you work at a desk all day. Very easy to get that stress around the neck and shoulders, so, beautiful way to release this. Remember, with these kind of stretches you can do them any time, any place, anywhere. Bring that in.

We're going to work into the shoulder. Lift the head up. We're going to take the arm across the chest. Doesn't matter which one you use. If you're on the same as me, that's good. If not, just remember to alternate. You're taking a hold just above the elbow and squeezing it a little further across. Don't let the body twist, but you'll feel this now getting into the shoulder. Ease into your stretch position to the point where you feel the mild tension and then hold it there. Good.

Keep your breathing nice and relaxed, and just enjoy being at peace for a moment. We'll swap that over to the other side. Bring it across.

So, we're working through a whole range of stretches here, just above the elbow, squeeze it in. The beauty of these standing ones, you could be standing at the photocopier at work and you could do these stretches. When you get a moment, why not have a stretch? Open that out.

Let's work into the chest. We're going to take the hands behind. We're going to put the palms together. We're going to lift away slightly from the backside and squeeze the shoulder blades together. Now, this is a great stretch for the pecs but also gets into the front of the shoulder. Try not to arch your back. Try not to stick your chin out. Remember we just had a relax through the neck. So, just feel that stretch through the chest.

Again, really try to get, just as when we do our workouts with the flexibility work, it's just as important to get your mind and muscle. Try to think about the chest. Try to picture the chest muscles stretching gently. Imagine those elastic fibers just stretching out. Breathing is nice and relaxed. And we'll ease that off and do the opposite of that.

Bring the hands up to the front. You can either interlock the fingers or put one on top of the other. The arms stay slightly bent, and now we're stretching forwards. So, the aim here is to reach your hands forwards and to really round the back. We're trying to pull those shoulder blades apart, really stretching through those muscles in the upper back. A great stretch. Really feel those shoulder blades pull apart. You can drop the chin down onto your chest even. That will be a trick. And ease your head up and drop them down. Beautiful.

We're going to shift on to the triceps at the back of the arm. Take one arm—again it doesn't matter which one. Drop it down behind. Now, what you're looking to do here is to put the hand on the fingers down, pointing down onto the back of the spine there. What we're going to do is put the hand on top of the elbow and simply encourage that hand to walk a little further down the spine, and that'll stretch into the triceps at the back of the arm as we press down. Hold that stretch. Keep your abdominals in tight.

Now, remember what we're looking for here. I talked about collagen creep. The idea here is that once you stretch into this position, after about 6 or 8 seconds, if we hold it, you'll find that those connective tissues around the muscle will begin to ease off, will begin to stretch a little bit, actually begin to align themselves all in the same direction. And ease off.

So, I know that with each of these static stretches—let's swap over to the other side—that if you really focus on your mind and muscle, after about 6 seconds or so, it'll begin to ease off, and at that point we can then take it slightly further. So, really try to identify that on each of your stretches. Getting into your position, feel the mild tension, and it will subside, and then you'll be able to ease a little further into the stretch, and the best way to do that is to link that to your breath. Take a deep breath in, and when it eases off breath out as you stretch further into the position. Beautiful. Ease that off.

Let's bend the knees. Put your hands on top of the knees. We're going to work into the lower back. The stretch here is to pull the tummy button in tight, trying to lift your lower back up to the ceiling, really rounding through the lower spine there, really getting into those—hopefully you remember— those erector spinae muscles. Really pulling the lower back up to the ceiling. You're supporting the weight on the back by putting the hands on the thighs, and then we'll slowly curl ourselves back up. Beautiful.

We're working our way down through the body, so let's go on now to the hip flexors. So, I'm going to take the left foot back and put it on the ball of the foot. The hips, chest, and shoulders are staying facing the front. We're going to bend both knees down.

Now, the secret here is we're going behind and tilting the pelvis up and forwards. So, tilting up and forwards will give you that flex on the hip flexors here. Now, this is a really important stretch because if we're sitting—hold that position for me, please—if you're sitting a lot when you're working, these muscles are shortened. What that tends to do then is start to pull the pelvis into a position we don't really want it to be in, which can put a strain on the lower back.

This hip flexor stretch—feeling it on the front here; really push forwards with the hip there—is a really good stretch, really important stretch. And remember, you're looking for that point where it begins to ease off a bit so that you can take it a little bit further. Beautiful. Slowly ease out of that.

Let's swap over. Line the feet up. Take the right foot back. Put it on the ball of the foot. Sink the knees down, keeping the abs in tight. Let's tilt the pelvis up and forwards. Let's really get into that stretch on the front here on the hip flexors, the iliopsoas muscles there. Also getting into the top of the quadriceps muscles there. Fabulous. Hopefully you can feel that. And we'll ease out of that.

Then go a little bit further down. Let's work from the hip flexors down into our quadriceps. Okay, so, let's set our balance up. The way we're going to do this is take a hold of the left foot. You're looking to squeeze the heel close to the backside, but be careful. Don't squeeze the heel right into the backside. What I'd like you to do here is hold it just a little bit away from the backside and then push the hip forwards. Okay? Now, the reason for that is that if you really squeeze the heel into your backside, what it does here is remember this is a synovial joint. We talked about them in our lecture on joints, and what that means is there's a sac of fluid here. If you squeeze this and it pushes it all forwards, puts a lot of pressure under the patella tendon. So, what I'm trying to do here is get that stretch on the quads but in not too extreme a position for the knee. So, we're keeping the heel a little bit further back, but as you push forwards you'll still feel that on the quadriceps.

Let's swap over to the other leg. Remember, for your balance you can bend the supporting knee, or for some reason—I'm not quite sure why—we take a hold of the earlobe, and that might help you with your balance. But you know what? If you're struggling with your balance, you can hold onto something or you can reset yourself if you wobble. That's okay.

Remember from our balance lecture this is one of the things that we look to improve over time. Pushing that hip forwards, can we feel that stretch on the front of the thigh in those quadriceps, those 4 muscles, powerful muscles on the fronts of the thigh that we use when we're squatting, when we're lunging, when you're walking upstairs for sure. And let's put that one down.

Let's move on. Remember we talked about our opposing muscle groups. So, from the quadriceps at the front of the thigh, let's move to the hamstring at the back. Left foot first. Heel down. Bend the other leg.

Now, what I want to do is put the hands on this right thigh because then what I'm going to do is try not to round your spine but take your chest forwards. As you drop the chest you'll start to feel that stretch into the hamstring into the back of the thigh. Again, this is a great one to get down there, feel the mild tension and hold it. Take a couple of deep breaths. Sometime around now we'll get that collagen creep, and if you take a deep breath and exhale you will find, as if by magic, you can go a little bit further. Really focus on the muscles that you're stretching. The chin is on the chest. Slowly roll yourself up, and swap over to the other side.

Now, while we're flipping side to side, try to be aware if you've got difference from one side to the other. If you've got one side particularly tight, it might need a bit of extra stretching. Bend down, hands onto your left thigh, chest dropped forwards, keeping your abs in tight. Nice, natural curve in your lower spine, and then we'll start to get that stretch into the back of the thigh into the hamstring there. Let the top of your head drop forward as well. We don't want an uncomfortable position in your neck. Remember, we've already stretched out the neck at the top. Put that tow down, chin on your chest, and slowly curl back up. Beautiful.

We're going to move onto your inner thigh, so you might straddle the mat now because we're going a little bit wider. We're going to point the toes out. We're going to point the knees out on that line. We're going to sit down. Hands are just above the knees, and push backwards, pushing backwards now.

We'll begin to open out through the inner thigh, give us that stretch for the adductor muscles, the hip adductors. These are the muscles that bring the legs in towards the center line of the body. We're not just resting the hands. We're pushing them backwards. Make sure we can feel that stretch on the inner thigh. Keep your breathing nice and relaxed. You're okay to forward body hinge on this a little bit. Try and keep your shoulders relaxed. Again, our target is about 15 seconds at least. If you've got time to hold it for longer, that's even better. And slowly come up out of that and walk them in. Fabulous. This is what we're going to do. We're going to take your left foot over your right. Okay, so, looking for a little bit of stretch into the outer thigh, into the iliotibial band. This is a really important one for runners.

What we're going to do here is take this left hand up, and I'm actually going to displace the hip here. What I'm going to ask you to do is to lean this way and physically push your hip in this direction as well at the same time. So, you're pushing the hip across as well as leaning at the same time. So, we're really getting into this lateral complex on the hip there, working a little bit through your smaller glute muscles but also particularly into the ITB down the side.

Bring that back up to the top. Let's swap over the other way. Keep everything balanced. We're taking the right foot over, bringing the right hand up, and push the hip that way, and that slight lean. Fabulous. Looking to feel that down the outside here. Remember, we're still after that. Hold it for a few seconds; see if we can feel it ease off a little bit. Perhaps it'll go a little bit further. And ease out of that position.

Okay, so, for our calf we have 2 muscles in the calf—the gastrocnemius and the soleus. We talked about them in our muscles lecture. Let's take the left foot back. Now, for this one we need to keep the feet facing forwards. So, make sure your feet are facing me. You're going to sink onto your front leg and keep your heel down at the back.

You're looking to keep that heel down, but can we shift the weight forwards, really getting that stretch. You might need to support your weight on the front leg. Really get that stretch into the calf muscle at the back.

Now, this one is particularly important for girls if you wear high heels, or even for guys if you wear high heels.

So, now we're going to change that to get a little lower. Just ease off down into the soleus and also into the Achilles. We ease out of the stretch slightly, but now I'm going to ask you to bend the knee. As you start to bend the knee, you'll feel that going a little lower down. So, we're still in the gastrocnemius, but we're really now getting down into the soleus underneath here and down into the Achilles. Beautiful stretch. For you runners, sports jocks, this is particularly important. Achilles does a lot of work. And east that off. Should we swap over to the other side?

So, you're taking your right leg back this time. Make sure your feet are about hip width apart for your balance. Shift the weight forwards. Keep the heel down at the back, the leg straight. Let's start to get that stretch through the calf, and interestingly, the calf muscle, the bigger calf muscle, the gastrocnemius, actually attaches at both of the knee. So, it assists when you're doing knee flexion exercises, when you're bending your knee.

Now, ease out of that stretch slightly, and now push that knee down to the ground, but keep the heel down, and you'll really feel that get a little lower down into your Achilles. It's a great stretch. And we'll ease that off.

You'll be pleased to know we're going to hit the floor now. So, there are your standing stretches. Beauty of those: You can do them absolutely anywhere. We're going to get down onto all fours, do a little bit of work for our lower back, obviously a key area for lots of us.

So, we're going to get the hands directly under your shoulders, the knees directly under your hips, and all I'm looking for there is that lower back stretch, dropping the chin down and lifting the tummy button. Pull it in as much as you can so that we're really pulling the lower back up towards the ceiling, really trying to round through the spine there, really get this flexed position and feel that stretch through the muscles, particularly in the lower back. Excellent stuff. And we'll ease ourselves out of that.

We're going to take your left arm, simply reach it down. Now, can we get down onto this shoulder and hold that position there. Feel that stretch across the shoulder a little bit into the upper back. Hold that position. Try and keep your breathing nice and relaxed, feeling that stretch through the shoulder, also, a little bit of rotation there stretching through the upper back as well, holding it for at least 15 seconds. A little longer is better.

We'll come out of that and swap it over to the other side. Try to keep your hips over your knees as we drop under. Try and let that shoulder go down, if you want to turn your head as well into that position. It's a beautiful stretch through the shoulder. Great stuff. Keep your breathing nice and relaxed. And ease yourself out of that.

And we're going to do completely the opposite of that now. So, again, reset yourself, hands under the shoulders, knees under the hips. Let's take the left hand, only this time keep looking at the hand, keep looking at the hand. Lift it up and keep looking at the hand. Okay? Doesn't matter where you go to, as long as you go to the point where we can feel that rotation through the lower spine. We're getting that stretch through the muscles, through the lower back. We're also releasing through the shoulder, releasing through the chest here. Doesn't have to be pointing up to the sky. You can be reaching across there, as long as you're working to your comfortable range of motion. Good. Should we ease that down and swap it over to the other side.

Set yourself first. Try not to sit backwards when you do this one. Keep your weight forwards. Press into your left hand so that your right hand is released. Keep your weight forwards. Don't sit back, just as far as is comfortable. Feel it open through the chest. Try and keep your breathing nice and relaxed. Beautiful. Rotating through that lower spine.

Again, particularly if you're sitting down an awful lot, you'll find that you can be in an unnatural position. It can cause a little bit of stiffness around the lower spine. This is a great way to release it. And we're going to ease that down.

Let's take this a step further. We're going to go into our upward dog position, those of you who are yoga disciples. Let's take the feet behind. Now, for the cobra you'll keep your hips down, but for the upward dog, we're actually going to lift the hips up off the floor. Lift up. Lift the face up and forwards. So, we're really working through that backbend, really trying to extend through the spine, but not backwards but up and forwards. Lift your face up and forwards. Shoulders are back and down. The hips are off.

Looking for that nice lengthening through the whole of the spine, from the top of the head right down to your tailbone. Remember, your back is designed, as we talked about when we looked at the spine, our lecture looked at the way it moved, and we talked about flexion and extension and also what is referred to as hyperextension, like this, where we go back slightly beyond the norm.

We're going to sit that back down now and take it back into our child's pose. Now, this is a great position—sit it back into child's for me, please—because it can affect different people in different ways. So, you might be feeling a little bit of a stretch through the lower back into the glutes, or it's possible that you could be feeling it if you're sitting your hips back into the quadriceps on the front of the thigh. You might actually be feeling it if you press down through the armpits to the floor, feeling it a little bit more in the chest towards the front of the shoulders also.

So, the great thing about this pose is it offers us many benefits, but sometimes it's worth experimenting with it. Sometimes sit with your feet together resting onto your feet. Sometimes sit with your feet apart and sit between your feet. Sometimes experiment with the post to see how it works for you.

We'll come out of that and come back onto all fours, and we're going to change slightly now into a swan position. What I'm going to ask you to do is bring your left foot forwards. Bring the knee up and turn it slightly to the side. We're now going to sit back, and again, this one has many benefits. Pushing this hip down we might feel it on the front here. We might feel it here into the glutes, depending on where you put this foot. If we move it a little further across you'll feel it a little more into the glutes here. If you need to support your weight, that's fine. I'm just looking really to get this hip down and this hip down.

Hold that position. Try to keep the upper body relaxed. Remember, we've had a nice stretch for the neck and shoulders already. And we'll ease out of that. Swap over to the other side.

Now, for me I don't know why it is—it might just be me—but more than any other stretch I feel a difference from one side to the other on this one. So, see how it works for you. We're bringing this foot across. We're trying to push this hip down to get a stretch into here, and then turning this forwards, getting a stretch into that hip flexor as well. It's a great combination stretch. Particularly, again, if your job involves you sitting, if it's driving or office-bound, it's great to get this stretch.

Let's ease ourselves out of that. We're going into wide leg stretch now, so if you guys both face that way for me, and I'll do it to the front, and then everybody at home can see what we're doing.

Taking the legs out wide, just as wide as it's comfortable; hands are down in the center. Lift the head up tall. Nice long back. Now, we're hinging from the hip, so don't round your shoulders. Just walk the hands forwards a little bit so that we start to get that stretch through the inner thigh just as far as it's comfortable for you, and hold that position. Try not to round the shoulders too much. Can we feel that on the inner thigh? Hold it there and remember, 6, 8 seconds. We'll start to get that collagen creep. We'll take a deep breath and ease a little further into that. Beautiful. Hopefully you can feel that.

We're going to walk the hands back out of that, and guys, you get the best part now because what you're going to do is turn your feet to the back, head down this way, and just lie down in the corpse pose for me for a second.

So, always a good idea at the end to have a lie down, have a little relax. Enjoy the moment, and also take a moment there while you're relaxing to just be aware now of how loose you feel through the body. Hopefully you should be feeling a little more supple now, a little free of tension, but also maybe a little bit energized as well.

So, just as a reminder, here are some guidelines for stretching. Try to stretch regularly, daily if you can. We're holding static stretches to the point of mild tension to around 15 seconds to maintain your flexibility and 30 seconds to improve it. Always ensure you're warm before you start, even with a bit of cardio or even if you're fresh out of a hot bath. Be aware of your posture. Important to ensure you're focusing on the target muscles. And perform the stretches that target the joints where you feel particularly stiff. Remember, we went from side to side so that you can check if you have any weak areas.

Always use deep breathing and maybe some suitable visualization. Imagine lengthening the elastic muscles. However, if at any time you feel any sharp or stabbing pain, you really must release that stretch immediately.

That brings us to the end of our series, and if you've been with me the whole way through, I really hope you've enjoyed the journey; but remember, this particular workout, the stretch workout, you can use at the end of the other workouts. We only did a little, very quick cool down at the end, in some cases none at all. So, this stretching, this flexibility workout, you can actually use in combination with the others to get a really good workout. Remember, they're only 30 minutes, so you've got the time to do that.

Also, importantly, remember in terms of those workouts, you now have the knowledge. We've talked about progressive overload. We've talked about how the muscles and the bones adapt. So, this is not just a one-off deal. These workouts we talked about increasing the resistance or increasing the time you're working, reducing the rest in between, or maybe instead of doing 1 set of the workout, you could do the whole routine twice or the whole routine 3 times, which we did a couple of times, for instance the plyometric workout. We did that 3 times.

So, you've got the opportunity to progress. The journey doesn't stop here. And remember, in one of our lectures you may remember the line we pinched from one of the sportswear giants. We said that fitness is a race that has no finish line. Hopefully now that you've got that extra knowledge, you know how to achieve fitness, why we're doing it in a certain way, then hopefully you're going to be running that race for some time to come.

Muscles of the Human Body

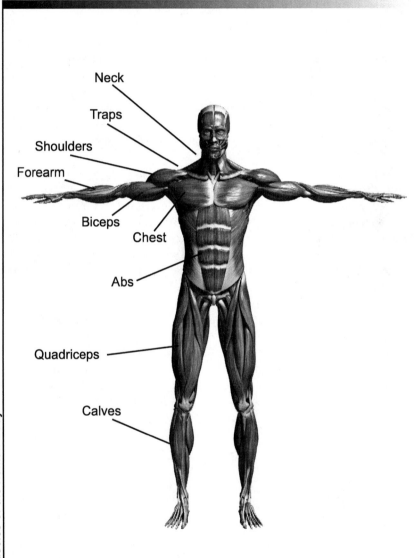

Neck

Traps

Shoulders

Forearm

Biceps

Chest

Abs

Quadriceps

Calves

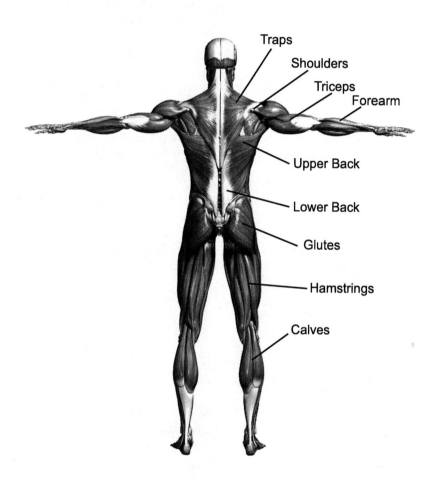

Glossary

1-repetition maximum: The maximum amount of resistance that a person can lift just once.

abduction: The movement of a limb away from the midline of the body.

Achilles tendonitis: A condition characterized by soreness and stiffness at the back of the ankle—in the Achilles tendon.

active isolated stretching: A stretching technique that uses the synchronization of paired muscles to allow for coordinated movements and is performed with a partner.

adduction: The movement of a limb toward or across the center line of the body.

adenosine triphosphate (ATP): The chemical in your muscles that breaks down to produce energy and, in turn, relies on the breakdown of carbohydrate, fat, and protein.

adipocyte: A fat cell.

aerobic: With oxygen.

aerobic capacity: Maximal oxygen uptake.

agility: The ability to change direction of the body or parts of the body, incorporating elements of deceleration and acceleration.

anaerobic: Without oxygen.

anaerobic threshold: The point at which lactic acid builds up in the body when a person starts to fatigue.

anatomy: The study of the bones, muscles, and other components that form the human body.

android: The apple shape associated with men's bodies.

aponeurosis: A sheath in the abdomen that is divided by tendon insertions that run across it and, more noticeably, centrally to give the appearance of separate blocks.

arthritis: An umbrella term for a large number of rheumatic diseases that affect the joints and the soft tissues around them, including conditions such as childhood arthritis, fibromyalgia, and lupus.

asana: The practice of physical poses—the poses that are assumed during yoga practice.

asthma: A condition whereby the tubes that carry air to the lungs become irritated, which sometimes narrows and perhaps produces more mucus than normal, restricting the ability to breathe.

atrium: One of the 2 upper chambers of the heart.

balance: The ability to maintain both static and dynamic equilibrium of the body parts as well as the whole body.

ballistic stretching: A type of stretching that involves swinging or bouncing a limb into a position beyond the normal joint range, thereby lengthening the associated muscles.

bioelectrical impedance analysis: A method of measuring body composition that involves passing a small electric current through the body and measuring the resistance to its flow to determine body fat.

blood pooling: The term given to blood remaining in the extremities, which can cause dizziness.

body composition: The proportional segmentation of body weight into lean and fat constituents.

body mass index (BMI): Calculated as your weight in kilograms divided by the square of your height in meters.

brain stem: The lower part of the brain that connects to the spinal cord and is responsible for the body's heartbeat, breathing, digestion, and circulation of the blood around the body—and for keeping a person awake and alert.

buoyancy: The degree to which your body floats when it's immersed in water.

calcitriol: A hormone that governs the flow of calcium into and out of the bone tissue.

cardiac cycle: A cycle that includes the duration of 1 heartbeat and the rest period that immediately follows it.

cardiac output: A term that quantifies the workload of the heart that is calculated as the sum of the stroke volume multiplied by the pulse rate.

cardiovascular endurance: The capability of the heart, lungs, and circulatory system to take in, absorb, and use oxygen.

central fatigue: The effect of messages in motor pathways from the brain and spinal cord to the muscles that leads to a reduction in effort or complete cessation of activity.

cerebellum: The bottom rear portion of the brain that governs movement by controlling balance and muscle contractions.

chi: A healthy flow of this internal energy is believed in Eastern cultures to reflect optimum balance in mind, body, and spirit.

chronic obstructive pulmonary disease (COPD): An umbrella term covering a number of conditions, such as emphysema—where the alveoli lose their elasticity and, therefore, their ability to take in oxygen—and bronchitis, which involves a buildup of phlegm that causes coughing.

circumduction: The act of performing a full circle that is unique to the shoulder joint.

collagen: The main component of connective tissue.

concentric contraction: The contraction that occurs when a muscle develops tension as it shortens.

continuous training: Training that is based on working out at a constant intensity for a specific duration of time.

coordination: The ability to perform a range of simple to complex movements with precision, timing, and continuity.

core strength: The strength that results from the muscles in your back, abs, and pelvis working together.

cortical bone: The type of bone that is the exterior of bone that is dense and strong—also known as compact bone.

creatine phosphate: A compound of creatine and phosphoric acid that can donate a phosphate molecule to ADP, making it ATP.

cross-training: Training that involves using different cardio workout modes either on different days or even within the same workout.

deep vein thrombosis (DVT): A clot in the leg or groin.

depression: The act of pulling a joint down.

dharana: Mental concentration.

dhyana: Meditation.

diastasis: The separation of parts that are normally joined together.

diastole: The stage of the cardiac cycle in which the pressure on the heart walls is at its lowest.

diastolic pressure: The pressure inside the arteries when the heart is between beats—during the relaxed phase of the cardiac cycle.

dorsiflexion: Pulling the toes upward, toward the body.

dual-energy X-ray absorptiometry: A very accurate method of measuring body composition that involves passing 2 types of X-rays through the body and uses a special scanner that is able to differentiate between fat, bone, and muscle tissue.

early flatfoot stage: The stage of walking at which the whole foot is in contact with the ground. This is an important stage because this is where shock absorption takes place, which is a key to preventing injury.

eccentric contraction: The contraction that occurs when a muscle actively lengthens.

elevation: The act of raising a joint.

endomysium: The connective tissue that covers the bundles of muscle fibers that are found within the perimysium.

epimysium: A strong connective tissue that surrounds the whole muscle.

epinephrine: A hormone that increases in concentration during cardio exercise.

erector spinae: A group of deep back muscles—including the iliocostalis, longissimus, and spinalis muscles—that are of varying lengths and run down both sides of the spine, from the cervical all the way down to the lumbar regions. This group produces movements including lifting you from a bent position, bending the trunk to the side, and rotating your upper body.

essential fat: The amount of fat that is needed and is found in the bone marrow and the organs.

excess postexercise oxygen consumption (EPOC): The number of calories that are burned immediately after exercise has ceased—due to the increased metabolic effect of your body removing waste products from the cells and then refueling.

extension: Increasing the angle at a joint, or straightening.

fartlek training: Training that introduces short, fast bursts between periods of average exercise.

fascia: The soft layer of connective tissue that surrounds muscles.

fast-twitch fibers: Muscle fibers that are white in color and hold low levels of mitochondria. They contract quickly, but they also tire equally rapidly, so they're suited for activities that are high in intensity but short in duration.

fatigue: An exercise-induced reduction in the ability to generate force or maintain an exercise intensity.

fibroblast: A type of cell that breaks down the clot that is formed by platelets once the damaged cells in an area of injury have been cleared, allowing scar tissue to be laid down.

fitness: A subjective state that is related specifically to an individual's personal medical history, current health status, socioeconomic situation, and perhaps sporting aspirations. In addition, fitness could be considered in emotional, mental, and even spiritual dimensions.

fitness yoga: A practice that combines centuries-old yoga poses with a modern approach to improving well-being, primarily through enhancing both postural awareness and core strength capabilities.

flexibility: The mobility of the joints and their associated soft-tissue structures.

flexion: A reduction in the angle at a joint, or bending.

floating stage: The moment for runners at which both feet are momentarily off the ground.

frontal lobe: The top front portion of the brain that determines emotions and is the logical part involved in solving problems, planning, and organizing.

functional fitness: The fitness that is relevant to day-to-day living.

glucose: The form of sugar that's transported and used by your body for energy.

glycolysis: The process through which glucose can produce ATP without oxygen.

Golgi tendon organ reflex: An automatic relaxing within the muscle that is a response to a change in muscle tension.

goniometry: The art of measuring flexibility.

gynoid: The pear shape associated with women's bodies.

hatha yoga: The most popular form of yoga that is described as the union of 2 opposites—with "ha" meaning "Sun," which relates to passion, energy, and positivity, and "tha" meaning "Moon," which suggests cool and reflective negativity.

heel strike: The split second at which the foot first touches the ground when walking.

high-density lipoprotein (HDL): The "good" cholesterol.

hip hitch: The act of lifting the hip away from the floor and back down.

hippocampus: The part of the brain that plays a role in memory function.

homeostasis: When the body's many systems function in harmony, causing the body to operate most efficiently.

horizontal extension: A backward movement in a horizontal plane.

horizontal flexion: A forward movement in a horizontal plane.

hormone-sensitive lipase: An enzyme that is located in the fat cell and acts to break apart the triglyceride, releasing the 3 fatty acids into the bloodstream.

hyaline cartilage: The material that covers the ends of most bones and acts to both assist shock absorption and reduce friction between articulating bones.

hydrostatic pressure: The constant pressure exerted by the water equally around the body.

hydrostatic weighing: A method of measuring body composition that is based on the premise that fat—being less dense than lean body tissue such as muscle and bone—is more buoyant, allowing a comparison of dry land and underwater weights to be used in calculating fairly accurate percentages for each.

hyperextension: The continuation of extension beyond the anatomical position.

hypertonic drink: A beverage that contains a higher percentage of carbohydrates; it is useful for recovery after a long workout or an endurance event.

hypotonic drink: A beverage that has a low carbohydrate concentration; it is useful for sports participants to rehydrate when lots of energy is not required.

iliotibial band syndrome: A friction problem between the thick band of fascia that runs down the outside of the knee and the lateral femoral condyle, or bottom end of the thigh bone.

imagery: The act of using some or all of your senses to create an experience in your mind.

immediate recovery: The type of recovery that begins during exercise.

intercostal muscles: The small muscles that are located between the ribs and aid in breathing.

interval training: Training that features spells of exercise interspersed with low-intensity periods to allow for recovery before the next period.

intervertebral disk: A fibrous cartilage mass that forms the cushioning between the bones of the spine to allow movement, acting as a shock absorber.

involuntary muscle: The type of muscle that is smooth in appearance and is not contracted intentionally—also known as visceral muscle.

isometric contraction: The contraction that occurs when a muscle doesn't shorten or lengthen.

isotonic drink: A beverage that has a similar concentration of carbohydrates to body fluids, so it is quickly absorbed; it is useful for tackling thirst during a workout or sports participation.

kyphosis: An exaggerated rounding of the thoracic spine—a hunched position sometimes known as dowager's hump—that can result from growing issues during adolescence, degenerative disease such as arthritis, compression fractures, prolapsed disks, and even lazy posture.

lamina flow: The smooth flow of water molecules.

larynx: The voice box.

late flatfoot stage: The stage of walking at which the center of gravity passes forward of the neutral position, and subconsciously, the whole body structure changes from being flexible, in order to absorb shock, to being more rigid, enabling the body to propel forward.

lateral extension: The return from a sideways position.

lateral flexion: Sideways bending.

latissimus dorsi: A surface back muscle that comes up from the iliac crest of the hip, connects through the vertebra T7 up to L5—lumbar 5—passes across the lower ribs, and eventually inserts into the upper arm. It's predominantly responsible for bringing your arm back down to your side, but it's also responsible for inwardly rotating the arm.

levator scapula: A surface back muscle that reaches from vertebra C1 to C3, sometimes to C4, and onto the upper part of the shoulder blade. In addition to assisting the trapezius in lifting, it tilts your head to the side.

ligament: A thick cord that connects bones together and gives the joints stability.

linea alba: The tendinous line in the middle of the abdominals.

lipoprotein lipase: An enzyme that draws fat out of the bloodstream for use as fuel.

lordosis: A curvature of the lumbar spine that makes the backside stick out and can be caused by poor posture.

low-density lipoprotein (LDL): The "bad" cholesterol.

lumbar stenosis: A back condition characterized by pain that is caused by a narrowing of the neural foramen, which could be caused by extra bone growth due to arthritis or advanced wear and tear leading to pressure on the nerve. Pain is particularly felt when standing and walking.

lumbopelvic area: The area of the body that includes the lumbar, stomach, pelvis, and hips.

lung cancer: A type of cancer that develops when cells change shape and grow, linking with other damaged cells to form a tumor that can then grow and spread to other parts of the lung and beyond—usually very slowly.

maximal oxygen uptake: The body's ability to take in oxygen and transport it to the working muscles.

meditation: A form of mental exercise that is based on the belief that the mind determines the quality of life.

mobilizer muscle: An abdominal muscle that brings about movement.

motor unit: A group of muscle fibers and the nerve that links them to either the central nervous system or the spinal cord.

muscular endurance: The capacity of a muscle, or a group of muscles working together, to maintain continued contractions against a low or moderate resistance.

myocardial infarction: A complete blockage of the blood flow to the heart—a heart attack.

myocardial ischemia: A partial disruption in blood flow to the heart.

myocardium: The heart muscle, or cardiac muscle.

myofibroblast: A type of cell that works to glue together the torn structures within an injury.

myotatic reflex: An automatic contraction within the muscle that is a response to a change in the length that is detected by muscle spindles.

naturopathic pain: A type of pain that relates to damage to the peripheral nerves or even to the central nervous system that manifests itself in contrasting ways—it could be sharp or numbing.

near-infrared interactance: A method of measuring body composition that uses a device that shines an infrared beam on the front of the arm, and the amount of light that bounces back from the bone is measured as an indication of the amount of fat present.

neuron: A cell that combines to form the nervous system and transmit information through both electrical and chemical means and is responsible for the estimated 70,000 thoughts we have each day.

neurotransmitter: A chemical that is responsible for conveying nerve impulses between neurons in the brain.

neutral spine: The natural, comfortable curve of your spinal alignment.

niyamas: Personal disciplines, such as cleanliness, contentedness, self-discipline, and self-study.

non-exercise activity thermogenesis (NEAT): The act of finding ways to introduce exercise into your daily routine.

occipital lobe: The back region of the brain that is responsible for the processing of visual information.

ossification: The buildup of calcium and magnesium salts that is deposited at a particular location, resulting in bone growth.

osteoarthritis: The form of arthritis that is caused by the degeneration of the hyaline cartilage, which is a key shock absorber on the end of bones when they come into contact with one another.

osteoblast cell: A cell that deposits mineral salts to promote new bone growth.

osteoclast cell: A cell that breaks down and absorbs old bone, allowing calcium, potassium, and phosphate compounds to be released from the bone into the bloodstream.

osteoporosis: A skeletal disease characterized by low bone mass and microscopic deterioration leading to increased susceptibility to fractures.

parietal lobe: The top region of the brain that is split into 2 sections, the right and left, and is concerned with spatial awareness on the right side and with language on the left side.

patella tendonitis: An inflammation below the kneecap that is usually noticed when walking down the stairs.

pericardium: The double-lined sheath in which the heart muscle is enclosed.

perimysium: The connective tissue that covers the bundles of muscle fibers that are found within the epimysium.

periosteum: The layer of connective tissue that coats the outer surface of bone and has a rich supply of blood vessels that provide nutrients for the growth phase and also for repair after injury.

peripheral fatigue: The point at which the protein filaments in the muscle fibers that are responsible for contraction cease to respond to neural stimulation. This is then combined with the depletion of glycogen stores in the muscle, so no fuel is available to prolong the exercise efforts.

peripheral heart action (PHA) training: An approach to circuit training that involves alternating upper- and lower-body exercises at stations next to each other. This format requires the blood to constantly shift oxygen-carrying blood from one part of the body to the next, leading to a greater calorie burn.

phagocytes: A type of cell that is attracted to the area of injury and absorbs the damaged cells that can no longer perform their functions.

physiology: The study of the interaction of the bones and muscles, along with the nerves, tendons, veins, arteries, heart, lungs, and thousands of complex systems working together to enable human beings to move and live.

piriformis muscle: A muscle located deep in the buttock that reaches from the pelvis, or sacrum, to the femur, or upper part of the thigh bone.

pituitary gland: The glad that controls the action of the kidneys.

plantar fasciitis: A strain of the connective band that maintains the longitudinal arch on the base of the foot, which is stretched basically every time the foot bears weight.

plantar flexion: Pointing the toes downward, toward the soles.

pneumonia: An infection that's transmitted by breathing in germs, which causes the alveoli to become filled with fluid and then inflamed, restricting the ability to transfer oxygen into the bloodstream.

postural hypotension: The drop of blood pressure that occurs when standing up quickly from a sitting or lying position.

power: The ability to achieve optimal force development of the voluntary muscles—but in a minimal time period.

pranayama: Breathing exercises.

pratyahara: The detachment from worldly activities or withdrawal of the senses.

primary sensory cortex: The part of the brain that controls the sense of touch and is located within the parietal lobe.

pronation: The inward turning of the palms.

proprioception: The body's ability to know where it is in space.

proprioceptive neuromuscular facilitation (PNF): A stretching technique that works by using the body's nervous system to encourage extended lengthening of the muscles.

protraction: The act of extending a body part forward.

reaction speed: The ability to recruit selected neuromuscular responses with a minimal time delay.

reciprocal inhibition: The process in which one muscle relaxes to some degree if its cooperating pair contracts.

recovery: The ability of the human body to meet the demands of future activity. In physiological terms, it's a multifaceted concept that includes the lowering of the blood pressure, the return to normal of the cardiac cycle, the replenishment of blood glucose and muscle glycogen energy stores, and the replacement of key cellular enzymes that govern the use of fuel sources.

rectus abdominis: The most visible mobilizer that stretches from the xiphoid process, where the ribs meet at the sternum, and ribs 5 to 7 down to the pelvis through a sheath, or aponeurosis, that joins to the symphysis pubis.

relaxation: A practice that is primarily aimed at and also benefits the body.

relaxin: A hormone that has the effect of loosening the ligaments.

retraction: The act of pulling a body part backward.

rheumatoid arthritis: An inflammation of the lining of the joint capsule that spreads to cause erosion of the cartilage and bone, leading to pain and stiffness—often in multiple joints—and often to visible deformity of the joint.

rhomboid: One of 2 surface back muscles that begin at vertebra C7, go down to T5, and attach to the inner border of the shoulder blade. The major and minor rhomboids retract your shoulder blade.

rotation: Movement that can be inward or outward.

rotator cuff: The small group of muscles around the shoulder girdle that connect the upper arm to the shoulder blade.

sacroiliac joints: The point at which the 3 pelvis bones meet.

sacrum: Connects the spine to the pelvis through the 2 sacroiliac joints; the point at which your upper body meets your lower body.

samadhi: Absorption with the Divine, God, or the Absolute.

sciatica: A back condition characterized by pain or perhaps numbness in the buttocks and rear of the lower leg caused by inflammation that is usually a result of a rupture of an intervertebral disk that begins to impinge on the nerve fibers. Pain is particularly felt when bending forward.

scoliosis: A side-to-side curve in the spinal column that leads to an "S" or "C" shape rather than a straight line when viewing from the rear and is usually due to a congenital defect but can also be caused by incorrect posture.

segmental muscle: One of a group of deep back muscles—the deepest, in fact—that only link from one vertebra to the next rather than connecting several. The interspinalis assists in extending the spine, and the intertransversarii assist in bending to the side—although all the muscles in these groups have a very limited amount of force.

serratus anterior: A surface back muscle that is situated on the front surface of the scapula and links to the 8th and 9th ribs. It draws the shoulder blades forward.

sesamoid bone: A bone that is housed within tendons at points of high physical stress and tension.

short-term recovery: The type of recovery that occurs between sets of exercises or between intervals in a session.

sinus: A cavity in the bone of the skull that is connected to the nose and nasal hairs.

skinfold caliper: A device used to take measurements at the waist, the back, and the front and rear of the upper arm to determine body composition.

Readings from the 4 sites are added together, and tables give an equivalent body fat percentage for these sums.

slow-twitch fibers: Muscle fibers that are red in color and contain a high concentration of mitochondria. These muscles fibers are slow to contract, but also slow to fatigue, so they're ideally suited for activities of a lower intensity and a longer duration.

SMART goal: An exercise-related goal that is specific, measurable, achievable, realistic, and timed.

somatic pain: A type of pain that is relatively easy to identify because the injured party can usually point to the exact location, and it can hurt to touch.

somatosensory system: The system that relies upon the sensors in the skin and the muscles to relay information to the brain regarding pressure, touch, and the position of your limbs.

splenius muscle: A deep back muscle that attaches from cervical to thoracic vertebrae and is responsible for lifting your head when it's down.

stabilizer muscle: An abdominal muscle that works to fix body parts in place.

static stretching: The most common method of stretching that requires a gentle movement toward the end position that slowly lengthens the muscle. Then, you hold the point at which there's mild tension for between 15 and 30 seconds.

steady state: The point at which the rate of lactic acid production exactly matches the rate of clearance of it from the cells. It is an intensity that feels comfortable and sustainable for some time.

strength: The force effectiveness of a muscle or a group of muscles.

subcutaneous fat: The unnecessary amount of fat that presents a risk factor and is stored beneath the skin.

supination: The act of turning your palm upward.

supine hypotensive syndrome: A condition in which lying on the back can result in the weight of the baby resting on the main blood vessels, causing them to pinch, which could temporarily restrict the blood supply flowing back up to the heart and, in turn, the supply to the mother and baby as a whole.

symphysis pubis: The point at which the 2 pubic bones meet.

synovial fluid: A vital lubricant secreted by the inner layer of the synovial membrane that helps reduce friction at the joint but also provides nourishment for the articular cartilage, which covers the end of the bone.

synovial joint: A freely movable joint.

synovial membrane: The inner layer of the fibrous capsule.

systole: The stage of the cardiac cycle in which the pressure on the heart walls is at its peak.

systolic pressure: The pressure inside the arteries as the heart is pumping.

temporal lobe: The middle region of the brain that is split into 2 sections, the right and left, and is concerned with visual memory on the right side and with verbal memory on the left side.

tendon: A fibrous connective tissue that connects the muscles to the bones.

tibialis anterior: A muscle that is located on the front of the shin and is responsible for raising the toes as the leg swings forward to ensure that the heel touches down first when walking.

tidal volume: The amount of air taken in with each breath.

toe-off stage: The stage of walking at which the swing of the leg begins.

trabecular bone: The type of spongy bone that is located on the inside and is where the red bone marrow that produces blood cells can be found—also known as cancellous bone.

trachea: The windpipe.

training recovery: The type of recovery that occurs between workouts, races, or matches.

transversospinalis muscle: One of a group of deep back muscles—including the semispinalis, multifidus, and rotator muscles—that lies deeper than and is generally shorter than the erector spinae, but it performs almost an identical function in extending, lateral flexing, and rotating the spine.

transversus abdominis: A stabilizer muscle that runs from the thoracolumbar fascia of the back and the iliac crest through the lower 6 ribs and into the linea alba. It is responsible for pulling in, compressing the abdominal cavity, and creating pressure that splints the lumbar spine as a result.

trapezius: A surface back muscle that runs from the base of the skull and vertebra C1 down to T12, inserting into the clavicle, acromion, and scapula at the back. It can lift and lower to retract the shoulder blade.

triglyceride: A group of 3 fatty acid molecules found within specific fat cells known as adipocytes.

trimester: A period of time that lasts 3 months and is used to divide a woman's pregnancy into 3 stages.

turbulent flow: The white water you see around you and the bubbles you feel against your skin when you move in the water, caused by molecules rebounding from an object in all directions.

vasoconstriction: The process in which blood vessels decrease in diameter.

vasodilation: The process in which blood vessels increase in diameter.

vastus medialis: The part of the quadriceps that is closer to the center and that helps to pull the kneecap back in line.

ventricle: One of the 2 lower chambers of the heart.

vestibular system: The system that refers to sensors in the inner ear that respond to the position of your head, causing your brain to send a message to your body to correct itself when you're off center, for example, when you stumble.

visceral pain: A type of pain that is characterized by cramping, a deep ache, or a dull throbbing that could be constant or intermittent. It's often a referred pain, so it can be difficult to pinpoint.

visual system: The system that provides information to your brain regarding where the body is in space, how fast it's moving, and details about possible obstacles in the immediate environment by using depth perception and peripheral sight skills.

voluntary muscle: The type of muscle that is controlled consciously by the nervous system and is also known as skeletal muscle, due to its attachment to the skeleton, and striated muscle, due to its striped appearance.

xiphoid process: The point at which the ribs meet at the sternum.

yamas: Individual practices that make us better human beings and contribute to a better world, including truthfulness, non-stealing, non-harming, leading a godly life, and non-grasping.

yoga: Means "union" or "yoke" and can be described as a unique system of physical, mental, and maybe even spiritual development that was developed about 3000 years ago.

Bibliography

Primary Sources

Delavier, Frédéric. *Strength Training Anatomy*. Paris, France: Éditions Vigot, 1998.

McArdle, William D., Frank I. Katch, and Victor L. Katch. *Essentials of Exercise Physiology*. 2nd ed. Philadelphia, PA: Lippincott Williams & Wilkins, 2000.

Wilmore, Jack H., David L. Costill, and W. Larry Kenney. *Physiology of Sport and Exercise*. 4th ed. Champaign, IL: Human Kinetics, 2008.

Additional Reading

American College of Sports Medicine. *ACSM's Guidelines for Exercise Testing and Prescription*. 8th ed. Philadelphia, PA: Lippincott Williams & Wilkins, 2010.

Brooks, George, Thomas Fahey, and Kenneth Baldwin. *Exercise Physiology: Human Biogenetics and Its Applications*. 4th ed. New York, NY: McGraw-Hill, 2005.

Everett, Tony, and Clare Kell, eds. *Human Movement: An Introductory Text*. 6th ed. New York, NY: Churchill, Living, Elsevier, 2010.

Golding, Lawrence A., Clayton R. Myers, and Wayne E. Sinning, eds. *Y's Way to Physical Fitness: The Complete Guide to Fitness Testing and Instruction*. 3rd ed. Champaign, IL: Human Kinetics, 1989.

Hamill, Joseph, and Kathleen M. Knutzen. *Biomechanical Basis of Human Movement*. 3rd ed. Baltimore, MD: Lippincott Williams & Wilkins, 2009.

Komi, Pavvo, ed. *Strength and Power in Sport*. Boston, MA: Blackwell Scientific, 1992.

MacIntosh, Brian, Phillip Gardiner, and Alan McComas. *Skeletal Muscle Form and Function*. 2nd ed. Champaign, IL: Human Kinetics, 2006.

Marieb, Elaine N., and Katja N. Hoehn. *Human Anatomy and Physiology*. 3rd ed. New York, NY: Benjamin Cummings, 1995.

Pollock, Michael L., Jack H. Wilmore, and Samuel M. Fox III. *Health and Fitness through Physical Activity*. New York, NY: John Wiley & Sons, Inc., 1978.

Rowell, Loring B. *Human Circulation: Regulation During Physical Stress*. New York, NY: Oxford University Press, 1986.

Silverthorn, Dee Unglaub. *Human Physiology: An Intergrated Approach*. 5th ed. Upper Saddle River, NJ: Benjamin Cummings, 2007.

Disclaimer

This series of lectures is intended to increase your knowledge of physiology, exercise, and health-related lifestyle choices and their basic effects on the human body. They are not designed for use as medical references to diagnose, treat, or prevent medical illnesses or trauma. Neither The Teaching Company nor Dean Hodgkin is responsible for your use of this educational material or its consequences. If you have questions about the diagnosis, treatment, or prevention of a medical condition or illness, you should consult your personal physician.

Notes

Notes

Notes

Notes